WASHINGTON DC
ACCESS®

W9-AOL-107

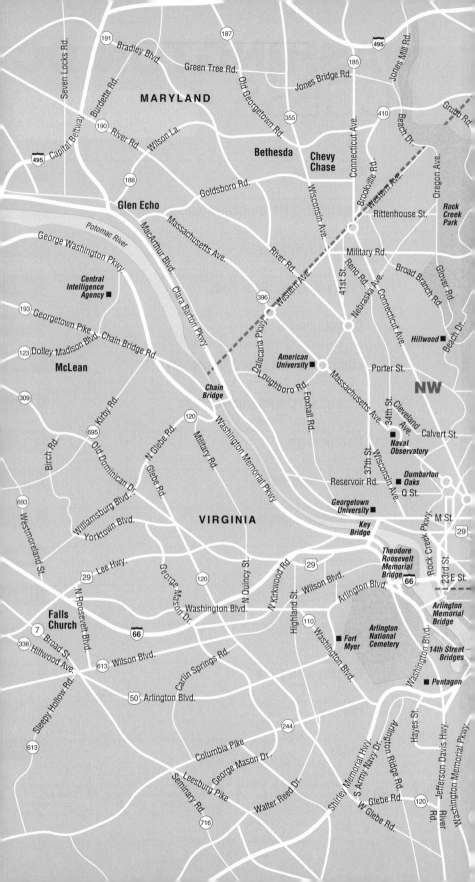

Orientation

It takes only an image or two to evoke Washington DC: the tiered dome of the **Capitol**, the tall white needle of the **Washington Monument**, or the Romanesque elegance of the **White House**. It's no wonder that first-time visitors to the city feel a sense of déjà vu: They've seen many of the sites countless times on TV, in editorial page cartoons, and in the movies.

Images of the capital possess a certain importance and formality: Imposing structures and institutions house a workforce with a single mindset—the governing of a nation. Along with this mission goes plenty of pomp—monuments, memorials, museums, and statuary. **The Mall** with its powerhouse sites—the **National Gallery** and the most popular museum in our country, the **National Air and Space Museum**—is certainly not to be missed. After all, it's also home to the cherished **Lincoln Memorial** and the poignant **Vietnam Veterans Memorial**, both deeply meaningful to our nation's history.

But after making the requisite pilgrimages, the visitor won't be long in discovering the "other Washington," a city of human scale. By law the skyline is low-level, to emphasize the **Capitol** and the memorials, and many of the city's neighborhoods reveal shady, quiet streets, lined with charming town houses—perfect for a stroll in spring or fall.

It also has more green space than you'd imagine possible in a city, from the remarkably pristine **Rock Creek Park** to **The Mall**, America's "backyard" and the scene of many political demonstrations and holiday celebrations. Transport yourself with a stroll through the lush, formal gardens of **Dumbarton Oaks;** a wonderland of terraces, pools, and arbors, it's DC's best-kept secret. On weekends at **Capitol Hill's Eastern Market**, Congressional representatives, TV newscasters, and other familiar faces may appear amid the crowd of regular city dwellers, here sampling a farmers' market chock-full of produce, picking over handmade crafts, or haggling with flea market merchants.

In terms of nightlife, it's true that Washington isn't red hot, like its northern neighbor, New York City. But DC's nightlife has its charms—from ethnic food sampling and bar hopping in funky, mobbed **Adams-Morgan**, to a performance in the **Kennedy Center's** elegant **Opera House**. Or maybe Georgetown's **Blues Alley** is your preference, with the hottest jazz and headliners around.

COURTESY OF THE WASHINGTON DC CONVENTION AND VISITORS ASSOCIATION

And don't confine your sense of Washington inside its famous **Beltway.** The nearby suburbs in **Maryland** and **Virginia** have their own rich history and other surprises, too, like a burgeoning collection of first-rate ethnic restaurants—especially those serving Southeast Asian cuisines. Not far away is **Baltimore**, a city with its own charms and plenty of gritty character. Catch a baseball game at **Camden Yards,** or visit the renowned **Baltimore Museum of Art** and the beautifully restored **Inner Harbor** with its sparkling waterfront and aquarium.

Although politics is the local sport, most Washingtonians do not live and die by which party is in power, and the viciousness that characterizes political rhetoric (remember the Clinton-Starr circus?) is remarkably absent in the District's citizenry. Just stop and ask someone for directions, and you're likely to get a detailed and friendly response. Summing up DC and its environs with a single image—no matter how powerful—could hardly do the area justice. The **Capitol**, the **Washington Monument,** and the **White House** are only just the beginning. The Washington described between these covers offers something for every taste—regardless of political stripe.

How To Read This Guide

ACCESS® **WASHINGTON, DC** is arranged by neighborhood so you can see at a glance where you are and what is around you. The numbers next to the entries in the following chapters correspond to the numbers on the maps. The text is color-coded according to the kind of place described:

Restaurants/Clubs: Red   **Hotels:** Blue

Shops/ 🌲 Outdoors: Green   **Sights/Culture:** Black

♿ **Wheelchair accessible**

Wheelchair Accessibility
An establishment (except a restaurant) is considered wheelchair accessible when a person in a wheelchair can easily enter a building (i.e., no steps, a ramp, a wide-enough door) without assistance. Restaurants are deemed wheelchair accessible only if the above applies and if the rest rooms are on the same floor as the dining area and their entrances and stalls are wide enough to accommodate a wheelchair.

Rating the Restaurants and Hotels
The restaurant star ratings take into account the quality, service, atmosphere, and uniqueness of the restaurant. An expensive restaurant doesn't necessarily ensure an enjoyable evening; however, a small, relatively unknown spot could have good food, professional service, and a lovely atmosphere. Therefore, on a purely subjective basis, stars are used to judge the overall dining value (see the star ratings below). Keep in mind that chefs and owners often change, which sometimes drastically affects the quality of a restaurant. The ratings in this guidebook are based on information available at press time.

The price ratings, as categorized below, apply to restaurants and hotels. These figures describe general price-range relationships among other restaurants and hotels in the area. The restaurant price ratings are based on the average cost of an entrée for one person, excluding tax and tip. Hotel price ratings reflect the base price of a standard room for two people for one night during the peak season.

Restaurants

★	Good
★★	Very Good
★★★	Excellent
★★★★	Extraordinary Experience
$	The Price Is Right (less than $10)
$$	Reasonable ($10-$15)
$$$	Expensive ($15-$25)
$$$$	Big Bucks ($25 and up)

Hotels

$	The Price Is Right (less than $80)
$$	Reasonable ($80-$120)
$$$	Expensive ($120-$180)
$$$$	Big Bucks ($180 and up)

Map Key

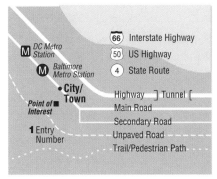

Area code 202 unless otherwise noted.

Getting to DC

Airports

Located 10 miles south of Baltimore and 32 miles north of Washington, **BWI** used to be called **Friendship International** (and still is by some old-timers). The main terminal is a two-level building with access roadways on each level. The bi-level design separates arriving and departing passengers. You can walk directly from individual airline entrances to ticket counters no more than 50 feet away. From there, all 40 departure gates are easily accessible.

Arriving passengers go directly to the lower level, where they find two baggage-claim areas, customs, car rentals, and ground transportation. Airport services include the usual complement of bars, restaurants, and a duty-free shop. For general nonflight airport information, call 410/859.7111 (Baltimore) or 301/261.1000 (DC area).

Airport Services

Airport Emergencies	410/859.7078
Business Service Center	410/859.5997
Currency Exchange	410/859.5997
Customs	410/859.3337
Information	410/859.7111
Interpreters	410/859.7111
Lost and Found	410/859.7387
Parking	410/859.9230
Police	410/859.7040
Traveler's Aid	410/859.7207

Airlines

Air Canada	800/776.3000
America West	800/235.9292
American	800/433.7300
British Airways	800/247.9297
Continental	800/525.0280
Delta	800/221.1212
Northwest	800/225.2525
Southwest	800/435.9792
TWA	800/221.2000
United	800/241.6522
US Airways	410/993.4976, 800/428.4322

An existing set of George Washington's false teeth is made of rhinoceros ivory and sealing wax, jointed by spiral springs.

Getting to and from Baltimore-Washington International Airport

By Bus and Van DC city buses don't go to and from this airport; however, the **SuperShuttle** (800/258.3826, 410/859.0803) leaves from the airport every half hour from 5:30AM to midnight. Purchase tickets ($28 one way, $56 round trip) at the **Transportation Desk** in the center of the airport near **Pier C.** In DC, the **SuperShuttle** drops off and picks up passengers at **Union Station** (50 Massachusetts Ave NE, at First St); it also offers door-to-door service. **BWI Airport Connection** (800/284.6066, 301/441.2345) offers door-to-door van service. The average cost is $35 for one person, $42 for two. Reserve at least 24 hours in advance.

By Car The drive between **Downtown** DC and **BWI** is about 45 minutes, except during rush hour, when the trip can take at least a half-hour longer. The most direct route to DC from BWI is to take **Interstate 195** north from the airport to the **Baltimore-Washington Parkway** (less than a mile) and proceed south. The BW Parkway ends just outside the District's limits; from there, **New York Avenue** leads into the Downtown area. An alternate route is to take Interstate 195 north to **Interstate 95** (about 6 miles) and proceed south to the **Capital Beltway** (where 95 continues). Continue to the BW Parkway heading south, or go west on the Beltway **(I-495)** and get off at any number of major exits (**Georgia** or **Connecticut** Avenues, Rockville Pike/Wisconsin Avenue) heading south to DC.

For those driving to the airport, a large parking garage is located close to the one and only terminal; satellite lots (which are cheaper) are a short shuttle bus ride away. For shuttle bus departure times, check with the airport's **Service Desk** or call **Hudson General** at 410/684.3904.

Rental Cars

The following rental car companies have 24-hour counters at the airport:

Alamo	410/850.5011, 800/327.9633
Avis	410/859.1680, 800/331.1212
Budget	410/859.0850, 800/527.0700
Dollar	800/421.6868
Hertz	410/850.7400, 800/654.3131
National	410/859.8860, 800/227.7368
Thrifty	410/859.1136, 800/367.2277

By Limousine The **Dulles Airport Express Taxi** (202/737.5500) serves all three Washington airports. **Triple Crown** (410/850.4100) offers door-to-door service throughout the Washington and Baltimore metropolitan areas. All major credit cards are accepted. Both services charge approximately $65 one way between **BWI** and Downtown DC.

By Taxi Taxi service is available from the airport to Baltimore and Washington. A dispatcher is always on duty; call 410/859.1100. For a 45-minute non–rush-hour ride to Downtown Washington, expect to pay upward of $45.

By Train Amtrak's **BWI Rail Station** is located two miles from the airport. Trains pass through on their way to such Northeast Corridor cities as Philadelphia, New York, and Boston; they stop at this station 13 times a day. One-way fare from the airport to DC's **Union Station** is $14. The airport runs a free shuttle bus (800/872.7245) to and from the **Amtrak** station every 20 minutes daily, starting at 6AM and stopping at midnight Monday through Friday, 1AM on Saturday, and 11:10PM on Sunday.

Washington-Dulles International Airport (IAD)

Eero Saarinen's expressive design for the main terminal epitomizes the joy of flight: This was the first airport (completed in 1962) designed for the jet age, and its airy main terminal is still spectacular. **Saarinen**'s other idea, mobile lounges designed to carry passengers to airplanes, has been altered somewhat by the surge in traffic. Now, most airlines use the lounges to carry passengers to midfield terminals, where they board through conventional gates. Long-range plans call for replacing the lounges with underground people movers.

International arrivals, customs, baggage claim, ground transportation, a bank, a post office, and 24-hour car rentals are on the ground floor. You also will find information and foreign language assistance services, a duty-free gift shop, an automated teller machine, and a barber shop. For general information, call 703/572.2700.

Airport Services

Airport Emergencies	703/572.2950
Customs	703/661.3632
Immigration	703/661.5101
Information	703/572.2700, 703/417.8000
Lost and Found	703/572.2954, 703/572.8479
Parking	703/572.5746
Police	703/572.2950
Traveler's Aid	703/572.8296

Airlines

AirTran	800/825.8538
American	800/433.7300
British Airways	800/247.9297
Canadian	800/426.7000
Continental	703/478.9700, 800/525.0280
Delta	800/221.1212
Northwest	703/471.7454, 800/225.2525
Qantas	223.3030, 800/227.4500
TWA	800/221.2000
United	800/241.6522
US Airways	800/428.4322

Getting to and from Washington-Dulles International Airport

By Bus Washington Flyer (703/685.1400) offers nonstop bus service from **Dulles** to Downtown, as well as to and from **National Airport**. Buses leave **Dulles** for the **Convention Center** (900 Ninth St NW, between H St and New York Ave) daily every half hour, at 20 and 50 minutes past the hour, from 5:20AM to 11:20PM. Every day except Saturday, they depart for **Union Station** (50 Massachusetts Ave NE, at First St) every hour, at 30 minutes past the hour, from 6:30AM to 9:30PM. The fare is $16 one way, $26 round trip. Buy tickets from the **Flyer**'s desk at the **Service Center** in the middle of the **Main Terminal.**

By Car To get to Downtown DC from the airport, take the **Dulles Access Road** going east (and avoid the **Dulles Toll Road,** a parallel road for local traffic) and watch for the signs connecting you to either **Interstate 66** or Interstate 495 (the Beltway). Interstate 66 will take you over the **Theodore Roosevelt Memorial Bridge** and into Downtown DC in about 45 minutes. It is the more direct route into town; however, during the morning rush hour (6AM-9:30AM) you must have at least two occupants in your car in order to use this road. If you take the Beltway, head north and take the **George Washington Memorial Parkway** exit, which follows the **Potomac River** (the views are spectacular). Follow the parkway to any of the four major bridges into town: the **Key** (into **Georgetown**), the Roosevelt Memorial or **Arlington Memorial** (into **Foggy Bottom,** just west of Downtown), or the **14th Street** (into **The Mall** and Downtown).

For those who are driving to the airport, short- and long-term parking lots are located just outside the terminal; other long-term lots (with cheaper rates) are a free shuttle bus ride away. Check with the airport's **Service Center** (703/572.5746).

Rental Cars

The following rental car companies have 24-hour counters at the airport:

Alamo	703/684.0086, 800/327.9633
Avis	703/661.3500, 800/331.1212
Budget	703/920.3360, 800/527.0700
Dollar	703/661.6630, 800/800.4000
Enterprise	703/478.2300, 800/736.8222
Hertz	703/471.6020, 800/654.3131
National	703/419.1032, 800/227.7368
Sears	703/920.3367, 800/527.0770
Thrifty	703/684.2054, 800/367.2277

By Limousine The **Dulles Airport Express Taxi** (202/737.5500) serves all three Washington airports. One-way fee from **Dulles** to Downtown DC is approximately $55.

By Taxi A taxi dispatcher is on duty at the airport 24 hours a day. Watch for the signs in the airport directing you to the taxi stands. As you approach, the dispatcher will give you a brochure, written in five languages, with estimated rates to various points in DC, suburban Maryland, and Northern Virginia. The cabs are metered. Expect to pay at least $45 for a trip to Downtown Washington.

Ronald Reagan National Airport (DCA)

Handling domestic and commuter flights, this is the most convenient airport to Downtown DC, just 3.5 miles or a 25-minute cab ride away. In 1997, a more efficient complex housing **Terminals B** and **C** opened next to what is now called **Terminal A.** The new layout has alleviated much of the former traffic and congestion problems, as well as added a pleasant, light-filled waiting area with shops, fast-food establishments, and a few restaurants.

Airport Services

Airport Emergencies	703/419.3972
Business Service Center	703/417.3200
Customs	703/927.6724
Ground Transportation	703/417.8400
Information	703/417.1808
Interpreters	703/419.3972
Lost and Found	703/417.8560
Parking	703/417.4300, recording 703/417.4311
Police	703/417.8560
Traveler's Aid	703/417.3975

Airlines

America West	800/235.9292
American	800/433.7300
Continental	703/478.9700, 800/525.0280
Delta	800/221.1212
Midwest Express	800/452.2022
Northwest	800/225.2525
TWA	800/221.2000
United	800/241.6522
US Airways	800/943.5436
US Airways Shuttle	800/428.4322

Poet Walt Whitman was an unorthodox Civil War nurse. He had little formal medical training, but would go from bed to bed dispensing cheer, an orange, a cigar, letter-writing paper and stamps—and a generous dose of his large personality. A wartime correspondent wrote, "His presence seemed to light up the place as it might be lighted by the presence of the God of love."

The Marine Band, which made its debut at the White House in 1801, is the oldest military band in the United States.

Getting to and from Ronald Reagan National Airport

By Bus **Washington Flyer** (703/685.1400) offers bus service from **National** to **Dulles**, and then into the city. Ticket offices are at the north end of the traffic circle in front of **Terminal A**, and on the baggage claim level of **Terminals B** and **C.** On Saturday and Sunday mornings between 6:30AM and 7:45AM, you can catch a **Metrobus** (637.7000) into Downtown DC from the **National Airport Metro** stop.

By Car As you leave the airport, you'll face a tangle of roads; if you're headed for DC, take care to follow the frequently appearing signs marked "EXIT TO WASHINGTON." This will put you on the George Washington Memorial Parkway heading north. Take the exit for **Interstate 395** north (it comes up quickly) to the 14th Street Bridge, which will lead you into the Downtown area.

If you're going to Foggy Bottom/West End or Georgetown, stay on the Parkway and follow the signs for Arlington Memorial Bridge, which will take you to the **Lincoln Memorial.** Bear left at the memorial and you'll be in Foggy Bottom; keep going and you'll arrive in Georgetown.

Each terminal at the airport has its own parking area, with pedestrian bridges connecting two garages to **Terminals B** and **C.** A third garage sits across the traffic circle from **Terminal A;** airport shuttle buses serve it as well as the more far-flung (and cheaper) satellite lots. For parking and shuttle bus information, call 703/271.4300.

Rental Cars

The following rental car companies have 24-hour counters at the airport:

Alamo	703/684.0086, 800/327.9633
Avis	703/661.3500, 800/331.1212
Budget	703/920.3360, 800/527.0700
Dollar	703/519.8700, 800/800.4000
Enterprise	703/553.7744, 800/736.8222
Hertz	703/419.6300, 800/654.3131
National	703/783.1590, 800/227.7368
Sears	703/920.3367, 800/527.0770
Thrifty	703/658.2200, 800/367.2277

By Limousine The **Dulles Airport Express Taxi** (202/737.5500) serves all three Washington airports. A one-way trip from **National** to Downtown DC is approximately $40.

By Taxi There are several taxi stands in the traffic circle in front of **Terminal A.** At **Terminals B** and **C,** the taxi stands are located just outside the baggage claim area on the lower level. Dispatchers are on duty at all stands. Expect to pay $15 for a trip to Downtown DC, which should take 25 minutes during non-rush hours.

By Train The **Metrorail** (637.7000) is without a doubt the cheapest way to get to or from **National**

Airport. The **National Airport Metro** station (on the **Yellow** and **Blue** lines) offers trains to Downtown DC; service begins at 5:30AM on weekdays and 8AM on weekends, and runs until approximately 11:40PM daily. **Terminals B** and **C** are connected to the **Metro** station by covered pedestrian walkways.

Bus Station (Long-Distance)

The only bus station in the DC area is the **Greyhound Station** (1005 First St NE, at K St, 289.5155) three blocks north of **Union Station,** just north of Capitol Hill. A taxi stand is right at the main entrance. The station's offices are open 6AM to midnight. For **Greyhound** schedules and fares, call 800/231.2222.

Train Station (Long-Distance)

Washington's **Union Station** (50 Massachusetts Ave NE, at First St, 371.9441) is one of the city's architectural jewels. Constructed in 1908, its soaring spaces are pretty much intact, thanks to a major restoration in the 1980s. (For a more detailed description of the building, see the "Capitol Hill" chapter.) The station is conveniently located just north of the **Capitol** (you'll see that familiar dome as you come out of the station's main doors). Most of the trains serve the Eastern seaboard, especially the Northeast Corridor (from Washington up to Boston). But there is service to the Midwest and connecting trains to other points. The station's offices are open from 5AM to midnight, although the building is open 24 hours a day. A **Metrorail** station is on the lower level, and a taxi stand is at the main entrance, where a dispatcher will guide you to a cab. For information on **Amtrak** schedules and fares, call 800/872.7245.

Getting Around DC

Bicycles and Mopeds Biking around DC can be thrilling—and dangerous. A ride along the bike paths of **Rock Creek Park** is glorious. But maneuvering around DC's angled streets and traffic circles, with confused tourists and reckless diplomats, is daunting even for residents. If you'd like to rent a bike or moped, try Capitol Hill's **Metropolis Bike & Scooter** (709 Eighth St SE, between I and G Sts, 543.8900) or Georgetown's **Big Wheel Bikes** (1034 33rd St NW, between the Chesapeake & Ohio Canal and M St, 337.0254). **Bike the Sites** (966.8662) offers two-hour tours of DC, with bike and helmet rentals; groups meet on **The Mall.**

By Bus More than 1,500 **Metrobuses** thread their way along about 400 routes in the DC area at speeds seldom exceeding 35 miles per hour. Many routes are designed to supplement and extend the reach of the rail system, but in some areas the bus is the sole source of public transportation. Buses are the only public transportation available to Georgetown, for example. Even-numbered *30* buses *(30, 32, 34, 36)* connect Georgetown to Downtown DC and **Upper Northwest.**

Bus-to-bus transfers are free within DC, with some surcharges on routes to the suburbs; get a transfer from the driver as you enter. The fare is $1.10; exact change is required and dollar bills are accepted. For more information, call the **Washington Metropolitan Area Transit Authority** (637.7000).

By Car DC is a somewhat bewildering place to navigate. The National Park Service's highway signs—easily read at horse-and-buggy speed—are often illegible to a harried motorist trying to find the right lane on the Rock Creek Parkway.

Unfortunately, you'll probably have ample time to read the signs, as the highways are crowded. The Beltway (Interstates 95 and 495) loops around the city's Downtown area and connects it to the suburbs. The few bridges over the Potomac (the **American Legion Memorial** and the **Woodrow Wilson Memorial Bridges** on the Beltway; the Roosevelt Bridge on Interstate 66; the Key and Arlington Memorial Bridges; and the popular 14th Street Bridge) quickly become rush-hour bottlenecks. Radio traffic reports on **WTOP** (1500 AM) are helpful.

In an attempt to handle Washington rush hours, certain traffic adjustments have been made. For example, Rock Creek Parkway becomes one way during rush hours, and some major thoroughfares, such as **Connecticut Avenue,** switch the direction of several lanes to match the traffic flow. Interstate 66 is restricted to car pools with two or more people inbound during morning rush hour and outbound in the evening; Interstate 395 has restricted car pool lanes during rush hours.

In addition to traffic woes, DC drivers have another worry: diplomats. Washingtonians have long cringed at the vehicular mayhem caused by some members of the diplomatic corps, who take advantage of the diplomatic immunity that protects them from criminal prosecution and civil suits resulting from an accident. Concern over these reckless drivers who refuse to heed parking regulations or speed limits has resulted in a law granting victims of diplomatic drivers some financial compensation in lieu of insurance payments. The State Department issues red-white-and-blue license plates to the diplomatic corps. You'd be wise to give them a wide berth.

Parking Be forewarned that the DC government is singularly efficient in its parking enforcement. Metered street parking generally runs for a two-hour maximum at a quarter for each 20 minutes; carry lots of quarters and return to the car on time. Expired meters incur a hefty ticket, and cars left in rush-hour zones are swiftly towed at painful cost. The DC police have also instituted strict weekend parking regulations in Georgetown in an effort to reduce congestion. Obey the special signs or risk having your car impounded. Parking on **The Mall** is free but scarce and is limited to three hours. All spaces for the disabled are monitored; if your car doesn't have a handicap license plate, don't try it. Your best bet is to leave your car in one of the downtown parking garages, which are plentiful but expensive, and use the **Metro** to get around from there. Given the high cost of tickets and towing, the garages could almost turn out to be a bargain.

Subways The steadily expanding **Metrorail** system—part subway, part surface transit—

9

comprises five color-coded lines that snake from the suburbs through Downtown DC and back (see map on inside back cover). Thanks to built-in quality control features by designer **Harry Weese,** travel by **Metrorail** is clean, comfortable, and usually very safe. More than 500,000 passengers use the system on an average day. Hours of operation are Monday through Friday from 5:30AM until midnight; Saturday and Sunday from 8AM until midnight. Most stations receive their last train at about 11:45PM; check "last train" posting at station kiosk. Station entrances are marked by a tall dark brown pylon, a large letter "M" displayed on all four sides. Brightly colored stripes beneath the logo indicate which lines serve that particular station. In addition to the color of the line, it is essential to know that train's last stop; trains on the same line may have different end points. The front of each train is clearly marked.

The fare you pay depends on where you get on and off and what time of day you travel. Rush-hour fares are in effect weekdays (excluding federal holidays) from 5:30AM until 9:30AM and again from 3PM until 7PM. A Farecard is a good way to deal with the cumbersome price hierarchy; you can get one that's good for up to $30 worth of travel. One-day or weekend family/tourist passes are available at the **Metro Center** station (12th and G Sts NW, 637.7000), at main transfer points, and at selected hotels.

Special discount fares for students, senior citizens, and the disabled are also available. (Although **Metrorail** is accessible to the disabled, its elevators are sometimes hard to find.) Up to two children age four or younger travel free with a paying customer. Ask about Flashpasses for various subway/bus combinations. (Free subway-to-bus transfers are available from machines inside your station of origin, but there are no bus-to-subway transfers.)

Don't be daunted; once you figure out how to use it, the subway is very convenient to most of the places you'll want to visit. If you have questions, go to **Metro Center,** the main transfer point on the **Blue, Red,** and **Orange** lines. An agent at one of the station windows at the **12th and F Streets** exit can help you or call 637.7000 for information about routes, fares (including disabled, student, and senior citizen), and parking; and how to get schedules by mail. Other help lines: bike-on-rail permits (962.1116); on-call service for the disabled (962.1825); TDD for the hearing-impaired (638.3780); lost and found (962.1195); transit police (962.2121). Visitors who plan ahead can call 800/METRO.INFO to request a **Metro** map and guides.

By Taxi DC's taxi system is a local embarrassment. Cabs are often dilapidated, and drivers are often rude, unscrupulous, and ignorant of the city's geography. The situation could be improved if Congress would legislate meters, and if the District would do something about the lax regulation of the taxi system. On the other hand, DC cabs are cheap and plentiful compared with those in other cities. There are about 8,000 cabs, so hailing one is rarely a problem.

DC cab fares are based on a zone system (the District is divided into eight zones), with an additional charge for each zone traversed. A surcharge is added onto the fare for additional passengers and during evening rush hours. Fare information, along with zone maps, should be displayed in each cab (be sure to specify which quadrant of the city you want). Unfortunately, this confusing system, in combination with the low fares, encourages drivers to overcharge. Caveat emptor: Drivers are allowed to pick up multiple fares as long as they take the original rider no more than five blocks out of the way of the original destination—great if it's a rainy day and you're the second or third fare; not so great if you're in a hurry. Fares from DC to the airports are based on mileage.

The three largest DC cab companies are **Yellow Cab** (544.1212), **Diamond** (387.6200), and **Capitol** (546.2400); they're all radio-dispatch cabs. Maryland and Virginia cabs use meters; they can take you in and out of DC, but not between spots within DC itself.

Tours For a walking tour of Washington contact **A Tour de Force** (703/525.2948), **TOUR DC** (301/588.8999), or **DC Heritage Tours** (639.0908). If you'd rather ride, the **Gold Line/Gray Line** (301/386.8300) offers a variety of tours on large air-conditioned buses. Roll by the major sites with **Old Town Trolley Tours of Washington** (832.9800) or **Tourmobile** (554.7950). **DC Ducks** (966.DUCK) lets you cruise both the streets and the Potomac—without leaving your seat—in a World War II amphibious vehicle. They operate from April to mid-November. For a cruise up the Potomac, contact **The Dandy** (703/683.6076), which offers lunch and dinner cruises daily year-round. If you'd like to try cycling around DC, **Bike the Sites** (966.8662, info@bikethesites.com) offers several tours geared to different abilities. Fun, educational itineraries can be custom-designed for your family by the **Children's Concierge** (301/948.3312, sdhoff@kidsgotoo.com). Outside the city, you can tour the **Miles River** to see nesting ospreys, historic houses, and Navy Point on the *Patriot of St. Michael's* (Navy Point, St. Michael's, Maryland, 410/745.3100).

Walking There's an easy and inexpensive way to see Washington: on foot. Walking around **The Mall** on a lovely day is a pleasure few other cities can offer; so many attractions are near one another and the broad lawn and shady trees provide a buffer to all that concrete and marble. A number of neighborhoods—Georgetown, Adams-Morgan, Capitol Hill, Foggy Bottom—were made for strolling, with their fine architecture and plentiful diversions, restaurants, and shops. When walking in unfamiliar areas, however, don't wander too far from popular attractions, and exercise extra caution at night.

In the late 1890s, luxury apartments rented for $35 to $50 a month in DC's most fashionable buildings. Current lessees have to shell out upwards of $2,000 per month.

FYI

Accommodations DC's many hotel rooms are at times occupied by almost as many visitors as conventioneers. In early spring, around the time the cherry blossoms bloom, rooms can be hard to come by, unless you're willing to settle for modest lodgings in areas less convenient to attractions. For help finding the right hotel, contact **Washington DC Accommodations** (800/554.2220) or **Capitol Reservations** (800/554.6750). For information about bed-and-breakfast accommodations, contact the **Bed and Breakfast/Sweet Dreams & Toast** (PO Box 9490, Washington, DC 20016, 363.7767) or **Bed 'n' Breakfast, Ltd.** (PO Box 12011, Washington, DC 20005, 328.3510, www.bnbaccom.com).

Climate DC is a temperate city, except during the summers, when the heat and humidity can wilt even the hardiest soul. Thunderstorms are frequent during the summer, and about 18 inches of snow falls during an average winter—just enough to send Washington drivers into a tizzy. Spring and fall are the best times to visit; during these seasons a sweater or jacket should be just right.

Months	Average Temperature (°F)
December-January	37
March-May	56
June-August	75
September-November	58

Drinking The legal drinking age in DC, Maryland, and Virginia is 21. Bars in the District can serve liquor until 2AM Monday through Thursday and Sunday, and until 3AM Friday and Saturday. Retail liquor store prices are generally cheapest within DC. Beer is sold in liquor stores, supermarkets with liquor departments, and the occasional market. Liquor stores close on Sunday.

Hours Throughout this guide, opening and closing times for shops, attractions, coffeehouses, and other establishments are listed by days only, if normal business hours apply (opening between 8AM and 11AM and closing between 4PM and 7PM). Otherwise specific hours are given (e.g., Su noon-5PM or daily 24 hours).

Money Banks are generally open Monday through Friday from 9AM to 3PM, with longer hours on Friday. Weekend hours are rare. Cash machines are plentiful, and can be found not only at banks but in public places like **Smithsonian** museums, supermarkets, and some **Metrorail** stations. **Thomas Cook Foreign Exchange** exchanges foreign currency, as do several major banks. Travelers checks are available at most local banks.

Personal Safety The city's reputation for street crime is in some ways well earned, but most of the personal crime takes place in neighborhoods far away from the tourist attractions. Even so, it's important to stay alert. Pickpockets are not unusual on crowded **Metro** trains and muggers can lurk in the shadows on lovely side streets. The **Metrorail** system has an exemplary safety record, with a strong police presence and attendants at each station to assist you. **Metrobuses** are not as well monitored. Car break-ins are not uncommon, so don't leave any possessions visible in your car when you park it. You can hail cabs in the more populous areas, or ask your hotel's concierge or a restaurant maître d' to call a cab.

Publications *The Washington Post* is the region's major daily; *The Washington Times* offers a conservative slant. The free weekly *City Paper* is particularly good for tracking the local entertainment scene, as is the *Post*'s "Weekend" section, published every Friday. *The Washingtonian* is a monthly magazine that covers the lifestyles of DC's movers and shakers. The new *Capital Style* monthly magazine also has its finger on the pulse of the nation's capital. The weekly *Capital Spotlight* offers an African-American perspective on local and national events; the *Current* newspapers, with weekly editions for Northwest, Georgetown, and Rock Creek, cover music, lectures, and shops in their respective areas. *Washington Review* offers insight into the cultural scene on a bimonthly basis.

Radio Stations Station formats can change with the seasons; don't be surprised if what you hear is not what you expected.

AM:		
570	WTEM	Business
630	WMAL	News/Talk/Sports
1260	WWDC	Big Band/Original Hits
1500	WTOP	News Radio
FM:		
88.5	WAMU	News/Talk/Music (NPR)
89.3	WPFW	Jazz/Community Radio
90.9	WETA	Classical (NPR)
93.9	WKYS	Urban Contemporary
94.7	WARW	Classic Rock
95.5	WPGC	Contemporary/Top 40
96.3	WHUR	Urban Adult
97.1	WASH	Soft Rock
98.7	WMZQ	Country
99.1	WHFS	Alternative
99.5	WGAY	Soft Rock/Contemporary
101.1	WWDC	Rock
103.5	WGMS	Classical
107.3	WRQX	Adult Contemporary

Restaurants Since you'll be vying for a table with Washington's ever-burgeoning dining-out population, it's wise to make reservations. Dress at most restaurants is relaxed, but it never hurts to double-check; for example, summer attire such as shorts and sandals may not pass muster. A few restaurants in the Foggy Bottom area (near the **Kennedy Center**) and Downtown (near the **Shakespeare Theatre**) offer menus for pre-theater diners, and some of the city's tonier spots offer prix-fixe menus; ask about special menus when making reservations. Regarding late-night meals: In this hard-working town, most people hit the sack early (even on weekends), so you may have to look around for restaurants that stay open late; these are likeliest to be in Georgetown and Adams-Morgan.

Shopping Downtown used to be the place to shop in Washington, and there is still some good shopping at the **Shops at National Place** (F St NW, between 13th and 14th Sts), but more fertile fields lie along lower Connecticut Avenue (between K St and Florida Ave), in Georgetown (along Wisconsin Ave and M St), and in Adams-Morgan (along 18th St and Columbia Rd). Upper **Wisconsin Avenue,** near the Maryland line, is home to two city malls: **Mazza Gallerie** and **Chevy Chase Pavilion,** catering to shoppers with deeper pockets. The best place to shop ethnic, especially Latin, Caribbean, and African, is in Adams-Morgan. And don't forget the **Smithsonian** shops, all of which offer good selections of souvenirs and one-of-a-kind gifts adapted from the museums' collections.

Smoking It is illegal to smoke on public transportation, in theaters, outside of designated smoking areas in restaurants, and in most shops.

Street Plan DC is a rectangle bordered on the southwest by the Potomac River and the other three sides by the state of Maryland. Within the city are four quadrants: Northwest (largest, most of Downtown), Northeast (mostly residential), Southwest (smallest, government buildings, the Potomac waterfront), and Southeast (Capitol Hill and residential). The **Capitol** is at the "center" of the city and the quadrants are determined in relation to it. Not all the quadrants are the same size, so some have many fewer streets than others. The directions in which they branch off determine the street names, i.e., there are four **First Streets** in Washington: NW, NE, SW, and SE.

Within the quadrants, streets form a grid: Those running north–south are numbered and east–west streets are lettered. Avenues—many named for states such as Pennsylvania, Connecticut, and New York—run on diagonals through the grid. Avenues intersect at traffic circles (**Dupont Circle,** where Massachusetts, Connecticut, and New Hampshire Avenues intersect, is the best known).

It is a popular delusion that the government wastes vast amounts of money through inefficiency and sloth. Enormous effort and elaborate planning are required to waste this much money.

P.J. O'Rourke
Parliament of Whores

Taxes The hotel tax is 14.5 percent in DC, 9.75 percent in Virginia, and 12 percent in Maryland. Restaurants charge a 10 percent tax on meals in DC, 8.5 percent in Virginia, and five percent in Maryland. The sales tax is six percent in DC, 4.5 percent in Virginia, and five percent in Maryland.

Tickets Most theaters in the Washington area sell advance tickets over the phone, charged to your credit card for a small fee. When you call, ask about student and senior citizen discounts. **Ticketmaster** (432.7328) has a monopoly on many big-event tickets, although tickets for sellout events such as **Washington Redskins** games are often available at hefty markups through classified ads in *The Washington Post* as well as through other ticket brokers. For tickets to **Orioles** games, try the **Orioles Baseball Store** (925 17th St NW, between I and K Sts, 296.2473). No telephone charges are accepted. **Ticket Connection** (8121 Georgia Ave, between Sligo and Silver Spring Aves, Suite 101, Silver Spring, Maryland, 301/587.6850) sells tickets to concert, theater, and sporting events. **Ticket Finders** (7833 Walker Dr, off Greenbelt Rd, Suite 510, Greenbelt, Maryland, 301/513.0300) specializes in tickets for sellout events, including concerts and **Redskins** games; cost rises with the popularity of the event. **The Ticket Outlet, Inc.** (105 E Annandale Rd, at S Washington St, Suite 208, Falls Church, Virginia, 703/538.4044) brokers tickets for **Redskins** games, concerts, and other high-demand events; price is based on the event's popularity. Located in the Old Post Office Pavilion, **TicketPlace** (1100 Pennsylvania Ave NW, at 11th St, 842.5387) sells half-price tickets the day of the show for local theaters, including the **Arena Stage, Kennedy Center,** and **Warner** and **National Theaters.** Only cash or traveler's checks are accepted, and a service charge is added. Full-price tickets are available in advance and can be charged to a credit card for a fee. **Top Centre Ticket and Limousine Service** (2000 Pennsylvania Ave NW, at 20th St, 452.9040) sells tickets for **Redskins** games and other sporting events, concerts, and theatrical performances. A service charge is added. **Washington Performing Arts Society** (2000 L St NW, at 20th St, 833.9800), the city's largest nonprofit arts organization, sponsors concerts at the **Kennedy Center, Dance Place,** and **Lisner Auditorium,** with offerings ranging from foreign orchestras **(Warsaw Philharmonic, Vienna Symphony Orchestra)** to folk music, dance, jazz, and gospel. If all else fails, ask your hotel's concierge, who may have his or her own resources.

Time Zone Washington is in the Eastern Time Zone, same as New York City, and three hours ahead of California.

Tipping A 15-percent tip is standard in restaurants; the meal tax is 10 percent, so increase the tax by half, unless you feel like being generous. Taxi drivers are also tipped 15 percent of the fare. Hotel and station porters generally expect one dollar per bag; maids should get at least two dollars a day, depending on the size and accoutrements of the room.

Visitors' Information Center The Washington DC Convention and Visitors Association (1212 New York Ave NW, between 12th and 13th Sts, Suite 600, 789.7000, www.washington.org) coordinates all tourist information from their Downtown office. Stop in for detailed maps, suggestions on where to stay, eat, and shop, as well as information on DC's famous and not-so-famous sights. The center is open weekdays from 9AM to 5PM.

Phone Book

Emergencies

AAA Emergency Road Service	703/222.5000
Ambulance/Fire/Police	911
Auto Impound	727.5000
Auto Theft	727.1010
Dental Emergency	301/770.0123

Hospitals

George Washington University	994.1000
Georgetown University	784.2000
Sibley Memorial Hospital	537.4000
Washington Hospital Center	877.7000
Locksmith (AAA 24-hour)	547.8236
Pharmacy (24-hour)	785.1466
Poison Control Center	625.3333
Police (non-emergency)	727.1010

Visitors' Information

AAA Road Conditions Information	703/222.5000
American Youth Hostels	783.4943
Amtrak Railroad Service	800/872.7245
Better Business Bureau	393.8000
Disabled Visitors' Information	789.7000
Greyhound Bus	800/231.2222
Metro Transit (Washington Metropolitan Area Transit Authority)	637.7000
US Customs	927.6724
US Passport Office	647.0518
Weather	936.1212

Capital Celebrations

Washingtonians love a parade—or a street fair or festival or any excuse to party and, not incidentally, be given a day off from work. (After all, this is the only place in America where workers get a holiday every fourth 20 January—Inauguration Day.) Planning a trip to Washington on any major holiday guarantees you can get in on the fun. Read on for details on those celebrations and a few others throughout the year. Admission to all events is free unless otherwise noted.

January

Inauguration Day

As mentioned, every four years on 20 January, a new term of office begins for a US president, and the city is packed with well-wishers from the winning party. Private parties are the order of the day, but there are usually public events on **The Mall** and you can stand along **Pennsylvania Avenue** and watch the president lead an impressive parade of bands from just about every state. There's usually a terrific fireworks show in the evening. Just bring your winter woolens; this is the coldest time of the year.

February

Chinese New Year Parade Washington has a tiny **Chinatown,** but that doesn't dampen the enthusiasm or turnout for this annual affair, complete with colorful dancing dragons and street-level fireworks. The parade travels along **H Street Northwest**

between **Sixth** and **Seventh Streets.** Call 789.7000 for the exact date.

Washington's Birthday Parade On the Saturday closest to 22 February, **Old Town Alexandria** throws a big party for our nation's first chief executive, whose **Mount Vernon** home is just down the road. Locals turn out in colonial costume, bands play, and there are even a few floats, though this will never be mistaken for the Tournament of Roses parade. Call 703/838.9350 for schedule of events.

March

Smithsonian Kite Festival On the last Saturday of March, the skies around the **Washington Monument** are filled with colorful, high-flying contraptions of paper and light wood. Competitions in design, performance, and other categories are held, but winning is secondary to the exhilaration of being outdoors on an early spring day. For more information, call 357.2700.

April

Cherry Blossom Festival Spring officially kicks off with this festival, which seems to grow larger every year. The blossoms usually bloom the first week of April, with two weeks of celebration offering a wide variety of events. Concerts and a big parade (usually the first Saturday of April) are the highlights. Call 547.1500 for a schedule of events.

White House Easter Egg Roll On the Monday after Easter, children ages 3 through 6, accompanied by an adult, are invited to assemble on the **South Lawn** of the **White House.** Participation is limited to this event, but a larger party also takes place across the street on the **Ellipse.** For more information, call 456.7041.

Georgetown Garden Tour On a Sunday in late April, tour the backyards of the Rich and Possibly Famous during this annual event. Call 333.6896 for the exact date.

May

Filmfest DC For two weeks during spring, Washington turns into a modest approximation of Cannes, with screenings of films from a variety of countries, as well as parties and receptions—all open to the public. Events are held at several commercial theaters and a few of the not-for-profit venues like the museum theaters. Admission is charged. Call 274.6810 for more information.

Preakness Celebration In mid-May, **Baltimore**'s biggest party of the year celebrates the second jewel in racing's Triple Crown. Balloon rides, concerts, tall ship–viewing in the harbor, and hearty partying are just some of the highlights of this nine-day event. The race comes almost as an afterthought. Call 410/542.9400 for a schedule of events.

Memorial Day Ceremonies Arlington National Cemetery (703/695.3175), the **Vietnam Veterans Memorial** (619.7222), and the **US Navy Memorial** (433.2525) are the sites for solemn ceremonies to honor the nation's war dead. Call for ceremony schedules.

June

PGA Kemper Open Early in June, the area's premier golf course, the **Tournament Players Club** at Avenel (in Potomac, Maryland) hosts this stop on the PGA Tour. The long and demanding course is laid out stadium-style, with tiered areas around the greens to give spectators better vantage points on the action.

Admission is charged. Call 301/469.3737 for exact dates.

Festival of American Folklife For the last weekend in June and first in July, the **Smithsonian**'s museums put on the summer's best show. **The Mall** becomes home to craftspeople, musicians, and, perhaps most important, cooks from a trio or quartet of American and foreign cultures. Each year focuses on different regions of the US and one foreign country. Call 357.2700 for more information.

July

Fourth of July Celebration A huge **Independence Day** parade kicks off Washington's biggest party. **The Festival of American Folklife** concludes on this day, and in the early evening the **National Symphony** presents a free concert on the **West Lawn** of the **Capitol.** Get there early with your blanket and picnic supplies. Finally, there's the mammoth fireworks display centered at the **Washington Monument,** but visible from many areas of the city. For more information, call 416.8100.

Bastille Day On 14 July, French Independence Day is celebrated with a race featuring waiters and waitresses carrying trays of Champagne along 12 blocks of Pennsylvania Avenue. Live entertainment and food keep the celebration going into the night. For more information, call 296.7200.

August

Maryland State Fair Maryland's own piece of Americana doesn't change much from year to year, and most people like it that way. The fair is held late in the month at the **Timonium Fairgrounds,** north of Baltimore. Admission is charged. Call 410/252.0200 for exact dates.

September

National Symphony Concert On Sunday of **Labor Day** weekend, the end of summer is marked by this big outdoor concert, held on the **West Lawn** of the **Capitol.** Crowds are more modest and temperatures more reasonable than at the **Fourth of July** affair. For more information, call 416.8100.

Adams-Morgan Day This weekend event in mid-September is the urban equivalent of a state fair, with games, music, crafts, and plenty of food in Washington's most ethnically diverse neighborhood. Call 332.3292 for a schedule of events.

Maryland Renaissance Festival This annual event has grown from a single weekend to stretch over nearly two months (beginning in September) of Saturdays and Sundays. Medieval games, food, entertainment, and the ever-popular jousting keep crowds coming back for more. The festival takes place in **Crownsville,** Maryland. Admission is charged. Call 800/296.7304 for exact dates.

October

Taste of DC For one weekend early in the month, Pennsylvania Avenue is closed to cars and open to booths with samplings of many of the area's best restaurants. Live entertainment adds to the fun. This is a great way to decide where you want to eat during your visit. For more information, call 347.2873.

Marine Corps Marathon The Marines only run the race, they don't run in it. On a crisp fall Sunday in late October, you get to cheer on some of the country's best long-distance runners—and take some inspiration for your own fitness regimen. Call 703/784.2225 for the exact date.

Halloween in Georgetown Not a scheduled event, but more of a happening on the 31st. Thousands of people congregate at **Wisconsin Avenue Northwest** and **M Street** to parade their costumes, which are often of the political bent: 1998 had a surfeit of bereted Monica Lewinskys and prison-garbed Bill Clintons.

November

Veterans Day On 11 November, wreaths are laid at the **Tomb of the Unknowns** (703/695.3175) and ceremonies are held at the **Vietnam Veterans Memorial** (619.7222), as thousands of vets come to Washington to honor their fallen comrades. Call for ceremony schedules.

December

Scottish Christmas Walk On the first weekend of the month, Alexandria's annual parade and festival honors Celtic traditions. Crafts and food will get you in the holiday mood. For more information, call 703/549.0111.

The Pageant of Peace Also early in the month, the lighting of the National Christmas Tree on the **Ellipse,** with music and caroling, is the official kickoff for the holiday season. Call 619.7222 for the exact date.

New Year's Eve Celebrations As part of a growing trend, many cities in the Washington-Baltimore area are holding nonalcoholic, family-oriented festivals featuring music, dance, and other performances. Among the participating communities (and phone numbers for information) are Alexandria, 540/835.1526; and Baltimore, 800/282.6632.

Capitol Hill/
Northeast/
Southeast

50

DOWNTOWN

NORTHEAST

CAPITOL HILL

SOUTHWEST

SOUTHEAST

The Mall

Union Square

Spring Grotto

Union Station

Judiciary Sq

Federal Center SW

Capitol South

Eastern Market

Waterfront

Navy Yard

Anacostia

Lincoln Park

Potomac Ave

Marine Corps Museum

Navy Museum

U.S.S. Barry

Anacostia Bridge

11th Street Bridge

Anacostia River

Frederick Douglass Memorial Bridge

U.S. Naval Reservation

Florida Ave. NE
Mount Olivet Rd.
West Virginia Ave. NE
Queen St. NE
Montello Ave. NE
Trinidad Ave.
Oates St.
Neal St.
Morse St.

M St. NE
L St. NE
K St. NE
I St. NE
H St. NE
G St. NE

New Jersey Ave. NW
N Capitol St.
1st St. NE
3rd St. NE
7th St. NE
8th St. NE

F St. NE
E St. NE
D St. NE
C St. NE

Maryland Ave. NE
Massachusetts Ave. NE
Tennessee Ave. NE

1st St. NW
Louisiana Ave.
Delaware Ave.

Pennsylvania Ave. NW
Constitution Ave. NE
A St. NE
E Capitol St.
A St. SE

Maryland Ave. SW
Independence Ave. SE
North Carolina Ave. SE
South Carolina Ave. SE
Kentucky Ave.

Canal St. SW
S Capitol St.
1st St. SE
2nd St. SE
4th St. SE
5th St. SE
6th St. SE
7th St. SE
9th St. SE
10th St. SE
11th St. SE
12th St. SE
13th St. SE
14th St. SE
15th St. SE

D St. SE
E St. SE
F St. SE
G St. SE

Virginia Ave.
Pennsylvania Ave. SE

Southeast Fwy.
I St. SE
K St. SE
L St. SE
M St. SE
Potomac Ave.

395

4th St. SW
Delaware Ave. SW
Half St.
New Jersey Ave. SE
M St. SW
N St. SW
O St. SW
P St. SW

Potomac Ave. SE

1st St. SW

Ridge Pl. SE
S St. SE
Good Hope Rd. SE
U St. SE
13th St.
V St. SE
W St. SE
14th St.

Martin Luther King Jr. Ave. SE

1 2 3 4 5 6 7 8 9 10 11 12 13 14 15 16 21 22 23 24 25 26 27 28 29 30 31 32 33 34 35 36 37 38 39 40

N

km   1/2   1
mi 1/4   1/2

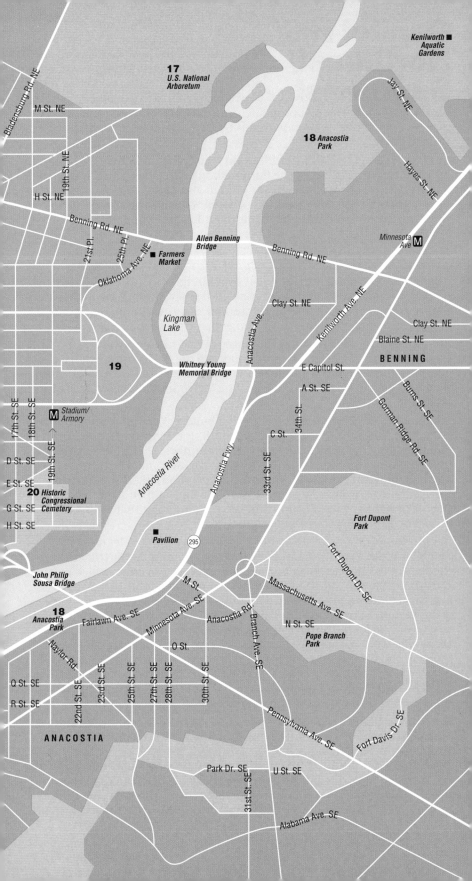

Kenilworth ■
Aquatic
Gardens

Jay St. NE

17
U.S. National
Arboretum

18 Anacostia
Park

Bladensburg Rd. NE

M St. NE

Hayes St. NE

19th St. NE

H St. NE

Minnesota Ave ⓂＭ

Benning Rd. NE

21st Pl.

25th Pl.

Allen Benning
Bridge

Benning Rd. NE

Oklahoma Ave. NE

■ Farmers
Market

Clay St. NE

BENNING

Anacostia Ave.

Kenilworth Ave. NE

Clay St. NE

Kingman
Lake

Blaine St. NE

19

Whitney Young
Memorial Bridge

E Capitol St.

A St. SE

Burns St. SE

34th St.

Gorman Ridge Rd. SE

17th St. SE

18th St. SE

ⓂＭ Stadium/
Armory

C St.

33rd St. SE

19th St. SE →

D St. SE

Anacostia River

E St. SE

20 Historic
Congressional
Cemetery

Fort Dupont
Park

G St. SE

Anacostia Fwy.

H St. SE

■ Pavilion

Fort Dupont Dr. SE

295

John Philip
Sousa Bridge

M St.

Massachusetts Ave. SE

18
Anacostia
Park

Fairlawn Ave. SE

Minnesota Ave. SE

Anacostia Rd.

Branch Ave. SE

N St. SE

Pope Branch
Park

Naylor Rd.

O St.

Q St. SE

22nd St. SE

23rd St. SE

25th St. SE

27th St. SE

28th St. SE

30th St. SE

R St. SE

Pennsylvania Ave. SE

Fort Davis Dr. SE

ANACOSTIA

Park Dr. SE

U St. SE

31st St. SE

Alabama Ave. SE

Capitol Hill/ Northeast/ Southeast

Although Capitol Hill may not lie in the exact geographical center of Washington, it is, nonetheless, the heart of the city. Whether you're involved in government or not, there is a permeating sense that much of what happens in this town either starts or concludes on "the Hill." Appropriately, the directionals at the end of every DC street name give its relation to this country's seat of democracy with its familiar dome.

In 1790, when **Pierre-Charles L'Enfant**, the Frenchman hired to design a capital city on the banks of the **Potomac**, spied the grassy rise, it was called **Jenkins Hill. L'Enfant** had already chosen a site a few miles to the west for the presidential residence, so this "pedestal waiting for a superstructure" would be the home of what he modestly called "the congressional building."

Ten years later, as the building, now known as the **Capitol**, was under construction, Secretary of the Treasury Albert Gallatain described the neighborhood around the **Capitol** as containing "seven or eight boarding houses, one tailor, one shoemaker, one printer, a washing woman, a grocery shop, a pamphlets and stationery store, and an oyster house," and considered it "far from being pleasant or even convenient."

Almost 200 years later, Capitol Hill, the area that fans out eastward from the **Capitol**, and the adjoining neighborhoods to the north and south have become quite pleasant, with a few more merchants and places to eat and stay than in Gallatain's day; and thanks to the **Metro** subway system, it is easily accessible.

Surrounding the **Capitol** are several other buildings, familiar perhaps more by name than by sight. To the immediate south sit three huge House office buildings (the **Rayburn, Longworth,** and **Cannon**); to the north, three more office buildings for the Senate (the **Russell, Dirksen,** and **Hart**). To the east are the **Library of Congress**, whose ever-expanding collections have filled three buildings, and the **Supreme Court**, the final arbiter of legal disputes. To the north is the splendid **Union Station**, a train station that's filled to the brim with intriguing shops and eateries.

Beyond these impressive structures lies the "real Hill," a quiet residential neighborhood of neatly maintained row houses, most dating from the turn of the century, some back even further. **Pennsylvania Avenue**, which extends southeast from the **Capitol**, is the Hill's main street, home to many businesses and restaurants (but, alas, no oyster house). At the heart of the Hill is the **Eastern Market** on **Seventh Street Southeast.** The lone survivor of the city's three major food markets from the late 19th and early 20th centuries, the market offers farmers' produce, crafts, and delicious crab cakes; it also serves as a weekend gathering place for residents to catch up with each other after a week of political posturing. Capitol Hill's boundaries depend on who does the mapping—real estate folks, mindful of the cachet the Hill's name holds, throw the net farthest into Northeast and Southeast territory.

Northeast is home to two universities and a college—including **Gallaudet University**, a leader in educating the deaf since 1857, and **Catholic University of America**, since 1887 a bastion of Catholic higher learning. On the grounds of **Catholic University** sits the impressive **National Shrine of the Immaculate Conception. Trinity College** has been offering women a liberal arts education for about a century. Northeast also boasts two glorious refuges, the **US National Arboretum** and the **Kenilworth Aquatic Gardens.**

Southeast is divided by the slow-moving waters of the **Anacostia River.** On the Capitol Hill side are blocks of residences and two military facilities, the tidy **Marine Corps Barracks** complex and the sprawling **Washington Navy Yard.** Across the river lies **Anacostia,** a neighborhood whose hills afford some of the best views of the city. Isolated and more self-contained than any other Washington neighborhood, Anacostia boasts two of the city's most important cultural institutions of African-American history: the **Anacostia Museum,** located in what was once known as Uniontown, a community settled after the Civil War by freed slaves; and **Cedar Hill,** the home of Frederick Douglass, onetime slave and eloquent leader of the abolitionist movement. Douglass's home has been restored by the National Park Service and is now a National Historic Site and museum.

1 Capitol George Washington officiated when the building's cornerstone was laid in 1793, but it was not until 22 November 1800 that the House and Senate moved in and officially called the first joint session of Congress to order. **Dr. William Thornton**'s building at that time was a two-story square construction. By 1807 a similar edifice had been built for the House of Representatives, with a wooden walkway linking the two buildings. British troops invaded Washington on 24 August 1814 and convened a session of their own in the Senate building. They decided that day to burn the building down along with other federal structures; only a sudden summer rainstorm spared the building from total destruction. Five years later, it was repaired, and Congress returned home. What you see today (see the illustration below) is an outgrowth of that 1819 restoration. (Incidentally, by law no structure in DC can be higher than the Capitol.)

Most visitors enter the building via the **East Front,** where every four years on 20 January—with rare exceptions, such as Ronald Reagan's two inaugurations—a presidential inauguration ceremony takes place. As you go up the steps toward the magnificent bronze **Columbus Doors,** pity the poor souls standing here for one and a half hours while William Henry Harrison delivered the longest inaugural speech on record in a drizzly downpour; he died of pneumonia three weeks later. Here, too, Franklin D. Roosevelt reassured an economically depressed nation, by declaring that "the only thing we have to fear is fear itself." From the steps of the **East Portico** John F. Kennedy uttered the famous words: "Ask not what your country can do for you; ask what you can do for your country."

A small wooden dome sheathed in copper once crowned the **Capitol,** but in the 1850s Congress decided it was unsafe and badly proportioned. A much bigger one, designed by **Thomas U. Walter,** was commissioned and was to be raised, topped with a sculpture, with the engineering expertise of General Montgomery Meigs. But erratic financing followed by the Civil War slowed construction. When the secretary of war wanted to divert the iron and manpower involved to the war effort, it seemed likely that the project would be scrapped.

At the time, Washington was a shambles, and morale was low. The **Capitol** building was

Capitol Building

COURTESY OF THE BUREAU OF ENGRAVING AND PRINTING

19

doing double duty as a field hospital. Abraham Lincoln appraised the situation and, ignoring criticism, decided construction must go on "as a symbol that our nation will go on." And so, while doctors and chaplains ministered to the wounded, builders hammered overhead. Late in 1863, amid tremendous fanfare, the 19.5-foot statue of *Freedom* was raised to the top of the nine-million-pound cast-iron dome. From a distance, the figure resembles a Native American: She wears a helmet rimmed by stars and finished with an eagle's head (actually symbols from ancient Western mythology).

Much of the artwork in the **Rotunda** and throughout the **Capitol** is a testament to one man, Constantino Brumidi. A political refugee from Italy, he spent 25 years (1852-77) painting the **Capitol**'s interior as a way of thanking his adoptive homeland. Brumidi created the fresco, *Apotheosis of Washington,* in the center of the dome, which represents the 13 original states. He began painting the massive frieze around the Rotunda—a portrayal of 400 years of American history— but, tragically, he nearly fell off his scaffolding and died from the shock of it a few months later. Fellow Italian Filippo Costaggini continued the work; it was finally completed in 1953 by Allyn Cox. Four of the eight large oil paintings lining the **Rotunda**'s walls are the work of John Trumball, an aide to then-General George Washington. Trumball had witnessed each of the Revolutionary War scenes he depicted. When torrents of water flooded the **Rotunda** during a thunderstorm in 1990, it became clear that the dome needed renovating. Several years and temporary fixes later, a major $30-million overhaul was begun in January 1999; during repairs, the area will remain open to visitors.

In 1864, each state was asked to contribute statues of its two most celebrated citizens for exhibition in the **Capitol**. Ninety-two figures, including likenesses of such people as Robert E. Lee (Virginia) and Brigham Young (Utah), are displayed in **Statuary Hall,** south of the **Rotunda.** The House of Representatives met here until 1857. An acoustical phenomenon of **Statuary Hall**'s design was discovered by John Quincy Adams, while serving in the House in his postpresidential years: It seems that at certain spots in the hall you can clearly hear conversations taking place across the room, while those standing in between hear nothing. In 1848, Adams suffered a stroke in this chamber, and a small gold star on the floor designates where the sixth president died.

Public areas north of the **Rotunda** include the **Old Senate Chamber,** the **President's Room,** and the **Old Supreme Court Chamber.** If you're not on the official **Capitol** tour but wish to sit in the **Visitors Galleries** in either the **Senate Chamber** or the **House Chamber,** stop by the office of your senator or representative (depending on which chamber you wish to observe), and pick up a gallery pass. If you don't know your representative's name or office location, call the **Capitol** switchboard (224.3121). Foreign visitors can enter the galleries by showing their passports. Space is reserved in each gallery for visitors with disabilities. An American flag flying over the chamber (south is the House; north, the Senate) means that that legislative body is in session, and a lantern glowing from the **Capitol** dome signals that at least one of the chambers is at work. To find out what's on the day's agenda call 225.6827 or check *The Washington Post*'s daily "Today in Congress" column. The action on Capitol Hill intensifies during December, when elected officials tie up loose ends so they can go home for the holidays. If you want to see Congress in action, this is the time. Although a visit to the chamber galleries is pro forma, those seeking drama during the rest of the year should observe at least one committee meeting. Schedules are also listed in *The Washington Post.* If it's an open meeting, you're free to show up—get there 15 to 30 minutes early.

The Senate cafeteria, on the first floor, is open to the public from 7:30AM to 3:30PM (you may see some familiar faces). The famous Senate bean soup has been served daily since 1901. Visitors are also allowed to ride the subway that links the House and Senate with the Congressional office buildings. During the summer, the **Capitol**'s **West Terrace** hosts free concerts, beginning at 8PM: Monday, **US Navy Band;** Tuesday, **US Air Force Band;** Wednesday, **US Marine Band;** Friday, **US Army Band.** Special concerts take place on Memorial Day weekend, the Fourth of July, and Labor Day weekend. At all times, the **West Terrace** affords an outstanding view of the city and a close-up of the original sandstone **West Front,** which was handsomely restored. When the House or Senate is in night session, that wing remains open.

Tours of the **Capitol** are given daily from 9AM until 3:45PM; they last 45 minutes and leave from the **Rotunda** every 15 minutes. Enter at the East Central staircase (across from the Supreme Court) for the tours. Write your senator or representative in advance to arrange a VIP tour. The address for senators is Senate Office Building, Washington, DC 20510; for representatives it's House Office Building, Washington, DC 20515. ♦ Daily. East Front entrance at Capitol Plaza (between New Jersey Ave SE and Delaware Ave NE). 225.6827 & Metros: Capitol South, Union Station

The Secret Service

Secret Service agents always surround the President of the United States. They are the discreet Men in Black who are sworn to protect him and his family, to literally throw themselves in front of an assassin's bullet.

But protecting the first family was not the original mission of the Secret Service. Immediately after the Civil War the US confronted a currency crisis: Between a third and a half of all its circulating paper money was counterfeit. Enter the Secret Service, created under the Department of the Treasury, whose special task became combating the production of funny money. Within a decade, counterfeiting was severely curtailed (but has yet to be completely eliminated).

Soon the agency broadened its purpose to investigate other government problems: the Teapot Dome Scandals, the Ku Klux Klan, land fraud, and espionage cases. Beginning in 1894, Secret Service agents began guarding President Cleveland on a part-time basis. Then the 1901 assassination of William McKinley, the third president to be assassinated in less than 50 years (Lincoln and Garfield had preceded him), forced the issue of full-time presidential protection. Congress mandated that responsibility be turned over to the Secret Service in 1906. By 1917 three or four men were assigned to the **White House,** while the majority of agents still served the Treasury's anti-counterfeiting force. Though the number of agents guarding the president today has increased, the Secret Service won't reveal any figures.

In 1930, after an unknown intruder managed to walk into the presidential dining room undetected, the **White House** police were placed under the supervision of the Secret Service. Two decades later, officer Leslie Coffelt was shot and killed by Puerto Rican nationalists while protecting President Truman at **Blair House.** Triggered by that attack, Congress enacted legislation that permanently authorized the Secret Service to protect the president, his immediate family, and the vice president, if he wishes. After the assassination of John F. Kennedy in 1963, Congress passed a special act authorizing Jacqueline Kennedy and her two children to be protected by the Secret Service for two years. Then in 1965 that protection was extended to all former presidents and first ladies for life, and children up to the age of 16 (but not first pets: Buddy and Socks are on their own when the Clintons leave office). Interestingly, the widow of a president loses her protection if she remarries.

As a result of Robert F. Kennedy's assassination in 1968, Congress authorized protection of major presidential and vice-presidential candidates. "Major" candidates are those who have qualified for federal campaign matching funds of at least $100,000, have received at least $2,000,000 in contributions, and score at least 5 percent of the vote in major polls and 10 percent in consecutive

primaries. The campaign trail—with multiple stops and staff intent on exposing their candidate to as many voters as possible—can be especially grueling for agents. Twenty-hour days are not unusual. During the 1976 campaign for the Democratic nomination, presidential hopeful Mo Udall and his wife, Ella, showed their appreciation by sharing a nightcap with their Secret Service agents at the end of each day.

On 5 September 1975 President Ford escaped harm when a Secret Service agent grabbed a pistol aimed at him by Lynette (Squeaky) Fromme, a Charles Manson follower, in Sacramento. Less than three weeks later, agents again came to Ford's rescue when political activist Sara Jane Moore fired a revolver, unsuccessfully, at the president. Ronald Reagan was the only president to be hit by a bullet and survive. John Hinckley got off six bullets on 30 March 1981, wounding Reagan in the chest and disabling press secretary Jim Brady before Secret Service agents were able to push them into the limousine and rush to **George Washington University Hospital** (where the emergency unit has since been renamed the Ronald Reagan Emergency Room).

Today the agency has 4,600 employees, 2,000 of whom are special agents assigned to investigative and protective services. Their recruits hail from many areas of expertise: forensics, communications, psychology, intelligence, and communications, to name a few. Among the various divisions are a bicycle unit that patrols the **White House** grounds and a K-9 unit. Founded in the 1970s, the K-9 division originally used German Shepherds but has since switched to Belgian Malinois (from Holland), a breed known for their stamina and adaptability to new environments. At night, the dogs go home with their handlers as part of the family.

Agents not only protect the president and vice president, but also the Treasury, embassies, and diplomats. They may also be called on to guard an item of importance—which have included the Gutenberg Bible, the *Mona Lisa*, the Declaration of Independence, and the US Constitution. The Secret Service will not discuss its methods, other than to say that it works in concert with other public service personnel, including fire and rescue divisions and branches of the law enforcement community.

2 Spring Grotto Visit this cool and quiet hideaway on a hot summer day. Frederick Law Olmsted—best known as the creator of New York's Central Park—designed it in 1875. ◆ Constitution Ave NW (between New Jersey Ave and First St). Metros: Federal Center SW, Judiciary Sq

3 Peace Monument Franklin Simmons designed this marble memorial in 1877 to commemorate sailors slain in the Civil War. Neptune, Mars, Victory, and Peace comfort America as she weeps on the shoulder of History. Inscribed in America's book: "They died that their country might live." ◆ Pennsylvania Ave NW and Union Sq. Metros: Federal Center SW, Judiciary Sq

4 General Ulysses S. Grant Memorial Henry Schrady's statuary in Union Square is the world's second-largest equestrian monument. At the center is a 17-foot bronze of Grant. To the north is the Cavalry Group; seven mounted men prepare to charge as their officer brandishes a sword, his mouth wide open as he shouts the advance. To the south of Grant's statue is the Artillery Group. Three horses, one with a rider, pull a cart holding a cannon and three soldiers, each of whom reveals a different face of battle: One is ready, another frightened, a third weary to the bone.

Schrady was only 31 years old and largely unknown when a jury of the most respected sculptors of his day—among them Augustus Saint-Gaudens and Daniel Chester French—commissioned him for this work. It was dedicated in 1927, though he died before it was completed. The six-acre Reflecting Pool at the foot of the memorial reflects the entire Capitol dome. ◆ Union Sq (between Maryland Ave SW and Pennsylvania Ave NW). Metros: Federal Center SW, Judiciary Sq

5 Library of Congress Ensconced within this institution is the largest library collection in the world, with some 100 million items (and growing). Among its treasures are Jefferson's first draft of the Declaration of Independence, Pierre L'Enfant's original design for Washington, five Stradivarius violins, and one of three perfect Gutenberg Bibles (circa 1455) in existence. Other holdings include rare books, photographs, films, sheet music, maps, and the world's largest collection of comic books.

Funded in 1800 with a mere $5,000, the collection began as a single reference room for Congress. When the British burned it down in 1814 (in retaliation for the library US troops had just burned in Canada), Thomas Jefferson sold his fine private collection to the government as a replacement. The **Jefferson Building,** constructed in 1897 by **Smithmeyer and Pelz,** is an ornate Italian Renaissance/

Beaux Arts confection originally criticized for being too over-the-top. Most striking is the **Main Reading Room,** which is crowned by a soaring, domed octagon in three colors of veined marble. At the entrance, the **Great Hall** is magnificently outfitted with marble columns, arches, mosaics, and paintings. Roland Hinton Perry's whimsical fountain, **The Court of Neptune,** bubbles next to the building's front steps. Twice in the past 60 years the library has been expanded: first the white Georgia marble **John Adams Building,** developed in 1939 by **Pierson and Wilson** (Second St and Independence Ave SE), which focuses on science, technology, and business; then the six-story, 46-acre **James Madison Memorial Building** (101 Independence Ave SE), which houses part of the library's collection of more than 13 million photos and prints, including Mathew Brady's Civil War photographs. The **Madison Building** (designed in 1980 by **DeWitt, Poor, and Shelton**) contains the nation's largest film archive, while its jewellike **Mary Pickford Theatre** screens classics at no charge; call 707.5677 for the schedule.

Specialized collections include the **Manuscript Division,** which comprises volumes from many former presidents' private libraries; the **Local History and Genealogy Division,** where family records may be researched; extensive Asian and European collections; and the **National Library Service for the Blind and Physically Handicapped.**

Concerts are offered in various locations year-round; call 707.5502 for the schedule. Fortunate visitors will catch the **Juilliard String Quartet** playing the library's collection of fine stringed instruments. From October through May, literary events are held in the **Madison Building** and feature noted poets and authors; call 707.5394 for more information.

The **Library of Congress** is open to all researchers over 18 years of age (younger visitors are welcome to see the hallway displays but are not allowed in the reading rooms). A 22-minute orientation film runs in a theater on the **Madison Building**'s first floor every half hour Monday through Friday from 8:30AM to 9PM; Saturday from 8:30AM to 5:30PM. The **Jefferson Building** offers free guided tours Monday through Saturday at 11:30AM, 1PM, 2:30PM, and 4PM. For these tours, visitors should enter through the West Front entrance (across from the **Capitol**). Same-day tickets are dispensed beginning at 10AM. For more information, call 707.5458. A gift shop in the **Madison Building** sells books, cards, and crafts. ◆ Free. M, W, Th 8:30AM-9:30PM; Tu, F, Sa 8:30AM-5PM. 707.5000, reference 707.6500, reading room 707.6400. Jefferson Bldg, First St SE (between

Independence Ave and E Capitol St) ও Metro: Capitol South

Within the Library of Congress:

Madison Building Cafeteria ★$ On the sixth floor of the **Madison Building** is one of the Hill's best restaurant bargains, with high-quality soups, salads, sandwiches, and heavier entrées served in an attractive dining room commanding a panoramic view of the city. ♦ American ♦ M-F breakfast and lunch. No credit cards accepted. 707.8300

6 Supreme Court Armed only with the US Constitution and a carefully delineated authority, the highest court in the land steers the direction of American society perhaps more than any other single power. Thus, anyone who comes to Washington to explore the federal government will find a session at the **Supreme Court Building** one of the city's most rewarding experiences. The nine justices are called into session the first Monday in October. They hear cases for two weeks, then retire to formulate their decisions for another two weeks, continuing this pattern through April. The court's hearings during in-session weeks are open to the public (Monday through Wednesday) on a first-come, first-served basis. Call 479.3030 for more information, as days and times change. There are two lines: a "three-minute line," which admits people for three minutes only; and a "regular line," which allows visitors to sit through an entire argument. *The Washington Post* reports the cases due for review on in-session days. If possible, visit on Monday, because, following discussion, the court takes the bench every Monday (usually until 4 July) to hand down orders and opinions. When the Supreme Court is out of session, courtroom lectures are given Monday through Friday every hour on the half-hour from 9:30AM to 3:30PM. In addition, a half-hour film features the chief justice and others on the bench explaining the history and day-to-day workings of the court.

The Supreme Court began hearing cases in 1790, but the tribunal so lacked prestige that its first chief justice, John Jay, resigned to become governor of New York. Almost 150 years passed before the court was deemed worthy of its own home, a dazzling white Neo-Classical edifice designed in 1935 by **Cass Gilbert.** The building, made of Vermont marble, is fronted with bronze doors that weigh 13,000 pounds each; they depict the history of the legal system from ancient times to the present.

On a less historic note, the **Supreme Court Building** happens to have one of the government's best cafeterias. ♦ Free. Court: M-F. Cafeteria: M-F 7:30-10:30AM, 11:30AM-2PM. First St NE (between E Capitol St and Maryland Ave). 479.3211 ও Metros: Capitol South, Union Station

7 Sewall-Belmont House The National Women's Party bought the house in 1929 for its headquarters, eventually converting it into a museum of American women's political achievements. Its displays commemorate Alice Paul, author of the original Equal Rights Amendments. Exhibits trace the history of the women's movement from its bid for suffrage to the present.

Supreme Court

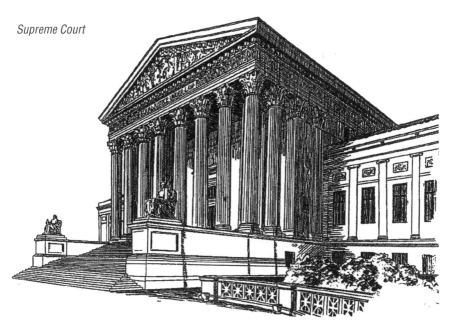

The original structure dates from the late 1600s; additions were made in 1800, and the British burned parts of the house in 1813. Numerous remodelings reflect Queen Anne, Georgian, Classical, and French influences. Albert Gallatain, secretary of the Treasury under both Jefferson and Madison, is purported to have worked out the details of the Louisiana Purchase here. ♦ Free. Tu-F 11AM-3PM; Sa noon-4PM. 144 Constitution Ave NE (at Second St). 546.3989. Metros: Capitol South, Union Station

8 2 Quail ★$$ Creative but uneven New American cuisine is served in three intimate rooms, all quirkily furnished with a collection of mismatched chairs and silverware. Featured entrées are grilled tuna and rainbow trout stuffed with spinach or crabmeat. Among the homemade desserts, the Key lime cheesecake stands out. ♦ Nouvelle American ♦ M-F lunch and dinner; Sa-Su dinner. Reservations recommended. 320 Massachusetts Ave NE (between Fourth and Third Sts). 543.8030. Metro: Union Station

8 Cafe Berlin ★★$$ Dine inside or out on stick-to-your-ribs dishes such as sauerbraten with potato dumplings and red cabbage, or beef goulash with spaetzle. The best choices on the huge dessert menu are apple strudel, Black Forest cake, and linzer torte. ♦ German ♦ M-Sa lunch and dinner; Su dinner. Reservations recommended. 322 Massachusetts Ave NE (between Fourth and Third Sts). 543.7656. Metro: Union Station

9 La Brasserie ★★$$ A charming town house is the setting for tasty nouvelle and classic country fare, from quiche to grilled salmon fillet. The crème brûlée with fresh raspberries is superb. In warm weather, the outdoor terrace is open for dining. ♦ French ♦ M breakfast and lunch; Tu-Su breakfast, lunch, and dinner. Reservations recommended. 239 Massachusetts Ave NE (between Third and D Sts). 546.6066 ᕃ Metro: Union Station

10 The Monocle ★★$$$ Traditionally an after-work watering hole for Senate-side powerbrokers, this spot also serves good pasta, steaks, and seafood. The place is particularly pleasant when Congress is not in session. ♦ American ♦ M-F lunch and dinner. Reservations recommended. 107 D St NE (between Second and First Sts). 546.4488. Metro: Union Station

11 Union Station Architect **Daniel Burnham**'s magnificent Beaux Arts monument to the optimism of the early 1900s is back on track, after a bumpy ride through the latter part of the century. The restoration of the station, along with the opening of stores and eateries within the building, has also pumped economic life into the surrounding area. The 1908 marble-sheathed railroad terminal (pictured on page 25), based on the Arch of Constantine (outside) and the Baths of Diocletian (inside), originally had its own bowling alley, mortuary, icehouse, and swimming pool. In 1937, at its apogee, as many as 42,000 travelers passed through the concourse daily.

With the decline of rail travel, however, the station was allowed to crumble. A leaking roof caused huge chunks of plaster to fall from the ceiling, water pipes burst repeatedly, and toadstools sprang from the muddy floor. In 1976 railroad operations were moved to a squalid temporary terminal behind the station, and the original vaulted waiting room was converted to a bicentennial visitors' center, with a giant pit dug into the floor. After further decay, a $181-million public/private partnership came to the building's rescue. Its 1988 reopening resurrected the grandeur **Burnham** had intended. The original walls, columns, and windows were restored, and much of the space is now given over to office and retail use. A large portion of the painting, stenciling, and restoration of the moldings and *scagliola* (imitation marble) is the work of master craftsman John Barianos, whose artistry can also be seen at the **Willard Inter-Continental Hotel,** in Downtown DC, and at the **Capitol.**

The **Main Hall,** with a majestic 96-foot-high barrel-vaulted coffered ceiling, contains a newsstand, a concierge station, and several cafes and restaurants, including **Sfuzzi,** an offshoot of the popular New York chain, and **America** (see page 25). The **West Hall** and the two-level **Station Concourse** behind the **Main Hall** contain over 60 shops, among them **Cignal, Ann Taylor, The Limited, Nature Company, Putumayo, Godiva Chocolatier,** and **Victoria's Secret.** The **East Hall** offers kiosks selling unusual handmade jewelry, crafts, and antique watches. The **Train Concourse,** just north of the **Station Concourse,** provides access to **Amtrak** trains and connects the station to the 1,381-space parking garage behind it (parking is free for one hour of shopping or three hours of moviegoing, with validation). Travelers will find an entrance to the **Metro** on the lower-level **Metro Concourse,** where about 25 international fast-food shops and a nine-screen movie theater complex are dramatically positioned among 25-foot-deep piers and arches. ♦ Station: daily 24 hours. Stores: M-Sa 10AM-9PM; Su noon-6PM.

Restaurants: hours vary. 50 Massachusetts Ave NE (at First St). 371.9441 & Metro: Union Station

Within Union Station:

★ AMERICA ★

America ★$$ A real Yank extravaganza, this restaurant accommodates 700 people with both indoor and outdoor seating. On its menu are nearly 200 items, including specialties from virtually every state in the union. Some popular dishes: New Orleans fried oyster po-boy; and blue-corn enchiladas with Gulf shrimp and chili sauce. Finish up with Death by Chocolate if you think you can survive the dense, five-layer concoction of semisweet and bittersweet chocolate. ♦ American ♦ Daily lunch and dinner. Street level. 682.9555 &

The Great Train Store A continuously chugging model train beckons window-shoppers who, once inside, discover railroad caps, railroad books, shot glasses etched with railway logos, and all kinds of fantastic trains.

Parents are free to browse while their kids are bewitched by the assembled wooden Brio train set. ♦ M-F 8AM-9PM; Sa 10AM-9PM; Su noon-6PM. Station Concourse. 371.2881; www.greattrain.com &

Brookstone Talk about gadgets—this shop would've made *Get Smart* proud. Items include automatic plant-waterers, feet massagers, snore stoppers (don't ask, it's complicated), clocks for the shower, all sorts of tools, Swiss Army watches, and high-tech games. ♦ Daily. Station Concourse. 289.3553 & Also at: 1140 Connecticut Ave NW (between L and M Sts). 293.9290. Metro: Farragut North

Proper Topper This shop offers hats for every head and occasion—and a fun way to pass the time while waiting for a train. ♦ Daily. West Hall. 371.0639; www.propertopper.com &

12 National Postal Museum The Smithsonian's newest museum (opened in 1993) is housed in the building that served as Washington's main post office from 1914 to 1986, when it was known as the **National Capital Station.** Designed in 1914 by **Graham and Burnham** to complement nearby **Union Station,** this smaller, less opulent Beaux Arts building is rendered in white Italian marble and trimmed with an Ionic colonnade. There's still a working post office on the first floor, and the lobby's marble and fixtures are restored to gleaming brilliance. On the lower atrium level is the world's largest collection of stamps and other philatelic items, drawn from the Smithsonian's **National Museum of American History.** Exhibits trace the history of postal collection, sorting, and delivery. The

Union Station

M. STORRINGS

Library Research Center, open by appointment Monday through Friday, and the educational **Discovery Center,** with activity kits and games, is not always open; call ahead for schedule information. ♦ Free. Museum: daily. Post office: M-F 7AM-midnight; Sa-Su 7AM-8PM. 2 Massachusetts Ave NE (at N Capitol St). 357.2991 ♿ Metro: Union Station

13 Capital Children's Museum (National Learning Center) Learning and playing come together in this fine museum, where children explore other cultures by trying on the clothes and sampling the foods of foreign lands. They can also discover how to traverse the city by play-riding in a bus or taxi. The idea is to learn by doing, whether the activity is computing, building, or painting. Even grown-ups find it hard to resist being captivated by the touchy-feely gizmos and climb-on constructions. The gift shop sells all kinds of toys, most as educational as they are fun. ♦ Admission; children under 2 free. Daily. 800 Third St NE (at H St). Information 675.4120, recording 675.4125 ♿ Metro: Union Station

14 Union Market (Florida Avenue Farmers Market) Open year-round, this shoppers' mecca comprises several wholesale warehouses that carry fresh meats, eggs, and fish, plus choice fruits and vegetables. Ethnic foods predominate. Several vendors prepare sandwiches, baked goods, and more for takeout. ♦ M-Sa. Florida Ave NE (between Fifth and Fourth Sts) ♿ Metro: Union Station

15 Gallaudet University Edward Miner Gallaudet, the youngest son of Thomas Hopkins Gallaudet, founder of the first deaf school in Connecticut, helped establish this beautiful Gothic-style campus as a higher-learning institution for the deaf. Founded in 1867, the world's only accredited liberal arts college for the hearing-impaired enrolls 2,200 students. Its formal Victorian stone structures are laced with points and arches, and the grounds reflect the master touch of landscape architect Frederick Law Olmsted. Arrange tours of the campus through the **Visitors Center.** ♦ 800 Florida Ave NE (between West Virginia Ave and Sixth St). Visitors Center and TDD (for the hearing-impaired) 651.5505; www.gallaudet.edu ♿ Metro: Union Station

16 Trinity College Founded in 1897 by the Sisters of Notre Dame de Namur, this liberal arts college for women has nearly 1,000 registered students. A strong continuing-education program for working women is included in the curriculum. The granite **Main Hall** is a Northeast landmark with its marble parquet and stained glass, culminating in a four-story atrium. ♦ 125 Michigan Ave NE (between Franklin and Fourth Sts). 884.9000; www.trinitydc.edu ♿ Metro: Brookland/CUA

Within Trinity College:

Chapel of Notre Dame The college's Byzantine house of worship has a 67-foot dome. Inside is Bancel La Farge's *Coronation of the Virgin,* a mosaic inspired by the scene from Dante's *Divine Comedy.* ♦ By appointment only. 884.9199

16 Catholic University of America Past and future meet at this century-old coeducational institution, founded by the Catholic bishops of the US. While some students pursue the university's highly respected traditional ecclesiastical curriculum, others work with researchers in biomedical engineering, physics, and biochemistry. The university's School of Philosophy is renowned, too. Guided campus tours can be arranged by appointment; call 319.5305. ♦ 620 Michigan Ave NE (between John McCormack and Harewood Rds). 319.5000 ♿ Metro: Brookland/CUA

Within Catholic University of America:

National Shrine of the Immaculate Conception The key word here is "huge": The church is about 460 feet long, 157 feet wide, and 329 feet high and can hold about 3,000 people. This magnificent edifice attests to the Catholic devotion to the Virgin Mary. Construction started in 1914, when the rector of Washington's **Catholic University of America** obtained papal sanction for a new monument dedicated to the "Heavenly Patroness of the US" (as she was decreed by Pope Pius IX in 1847). Completed in 1959, the world's seventh-largest church (and the largest Catholic church in the Western hemisphere) is a modern cruciform giant with both Byzantine and Romanesque elements. Thirty-two chapels in the upper church contain bright mosaic altars portraying interpretations of the Virgin from all around the world. Light streams through 200 stained-glass windows to wash over an immense mosaic shrine whose construction depleted an entire Italian quarry. The church's real masterpiece, though, is probably Millard Sheet's colossal mosaic *Triumph of the Lamb,* which is affixed to the sanctuary dome.

Since every parish in the US contributed to the building fund, the shrine belongs to every American Catholic. With this in mind, the church administration actively encourages pilgrimages, and Communion is celebrated daily. There is a gift shop downstairs. ♦ Tours (usually given on the hour): M-Sa 9AM-3PM; Su 1:30-4PM. Harewood Rd NE (between Michigan Ave and Taylor St). 526.8300 ♿

Hartke Theatre This 600-seat theater is justly acclaimed for the quality of the plays produced on its stage, which range from Greek and Shakespearean dramas to opera and American musicals. Thespian alumni include Susan Sarandon, Jon Voight, and playwright Jason Miller. ♦ Box office: M-F. Harewood Rd NE (between Michigan Ave and Taylor St). 319.5367

16 Dance Place For 42 weeks every year, the area's largest producer of contemporary and avant-garde dance puts on weekend performances by national and international troupes such as the **Lesa McLaughlin** group, **Liz Lerman,** and **Memory of African Culture.** Ongoing modern-dance classes are offered, and an African Dance Festival takes place in June. The theater seats 200 people, and the box office opens one hour before showtime; call to reserve seats in advance. ♦ Box office: M-Th noon-7PM, F-Sa noon-5PM. 3225 Eighth St NE (between Franklin and Monroe Sts). 269.1600; danceplace@danceplace.org; www.danceplace.org ♿ Metro: Brookland/CUA

16 Colonel Brooks' Tavern ★$ It's tough to find a restaurant in the largely residential Brookland area, so this casual, reliable place is something of an oasis. Good burgers, sandwiches, egg dishes, and desserts round out the seasonal menu. Customers can complement their meals with dark or light ales from a list of about 15 drafts. Local Dixieland bands take the stage on Tuesday nights. ♦ American ♦ M-Sa lunch and dinner; Su brunch and dinner. 901 Monroe St NE (at Ninth St). 529.4002 ♿ Metro: Brookland/CUA

16 Franciscan Monastery Officially the "Commissariat of the Holy Land for the United States," this monastery provides a fascinating glimpse of cloistered life. The enterprising mendicants here, who belong to the Order of the Friars Minor, raise funds to preserve shrines in the Holy Land; closer to home, they also maintain the beautiful grounds surrounding the monastery. A 45-minute tour of the rose garden and the early–Italian Renaissance church, completed in 1899, includes faithful replicas of several Holy Land shrines. Also on the tour (the only way to see it) is a small, authentic reproduction of a Roman catacomb beneath the church illustrating the plight of early Christian worshipers. ♦ Tours: on the hour M-Sa 9-11AM, 1-4PM; Su 1-4PM. 1400 Quincy St NE (at 14th St). 526.6800. Metro: Brookland/CUA

17 US National Arboretum Few locals seem aware of this 440-acre plot of garden and woodland (see map below) overlooking the Anacostia River, which is practically deserted except for the few weeks in spring when the azaleas (and tourists) run wild. So much the better for the cognoscenti, since this semisecret garden is a lovely place.

Established by Congress in 1927 as a research institution, the arboretum harbors such rare plants as the Siberian larch and Manchurian lilac, as well as thousands of

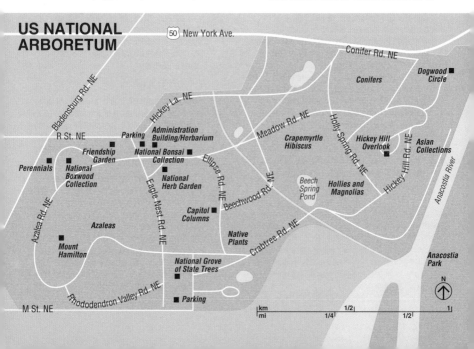

US NATIONAL ARBORETUM

azaleas, ornamental crab apples, cherries, and dogwoods. During Washington's languorous spring, each week brings a new cascade of color and fragrance. Amid all this life rises an incongruous stand of Neo-Classical columns, salvaged from a renovation of the **Capitol** and erected here in the late 1980s. Also on the vast grounds is the **Herbarium,** filled with a "library" of more than 500,000 dried plants.

Perhaps the arboretum's most prestigious feature is the *National Bonsai Collection,* valued at more than $5 million (and protected by an elaborate alarm system). A gift from the people of Japan, the plants are housed in a pavilion next to the **Administration Building.** The 200-plus trees, representing a wide variety of species, range from 30 to more than 350 years old. The bonsais, artfully stunted in shallow pots, stand no more than two feet high.

The arboretum's peak season is the spring, when crowds can reach 20,000 daily. In winter, the austere scene is populated mainly by 1,500 dwarf and slow-growing conifers assembled on a hill. The arboretum regularly presents special demonstrations, films, and flower shows. Arrange group tours for 10 or more by calling at least three weeks in advance. ♦ Free. Daily. Bonsai collection: daily 10AM-3:30PM. Entrances at 3501 New York Ave NE (between South Dakota Ave and Bladensburg Rd) and R St NE (east of Bladensburg Rd). 245.2726. Metros: Stadium/Armory, Rhode Island Ave

18 Anacostia Park Extending eight miles along the Anacostia River, these 1,300 acres qualify more as a natural preserve than as a conventional park, with mostly fertile marshland and small, sunny glades hidden in the forests. In the northeast are **Kenilworth Aquatic Gardens** (see below); adjacent to the gardens are approximately 70 acres of wetlands inhabited by songbirds and wading birds, such as green and great blue herons. During the winter migrating season, hordes of ducks and geese also congregate in the park. You can walk almost anywhere, except to the river's upper reaches, where its natural wild state renders the area inaccessible. A multipurpose pavilion at the south end of the park offers environmental-education programs, community exhibitions, and a roller-skating rink. ♦ Fairlawn Ave SE (between Pennsylvania Ave and 16th St). 472.3873. Metro: Anacostia

---

Abraham Lincoln lived in Mrs. Spriggs's boarding house on Capitol Hill while he was a member of Congress. From his window he could see slaves being bought and sold in an active slave market on Capitol Hill. The site is now the Library of Congress.

Within Anacostia Park:

18 Kenilworth Aquatic Gardens Fourteen acres of water-loving flora and fauna are hidden within this seldom-visited marshland in the northeastern part of **Anacostia Park.** War veteran W.B. Shaw began the gardens' evolution in 1882 with a few water lilies from Maine. Native willow oaks, red maples, and magnolias sheltered the ponds, which attracted a variety of water dwellers; today, muskrats, raccoons, and opossums coexist with frogs, toads, and turtles. Visit early in the morning, since many of the night-blooming lotuses close during harsh daylight. Group tours are possible with advance notice. ♦ Daily 7AM-4PM. Anacostia Ave NE (between 40th and Quarles Sts). 426.6905. Metro: Deanwood

19 RFK Stadium/DC Armory Hall Two impressive structures—the **RFK Stadium** and the **DC Armory Hall**—compose this huge concert, trade-show, and sports complex, also called **Starplex.** The circular, five-tier amphitheater seats 55,000. Various athletic events, rock concerts, and even religious convocations alternately fill the arena. Though **Redskins** fans now watch their team at the new **Jack Kent Cooke Stadium** (see page 167) in Landover, Maryland, the **DC United** soccer team still draws its share of spirited fans here.

Next to RFK stadium is the **DC Armory Hall,** a domed structure whose two levels comprise a total of more than 133,000 square feet of space. The adaptable main hall hosts events as diverse as the "Holiday on Ice" show and political conventions; the resourceful **Starplex** technicians have at various times transformed the **DC Armory Hall** into skating rinks, circus arenas, and ballrooms. ♦ Box office and information office: M-F. 2001 E Capitol St (between the Anacostia River and 19th St SE). Stadium and armory information 547.9077 Starplex ticket office 547.9077, ♿ Metro: Stadium/Armory

Within RFK Stadium:

Farmers Market Local farmers set up shop in the parking lot north of the stadium to sell their superfresh produce, cheese, and bread. The DC government sponsors the market. ♦ Tu, Th 7AM-5PM; Sa 7AM-4PM. Parking Lot 6 (off Benning Rd NE) ♿

20 Historic Congressional Cemetery "Being interred beneath these grounds adds a new terror to death" is how one US senator described the oppressive solemnity of this final resting place, reserved for diplomats, senators, and other prominent citizens. The process of filling the burial reservations of Washington's eminent started in 1807. Seventy years later, Capitol Hill architects **William Thornton** and **Robert Mills,** a Choctaw chief, and John Philip Sousa were among the last to find their places under Benjamin Latrobe's stern, predesigned gravestones. Also laid to rest here were J. Edgar Hoover and photographer Mathew Brady. The gatekeeper will provide information and memorial maps. ♦ 1801 E St SE (at 18th St). 543.0539 ♿ Metro: Potomac Ave

21 Lincoln Park Two of the city's finest and most affecting statues grace this compact urban park. The *Emancipation Monument,* sculpted in 1876 by Thomas Ball and funded by former slaves, depicts a life-size Abraham Lincoln holding the Emancipation Proclamation. At Lincoln's feet, a slave is rising, his chains finally broken. Ball modeled the man's face after a photo of Archer Alexander, the last person to be taken under the Fugitive Slave Act. The heartening sculpture of black educator/activist Mary McLeod Bethune portrays the former adviser to Franklin D. Roosevelt passing her legacy to two children: It reads in part, "I leave you a thirst for education. I leave you a respect for the use of power. I leave you faith. I leave you racial dignity. I leave you a desire to live harmoniously with your fellow man." ♦ E Capitol St (between 13th and 11th Sts). Metro: Eastern Market

22 Frederick Douglass Museum and Hall of Fame for Caring Americans Located in the restored Capitol Hill home of abolitionist, publisher, and orator Frederick Douglass, this museum houses art exhibits and a permanent collection of Douglass memorabilia. There is also a memorial dedicated to those who have spent their lives in service to others. ♦ Admission. Visits by appointment 24 hours in advance. 320 A St NE (between Fourth and Third Sts). 547.4273; www.caring-institute.org. Metros: Capitol South, Union Station

23 Folger Shakespeare Library Founded in 1930 by Henry Clay Folger, a Standard Oil executive and Shakespeare maven, the library contains the world's largest collection of plays and poetry by the Bard, including several copies of the 1623 First Folio, the original printed collection of Shakespeare's plays, and the only surviving quarto of *Titus Andronicus.* Selected works from the collection are displayed in the gallery.

The building, one of **Paul Philippe Cret**'s finest designs, reconciles a Greek-influenced Art Deco exterior (its nine bas-reliefs depict Shakespearean scenes) with an Elizabethan interior. The late-1970s additions are tasteful and well done. The museum shop sells all kinds of souvenirs sporting Shakespeare's image or his words. A full-scale model of an Elizabethan theater, with seating for about 250, is home to occasional musical performances. It also used to be the home of

the **Shakespeare Theater,** which has since moved to Seventh Street NW. Literary readings are held here irregularly; check Friday's *The Washington Post* "Weekend" section or Sunday's "Book World" for details. An open house celebrating the Bard's birthday takes place here every April. ♦ Free. M-Sa. Tours: 11AM-1PM; group tours are given by appointment. 201 E Capitol St (at Second St SE). 544.4600; www.folger.edu ♿ Metros: Capitol South, Union Station

24 Le Bon Café ★★$ The tables are set too close together, but the fresh sandwiches and pastries, best followed up with a bowl of frothy cappuccino, outweigh this cafe's inconveniences. For that extra soupçon of European flavor, outside seating is available when weather permits. Place your order at the counter; there's no table service. ♦ French ♦ Daily breakfast and lunch. 210 Second St SE (between C St and Pennsylvania Ave). 547.7200. Metro: Capitol South

24 Chesapeake Bagel Bakery ★$ New York–style bagels are served hot out of the oven here, with the requisite spreads and sandwich fillings. Carry out or eat indoors, where you can peruse the notice-laden bulletin board. ♦ Deli ♦ Daily breakfast, lunch, and dinner. 215 Pennsylvania Ave SE (between Third and Second Sts). 546.0994. Metro: Capitol South. Also at: 1636 Connecticut Ave NW (between Hillyer Pl and R St). 328.7985 ♿ Metro: Dupont Circle; 4000 Wisconsin Ave NW (at Rodman St). 966.8866 ♿ Metro: Tenleytown/AU; 818 18th St NW (between H and I Sts). 775.4690 ♿ Metro: Farragut West

24 Trover Shop A pleasant place to browse, this two-floor shop has a comprehensive selection of political books, best-sellers, and classics, as well a number of out-of-town newspapers. Cigar connoisseurs can select from an abundance of stogies. ♦ M-F 7AM-9PM; Sa 7AM-7PM; Su 7AM-3PM. 221 Pennsylvania Avenue SE (between Third and Second Sts). 547.BOOK; www.trovershop.com ♿ Metro: Capitol South

Washington Between the Covers

Washington has been the scene of so much history that most books on US politics are bound to include it as a backdrop at some point. The following volumes put the city and its machinations front and center:

Cupid and Diana by Christina Bartolomeo (Scribner, 1998). In this novel, heroine Diana Campanella searches for the right man, the right career, and the right outfit. Along the way, readers get a glimpse of everyday Washington off the tourist beat.

Democracy by Henry Adams (New American Library, 1983). This descendant of two presidents carved his own niche as a historian and man of letters. Written in 1880, his scathing novel of the scandal-ridden Grant administration is a cautionary tale that too many politicians have since ignored.

Lost in the City by Edward P. Jones (Morrow, 1992). A collection of stories about the "other" Washington, the African-American residents whose lives are rarely affected by the doings at either end of **Pennsylvania Avenue.** Jones writes with humor and compassion about lives often torn, and occasionally enriched, by the day-to-day struggles of urban life.

The Man Who Loved Children by Christina Stead (Holt, Rinehart & Winston, 1940). Australian novelist Stead spent enough time in Washington in the late 1930s to write this brilliantly perceptive tale of a domestic situation that appears idyllic at first glance, then gradually reveals itself to be dark and finally, tragically flawed. Samuel Clemens Pollit, the easy-going protagonist, who tends his brood in a rambling house north of Georgetown, is a fine literary creation.

Patron Saint of Unmarried Women by Karl Ackerman (St. Martin's Press, 1994) This wry and funny first novel captures Washington as hometown. Jack Townsend, a landscape architect, and his girlfriend, artist Nina Lawrence, lead readers away from Washington's monuments and into the city's funkier neighborhoods.

Primary Colors by Anonymous (Random House, 1996). *Newsweek* columnist Joe Klein got himself in hot water when he was revealed to be the author of this best-selling novel about a southern governor who runs for president. The unflattering and thinly veiled portrait is reputedly based on Clinton's rise to power.

Reveille in Washington: 1860-1862 by Margaret Leech (Carroll and Graf, 1991). Written in 1942, this engaging history of Washington during the Civil War reminds us that the capital of the United States was south of the Mason-Dixon Line and only 120 miles north of Richmond, the capital of the Confederacy. Mixed loyalties and intrigue abound, and the towering presence of Lincoln hovers over all.

Strange and Fascinating Facts About Washington, DC by Fred L. Worth (Bell, 1988). Just what the title says: plenty of trivia, but also lots of substantial information about nearly every aspect of life in DC.

Twilight at Mac's Place by Ross Thomas (Mysterious Press, 1990). A former CIA man, Thomas writes some of the most literate cloak-and-dagger fiction around. A number of his thrillers are set in Washington; this one revolves around the intrigue at a **Dupont Circle** bar.

Waking the Dead by Scott Spencer (Knopf, 1986) Neither a horror story nor religious tract, this is the tale of a thirty-something Congressional wannabe. The Washington scenes capture the city well, which isn't surprising, since the author is a DC native.

Washington: A History of the Capital, 1800-1950 by Constance McLaughlin Green (Princeton University Press, 1961-1963). Originally published in two volumes (the first won a Pulitzer Prize), this magisterial look at the city's first 150 years also manages to be readable and entertaining. A one-volume edition is available in paperback.

Washington, City and Capital by the Federal Writers Project (US Government Printing Office, 1937). From the famed Depression-era series of American guidebooks funded by the New Deal's Works Projects Administration, this is time-capsule history at its best: informative, occasionally opinionated, and incredibly detailed.

Washington, D.C. by Gore Vidal (Little, Brown, 1967). No novelist of the past 30 years has written so well about Washington's recent and more distant past. This novel, which Vidal started when John F. Kennedy was still alive and finished when the Vietnam War was in full swing, reflects his growing disillusionment with the political process. Also recommended are Vidal's *Burr* (Random House, 1973) and *Lincoln* (Random House, 1984).

Washington Itself by E.J. Applewhite (Knopf, 1981). The longtime Washington resident and former CIA executive offers what he calls an "informal guide" to Washington, with an emphasis on architectural details of the city's many historic buildings. The author isn't always impressed with what may appear to some as grand designs, but that's part of the informative and engaging charm. The line drawings are lovingly rendered by Fred H. Greenberg.

24 Sherrill's ★$ The Hill has its very own time machine: Step inside, and you'll swear Harry Truman is still president. A grumpy waitress will serve you a luncheon of meat loaf and gravy while you sit in a dark wood booth, or you can take out a bag of doughnuts from the bakery. An Oscar-nominated 1989 documentary, *Fine Foods, Fine Pasteries, Open 6 to 9,* testified to **Sherrill's** unique place in Washington. ♦ American ♦ Daily breakfast, lunch, and dinner. No credit cards accepted. 233 Pennsylvania Ave SE (between Third and Second Sts). 544.2480 Ꭽ Metro: Capitol South

25 Capitol Hill Suites $$ A former apartment building on a quiet residential block just three blocks from the **Capitol,** this hotel offers 152 suites—some nonsmoking, some with fully equipped kitchens. Continental breakfast and free happy hour add to the appeal; there's no restaurant. ♦ 200 C St SE (at Second St). 543.6000, 800/424.9165; fax 547.2608; CapitolHillSuites@erols.com Ꭽ Metro: Capitol South

26 Taverna the Greek Islands ★★$ Try the moussaka (a layered casserole of ground meat, sliced eggplant, and béchamel sauce), lamb pie, stuffed grape leaves, kabobs, and other specialties, as well as one of several varieties of Greek wine. ♦ Greek ♦ M-Sa lunch and dinner; Su dinner. 305 Pennsylvania Ave SE (between Fourth and Third Sts). 547.8360. Metro: Capitol South

Hawk 'n' Dove

26 Hawk and Dove ★$ An intriguing mix of Hill insiders, Georgetown law students, and local rugby players people this dark, archetypal burger-and-brew joint. ♦ American ♦ Daily lunch and dinner. 329 Pennsylvania Ave SE (between Fourth and Third Sts). 543.3300. Metro: Capitol South

26 Tune Inn ★$ This preppy hangout is a legendary landmark for cheap beer, greasy burgers, and cantankerous help. Don't miss the stuffed deer derrières over the bathroom doors or the jukebox with plenty of country classics. ♦ American ♦ Daily breakfast, lunch, and dinner. 331½ Pennsylvania Ave SE (between Fourth and Third Sts). 543.2725. Metro: Capitol South

27 Bullfeathers ★$$ Congressional staffers throng here for the Happy Hour. Otherwise, this Victorian-style pub is a relatively calm place to come for hearty American fare, including burgers, crab cakes, and steaks. At brunch there's a full bar, featuring Bloody Marys that you can fix yourself. ♦ American ♦ M-Sa lunch and dinner; Su brunch and dinner. Reservations recommended. 410 First St SE (between North Carolina Ave and D St). 543.5005 Ꭽ Metro: Capitol South

28 Eastern Market Inside the **Adolph Cluss**–designed structure (1873), greengrocers and butchers offer the freshest food money can buy—they'll even handpick each item, and wrap it as if they were serving royalty. The prices they charge, however, may seem like a king's ransom. Outside, farmers from West Virginia, Pennsylvania, Virginia, and Maryland sell produce, cider, flowers, and baked goods. Saturday mornings are the most energetic, as Capitol Hill residents crowd the market and craftspeople take over the north sidewalk plaza. On Sundays, the food stalls are replaced by an ad hoc flea market selling knickknacks and old furniture. One Sunday every May the market becomes the site of a street festival called Market Day, in celebration of spring. Several blocks of Seventh Street are closed to cars, which are replaced by live music performances, ethnic food stalls, and crafts of all descriptions. ♦ Tu-Th 7AM-6PM; F-Sa 6AM-7PM; Su 8AM-5PM. 225 Seventh St SE (between C St and North Carolina Ave) Ꭽ Metro: Eastern Market

Within Eastern Market:

Market Lunch ★★$ The name may say "lunch," but lines snake out the door Saturday mornings for breakfast, and with good reason. On the other hand, lunch has its benefits, too, namely fabulous crab cakes, served on homemade bread with coleslaw and hot sauce. Stop in during the week when it's less crowded. ♦ American ♦ Tu-Sa breakfast and lunch. No credit cards accepted. 547.8444 Ꭽ

29 The Village Around the corner from **Eastern Market,** this wonderful gift shop carries ornaments, cards, nativities, pottery, and more from South America, Asia, and India. ♦ Daily. 705 North Carolina Ave SE (between Independence Ave and Seventh St). 546.3040. Metro: Eastern Market

30 Misha's Deli ★$ A little bit of New York's Lower East Side, this friendly, tiny Russian deli offers tasty sandwiches, schnitzel, blinis, and soups you can eat at a table or take with you. Have a craving for knishes or pierogi? Just ask. ♦ Russian ♦ Daily lunch and dinner. 210 Seventh St SE (between C St and North Carolina Ave). 547.5858 Ꭽ Metro: Eastern Market

Restaurants/Clubs: Red   Hotels: Blue
Shops/ 🍴 **Outdoors:** Green   **Sights/Culture:** Black

30 Prego Deli ★$ The overstuffed sandwiches at this Italian deli run by a Korean and staffed by African-Americans and Latinos make for a delicious defense of multiculturalism. A fine selection of wines, cheeses, and gourmet foods is also available. ♦ Deli ♦ Daily lunch and dinner. 210 Seventh St SE (between C St and North Carolina Ave). 547.8686. Metro: Eastern Market

30 Tunnicliff's ★$$ Scenes of the old **Eastern Market** are etched on the glass dividers decorating this place. The Cajun specialties, fresh fish, and steaks can be savored outdoors in warm weather. ♦ American ♦ M-F lunch and dinner; Sa-Su brunch and dinner. Reservations recommended. 222 Seventh St SE (between C St and North Carolina Ave). 546.3663; BigEasyDC@aol.com; www.tunnicliffs.com & Metro: Eastern Market

31 The Fairy Godmother Books, toys, and music crowd this microscopic shop, where European toys, audio tapes, and a special bilingual section make this spot a charming alternative to Toys 'R' Us. ♦ M-Sa. 319 Seventh St SE (between Pennsylvania Ave and C St). 547.5474. Metro: Eastern Market

31 A Man for All Seasons The city's best source for men's secondhand clothing stocks classic and contemporary suits, ties, shoes, shirts, and casualwear. It just may be possible that a $60 suit here once made an appearance on the Senate floor. ♦ Tu-Th, Sa; Su 12:30-4:30PM. 321 Seventh St SE (between Pennsylvania Ave and C St). 544.4432. Metro: Eastern Market

ROASTERS On The HILL

31 Roasters on the Hill With generic coffee bars multiplying like rabbits across the land, this is the one and only as far as the Hill is concerned. An indoor bar and outdoor tables are available for those who want to start sipping their java right away. ♦ Daily. 666 Pennsylvania Ave SE (at Seventh St). 543.8355 & Metro: Eastern Market

31 Bread & Chocolate ★★$ After a whirl through Eastern Market, this spot is the perfect place to stop for an espresso and some biscotti. Scrumptious offerings, such as fruit tarts, crepes, and specialty sandwiches are sure to tempt. In warm months, you can dine alfresco and soak up the Capitol Hill scene. ♦ Cafe ♦ Daily breakfast, lunch, and dinner. 666 Pennsylvania Ave SE (at Seventh St). 547.2875. Metro: Eastern Market

32 Trattoria Alberto ★★$$ Friendly and slightly kitschy, this honest-to-goodness trattoria serves good, cheap wine and ample portions of homemade pasta, as well as some tender veal dishes. ♦ Italian ♦ M-F lunch and dinner; Sa dinner. Reservations recommended. 506 Eighth St SE (between G and E Sts). 544.2007 & Metro: Eastern Market

32 Banana Café ★$ The kitchen offers a variety of Latin-influenced dishes, with Tex-Mex, South American, and Spanish accents. The fajitas are excellent. ♦ Mexican ♦ M-F lunch and dinner; Sa-Su brunch and dinner. 500 Eighth St SE (at E St). 543.5906 & Metro: Eastern Market

33 Newman Gallery & Custom Frames Offers rotating exhibits of original work by local artists. ♦ Tu-Sa. 513 11th St SE (between G and E Sts). 544.7577; Newmanglry@aol.com; www.gallerynewman.com. Metro: Eastern Market

34 Christ Church, Washington Parish With this Episcopal church, **Benjamin Latrobe** became one of the first architects in the country to use a Gothic Revival design (the original scheme has since been significantly altered). Built in 1806, it's probably the oldest ecclesiastical edifice in the District. Over the years, the congregation has included many of Washington's leading citizens, among them presidents Thomas Jefferson, James Madison, and John Quincy Adams. ♦ Tours by appointment only. 620 G St SE (between Seventh and Sixth Sts). 547.9300 & Metro: Eastern Market

35 Marine Corps Barracks America's first marine post is still home to the "Eighth and Eye" Marines. The **Commandant's House,** with its classical overtones and bay windows, is the only original building standing on the grounds. The Marine Corps holds parades in the barracks courtyard on Fridays at 8:45PM mid-May through early September. It's a great spectacle, even for those not wild about rifle drills and precision marching. Reservations are required three weeks in advance. (If you can't get in, a shorter, sunset version of the parade is performed Tuesday evenings at 7:30PM the last week of May through mid-August on the grounds of the **Iwo Jima Memorial** in Arlington.) ♦ Eighth St SE (between I and G Sts). 433.6060 & Metro: Eastern Market

36 Washington Navy Yard

Kids of all ages play and learn simultaneously in this historic precinct, which served as the **Naval Gun Factory** during the 19th century. The distinguished architect-engineer **Benjamin Latrobe** came up with the original plan; while various refurbishings have eroded signs of his influence, the main gates still evoke his style. (Some speculate that he designed the **Commandant's House** as well.) Splendid officers' mansions once lined the waterfront here; now the functional factory and warehouse buildings stand in their place.

The **Navy Museum** illuminates a more-than–200-year history of naval weapons, famous ships, and battle scenes, from the US Revolutionary War through Desert Storm. Its exhibitions are designed for the young and energetic: Gun turrets revolve, periscopes rise, and ships stand at the ready for boarding by boisterous young admirals. Claustrophobes should avoid the authentic submarine room and content themselves with the large dioramas depicting heroes damning the torpedoes and going full speed ahead. A decommissioned Vietnam-era destroyer, the *USS Barry,* can also be toured. High-tech fans will want to seek out the inertial guidance systems; fashion followers will want to check out the display of World War II uniforms by naval couturier Captain Guy Molyneux.

Buffs of military pomp and protocol should visit the **Marine Corps Museum,** where flags, trophies, and the personal effects of famous marines are displayed. At the **Parade Grounds,** a free audiovisual presentation of our country's naval history and lore is given on Wednesday evenings during the summer (reservations are recommended). ♦ Free. Navy Museum: daily. Marine Corps Museum: daily. Ninth and M Sts SE. Navy Museum 433.4882, Marine Corps Museum 433.3534, audiovisual presentation information 433.2218 ♿ Metros: Navy Yard, Eastern Market

37 Tracks

This gay-oriented nightclub has a huge dance floor and irresistible deejay-spun music. There's outdoor volleyball in good weather. Many of the Washington gay community's events are held here, but everyone is welcome. ♦ Cover after 9PM. Th-Sa 6PM-very late; Su 4PM-very late (sometimes open all night). 1111 First St SE (between M and L Sts). 488.3320; Info@Tracks2000.com; www.Tracks2000.com ♿ Metro: Navy Yard

38 Capital Ballroom

Though Washington isn't known for its nightlife, this large club, which opened in 1995, filled the gap for techno and rock music. Located in a former boiler works, it contains two main rooms separated by a long bar. The main **Ballroom** is like a large gymnasium (1,500 capacity) with great sound and light systems for live shows; the smaller **Half Street Club** plays recorded music. Both spaces are dark and starkly industrial, with plenty of room for dancing. With the **Metro** nearby, club management tends to end performances by midnight (when the subway closes). ♦ Admission for live shows. Call for show times. 1015 Half St SE (between L and K Sts). 554.1500, tickets 703/549.7625 and 432.7328. Metro: Navy Yard

39 Frederick Douglass National Historic Site (Cedar Hill)

Abolitionist and statesman Frederick Douglass resided at this simple white Victorian house from 1877 until his death in 1895. Douglass, who was born a slave on a Maryland plantation in 1817, escaped at the age of 21 and eventually became an adviser to four presidents and an eloquent spokesman for the antislavery movement. During the Civil War, Douglass counseled President Abraham Lincoln and supported postwar constitutional amendments that gave blacks citizenship and the right to vote.

Cedar Hill, built in 1854, rests on a hilltop. Its large, airy porch, punctuated by Doric columns, offers breathtaking vistas of the **Capitol** and its vicinity. Much restored to its original appearance, Douglass's home holds furniture and several gifts from Lincoln and other contemporaries, including Harriet Beecher Stowe and William Lloyd Garrison. One remarkable feature is the self-taught philosopher's personal library, containing more than 1,200 volumes.

The **Visitor Center,** which contains Ed Dwight's life-size statue of Douglass, is located at the bottom of the grounds so as not to obstruct the view from the house. An accurate and affecting picture of Douglass's work is captured in a short film, shown every hour on the hour. Tours are given on the hour, and group tours can be arranged by calling in advance. Limited parking is provided. ♦ Free. Daily. 1411 W St SE (between 16th and 14th Sts). 426.5960; www.nps.gov ♿ Metro: Anacostia

40 Anacostia Museum

Founded in 1967 as a branch of the **Smithsonian Institution,** this museum displays exhibits on African-American history in the Upper South. There are also art displays and, at times, educational lectures, films, and concerts, as well as demonstrations of black music and dance. On the grounds is a picnic area with tables and grills. Groups of 15 or more may arrange tours by calling in advance. ♦ Free. Daily. 1901 Fort Pl SE (at Erie St). 287.3369; www.sil.si.edu ♿ Metro: Anacostia

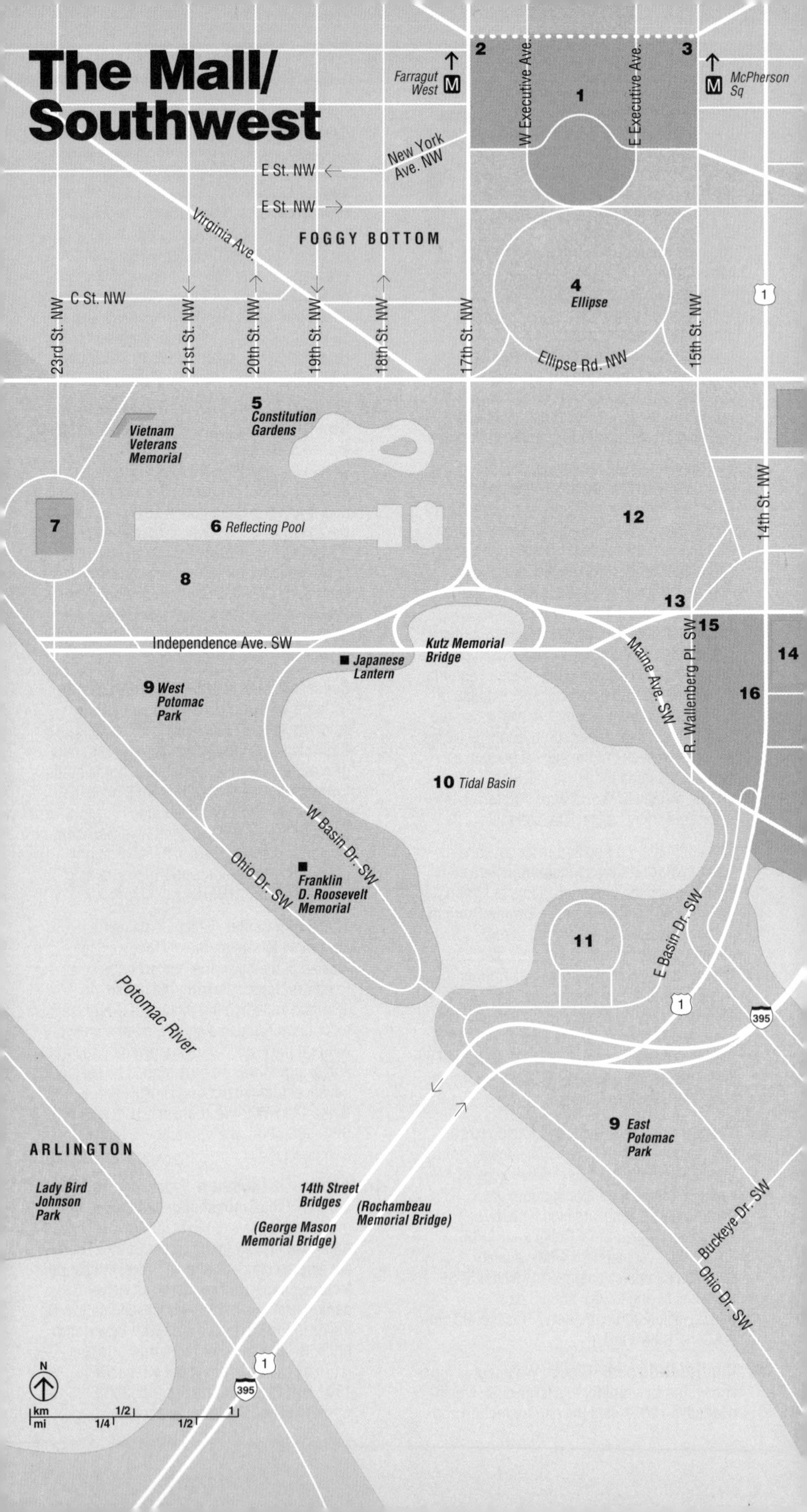

The Mall/
Southwest

↑ Farragut West Ⓜ

2

W Executive Ave.

1

E Executive Ave.

3 ↑

Ⓜ McPherson Sq

↑ Farragut West Ⓜ

New York Ave. NW

E St. NW ←

E St. NW →

FOGGY BOTTOM

Virginia Ave.

C St. NW

23rd St. NW

21st St. NW

20th St. NW

19th St. NW

18th St. NW

17th St. NW

15th St. NW

4
Ellipse

Ellipse Rd. NW

1

14th St. NW

5 *Constitution Gardens*

Vietnam Veterans Memorial

7

6 *Reflecting Pool*

8

12

13

Independence Ave. SW

Maine Ave. SW

15

R. Wallenberg Pl. SW

Kutz Memorial Bridge

14

■ Japanese Lantern

16

9 *West Potomac Park*

10 *Tidal Basin*

W Basin Dr. SW

Ohio Dr. SW

■ Franklin D. Roosevelt Memorial

E Basin Dr. SW

11

1

395

Potomac River

9 *East Potomac Park*

ARLINGTON

Lady Bird Johnson Park

14th Street Bridges

(Rochambeau Memorial Bridge)

(George Mason Memorial Bridge)

Buckeye Dr. SW

Ohio Dr. SW

N
↑

1

395

| km | | 1/2 | | 1 |
| mi | 1/4 | | 1/2 | |

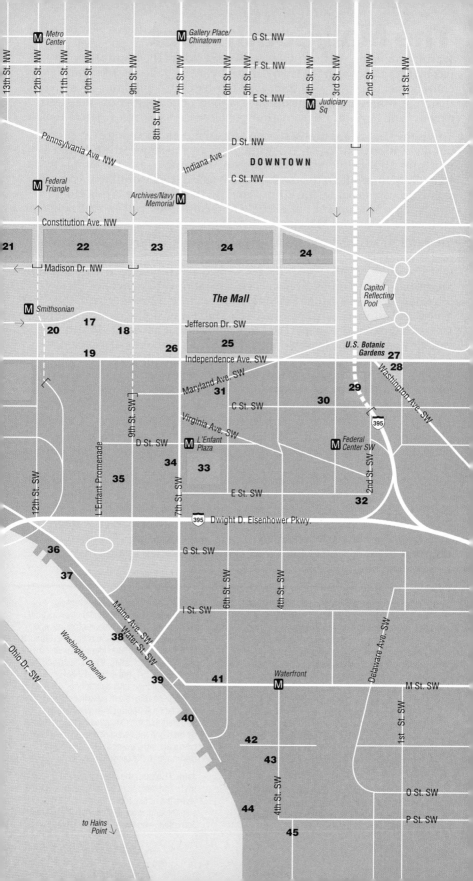

The Mall/Southwest

It is a view even the most jaded Washingtonian never tires of: From the west side of the **Capitol** is a rectangular carpet of green lawn flanked by small groves of trees and a collection of impressive—if somewhat mismatched—buildings, each no more than four stories high. In the distance, a spiky obelisk rises from the green expanse and beyond, a long, narrow pool leads to a columned, Greek temple.

This is the Great American Mall—no, not an indoor shopping extravaganza, but our National Backyard. Those buildings are the major **Smithsonian** museums, the obelisk is the **Washington Monument**, and the temple is the **Lincoln Memorial**. To the north of the **Washington Monument** is another, smaller, grassy expanse, the **Ellipse**, and north of that, the **White House**. South of the **Monument** is the stately **Jefferson Memorial** and the poignant **Holocaust Memorial Museum**.

The **Mall** and its environs are the magnetic center of Washington, drawing millions of visitors every year, as well as throngs of proud locals. The Pope said Mass here, Martin Luther King delivered a historic speech at the **Lincoln Memorial**, and countless political demonstrations have engulfed this legendary lawn. Every June the **Smithsonian** hosts a summer bash, the American Festival of Folklife, when **The Mall** is transformed into a county fair, with dancing, live music, and food booths that hawk the cuisine of various states. On the Fourth of July, **The Mall** is the scene of a daylong birthday blast, culminating in a mammoth fireworks display. With all this activity, it's a wonder that by summer's end there's any grass left. But every fall the National Park Service dutifully reseeds the bare patches, and each spring the green carpet rolls out again.

Tucked between The Mall and the **Potomac River** is Washington's smallest quadrant: Southwest. Unlike the rest of the city, its buildings seem to have been almost wholly created within the last 30 years. During the 19th century, when its waterfront location was prime real estate for Washington's commercial interests, Southwest was an important business center. The 20th century brought a slow and painful decline to the area, but in the 1960s, Southwest became a testing ground for urban renewal, and now its waterfront is dotted with restaurants and also boasts a popular fish market. Farther inland are the nationally acclaimed **Arena Stage/Kreeger Theater**, the **L'Enfant Plaza** complex, and a mélange of row houses, apartment high-rises, and federal buildings.

1 White House When John Adams arrived at his new home on 1 November 1800, he found a shantytown of workers' shacks just outside the front door and unplastered walls inside. Not a single room was finished. The central staircase was a pile of timbers on the floor, and only with flames blazing in 13 fireplaces could Adams fend off the damp chill. That night, in a letter to his wife, Abigail, the nation's second president and the Executive Mansion's first tenant wrote, "I pray Heaven to bestow the best of blessings on this house and all that shall hereafter inhabit it. May none but honest and wise men ever rule under this roof."

Since that inauspicious first day, 41 families have called the White House home. The only US president not to list 1600 Pennsylvania Avenue as his address was George Washington, who served his term in Philadelphia while the capital city was under construction. It was Washington, however, who selected the location of the "President's Mansion," or the "President's Palace," as it was more often called. When he staked out the site in 1791, the city was a flat, unpopulated woodland with one distinguishable rise in elevation, which would later become **Capitol Hill**. Washington declared that the Executive Mansion should be built one mile west of the hill, to secure a commanding view of the Potomac and, beyond that, Alexandria.

James Hoban, the original architect, was Irish, and despite many alterations over the years the house today remains as crisp, elegant, and white as fine Irish linen. Thomas Jefferson, who lost the original design competition (he submitted it under a pseudonym), used his clout as the third president to tinker with the Georgian country-house design. Then, during the War of 1812, the British took its remodeling into their own vengeful hands by setting fire to the White House—a severe thunderstorm saved it from total destruction. The building's exterior was first painted white to cover the charring. It isn't known who coined the term "White House," but Theodore Roosevelt officially named it such in 1902, well after the moniker had become commonplace. **Hoban** was enlisted to help with reconstruction after the fire. Other alterations have included the front portico, which was added in 1829; the wings, which **McKim, Mead, and White** designed in 1902; and such modern amenities as running water (in 1833), gas (in 1848), bathrooms (in 1878), and electricity (in 1890). The house was remodeled in 1902, in conjunction with the wing additions. Then in the late 1940s, after it was discovered to be structurally unsound, the whole house was taken apart: The stone framing was replaced with steel and the original panelings and decorations were removed, restored, and reconstructed. The **White House** now contains 132 rooms.

Through the years, the mansion has witnessed one presidential wedding (Grover Cleveland and Frances Folsom), five first family weddings, 11 births, seven presidential funerals, at least 39 redecorations—and numerous scandals. Since it was designed to serve not only as the home but also as the office of the president, the two functions frequently got crossed. In 1902 the second floor was at last set aside for the exclusive use of the president's family, but as late as 1962 the first family's meals were still being served on the nonprivate first floor, because the second floor had no kitchen.

When Jacqueline Kennedy, wife of the 35th president, arrived at the **White House** in 1961, she found the interior decor to be a mishmash of at least 34 individual tastes, with few historically accurate (or original) objects left. Deciding that "everything in the White House must have a reason for being there," the first lady spearheaded an extensive restoration project aimed at returning to the **White House** furnishings and possessions used during previous administrations. Significant artifacts were scattered around the globe but could be retrieved. (After all, early in the 20th century, the descendant of a British soldier had graciously returned James Madison's medicine box, purloined during the fire in 1814.) Under Jackie's direction, people from all over the world pitched in. Thanks to these efforts and those of subsequent administrations, which have continued the project, today's **White House** is as much a museum of priceless American antiques as it is a home and an office.

The tour takes you through five rooms. The white-and-gold **East Room,** where Abigail Adams hung her laundry to dry and where Theodore Roosevelt's children roller-skated, is now used for receptions, press conferences, concerts, and dances. On the east wall is Gilbert Stuart's famous painting of George Washington, rescued by Dolley Madison when the British invaded the city in 1814. Seven presidents who died in office, including Lincoln and Kennedy, have lain in state in this room. Connecting doors lead from the **East Room** through the small reception chamber known as the **Green Room,** which has walls lined with green silk. This room is often the setting for presidential photo-ops with foreign heads of state. The oval-shaped **Blue Room,** which Grover Cleveland used as a wedding chapel in 1886,

White House

is where the **White House** Christmas tree stands during the holidays. Just off the **Blue Room** is the **Red Room,** where Dolley Madison held her legendary Wednesday night parties. The final tour stop is the **State Dining Room.** Note the inscription on the marble mantel, put there by Franklin D. Roosevelt: It's John Adams's **White House** prayer.

Each December, you can take a candlelight tour of the **White House** in all its Christmas glory. In the spring and fall, an afternoon Garden Tour opens the usually off-limits **White House** grounds to the public. And on Easter Monday, the traditional Easter Egg Roll takes place. Just show up on the **Ellipse** between 10AM and 2PM; some people arrive as early as 7AM.

Free, self-guided tours of the White House are organized by the National Park Service. No tours are offered during state visits—and delays and even cancellations may occur on short notice—so call ahead. Visitors may secure timed, same-day tickets at the **White House Visitors Center** (E St NW, between 14th and 15th Sts, 208.1631; Metro: Federal Triangle). The center is open daily from 7:30AM to 4PM; tickets are often gone by 9AM, so get there early. The center also houses a museum devoted to the **White House.** Tours are conducted Tuesday through Saturday mornings, when visitors have 15 to 20 minutes to view the five rooms described above. You can also contact your senator or representative 8 to 10 weeks before your visit to reserve tickets for a guided 30- to 40-minute tour Tuesday through Saturday.

Incidents at the **White House** during the early 1990s—one involving a suicidal pilot who crashed his light plane at the base of the Executive Mansion on the **South Lawn,** another in which a man sprayed the **North Lawn** with bullets—prompted a serious security review by the Secret Service. The April 1995 bombing in Oklahoma City further exacerbated fears of terrorist acts against government buildings. In May 1995, President Clinton approved a plan to close Pennsylvania Avenue NW from 15th to 17th Streets to vehicular traffic. The plan is to eventually build a pedestrian mall along this fabled stretch of Pennsylvania Avenue. Also, a short section of E Street NW—along the southwest perimeter of the grounds—is now closed to vehicles. In addition, be aware of recently changed one-way streets to the north of the **White House** and limited on-street parking to the south along 15th and 17th Streets. ♦ Free. White House: Tu-Sa 10AM-noon. Signed tours for the hearing-impaired may be arranged through your representative or senator. 1600 Pennsylvania Ave NW (between 15th and 17th Sts). Tours and events 456.7041 (recording), visitors center 208.1631 ♿ Metro: Metro Center

At the White House:

White House Grounds The 18 acres known as the **President's Park** contain more than 80 varieties of trees planted over the years by almost every presidential family. A seedling from John Quincy Adams's home in Massachusetts is now the giant American elm on the Center Oval. Andrew Jackson brought a magnolia from Tennessee as a memorial to his wife. The other magnolia, near the east entrance to the **White House,** was planted by Warren Harding in remembrance of animals killed during World War I. More recent trees include the Gerald Ford family's white pine, a giant sequoia set by Richard Nixon in the Center Oval, and little Amy Carter's tree house, built on poles and shielded by a magnificent silver Atlas cedar.

Perhaps the most famous part of the park is Ellen Wilson's rose garden, planted in 1913 and redesigned by Mrs. Paul Mellon at the request of John F. Kennedy in 1962. This rendition of an 18th-century garden also includes osmanthus and boxwood hedges, tulips, narcissus, chrysanthemums, and heliotrope.

The grounds are closed to visitors except during the **White House** garden tours and the annual Easter Egg Roll, the biggest and best-attended—and least formal—party the **White House** throws. Since grass stains are almost inevitable, jeans and sneakers are just fine. All children six years old and younger (and accompanied by an adult) are welcome.

The Easter Egg Roll's history, according to local legend, is as follows: More than a hundred years ago, egg rolling was very big with the kids of DC, and their favorite spot was the gentle slope of the **Capitol** lawn, which their egg rolling destroyed on an annual basis. One year, by chance, the wife of Rutherford Hayes was passing by just as the kids were being chased away. Taking pity on the crying youngsters, she invited them to the **White House** and they came back every year for more than 50 years.

During World War II, Franklin D. Roosevelt called the event off, and it remained suspended for 12 years, long after the war's end. Traditionally, the first lady hosts the event, and it was Mamie Eisenhower who decided that happy times warranted a comeback of the festive event. After more than a decade, no one knew quite what to expect. Yards of storm fencing were put up to protect flower beds and the president's putting green; rest rooms and drinking fountains were hastily erected. When the great day arrived, the lawn was mobbed. Kids threw more eggs than they rolled, and the Eisenhower children retreated speedily to the **White House.** Secret Service agents had to rescue the president, who was holding his baby granddaughter. Although the lawn became a matted mess of eggs, jelly beans, and marshmallows, the event was declared a huge success. These days, after so many years of experience, it has rarely taken more than an afternoon to return the lawn to its tidy state.

All egg rolling currently takes place in eight well-marked lanes, but real eggs and long-handled spoons are still used. Each recipient gets two eggs—one for practice. The Reagan administration added another spin to the festivities: All participants are awarded wooden eggs inscribed with the White House insignia as a prize. In addition, executive staffers send out thousands of eggs to politicians, athletes, and entertainers to be autographed and returned; these become treasures in the Easter Egg Hunt, which takes place at the same time as the egg roll in an enclosure at the side of the **White House.** Twenty-five young egg hunters at a time search this area. The **White House** has also begun sending eggs to respected American artists and foreign embassies for special decoration. Easter visitors can view the finished results, which are often quite wonderful, in a display case on the lawn.

2 Old Executive Office Building Originally designed to house the Navy offices and the departments of War and State, this outrageous French Second Empire building was so hated by the time of its completion in 1888 that no one wanted to pay architect **Alfred B. Mullett.** At the same time, nobody could justify the cost of demolishing the structure, which has four-foot-thick granite walls and an iron door and window frames, trimming, and baseboards, all cast in an on-site foundry. Newly restored, the building is used for senior-level **White House** offices. Particularly notable are the stained-glass skylights over the cantilevered staircases, the **State Department Library,** with four cast-iron balconies and Minton tile floors, and the **Indian Treaty Room,** with marble wall panels and elaborate ironwork. The **War Department Library,** now the **White House Law Library,** features eclectic cast iron, including Moorish, Gothic, Classical, and Baroque designs plated with bronze and brass. Although the building is not open to the public during the week, 90-minute Saturday morning tours are available by reservation; when arranging for a tour, you must supply your name and birthdate and you must bring appropriate ID for admittance.
◆ Free. Tours: Sa, by appointment. Reservations required. Pennsylvania Ave NW and 17th St. 395.5895 ⑂ Metros: Farragut West, Farragut North

Pennsylvania Avenue

As John Kennedy's inaugural motorcade rolled down Pennsylvania Avenue from the **White House** to the **Capitol,** the President-Elect took in "America's Main Street." He viewed an avenue in economic shambles with tacky souvenir shops and cheap restaurants. The once grand **Willard Hotel** was tattered; peep shows, pawn shops, and liquor stores had turned the avenue into a seedy strip. Supposedly, JFK declared, "It's a disgrace—fix it."

From Kennedy's orders grew a comprehensive redevelopment plan for Pennsylvania Avenue—although things did not improve immediately. Kennedy's assassination, the riots of 1968, and the building of the FBI headquarters (an architectural monstrosity that even J. Edgar Hoover called the ugliest building he'd ever seen), set planning back a decade.

In 1974 the **Pennsylvania Avenue Development Corporation (PADC),** established by Congress under President Nixon, issued its first report proposing parks, restored historic buildings, new federal buildings, and revitalized commercial space. Today, though some elements of the **PADC's** original proposal were changed, the plan's revitalizing spirit has persevered to create a grand Pennsylvania Avenue forged from the old and the new.

The **Willard Hotel** (1401 Pennsylvania Ave NW, at 14th St, 628.9100), which closed in 1968, was

reopened in 1986, meticulously restored. Both the **National Theatre** (1321 E St NW, between 13th and 14th Sts, 628.6161) and the **Warner Theatre** (13th and E Sts NW, 783.4000) are running full entertainment schedules. The old **Apex Liquor Store** at Pennsylvania Avenue and Seventh Street Northwest, with its often-photographed statue of *Temperance* out front, has been restored to its original name, **Sears House.** Now a small, private office building, the more than 120-year-old structure once housed photographer Mathew Brady's studio.

New construction has added 20th-century architecture to the avenue. **I.M. Pei** perfectly suited the **East Wing** of the **National Gallery of Art** (Fourth St NW, between Madison Dr and Constitution Ave, 737.4215) to its triangular site. Nearby, the Canadian Government built an award-winning chancery (501 Pennsylvania Ave NW, between Constitution Ave and Sixth St) where an old, nondescript library once stood. And most welcome to pedestrians are two parks—**Freedom Plaza** and **Pershing Park**—both near the **White House.**

Pierre L'Enfant, Washington's first city planner, envisioned Pennsylvania Avenue as a grand ceremonial boulevard, linking the **Capitol** and the presidential "palace." More than two hundred years later, the Avenue appears closer than ever to that goal.

3 Treasury Building After years of congressional foot-dragging, Andrew Jackson impatiently chose this site, even though the exquisite Greek Revival building raised here blocks **L'Enfant**'s intended view of the **Capitol** from the **White House.** The building, which took 33 years to complete (in part because of the Civil War), still houses the administrative offices of the Treasury Department; the interior has been restored to its former glory. The **East Wing,** designed by **Robert Mills,** was completed in 1842; the other wings were designed by **Thomas U. Walter,** with supervising architects **Ammi Young, Isaiah Rogers,** and **Alfred B. Mullett.** In 1989, the curator's office began offering 75-minute tours on Saturday mornings. Visitors must provide their birthdates when making reservations. Tours for the hearing-impaired are also available. ♦ Free. Sa 10, 10:20, 10:40, and 11AM. Reservations required. Pennsylvania Ave NW and 15th St. 622.0896 ♿ Metro: Metro Center

4 Ellipse The 52-acre oval yard south of the **White House** is best known as the site of the National Christmas Tree, which the president lights each December. Carolers and other yuletide celebrants fill the area with pageantry throughout the holiday season. In 1998 a menorah was added to the decorations, in honor of Hanukkah. During the rest of the year, vendors, chess players, softball players, and strollers enliven the park on sunny days. ♦ Bounded by 15th and 17th Sts NW, and Constitution Ave and E St ♿ Metros: Federal Triangle, Farragut North

5 Constitution Gardens This park is located between the **Washington Monument** and the **Lincoln Memorial,** where temporary Navy Department buildings from World War I stood until well after World War II. **Skidmore, Owings & Merrill** originally designed a 50-acre park, but the recessionary budget cuts of the 1970s marred the plan. Though some find the results disappointing, this spot is a lovely, little-known haven in the midst of the bustling tourist sites. Walking paths and bike trails surround the 7.5-acre lake and its landscaped island, where you can examine Joseph E. Brown's Memorial to the 56 signers of the Declaration of Independence. More than 5,000 trees create their own islands of shade. ♦ Just south of Constitution Ave NW ♿ Metro: Foggy Bottom/GWU

Within Constitution Gardens:

Anacostia, established in 1854, started off as Uniontown. So many towns were named Uniontown after the Civil War that in 1886 the area was rechristened Anacostia, for the river that flows nearby.

Vietnam Veterans Memorial In 1980, Congress authorized the construction of a memorial to the veterans of the Vietnam War on this plot near the **Lincoln Memorial.** After a national design competition with 1,421 entries, Congress unanimously chose a design by Maya Ying Lin, then a 21-year-old architecture student at Yale University. She conceived of the monument's polished black granite walls as a park within a park, a quiet place. The walls point to the **Washington Monument** and the **Lincoln Memorial,** and the 58,156 names of those killed in the war are inscribed in chronological order of the date of death, beginning at the walls' intersection, the memorial's deepest point. In a very real sense, the names become the memorial.

Lin's unconventional design stirred a storm of controversy. A flagpole and a more traditional bronze statue of three soldiers, by Washington sculptor Frederick Hart, were added nearby to mollify critics. The *Women's Memorial,* Glenna Goodacre's bronze sculpture of two uniformed women tending a wounded male soldier honors the estimated 10,000 women who served in the war. However, Lin's work has transcended the initial criticism. Her Vietnam memorial is one of the nation's most moving public monuments. Veterans' groups maintain vigils here, and those who lost loved ones leave flowers, medals, letters, and other tokens of remembrance. The National Park Service is saving these offerings in a large warehouse at 23rd and I Streets, and plans to display them in museum exhibits. Volunteers are available to help find names and a guard is on duty from 8AM until midnight. A directory of the inscribed names can be purchased by calling 347.2054. ♦ 634.1568 ♿

6 Reflecting Pool The glassy surface of this shallow, rectangular pool mirrors both the **Washington Monument** and the **Lincoln Memorial.** The pool, a third of a mile long by 180 feet wide and three feet deep, is bordered by tree-lined pedestrian paths—usually a peaceful oasis in this fast-paced city. However, many celebrations and demonstrations held here have disrupted the tranquil setting. The 1963 Civil Rights March on Washington climaxed with Martin Luther King Jr. giving his "I Have a Dream" speech (from the steps of the **Lincoln Memorial**) before 250,000 people crowded around, and in, the pool. ♦ ♿ Metros: Foggy Bottom/GWU, Smithsonian

7 Lincoln Memorial This structure (pictured on page 41), so perfectly etched on Washington's landscape—not to mention the penny and the $5 bill—was built only after much debate over its shape and location. Among the early design proposals were an obelisk, a pyramid, and—sponsored by car and real estate interests—a 72-milelong memorial parkway between Gettysburg and Washington. The flea-ridden, swampy site eventually chosen had to be drained and filled before construction could begin in 1914. And yet a better choice now seems unimaginable. **Henry Bacon's** classical memorial anchors the east-west axis of **The Mall.** A larger-than-life Lincoln gazes over the **Reflecting Pool** toward the **Washington Monument** and the **Capitol.** To the rear, an imaginary line connects the man who preserved the union with Robert E. Lee's final resting place in **Arlington Cemetery.** The memorial is essentially a Greek-style temple ("Coolly cribbed from the Parthenon," reported one critic) with a Roman-style attic or roof. The entrance is on the broad side facing **The Mall** rather than on one of the narrow ends, as would have been typical in antiquity.

Thirty-six Doric columns rim the building; they tilt inward so as not to create the optical illusion of a bulging top. Above the colonnade is a frieze inscribed with the names and admission dates of the 36 states in the union at the time of Lincoln's death. (The date for Ohio is off by one year.) Higher on the attic frieze are the names of the 48 states in the union at the time of the memorial's dedication in 1922.

Daniel Chester French's statue, often called "The Brooding Lincoln," looms from the center of the memorial. French designed the statue but only supervised the carving. The Piccarilli Brothers executed it in four years, using 28 blocks of white Georgia marble. The 16th president leans back in a monumental throne adorned with fasces, the Roman symbol of the authority of the state. From heel to head the seated statue measures 19 feet, and if this stone exaggeration of our tallest

president were to stand, it would tower above the crowd at a height of 28 feet.

Carved on the south wall is the Gettysburg Address, and on the north, Lincoln's second inaugural address. Above the texts are huge (12 feet high, 600 feet long) murals by Jules Guerin; one depicts the Angel of Truth liberating a slave, the other, the unity of North and South.

When the memorial was dedicated, one of the speakers was Dr. Robert Moton, the black president of Tuskegee Institute. Ironically, upon Moton's arrival, a Marine Corps usher escorted him from the dais to the all-black section, separated from the memorial and the rest of the audience by a roadway. In the years since, the memorial has become a powerful symbol of the struggle for racial equality. In the 1940s, when the Daughters of the American Revolution refused to allow a concert by Marian Anderson at Constitution Hall, Anderson sang instead before more than 75,000 people from the steps of the memorial.

A magnificent sight at all times, the **Lincoln Memorial** is most impressive at dawn and dusk. Note: The **Cave under Lincoln,** a vast stalactite- and stalagmite-filled cavern created by excavations for the building, and later by water dripping from the marble steps, contains the original substructure—columns more than 45 feet high support the 900-ton statue. The cave has been closed, however, since the discovery of asbestos there, and it is unlikely to reopen soon. ♦ Daily 24 hours. Ranger on duty 8AM–midnight. 23rd St (between Independence Ave SW and Constitution Ave NW). 426.6895 க Metro: Foggy Bottom/GWU

Lincoln Memorial

COURTESY OF THE BUREAU OF ENGRAVING AND PRINTING

Jefferson Memorial

8 Korean War Veterans Memorial Opened in July 1995, this tribute to the men and women who served in the "forgotten war" is located on the south side of the **Reflecting Pool,** complementing the **Vietnam Memorial** on the north side. The **Cooper-Lecky Architects'** design consists of two intersecting components: the triangular *Field of Service* and the circular *Pool of Remembrance.* Scattered on the field are statues, sculpted by Frank Gaylord, of 19 servicemen clad in foul-weather ponchos. Walkways lead pedestrians along two sides of the triangle to a point that intersects with the pool. Bordering one walkway is a granite wall with photographic images of the war taken from the National Archives. ♦ North of Independence Ave SW. 634.1568; www.nps.gov & Metros: Foggy Bottom/GWU, Smithsonian

9 East and West Potomac Park/Hains Point East Potomac Park is the island created by the Washington Channel; West Potomac Park encompasses the area between the **Tidal Basin** and the **Lincoln Memorial.** Together, these parks cover 700 acres at the west end of **The Mall.** Scattered with monuments, pools, and trees, they offer some of the city's best views. Come during cherry blossom time and enjoy almost 2,000 pink double-blossomed trees in bloom, generally two weeks later than those at the **Tidal Basin.** (Take the 14th Street Bridge and head south on Ohio Drive to the park.) Visitors can play golf at the public course, ride along the bike paths, paddle a boat, savor a picnic, or just enjoy the sunshine. At Hains Point, the peninsula's southern tip, check out *The Awakening,* Seward Johnson's unusual 1980 aluminum sculpture—a gigantic figure rising out of the ground as if coming to life. ♦ Ohio Dr SW (south of Independence Ave). Information 426.6841, tennis and golf information 554.7660 & Metro: Smithsonian

Within East and West Potomac Park:

Franklin D. Roosevelt Memorial Designed by architect **Lawrence Halprin,** this long-overdue tribute to the president who led America through the Great Depression and all but the last months of World War II opened in May 1997. It features four outdoor "rooms" (one for each of Roosevelt's terms in office), covering 7.5 acres. Incorporating fountains and gardens, it's very different in concept from the self-contained memorials to Lincoln and Jefferson. Studded with 10 bronze sculptures, this memorial goes beyond the celebration of one man and also honors the institution of the presidency, the human struggles of the Great Depression, the United States's emergence as a world power, and First Lady Eleanor Roosevelt. Despite efforts by members of the disabled community to have the president portrayed in his wheelchair, he is shown in a standing position. ♦ 619.7222 &

10 Tidal Basin Come here to picnic, jog, read, or enjoy the view. On the east side are gardens of seasonal flowers—especially brilliant in spring, when the tulips appear—and a concession stand that sells hot dogs and burgers and rents the little blue paddleboats that skim the lake. Near East Basin Drive is the **Japanese Pagoda,** and near the Kutz Memorial Bridge is the **Japanese Lantern.** This park and breeze-swept lake will take your breath away when the 600 surrounding cherry trees bloom (sometime between mid-March and mid-April, depending on the weather). The best way to experience blossom time is on foot. In fact, driving can be a miserable experience, with traffic jams and honking horns. Use public transportation to reach **The Mall,** then walk through the lovely park, where the crowds attract vendors and street performers. Other places to see Japanese cherry trees are the **Washington Monument**

grounds (see on the right) and **East and West Potomac Park** (see page 42). The basin was created in 1897 to collect water from the Potomac and empty it into the Washington Channel, possibly because the river is an estuary and rises with the tide. ♦ Boathouse/concession: daily 10AM-dusk Apr-Oct. 484.0206 ⅃ Metro: Smithsonian

11 Jefferson Memorial John Russell Pope's monument is a fitting tribute to a man who was an accomplished architect as well as a powerful and thoughtful statesman. Essentially an adaptation of the Roman Pantheon favored by Jefferson, the memorial recalls the third president's own designs for his home, **Monticello,** and for the rotunda of the **University of Virginia.** The circular building is rimmed by 54 Ionic columns and is fronted, on the side facing **The Mall,** with a classical portico and a pediment supported by even more columns. Three other entrances bring light and air into the gracefully proportioned chamber.

Like so much of **The Mall,** this site was under brackish water until the commencement of an eight-year dredging project. The reclaimed land couldn't support the memorial, whose every column weighs 45 tons, without a specially prepared foundation. Concrete-filled steel cylinders were driven 135 feet into the earth before reaching bedrock.

The interior of the coffered dome is of Indiana limestone. The walls are of white Georgia marble and the floors of pink-and-gray Tennessee marble. Standing in this grand setting is a majestic 19-foot-high statue of Jefferson—who stood 6 feet 2 inches in life. He wears knee breeches, a waistcoat, and a fur-collared greatcoat like the one that the Polish patriot Thaddeus Kosciuszko gave him. Rudolph Evans's design was chosen from more than one hundred submissions. During dedication ceremonies, officiated by Franklin D. Roosevelt in 1943, a plaster model represented the sculpture. It couldn't be cast in bronze until several years later when the wartime ban on the use of domestic metal was lifted.

The offerings at any local postcard stand will prove that the **Jefferson Memorial** is one of the most popular attractions in this monumental city. But at the time of its construction, the memorial was denounced as being too sweet and feminine. Its low circular shape prompted one critic to rename the memorial "Jefferson's muffin." Some parking is available near the memorial.
♦ Daily 24 hours. Ranger on duty 8AM-midnight. Rotunda open and lighted through the night. E Basin Dr SW (between Maine Ave and Ohio Dr). 426.6821 ⅃ Metro: Smithsonian

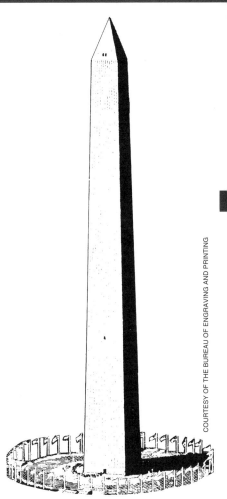

COURTESY OF THE BUREAU OF ENGRAVING AND PRINTING

12 Washington Monument The simple yet grand presence of this monument (pictured above) is, at 555 feet 5⅛ inches, the tallest structure in DC. It was the tallest in the world when it opened to the public in 1886. The "Monument Committee," which launched a nationwide competition to select a landmark for the capital, didn't favor **Pierre-Charles L'Enfant**'s equestrian statue of Washington that would have stood on the current site of the **Jefferson Pier.** Instead it preferred **Robert Mills**'s richly decorated obelisk, designed to rise like a giant birthday candle from behind a Greek-style circular temple that was to hold the tombs of Revolutionary War heroes. Plans also included a massive marble statue of Washington driving a quadriga (a Roman chariot pulled by four horses) in front of the monument. Lack of money and public support for these frills led to the establishment of the simple gleaming tower—a familiar symbol of Washington the City as well as Washington the Man.

Funds for the monument initially came from private groups that solicited $1 apiece from citizens across the nation. Construction proceeded smoothly for seven years—until a single block of marble was donated by Pope Pius IX. This infuriated the antipapist Know-Nothing Party, which stole the "Pope's stone" and sabotaged further fund-raising for the monument. Then the Civil War broke out, and the project was abandoned for almost 20 years.

In 1876—after the war and the US Centennial Exposition—public interest returned and construction was turned over to the Army Corps of Engineers. They strengthened the foundation (although it still sinks a quarter inch every 30 years) and redesigned the monument, much improving the original proportions. A slight change of color in the stone marks the point at which construction resumed. Four years later the obelisk was capped with a nine-inch tip made of solid aluminum (an exotic material at the time) and wired with 144 platinum lightning conductors. The government picked up the $1-million tab. At press time, a much-needed, $8-million restoration of the monument was near completion. During the project, an on-site interpretive center will use interactive exhibits to bring the history and restoration of this national treasure to life.

For a magnificent view of the city, take the 70-second elevator ride to the top. The National Park Service conducts "walking-down-step tours" on weekends, during which you'll see 188 carved memorial stones that various private citizens, societies, states, and nations donated in the 19th century. On Saturday or Sunday, call 426.6840 to see if a tour is offered that day. ♦ Free. Daily 9AM-5PM Labor Day–1st Su in Apr; daily 8AM-midnight 1st Su in Apr–Labor Day. West of 15th St. 426.6839 ♿ Metro: Smithsonian

The impressive Franklin D. Roosevelt Memorial is not what the former president had in mind. According to Supreme Court Justice Felix Frankfurter, Roosevelt told him "I am likely to shuffle off long before you kick the bucket. If they are to put any memorial to me, I should like it to be placed in the center of that green plot in front of the Archives Building. I should like it to consist of a block about the size of this." He pointed to his desk.

Douglas E. Evelyn and Paul Dickson,
On This Spot

Restaurants/Clubs: Red   Hotels: Blue
Shops/ 🍴 **Outdoors:** Green   **Sights/Culture:** Black

13 Sylvan Theater Weather permitting, this outdoor theater with a huge lawn regularly presents musicals, Shakespearean festivals, and concerts. Thousands of people flock to the small stage on hot summer evenings; the first to arrive claim the best spots by spreading picnic blankets or unfolding their own lawn chairs up front. Military- and big-band concerts are usually held Tuesday through Friday and Sunday at 8PM, Memorial Day through Labor Day. ♦ Free. 15th St SW and Independence Ave. 426.6841 ♿ Metro: Smithsonian

14 Department of Agriculture This was the first building erected by the McMillan Commission, which was charged at the turn of the century with resurrecting **L'Enfant**'s plan for a gracious, ceremonial capital city. ♦ Independence Ave SW and 14th St ♿ Metro: Smithsonian

15 United States Holocaust Memorial Museum Opened in 1993, this museum has established itself as one of the most moving memorials in Washington, if not the world. It tells the story of the millions of Jews, Gypsies, and other "undesirables" who were executed by the Nazis from 1933 to 1945. Give yourself ample time to experience this museum. **James Ingo Freed,** of **Pei Cobb Freed & Partners,** designed the building and his intelligence and creativity show in every detail, from interior lights that resemble watchtower spotlights to exits that look like prison doors. Through strange angles, slanted walls, and out-of-kilter staircases, the structure intimates that visitors are entering a world where sanity no longer prevails. The exhibits here build upon one another, augmenting the viewer's feelings of shock and horror and creating an unforgettable experience.

At the beginning of the tour visitors receive a card containing information about a particular Holocaust witness, thus allowing them to establish a bond with an individual from history. This helps most people feel the impact of a tragedy that affected millions. Be sure to save time (and energy) for the last exhibit—*Testimony,* an hourlong film—presented in a stark, open auditorium. Haunting accounts of the Holocaust are delivered by several of its survivors—a heart-wrenching yet inspiring experience. At the end of your tour, stop in the calmingly spare **Hall of Remembrance** to absorb all you've encountered. A computer learning center also provides electronic databases for those who want to conduct additional research.

Owing to the volume of visitors, tickets are required for the permanent exhibition. You can call any **Ticketmaster** outlet (Washington number is 202/432.7328), but they will levy a service charge. A limited number of same-day tickets are available at the museum beginning at 10AM; get here early. ♦ Free, with ticket. Daily. 100 Raoul Wallenberg Pl SW (at Independence Ave). 488.0400; www.ushmm.org & Metro: Smithsonian

16 Bureau of Engraving and Printing Once every fiscal year the Federal Reserve puts in an order at the **Bureau of Engraving and Printing**. The order is for a great deal of paper money—so much, in fact, that the presses must roll 24 hours a day all year to print it. In 1997, the bureau printed 4,646,400,000 notes in $1 denominations. To put this into perspective, if you had that much money and spent it at the reasonable rate of $1 per second, it would take you a little longer than 147 years to go broke. Of all the notes printed each year, 95 percent are used to replace notes already in circulation and nearly half are $1 bills.

Aside from a whole lot of bucks, the bureau prints treasury notes, military certificates, invitations to the White House, and 40 billion postage stamps every year. In the past it has turned out food stamps, and during the oil embargo of 1973, it had an order—never filled—to print coupons for gas rationing.

Watching crisp sheets of money roll off the presses is great fun for kids and fuels the fantasies of adults. The bureau offers a free 20-minute tour. Enter through the main lobby, where some of the bureau's products are displayed, including stamp sheets four times the size of those at your local post office, as well as part of a press plate and some first-rate examples of the nefarious art of counterfeiters. Continue to the gallery, which offers an excellent view of large sheets of money being printed, checked, overprinted with the treasury seal, cut, stacked, and bundled for shipment. A recorded explanation of the sights plays over a PA system here. The tour ends at the **Visitors' Center,** where presidential portraits and commemorative coins are displayed and sold. Additional exhibitions further explain the engraving process and the activities of the bureau. Buy a small bag of shredded money or a sheet of uncut currency for a unique souvenir.

Free tours are given Monday through Friday between 9AM and 2PM. Tickets are required and can be picked up at the ticket booth, located on the 15th Street side of the building

(at Raoul Wallenberg Pl); it opens at 8AM. ♦ Free. M-F 9AM-2PM. 14th St SW (between Maine and Independence Aves). 874.3188; www.moneyfactory.com & Metro: Smithsonian

17 Smithsonian Institution Building Popularly known as the "Castle" because of its marvelous spires, towers, turrets, and crenellated parapets, this was the **Smithsonian**'s first building. Designed by **James Renwick** in 1855, it is composed of red Seneca sandstone and widely recognized as one of the finest Gothic Revival buildings in America. The **Smithsonian**'s administrative offices and the headquarters of the Woodrow Wilson International Center for Scholars occupy the Castle. Also within is the **Crypt Room,** housing the tomb of the Smithsonian's British benefactor, James Smithson. It was his $500,000 bequest to the United States in 1838 that established the Smithsonian Institution. ♦ Free. Daily. 1000 Jefferson Dr SW (between Seventh and 12th Sts). 357.2700 & Metro: Smithsonian

18 Arts & Industries Building Restored in 1976, this 19th-century building houses one of the most extensive collections of American Victoriana in existence. Many of the items, collectively called "1876: A Centennial Exhibition," were displayed in the Philadelphia Centennial Exposition of that year: horse-drawn carriages, machinery, pistols, silverware, furniture, and unusual objets d'art, all celebrating the brassy glory of America during the 19th century. Even the building, designed as a partner to the administration building next door, is a Victorian fantasy: an elaborate polychrome/brick affair with giant industrial trusses and meandering iron balconies. The museum shop sells replicas of Victorian picture frames, paper-doll cutouts, and jewelry. The Smithsonian Resident Associate Program's **Discovery Theater** puts on programs that range from puppet shows to mime and dance troupes. ♦ Museum: free; Discovery Theater: admission. Daily. Shows: call for times. 900 Jefferson Dr SW (between Seventh and 12th Sts). Information 357.2700, theater tickets and reservations 357.1500 & Metro: Smithsonian

---

The obelisk has to my eye a singular aptitude in its form and character to call attention to a spot memorable in its history. It says but one word. But it speaks loud. If I understand this voice, it says, 'Here!'"

Horatio Greenough
The Architecture of Washington,
American Institute of Architects

19 Enid A. Haupt Garden Conceived by Smithsonian Institution Director Emeritus S. Dillon Ripley in 1987, the 4.2-acre garden is sandwiched between the **Sackler Gallery** and the **National Museum of African Art.** It's named after Enid Annenberg Haupt of New York, who contributed $3 million toward its establishment. The central Victorian parterre is a retreat from the museum bustle, with 40 antique wrought-iron park benches and beds of bright flowers that form patterns designed after the sunken garden at Philadelphia's 1876 Centennial Exposition. The main entrance, in front of the parterre, is known as the **Renwick Gate,** after "Castle" architect **James Renwick,** who sketched a carriage gate in 1849 that was never built. The entrance's four stone pillars are made from the same red Seneca sandstone that was used to build the Smithsonian Institution building. Two minigardens, one on either side of the parterre, reflect the styles of the museums below. The **Moongate Garden** near the **Sackler Gallery** features two nine-foot-tall pink granite "moongates," one on either side of a pool paved with half-round pieces of granite and shaded by two weeping cherry trees. The **Fountain Garden** near the **National Museum of African Art** is designed to be a haven on hot days, with a waterfall and thornless hawthorns. ♦ Daily 7AM-5:45PM Oct-May; daily 7AM-8PM Jun-Sept. Independence Ave SW (between Seventh and 12th Sts) & Metro: Smithsonian

19 The Quadrangle Pressed for more exhibition and office space, the Smithsonian Institution slipped a three-story complex below the **Enid A. Haupt Garden** (see above). Within this space, which is 96 percent below ground, is the **Smithsonian's Traveling Exhibition Service (SITES).** Also below ground level is the **National Museum of African Art** pavilion, whose domed roofs recall the arch motif of the **Freer,** and the **Arthur M. Sackler Gallery** pavilion, its pyramidal silhouette echoing the roof lines of the **Arts & Industries Building.** ♦ Independence Ave SW (between Seventh and 12th Sts) & Metro: Smithsonian

Within The Quadrangle:

National Museum of African Art The only museum in the US dedicated to the traditional arts of sub-Saharan Africa was founded by Warren Robbins in 1964 as a private institution in a series of connected row houses on **Capitol Hill** (one of which belonged to Frederick Douglass). It became a branch of the Smithsonian in 1979.

The collection demonstrates how the continent's 900 distinct cultures weave art into daily life, expressing religious beliefs and practices not only in masks and figures created for ceremonial purposes but also in everyday objects, such as splendid sculptures,

textiles, building tools, and household utensils. Most are made from impermanent organic materials, such as wood; therefore, the bulk of the collected works only date back to the late-19th and 20th centuries.

On the museum's first level is a gallery that includes one hundred of the collection's highlights, many of which have never been displayed before, as well as an exhibition of metal sculpture from Benin. The second level contains a gallery for temporary exhibitions and the museum's learning center, which offers programs, workshops, lectures, and the like sponsored by the museum's education department. ♦ Free. Museum: daily. Library: by appointment. Tours: M-F 1:30PM; Sa-Su 11AM, 1PM. 357.4600; www.si.edu/organiza/museums/africart &

Arthur M. Sackler Gallery The museum's two floors of below-ground galleries give the Smithsonian its first real opportunity to showcase its extensive collection of Eastern art. Dr. Arthur M. Sackler, a New York medical researcher, donated one thousand masterworks to found this collection. He also gave $4 million toward the construction of the museum. On display are Chinese bronzes from the Shang (circa 1523-1028 BC) through the Han (circa 206 BC-AD 220) dynasties, Chinese jades from 3000 BC into the 20th century, and Near Eastern works in silver, gold, bronze, and lesser minerals.

The first level holds Persian and Indian paintings, Chinese Ming dynasty furniture, and an exhibition of Chinese interpretations of animal motifs highlighted by a zodiac display. The second level presents Chinese bronzes and neolithic jades, some dating from the fourth millennium BC. The second-level library houses 35,000 volumes, half in Chinese or Japanese, and more than 200 periodicals. There are often free events, ranging from concerts to dance presentations. ♦ Free. Galleries: daily. Library: M-F. Tours: M, F, Sa 12:30PM. 357.2700 &

Smithsonian
Freer Gallery of Art

20 Freer Gallery of Art A four-year renovation (1989-93) of this Florentine building, which originally opened in 1923, not only retained but heightened its charm. An elegant little theater was added, display cases dramatically lit, explanatory texts expanded, and the entrance cleared of an intrusive gift shop. Housed within is an eclectic collection of Asian art and late 19th- and early 20th-century American art showing a Far Eastern influence. The late Charles Lang Freer, a wealthy Detroit businessman, began collecting Eastern art on the advice of his close friend, artist James McNeill Whistler. The flamboyant **Peacock Room,** painted by Whistler, is a highlight of the collection. ♦ Free. Daily. Tours: M-Tu, F-Su 11:30AM. Jefferson Dr SW (between Seventh and 12th Sts). 357.2700 ♿ Metro: Smithsonian

21 The National Museum of American History Celebrating the country's scientific, technological, political, and cultural heritage, this collection (see floor plan below) functions as the "attic" of America, storing all the outdated contraptions that remind us who we once were and how we've changed. In 1858, the US Patent Office transferred its overcrowded cabinet of curiosities to the Smithsonian. To this base was added a windfall of exhibitions from the Philadelphia Centennial Exposition in 1876. Today, behind its pink Tennessee marble exterior, the museum shelters the Country Store Post Office from Headsville, West Virginia, circa 1861 (you can still post your mail here, and it will go out with a special Smithsonian Station postmark); agricultural machinery from a time when farming was strictly a family business; a 1913 Ford Model T; one of Thomas Edison's first phonographs; the first typewriter (built in 1829); a 1790 chemistry lab that includes equipment used by Joseph Priestley; George Washington's false teeth; and a 280-ton steam locomotive. And that's just the first floor.

Among the many displays on the second level, you'll find a Foucault pendulum, which demonstrates the earth's rotation; the original "Star-Spangled Banner" that Francis Scott Key saw "by the dawn's early light" still flying over Fort McHenry in 1814; genuine home interiors dating from the 1600s to the 1900s and ranging from a colonial Virginia parlor to the farmhouse of a Delaware family; political campaign paraphernalia; and a pocket compass used by Lewis and Clark. In the museum's newest permanent exhibition, **Ceremonial Court**—a re-creation of **Cross Hall,** the grand front corridor of the **White House**—is a selection of first ladies' inaugural gowns.

The relocated and expanded **Museum Shop** features current titles published by the Smithsonian presses as well as handicrafts that relate to the exhibitions. ♦ Free. Daily. Constitution Ave NW (between 12th and 14th Sts). 357.2700 ♿ Metro: Federal Triangle

22 National Museum of Natural History/National Museum of Man This treasure chest of natural science displays dioramas, re-creations, prototypes, and artifacts used to study evolution, cultures, dinosaurs, fossils, amphibians, reptiles, birds, sea organisms, mammals, insects, plants, rocks, minerals, and meteorites—in short, the entire planet (see floor plan on page 48). There's too much here to digest in one visit, but some of the highlights are "Uncle Beazley," the life-size model of a triceratops dinosaur that greets you at the museum's Mall entrance; a 13-foot-tall African bush elephant (the largest known specimen of the largest land animal of modern times); a 3.1-billion-year-old fossil of a fig tree; dinosaur skeletons; an audiovisual show describing Ice Age glaciation effects on the earth's surface; and one of Easter Island's famous stone heads. Press onward, even if your senses are overloaded, because there is also a life-size model of a 92-foot-long whale; a living coral reef rocked by waves; and, in the renovated **Hall of Geology, Gems, and Minerals,** more than 1,000 precious and semiprecious stones—the star of which is the legendary Hope Diamond, a 45.5-carat dazzler. Another must-see is the **Insect Zoo,** which

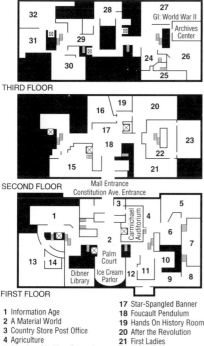

THIRD FLOOR

SECOND FLOOR

Mall Entrance
Constitution Ave. Entrance

FIRST FLOOR

1 Information Age
2 A Material World
3 Country Store Post Office
4 Agriculture
5 American Maritime Enterprise
6 Road Transportation
7 Railroads
8 Bridges & Tunnels
9 Power Machinery
10 Electricity
11 Engines of Change
12 Timekeeping
13 Science in American Life
14 Hands On Science Center
15 Field to Factory:Afro-American Migration 1915-1940
16 American Encounters
17 Star-Spangled Banner
18 Foucault Pendulum
19 Hands On History Room
20 After the Revolution
21 First Ladies
22 Ceremonial Court
23 From Parlor to Politics
24 Gunboat *Philadelphia*
25 Firearms
26 A More Perfect Union: Japanese Americans and the US Constitution
27 Armed Forces
28 Money & Medals
29 Textiles
30 Printing & Graphics
31 Musical Instruments
32 Ceramics

Looking at the proposed site for the nation's capital, designer Pierre L'Enfant proclaimed the land "a pedestal waiting for a monument."

features thousands of live bugs. Volunteers display these remarkable creatures. Children will especially enjoy the **Discovery Room,** located on the first floor near the North American mammal exhibition. Hundreds of specimens, from elephant tusks to crocodile heads to herb seeds, can be touched, smelled, and, in some cases, tasted. Even after you've taken an exhaustive (and exhausting) tour, the vast majority of the museum's 120 million objects remain stored unseen behind the scenes, where the museum's scientists have their laboratories. Free lectures or films are sometimes offered on Friday at noon. Receivers for a self-guided audio tour of the exhibitions are available on the first-floor rotunda for a fee. And there's a cafeteria and an excellent museum shop. ♦ Free. Daily. Tours: M, T, Th 10:30AM and 1:30PM; W 1:30PM; F 10:30AM. Passes for Discovery Room available at the door. Constitution Ave NW (between Ninth and 12th Sts). Mall entrance: Madison Dr NW (between Ninth and 12th Sts). Information 357.2700, reservations for groups of six or more 357.2747 ♿ Metros: Federal Triangle, Smithsonian

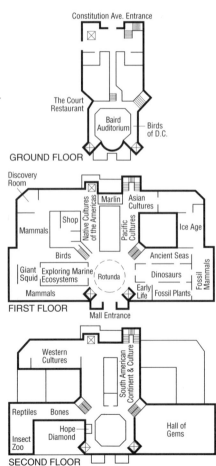

Constitution Ave. Entrance

The Court Restaurant

Baird Auditorium — Birds of D.C.

GROUND FLOOR

Discovery Room

Native Cultures of the Americas — Marlin — Asian Cultures

Shop — Pacific Cultures — Ice Age

Mammals

Birds — Ancient Seas

Giant Squid | Exploring Marine Ecosystems | Rotunda | Dinosaurs | Fossil Mammals

Mammals — Early Life | Fossil Plants

FIRST FLOOR

Mall Entrance

Western Cultures — South American Continent & Culture

Reptiles | Bones

Insect Zoo | Hope Diamond | Hall of Gems

SECOND FLOOR

23 Sculpture Garden Ice-Skating Rink For winter fun you can't beat the setting: right on **The Mall,** nestled between the **Museum of Natural History** and the **National Gallery,** just north of the **Hirshhorn Sculpture Garden.** Skate rental is available. ♦ Admission. Daily 9AM-midnight mid-Nov through mid-Mar. Constitution Ave NW (between Seventh and Ninth Sts). 737.6938 ♿ Metro: Archives/Navy Memorial

24 National Gallery of Art Here is one of the world's most exceptional collections of European and American painting, sculpture, and graphic art dating from the Middle Ages to the present. (Its core collection was the gift to the United States by Andrew Mellon, banker and onetime Secretary of the Treasury). The gallery's **West Building,** designed in 1941 by **John Russell Pope,** houses pre–20th-century art by Titian, Rembrandt, El Greco, Rubens, Van Eyck, Fragonard, Renoir, Monet, Whistler, Gainsborough, and Cézanne. Included here is Botticelli's priceless *Adoration of the Magi* and Raphael's *The Alba Madonna.* The *Ginevra de' Benci* by Leonardo da Vinci is the Italian master's only painting outside Europe. Grand spaces inside the simple Neo-Classical exterior (a Pope characteristic) set the stage for the art; the pantheonlike rotunda, with marble trim from quarries in the US and abroad, is particularly majestic. The new outdoor **Sculpture Garden** (at Seventh St), with an elegant fountain and winter ice-skating rink, features nearly 20 works by such celebrated artists as Roy Lichtenstein, Isamu Noguchi, and Louise Bourgeois.

Across the **National Gallery Plaza,** connected by an underground concourse, is the **East Building,** built in 1978 by **I.M. Pei and Partners,** where you will find distinguished 20th-century artworks such as Alexander Calder's last major mobile, *Untitled,* and Joan Miró's dramatic tapestry, *Woman.* Henry Moore's ever-changing sculpture, *Knife Edge Mirror Two Piece,* is stationed outside at the entrance portico. The **East Building** also showcases temporary exhibitions throughout the year.

Considered one of the best modern buildings in the city, the East Building's twin triangles fit together to fill the oddly shaped site, leaving only a narrow green belt around the perimeter. **Pei** designed the new gallery to blend with the mathematical harmonies of the older one— height, color, even the size of the marble blocks reflect the example of the **West Building.** The interior spaces are strong and dramatic, and the roofline is a wonderland of frames and towers.

In recent years, the **National Gallery** has hosted several prestigious shows, including Vermeer and Van Gogh. Though free, advance tickets may be required (the 1998 Van Gogh exhibition had people lined up as early as 6AM for same-day tickets). Beware hucksters selling tickets outside of the Gallery (for $20 and up); often counterfeit, these tickets will not be honored.

Sunday lectures, given in the **East Building** auditorium at 4PM, feature art historians discussing their own research or works in the museum's collection. Free Sunday evening concerts, performed by the **National Gallery Orchestra** or guest artists, begin at 7PM (seating begins at 6PM) in the **East Garden Court** of the **West Building** (no concerts are held in July, August, or September). Gallery Talks examine one type of painting or a special exhibition or a particular work in depth. Check the **Information Desk** for a schedule of upcoming talks. Introductory tours of the East and West buildings are given several times a day; call for times. Tours in

foreign languages or for groups of 15 or more can be arranged (842.6247).

Art documentaries and an adventurous program of feature films are screened, free of charge, in the 300-seat theater, just inside the Constitution Avenue entrance of the **West Building.** For inexpensive postcards or poster reproductions of works by artists from da Vinci to Picasso, the **National Gallery Bookstores** are incomparable. An excellent collection of art books is available at both the shop in the West Building and the one near the **Cascade Cafe** in the underground passageway between the West and East Buildings. ♦ Free. Daily. West Bldg: Constitution Ave NW (between Fourth and Seventh Sts). East Bldg: Fourth St NW (between Madison Dr and Constitution Ave). 737.4215 & Metro: Archives/Navy Memorial

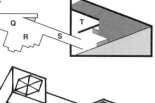

MAIN FLOOR

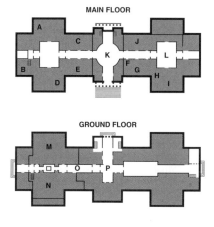

GROUND FLOOR

A 16th C Italian
B 17th-18th C Italian, Spanish, and French
C 13th-15th C Italian
D Netherlandish/German
E Dutch/Flemish
F 18th-19th C Spanish
G 18th-Early 19th C French
H British
I American
J 19th C French
K Rotunda
L East Garden Court
M Sculpture & Decorative Arts
N Prints & Drawings
O Central Galleries
P Garden Cafe
Q Bookstore
R Cascade Cafe
S Underground Walkway
T Auditorium
U Terrace Cafe

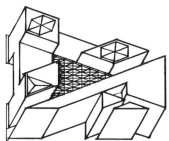

COURTESY OF THE OFFICE OF JOSEPH PASSONNEAU

National Air and Space Museum

M. STORRINGS

25 National Air and Space Museum This is rightfully one of the world's most popular museums (illustrated above). Its 23 exhibition areas overflow with reminders of the finest hours of aviation and space flight: the Wright Brothers' *Flyer;* Robert Goddard's early rockets; Charles Lindbergh's *Spirit of St. Louis;* Amelia Earhart's *Vega;* Chuck Yeager's *Bell X-1;* the Apollo 11 command module *Columbia;* and, as a fanciful tribute, the original model of the *USS Enterprise* from the "Star Trek" TV series. The "How Things Fly" exhibit incorporates a supersonic wind tunnel, a floor-to-ceiling

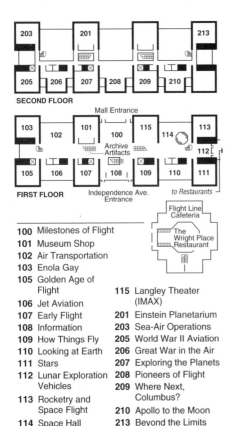

SECOND FLOOR

Mall Entrance

Archive Artifacts

FIRST FLOOR Independence Ave. Entrance

to Restaurants

Flight Line Cafeteria

The Wright Place Restaurant

100 Milestones of Flight
101 Museum Shop
102 Air Transportation
103 Enola Gay
105 Golden Age of Flight
106 Jet Aviation
107 Early Flight
108 Information
109 How Things Fly
110 Looking at Earth
111 Stars
112 Lunar Exploration Vehicles
113 Rocketry and Space Flight
114 Space Hall

115 Langley Theater (IMAX)
201 Einstein Planetarium
203 Sea-Air Operations
205 World War II Aviation
206 Great War in the Air
207 Exploring the Planets
208 Pioneers of Flight
209 Where Next, Columbus?
210 Apollo to the Moon
213 Beyond the Limits

sliding barometer, and a computer-aided spacecraft—all to help visitors understand gravity, thrust, and forward motion. Other exhibits include a touchable moon rock, simulated landings on an aircraft carrier deck, and a walk through Skylab. Tours are given daily at 10:15AM and 1PM.

One of the museum's highlights is the **Langley Theater**'s IMAX film projection system, with a five-story-high screen. An everchanging film schedule has included the classic *To Fly, Cosmic Voyage, Mission to Mir,* and *Everest.* The IMAX experience can be so realistic that some viewers may feel a little motion sickness, especially during *To Fly.* Tickets are available the day of the show (with daily screenings), and often sell out during the tourist season.

The museum's striking glass-and-steel restaurant is the largest public dining establishment in the District. The 800-seat **Flight Line** cafeteria on the main floor, open for lunch and dinner, serves burgers, homemade pizza, foot-long hot dogs, and salads. A mezzanine-level restaurant, the 180-seat **Wright Place,** serves seasonal specialties— from ceviche to crab cakes—and Cobb salad, as well as sandwiches, but is open for lunch only. There are three museum shops and a full-service bar, too. ♦ Free. Daily. Independence Ave SW (between Fourth and Seventh Sts). 357.2700 ♿ Metro: L'Enfant Plaza

26 Hirshhorn Museum and Sculpture Garden For the modern art enthusiast, this is the stuff of which dreams are made. The museum is, in fact, the realized dream of American immigrant and self-made millionaire Joseph Hirshhorn. The industrialist spent more than 40 years indulging his love of art and championing many yet-to-be-discovered American artists at a time when most Americans still looked to Europe for artistic legitimacy.

At its premiere, the Hirshhorn collection consisted of more than 6,000 pieces, including some 2,000 sculptures, and was estimated to be worth at least $50 million. Under the

Smithsonian's guidance, the collection has grown and now boasts sculptures by Auguste Rodin, Constantin Brancusi, David Smith, Alexander Calder, and Henry Moore. The museum's 19th- and 20th-century paintings are by Winslow Homer, Thomas Eakins, Jean Dubuffet, Josef Albers, Georgia O'Keeffe, Andy Warhol, Anselm Kiefer, and Jackson Pollock, to name just a few of the notables. The Hirshhorn also mounts several major loan exhibitions each year, concentrating on an artist, medium, style, or theme.

Gordon Bunshaft/Skidmore, Owings & Merrill's controversial doughnut-shaped building (the circular forms look concentric, but they're very slightly off center) aims to maximize wall space while minimizing sun damage to the art. So there are no exterior windows, but the third-floor balcony offers a great view.

Spend a moment in the sunken garden adjacent to the museum: The terraces, reflecting pool, and works by master sculptors make it one of the city's most evocative settings. A rewarding stop in the sculpture garden is Rodin's *Burghers of Calais*. This haunting piece dramatizes the moment when the town fathers of Calais, France, gave themselves up to British invaders so that their town might be saved. The six proud, anguished men wear nooses around their necks as they prepare to hand over the keys to the city.

On certain Thursday and Friday evenings at 8PM the Hirshhorn sponsors independently produced film shorts representing the best local, national, and international filmmakers (free, held from September to June). Special tour arrangements can be made by calling at least two weeks in advance. No baby strollers are allowed in the galleries; exchange them for infant backpacks loaned at the checkroom. Be sure to browse in the museum shop. ♦ Free. Daily. Tours of permanent collection: M-F noon; Sa-Su noon and 2PM. Outdoor cafeteria hours vary seasonally; call for schedule. Independence Ave SW and Seventh St. Information 357.2700, special tours, film and lecture schedule 357.3235 ♿ Metro: L'Enfant Plaza

27 US Botanic Gardens At press time this cast-iron-and-glass Victorian nursery—a 19th-century style epitomized by the Syon and Kew gardens in England—was closed for renovation. It will reopen in fall 2000. The gardens house ferns, succulents, cacti, orchids, palms, cycads, and other botanical collections, some of which get transplanted to congressional offices. Group tours are available; call for information. ♦ Daily. First St SW and Independence Ave. 225.8333 ♿ Metro: Federal Center SW

28 Bartholdi Fountain This 1,500-pound cast-iron extravaganza by Frédéric-Auguste Bartholdi, creator of the Statue of Liberty, was a prize-winner at the 1876 Centennial Exposition in Philadelphia. Three colossal women hold up a basin, rimmed with fanciful lamps. This was one of the first public displays of electric illumination. ♦ Independence Ave SW and First St ♿ Metro: Federal Center SW

29 Hubert H. Humphrey Building Marcel **Breuer**'s bold design is often compared favorably to his nearby **Housing and Urban Development (HUD)** building (see page 53). The carbon monoxide funnels for I-395 (which runs under Capitol Hill) are incorporated into the structure, so the building sometimes appears to smoke. The building is not open to the public. ♦ Independence Ave SW (between Washington Ave and Third St). Metro: Federal Center SW

30 Voice of America (VOA) This government-run radio station broadcasts US news and information through more than 112 overseas and North American transmitters. **VOA** announcers translate into 52 languages: you may hear broadcasts in Bengali, Urdu, or Albanian, depending on the time of day. Forty-five minute tours explain the role of the **VOA** and its parent organization, the US Information Agency. ♦ Free. Tours: M-F 10:30AM, 1:30PM, 2:30PM. Reservations required; groups limited to 25. C St SW (between Third and Fourth Sts). 619.3919 ♿ Metro: Federal Center SW

31 Vie de France Café ★★$ The food is French style, but the fast and furious service is American. Select baked goods and buttery croissants in the self-service section; the cafe has a variety of sandwiches, omelettes, and specials. ♦ French ♦ M-F breakfast, lunch, and dinner; Sa breakfast and lunch. Capital Gallery, 600 Maryland Ave SW (at Sixth St). 554.7870 ♿ Metro: L'Enfant Plaza

32 Market Inn ★$$ Settle into the music-filled dining room, or opt for a quiet, dimly lit booth in the bar. Then choose from a huge selection of fresh seafood, homemade soups, and other entrées. This is a favorite gathering spot for Washington oldtimers. ♦ Seafood ♦ M-F lunch and dinner; Sa dinner; Su brunch and dinner. Reservations recommended. 200 E St SW (at Second St). 554.2100 ♿ Metro: Federal Center SW

Thomas Jefferson called Washington "that Indian swamp in the wilderness."

Restaurants/Clubs: Red   Hotels: Blue
Shops/ Outdoors: Green   **Sights/Culture:** Black

51

Dramatic DC

Although it could be said that DC's best drama unfolds on the Congressional floor, Washington also has its share of legitimate theater. Home to the first lady of theater Helen Hayes, opera diva Denyce Graves, and film star Sandra Bullock, Washington nurtures a proud tradition of performing arts.

The John F. Kennedy Center for the Performing Arts (see page 64), an imposing monumental white structure that glistens over the **Potomac**, opened in 1971 and now attracts over 20 million visitors a year. Most come to tour the building, walking through the flag-adorned **Hall of States** or **Hall of Nations** and on to the **Grand Foyer**, a room 630 feet long and six stories high. Worth admiring are Robert Berks's enormous bust of President Kennedy, the 18 crystal chandeliers, and the view of the Potomac and downtown from floor-to-ceiling windows. Performances here include everything from the ballet and Broadway shows to comedy revue and college theater festivals held in one of the center's five stages: the **Opera House, Eisenhower Theater, Concert Hall, Theater Lab,** and **Terrace Theater.** Ticket prices run the gamut—from $10 for a senior/student concert ticket to $250 for a box seat at the opera. Standing room tickets are sometimes available on a limited basis. Free events are shown nightly on the **Millennium Stage.**

Arena Stage (see page 54), Washington's oldest repertory company, opened in 1950 under the direction of Zelda Fichandler. Now in Southwest DC near the waterfront, the complex houses three theaters: the 800-seat **Arena** theater-in-the-round, the **Kreeger,** and smallest of the three, the **Old Vat.** James Earl Jones and Jane Alexander got their starts here; both Kevin Kline and Stacey Keach have made frequent appearances. Each season showcases old standbys as well as "unjustly neglected works" and productions by new playwrights from around the world.

Both the **National Theatre** (see page 83), a block from the **Willard Hotel,** and the **Warner Theatre** (see page 83), book Broadway blockbusters. The **National,** Washington's oldest theater in continuous operation, opened in 1835, weathered five fires, was rebuilt, and later renovated in 1984. Free performances for children are shown on Saturday mornings. The fourth-floor archives collection houses 5,000 books related to theater.

Ford's Theatre (see page 94), where President Lincoln was shot, produces plays in an intimate setting. Closed after the assassination, the theater was later leased by the government. Then in 1964 a careful renovation began, including restoration of the presidential box; the stage reopened on 13 February 1968.

Each season the well-established **Shakespeare Theatre**'s (see page 93) repertory company presents three Shakespearean plays as well as two works by the Bard's contemporaries or playwrights he influenced. Under the direction of Michael Kahn, the company performs in a well-designed, 449-seat space—which also attracts such guest artists as Harry Hamlin, Patrick Stewart, Dixie Carter, and Kelly McGillis. Every June the company offers two weeks of free Shakespeare in the park at **Carter Barron Amphitheatre** (see page 151) in **Rock Creek Park.**

For a cutting-edge alternative to traditional Shakespeare, the **Washington Shakespeare Company** (Clark Street Playhouse, 601 Clark St, at Old Jefferson Davis Hwy, Arlington, 703/418.4808) presents audacious adaptations of the Bard as well as contemporary theater. In *A Winter's Tale*—one of Shakespeare's "problem" plays—the innovative company staged Bohemia as a 1950s beach party, complete with Autolycus dressed as Elvis Presley.

The **Studio Theatre** (see page 100), a 20-year-old repertory company, puts on contemporary works by such playwrights as August Wilson, A.R. Gurney, and Alfred Uhry. An extensive renovation has given the space a sleek, modern design that now houses two 200-seat theaters. The **Source Theatre** (see page 100), a smaller space close to the **U Street corridor,** presents contemporary works, world premieres, and reinterpretations of the classics. More avant-garde contemporary works can be seen at the **Woolly Mammoth Theater** (see page 100).

The latest Spanish-language performance by new playwrights, as well as concerts and classical works, can be seen at the **Gala Hispanic Theater** (see page 124). Simultaneous English translation is available through earphones.

If you're still begging for more, try: **The Improv** (see page 74) for political satire; **Discovery Theater** (see page 45) for children's plays, musicals, and puppet shows; and the many university theaters that present a wide range of theater, music, and opera. Check local newspapers—especially the *Washington Post*'s Friday edition, *City Paper,* and *Current*—for listings.

33 Department of Transportation (Nassif Building) Edward Durell Stone's insistent vertical lines and thin slab roof are rendered here in Carrara marble. The building is not open to the public. ♦ 400 Seventh St SW (at D St). Metro: L'Enfant Plaza

34 Department of Housing and Urban Development (HUD) The grid pattern in the exterior's beige concrete walls is relentless, despite an open ground floor. **Marcel Breuer**'s unusual double-Y layout (also used in his design for the NATO building in Paris) improves circulation within the building and helps minimize the alienation evoked by endless miles of office corridors. The building is not open to the public. ♦ 451 Seventh St SW (between I-395 and D St) & Metro: L'Enfant Plaza

35 L'Enfant Plaza Acres of red granite were intended to be the soil of a garden of urban delights watered by a splashing fountain, but so far nothing has taken root. All the shopping action is below plaza level in the **L'Enfant Plaza Promenade** (see below). One of the few highlights is the US Postal Service's **Philatelic Sales Center,** on the ground floor of the **West Building;** another is the yellow glow of the plaza's trademark globe lamps. ♦ L'Enfant Promenade (between Frontage Rd and D St) & Metro: L'Enfant Plaza

On L'Enfant Plaza:

LOEWS L'ENFANT PLAZA
H O T E L

Loews L'Enfant Plaza Hotel $$$$ Both sightseers and conventioneers appreciate this four-star quality hostelry with 392 spacious, contemporary rooms and suites. **Club 480** offers such VIP perks as express check-in and check-out, concierge service, a meeting parlor, and even fresh fruit, cheese, and Godiva chocolates waiting in your suite. Dining options include the formal **Terrace** restaurant, serving continental fare, and the **Lobby Café,** which offers lighter meals. There's also a state-of-the-art health club and rooftop swimming pool to help burn off those calories. Conference rooms, audiovisual services, and catering are among the special business amenities. Children under 14 stay free and receive "goodie bags" that include a kids' newsletter, crayons, and an access card for video games, books, and toys. Ask about weekend specials. ♦ No. 480. 484.1000, 800/23LOEWS; fax 646.4456; loewshotels@aol.com &

35 L'Enfant Plaza Promenade One flight below the hotel lobby is an underground mall with more than 50 shops (from **Hallmark** Cards to **Fannie Mae Candies**) and services (dry cleaners, beauty salons, post office, bank, and copy center), as well as a number of fast-food stands. ♦ L'Enfant Promenade (between Frontage Rd and D St). Metro: L'Enfant Plaza

Within L'Enfant Plaza Promenade:

Reprint Book Shop The best reason by far to visit **L'Enfant Plaza,** this store is one of the shopping center's originals (it opened in 1968) and it's still going strong with an excellent selection of general interest titles; special emphasis is on fiction and African-American studies. Note the weekday-only hours. ♦ M-F. 554.5070; swdcbooks@aol.com; www.reprintbookshop.com

36 The Fish Market Locals swear by the freshly caught and reasonably priced bounty trucked to this market from the Chesapeake Bay and the lower Potomac and Delaware Rivers. The market brings you the daily catches of more than a dozen fish peddlers, who set up shop along the Potomac's edge, some off the back of their boats, selling bushels of blue crabs, rockfish, oysters, shrimp—almost anything edible that swims in the region's waters. ♦ M-F. Maine Ave SW (between 9th and 12th Sts). Metro: L'Enfant Plaza

37 Le Rivage ★★$$$ A bright spot on the waterfront dining scene (and two blocks from the **Arena Stage**), this place specializes in fresh seafood served in an innovative French format: Trout stuffed with smoked salmon mousse is one creative dish. There's also a prix-fixe pretheater menu served from 5:30 to 6:30PM. Free parking is available. ♦ Seafood ♦ M-F lunch and dinner; Sa-Su dinner. Reservations recommended. 1000 Water St SW (off Maine Ave). 488.8111. Metro: L'Enfant Plaza

38 Hogate's ★$$ The traditional seafood menu is decent, if unspectacular, and draws steady tour-bus traffic. But upscale professionals favor the bar after work. In the summer, patrons can linger on the outdoor patio. ♦ Seafood ♦ M-Sa lunch and dinner. Su brunch and dinner. Reservations recommended. 800 Water St SW (off Maine Ave). 484.6300 & Metros: Waterfront, L'Enfant Plaza

39 Channel Inn $$ DC's only waterside hotel is set among the strip of restaurants along the Washington Channel. All rooms have balconies. The inn's **Pier 7** restaurant specializes in seafood, including Maryland crab dishes. The inn has an outdoor swimming pool, and live jazz is offered several days a week in the **Engine Room** lounge. Children under 12 stay free. ♦ 650 Water St SW (off Maine Ave). 554.2400, 800/368.5668; fax 863.1164; www.channelinn-pier7.com & Metro: Waterfront

40 Odyssey This mammoth cruise ship offers a different view of Washington and neighboring Virginia as it glides up and down the Potomac River. The only one of its kind in the US, this sleek craft boasts glass ceilings over the dining areas and plenty of outdoor deck space for strolling. Live jazz and dancing are highlights of Sunday brunch. ♦ M-Sa lunch and dinner; Su brunch and dinner. Jacket recommended for dinner. 600 Water St SW (off Sixth St). 488.6000; www.odysseycruises.com & Metro: Waterfront

40 The Spirit of Washington The Potomac is not an extensively traveled river, but it is still possible to view its quaint shoreline by taking a cruise. A 145-foot cruiser, it holds up to 600 passengers and travels past **Alexandria, Fort Washington, Fort McNair,** and **National Airport.** All trips feature live entertainment. ♦ Pier 4, Water St SW (off Sixth St). Information 554.8000, departures and ticket rates 554.1542; www.spiritcruises.com & Metro: Waterfront

41 Arena Stage and Kreeger Theater
From its first production in 1950 in a former burlesque house, the **Arena,** a theater-in-the-round, has grown into one of the nation's best regional theaters. Recently, with the debut of director Molly Smith, an emphasis has been placed on American playwrights. The **Kreeger** is a proscenium theater, and the **Old Vat Room** is a cabaret-style theater, where recent offerings have included *Shirley Valentine* with Greek taverna fare and *Christmas at the Old Bull and Bush* with English pub snacks and a pint before the show. Saturday morning tours of theaters and offices are available. ♦ Box office: M-Sa; Su noon-7PM. Maine Ave SW (between Sixth and Seventh Sts). Information 554.9066, box office 488.3300; www.arenastage.com & Metro: Waterfront

42 Thomas Law House This classic three-story Federal-style house was built by **William Lovering** in 1796. Once the home of George Washington's granddaughter, it may be rented today for parties and gatherings of up to 150 people. ♦ Free tours by appointment. 461 N St SW (west of Fourth St). 554.0309, tours 554.4844 & Metro: Waterfront

From the journal of Captain John Smith: "The fourth river is called Patawomeke, 6 or 7 myles in breadth. It is navigable 140 myles, and fed as the rest with many sweet rivers and springs, which fall from the bordering hills. These hills many of them are planted, and yeeld no lesse plentie and varietie of fruit, then the river exceedeth with abundance of fish."

43 Wheat Row Located in the shadow of the successful Harbor Square apartment complex urban renewal project, **William Lovering**'s **Wheat Row** is considered one of the best examples of the Federal style within DC. ♦ 1313-21 Fourth St SW (between P and N Sts) & Metro: Waterfront

44 Titanic Memorial Located in **Washington Channel Park,** just a slip of land, this memorial was sculpted by Gertrude Vanderbilt Whitney in memory of the men who gave up their places in the lifeboats when the famous ocean liner sank. The granite figure stands with arms outstretched in the shape of a cross. The sculptor's own brother went down in 1915 when the Kaiser's Navy sank the *Lusitania*. ♦ Washington Channel Park, Fourth St SW (between P and N Sts) & Metro: Waterfront

45 Fort Lesley J. McNair Over the years, the name and function of this strategic military post have changed. In 1791, **L'Enfant** intended it to be the main fortification point of the capital. As the **Washington Arsenal,** the fort was a major distribution center for government hand weapons and cannons in the early 1800s. Immediately after the 1814 Battle of Bladensburg, the British invaded the fort, only to lose 40 of their own men when a supply of gunpowder accidentally exploded. Discouraged, the British left the ruined fort. In succeeding years, the US continued to store and also produce weapons at the arsenal. By the time of the Civil War, the fort contained more than 800 cannons, 50,000 rifles, and hundreds of gun carriages. One more explosion finally convinced the government that the arsenal was unsafe: In 1864, an ignited rocket in a row of fireworks killed or maimed more than one hundred women who were making rifle cartridges in the laboratory.

The fort served as a warehouse and a small hospital until the **Army War College** was built on the milelong peninsula. Later merged with the **Industrial College of the Armed Forces,** the college is still housed in its original, disciplined Beaux Arts structure under the name of the **National Defense University.** The **Inter-American Defense College** and the headquarters of the US Army Military District of Washington are nearby; the Romanesque barracks and more sumptuous officers' quarters add a graceful note to the military primness. Old soldiers quarters have been preserved, making the beautiful grounds well worth a visit. ♦ Grounds: daily dawn-dusk. ID must be presented at gate. P and Fourth Sts SW. 703/545.6700 & Metro: Waterfront

Bests

Susan Stamberg
Special Correspondent, National Public Radio

Union Station: The ultimate gateway, a place to visit . . . arrive and depart. Built in 1907 in the heyday of rail travel, it was grand . . . By the time I moved here in the 1960s, **Union Station** had become just a serviceable transportation spot. The best thing about it was the throat-catching sight of the **Capitol** building as you walked out the station's front door. In the 1970s, **Union Station** sat and rotted. "That white elephant on Massachusetts Avenue," we called it. By 1981, it was closed.

Then, in the fall of 1988, after a $181-million renovation, it reopened, not just as a train station, but as a lively social center on **Capitol Hill,** a place to shop, eat, see a movie, meet a friend, and listen to what Washington writer Marita Golden once described as the "cacophony of good times": fountains, pianists, plus the always haunting sounds of the trains and the announcements of arrivals and departures.

The entrance hall is really the most spectacular part of **Union Station,** an enormous vaulted ceiling with geometric patterns and gold centers to each of the patterns . . . The special thing about the Roman warrior statues is that each one carries a shield, a big long thing, that goes from about waist length down to the ground and rests between their feet. Apparently some delicate-minded souls, around 1907 when **Daniel Burnham** did the design for **Union Station,** felt it would be unseemly for the scantily-clad Roman soldier to be seen frontally, so the shield was designed in order to give them the proper cover-up.

Eastern Market: The next place is **Eastern Market** at 7th and C Streets SE . . . the only remaining farmers' market of three that were in the original plan that **Pierre L'Enfant** did for the City of Washington . . . It was built in 1873, just after the Civil War when the city was really booming; the population doubled at that point. So there were all kinds of public works projects and **Eastern Market** is one of them. And this is the only building from that post–Civil War period that still survives on Capitol Hill. Suspended signs list the various vendors' names and what they sell: Smithfield Hams, that's a local favorite—we are near Virginia and Maryland, remember—slab bacon, smoked sausage. Down the line in the produce section, there are stalls jammed with deep purple eggplant, oranges, honey tangerines. You can work up an appetite there. **Eastern Market** is on the National Register of Historic Places and there's continual talk about restoring it, and what that might cost. Meantime, the old farmers' market just keeps going. Some of the vendors have been here for decades.

Washington Harbour: Fantastic. In **Georgetown** at the southern end of Wisconsin Avenue just at the edge of the **Potomac River, Washington Harbour** is glitzy, a complex of fountains, terraced steps banked with flowers in most seasons, restaurants, a few shops, and luxury condominiums, really luxury: $440 a square foot luxury. But you don't have to be rich to come here just to hang out, have a cup of coffee, check out the view.

In summer, **Washington Harbour** becomes our Venice, I think, and the river is our Grand Canal. All the fountains are going. The water's jammed with motorboats, canoes, mini-yachts. Across the Potomac, people are fishing on the Virginia shore. **Washington Harbour** has given us back our waterfront.

Rock Creek Cemetery: . . . established in 1719 in a corner of Northwest Washington off North Capitol Street. And there's an incredible sculpture there. It's absolute. It's like the visualization of silence and peacefulness. In a grove of holly a seated bronze figure larger than life, a woman shrouded in drapery, one hand at her chin, her eyes closed in reflection. She has a noble strength. Augustus Saint-Gaudens made this statue for Henry Adams, writer, historian, descendent of presidents, to mark the grave of his wife, Clover. She died in 1885. In 1918 it became Adams's burial place too. Eleanor Roosevelt came often during her White House years to take refuge in the serenity of this figure of repose.

Beth Joselow
Author/Associate Professor, Corcoran School of Art

Washington is a city of gardens. Some of the most lovely and expansive are: The **National Arboretum** off of New York Avenue, **Dumbarton Oaks** in Georgetown, and **Brookside Gardens** in Wheaton, Maryland. Each is easily worth an afternoon, and will make anyone feel far from the madding crowd.

Many of Washington's museums, those not a part of the **Smithsonian,** are worth visiting for their magnificent architecture alone: The **National Museum of Women in the Arts,** the **Corcoran Gallery of Art,** the **Phillips Collection,** the **Renwick,** and the **Textile Museum.** On the first Friday of each month, the art galleries that line the streets of **Dupont Circle** (especially R Street) host "First Friday," an evening of simultaneous openings of new shows by local and nationally known artists. The streets are crowded with art lovers and artists, many of whom are regulars at these events.

Have tea at **The Four Seasons Hotel** for an elegant late afternoon experience. First have lunch at **Café La Ruche** nearby, especially if the day is warm enough to sit in the garden.

Rent a canoe at **Fletcher's Boat House** and paddle the **Potomac.** Or just have a drink by the river at the foot of 31st Street in Georgetown. Take in the view of the **Watergate Complex** and the **Kennedy Center,** and the planes landing at **Reagan National.**

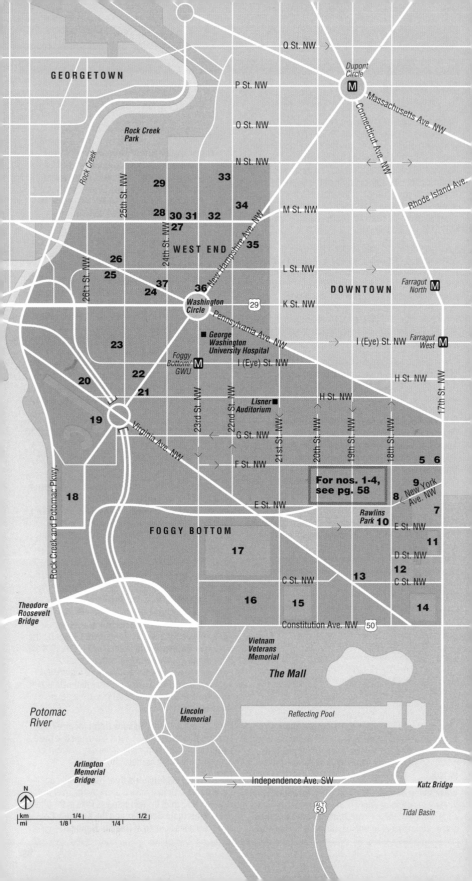

Foggy Bottom/West End

Wedged between Downtown and Georgetown are the revitalized neighborhoods of Foggy Bottom and West End. With the exception of the higher ground to the east, which is the site of one of DC's oldest residential enclaves and the home of Dolley Madison (the **Octagon House**), these once-swampy areas seemed almost an afterthought for Washington planners. During the last century and partway into this one, West End (north of **K Street**) was full of warehouses, while Foggy Bottom (south of K Street) contained a glass factory, a brewery, and a giant gasworks. The industrial fumes and smoke, along with the fog drifting off the **Potomac**, contributed to the neighborhood's name. From an industrial zone, the area deteriorated into one of DC's worst slums, which later became first on the city's list for urban renewal.

The turning point for DC's westernmost neighborhoods came in the 1950s, when the **State Department** established residence in a sprawling modern building along the west end of **Constitution Avenue**, and at long last the mist began to lift on development in Foggy Bottom. **George Washington University,** a longtime tenant, soon launched an ambitious expansion program, and in the 1960s, the brewery building was razed and the **Kennedy Center for the Performing Arts** took its place. This was followed by the construction of the luxurious **Watergate** complex of office space, condominiums, upscale shops, and a posh hotel. Not surprisingly, the value of historic row houses on the adjacent streets skyrocketed.

Foggy Bottom's modest size and the variety of its attractions—from the **Corcoran Gallery of Art** to the bustling campus of **George Washington University**—make it one of the most attractive areas of Washington for strolling. And it's also convenient to the West End, which caught Foggy Bottom's revival bug in the 1970s and 1980s. Gone are the warehouses of old and in their place are some of the city's most interesting attractions and plenty of fine dining to sustain you along the way.

Foggy Bottom

1 George Washington University With hopes of establishing a national university, the first president of the United States bequeathed his stock in the Potowmack Canal Company (the precursor of the company that built the C&O Canal) as an endowment. But members of Congress could not agree on the federal government's role in such an institution, and so the endowment was forfeited. President James Madison also pursued the issue but with the same results.

Finally, in 1821, the Baptist church raised funds to create the nonsectarian **Columbian College,** which less than a hundred years later was renamed **George Washington University.** Although it has a popular undergraduate program, "GW" (as the school is called around town) is probably better known for its fine schools of law and medicine, as well as the highly respected **George Washington University Hospital.** "GW" is the city's second-largest landholder (after the federal government), and therein lies much of its prestige. When the school settled here in 1912 (its third site), it wisely engulfed many of the neighborhood's fine old homes, converting them into offices and dormitories. Now 20 full blocks of central Washington are owned by the university, making it a one-institution urban renewal force. ♦ 2121 I St NW (between 21st and 22nd Sts). 994.4949 ₺ Metro: Foggy Bottom/GWU

Within George Washington University:

Lisner Auditorium of George Washington University A classic modern structure built during the 1940s, this theater is home to the **Christmas Revels,** who put on different shows each year, and the **Dimock Gallery** (994.1525), which exhibits works by university students and faculty as well as by locally prominent artists; exhibitions change monthly. On permanent display in the auditorium is an abstract mural by Augustus Tack, painted on the stage fire curtain. Independent production companies such as **Theatreworks USA** put on most of the performances here, but occasionally the university presents rock concerts, comedy shows, and other artistic events. The box office opens one hour before performances to offer last-minute tickets. Check local newspapers for event listings. The theater seats 1,500. ♦ 730 21st St NW (at H St). 994.6800, concert line 994.1500

2 2000 Pennsylvania Avenue The renovation by **Hellmuth, Obata & Kassabaum** of the **Lion's Row** town houses in 1983 won kudos for retaining the original brick facade. Within the building is a spiffy minimall that includes a coffee bar and a newsstand with out-of-town, including foreign, newspapers. ♦ 2000 Pennsylvania Ave (at 20th St) ＆ Metro: Foggy Bottom/GWU

Within 2000 Pennsylvania Avenue:

Kinkead's ★★★★$$$ Robert Kinkead— honored with the prestigious James Beard Mid-Atlantic Chef of the Year Award in 1995 and the DiRoNa (Distinguished Restaurants of North America) Restaurant Achievement Award in both 1996 and 1997—has gained a huge following at this two-level bistro specializing in seafood dishes. Downstairs is dominated by a huge and (in the evening) noisy bar; upstairs is more formal and more serene. Wherever you're sitting, start your meal off with a crab cake or chowder, and then move on to the roast monkfish with chorizo or the pepita-crusted salmon. The

crème brûlée is a must for dessert. There's also a popular carryout stand on the first level. ♦ American ♦ Daily lunch and dinner. 296.7700 ＆

Tower Records It's a trade-off; the prices are generally higher than those in most other music outlets in town; however, its broad selection may include the recording that's been eluding you for years. The two-story audio store is at the west end of the 2000 Pennsylvania Avenue complex, and an excellent video outlet is at the east end. ♦ Daily 9AM-midnight. 331.2400

Lindy's Bon Appétit ★$ Come here for hamburgers—22 charbroiled varieties—as well as hot dogs, pizza, fries, and sandwiches. This agreeably funky take-out place, popular with several generations of GW students, also offers a few outdoor tables. Enter outdoors on Eye Street. ♦ American ♦ M-F breakfast, lunch, and dinner; Sa lunch. 452.0055

3 Magic Gourd ★$$ Convenient to **George Washington University** and the **State Department** is this Chinese restaurant with a broad menu of Szechuan, Hunan, and Cantonese favorites. Try the hot-and-sour soup or firecracker shrimp. ♦ Chinese ♦ M-F lunch and dinner; Sa-Su dinner. Columbia

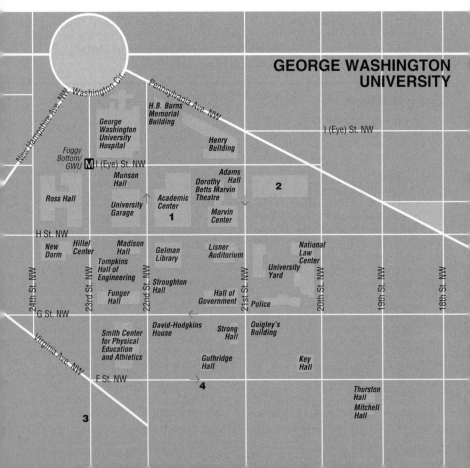

Corcoran Gallery of Art

M. STORRINGS

Plaza, 528 23rd St NW (between E St and Virginia Ave). 466.3995 ⅽ Metro: Foggy Bottom/GWU

4 Garden Cafe ★★$$ Located in the unremarkable **State Plaza Hotel,** this spot has become a favorite of both **George Washington University** students and **State Department** employees for its contemporary dishes and solid service. Peruvian fritters, stuffed with lobster and crabmeat, and steamed mussels marinara are recommended. A secluded courtyard is just the place for romantic dining. ♦ American ♦ Daily breakfast, lunch, and dinner. 2116 F St NW (between 21st and 22nd Sts). 861.0331. Metro: Foggy Bottom/GWU

5 Max's of Washington ★★★$$$ Near the **White House,** the former **Maison Blanche**'s luxuriously appointed dining room was a favorite with movers and shakers in the Reagan administration. In its new incarnation, the menu has shifted from French to American. Dessert is delicious here. Steaks are the order of the day, but the crab cakes are also highly recommended. Save room for profiteroles or the apple tart. ♦ American ♦ M-F lunch and dinner; Sa dinner. Reservations recommended; jacket and tie requested. 1725 F St NW (between 17th and 18th Sts). 842.0070 ⅽ Metro: Farragut West

6 Winder Building Built in 1848 by **William H. Winderin,** this five-story office building was the city's first high rise. It was also the first to use structural cast iron and central heating. The executive branch now has offices inside, but it's not open to the public. ♦ 604 17th St NW (between F and G Sts). Metro: Farragut West

7 Corcoran Gallery of Art In the late 1850s, banker William Wilson Corcoran commissioned architect **James Renwick** to create a suitable home for his paintings and sculptures, but the collection quickly outgrew that building (it's now the **Renwick Gallery,** just north on 17th Street). Today's **Corcoran** (see illustration above) is essentially Beaux Arts in design, but an American influence gives it cleaner lines and massing. Designed by **Ernest Flagg** in 1897, it was **Frank Lloyd Wright**'s favorite building in Washington. The **Clark Wing** was added in 1927 by **Charles Platt.**

With an emphasis on early portraiture, primitives, the Hudson River School, American Impressionism, Abstract Expressionism, the Ashcan School, Pop, and Minimalism, the **Corcoran** is a celebration of American art. Though William Corcoran's collection still forms the nucleus of the museum, two substantial bequests have added a small but impressive European collection. Works by Degas, Rubens, Rembrandt, Renoir, and Millet, as well as the breathtaking **Salon Dore** with its stunning collection of 16th-century Italian earthenware are must-sees. The impressive Evans-Tibbs collection of African-American art, which spans more than a century, was donated to the museum in 1996. Privately funded (it's not part of the Smithsonian empire), this museum has used its freedom to present some remarkable shows, including works by edgy performance artists and up-and-coming local talents, many of whom have studied or taught at the adjacent **Corcoran Art School.**

The **Armand Hammer Auditorium** offers talks by artists and art historians. The Frances and Armand Hammer Musical Evening Series presents chamber music (past highlights include the **Tokyo String Quartet** playing on the **Corcoran**'s prized Amati violins). A sprawling atrium cafe serves lunch (and on Thursdays, dinner). Every Wednesday there's a jazz lunch; and on Sunday, a gospel brunch. The **Gallery Shop** sells books, posters, reprints, and gifts. ◆ Donation. M, W, F-Su; Th 10AM-9PM. Half-hour tours of the permanent collection's highlights: M, W, F noon; Th noon and 7:30PM; Sa-Su 10:30AM, noon, and 2:30PM. 500 17th St NW (at E St). 639.1700 ও Metro: Farragut West

8 Octagon Museum Built in 1800 as a town house for Colonel John Tayloe III and designed by **Dr. William Thornton,** the Federal-style **Octagon** contains a small museum dedicated to architecture and design. The building was spared by the British-ignited fire that swept through the **White House** in 1814, and it served as President James and First Lady Dolley Madison's home during that fall and winter. Madison signed the Treaty of Ghent here, establishing final peace with Great Britain. For several decades afterward the building changed hands and deteriorated, but the **American Institute of Architects (AIA)** saved it from neglect in 1902.

A $5.5-million restoration in the early 1990s returned the house to its 1817 splendor. Original Chippendale and Federal-period furniture was placed in the high-ceilinged rooms; the cornices of the original English Coade stone mantels were restored; and the circular table believed to be the location of the treaty's signing was again set in Madison's study. In 1949 the **AIA** moved its headquarters to a new, adjoining building. The allegedly haunted **Octagon** is now a registered National Historic Landmark, owned by **The American Architectural Foundation,** an offshoot of the **AIA Foundation.** Tours are available on a walk-in basis; tours for hearing-impaired persons are also available on request. ◆ Admission. Tu-Su. 1799 New York Ave NW (at 18th St). 638.3105 ও Metro: Farragut West

9 American Institute of Architects Bookstore Just behind the **Octagon Museum** and across the street from the **Corcoran Gallery,** this store has all kinds of books relating to architecture—on history, construction, design, and graphics—as well as children's books, T-shirts, and mugs. It even sells ties with architectural themes. ◆ M-F. 1735 New York Ave NW (between 17th and 18th Sts). 626.7475 ও Metro: Farragut West

10 Rawlins Park Don't overlook this dainty park, where two shallow pools offer goldfish-watching on lazy spring days when the air is filled with the scent of tulip-tree magnolias. The park was named after President Ulysses Grant's chief of staff and, later, secretary of war. ◆ E St NW (between 18th and 19th Sts) ও Metro: Farragut West

11 National Red Cross Headquarters Clara Barton organized the US branch of this international service organization in 1881. The centerpiece of its three-building headquarters is the marble palace, built in 1917 by **Trowbridge & Livingston** to commemorate the women who ministered to Civil War wounded. Historical exhibitions fill the lobbies of all three floors; included is a collection of recruitment and public service posters. A trio of stained-glass Tiffany windows lights the second-floor lobby, and sculptures by such artists as Hiram Powers and Felix de Weldon decorate the buildings and grounds. To the south of the building, a small garden memorializes Red Cross workers killed in action. From this complex, more than 2,700 Red Cross chapters are coordinated to offer vital community services ranging from disaster relief and blood banks to children's swimming lessons. ◆ M-F. 430 17th St NW (between D and E Sts). 737.8300 ও Metro: Farragut West

12 DAR Museum/Continental Hall Members of the Daughters of the American Revolution (DAR) trace their lineages to the colonists who fought for independence. Their museum building, designed by **Edward Pearce Casey,** echoes that period; the elaborate four-story Beaux Arts affair is marked by a vast porte cochere supported by enormous Ionic columns.

Within, some 33 "period rooms" commemorate various states; there's the **Tennessee Room,** featuring **White House** furnishings from the Monroe presidency; the **Oklahoma Room,** displaying 18th- and 19th-century kitchen utensils; and the **Missouri Room,** with a Victorian parlor. Adults will marvel at the antique toys and dolls in the **New Hampshire Attic,** while children are encouraged to play with replicas of the toys in the **Touch of Independence** area.

The excellent collection of Revolutionary War–era artifacts includes silver by Paul Revere. The genealogical library (which you can use for a modest charge) is one of the best in the nation. The museum also presents changing exhibits. ♦ Free. Museum: M-F 8:30AM-4PM; Su 1-5PM. Tours: M-F 10AM-2:30PM; Su 1-5PM. 1776 D St NW (at 18th St). 628.1776 ᪵ Metro: Farragut West

12 Constitution Hall Architect **John Russell Pope** was a master of simple Roman forms, and this 1930 building is among his best, with its clear circulation patterns and acoustics, which Arturo Toscanini considered remarkable. The hall, which seats 4,000, reigned for many years as the city's major concert venue. Although it has been surpassed in popularity by the **Kennedy Center,** it still attracts its share of noteworthy performers. ♦ Box office open day of performance only; times vary. 1776 D St NW (at 18th St). 638.2661 ᪵ Metro: Farragut West

13 US Department of the Interior Museum This gallery is as multifaceted as the department itself, encompassing exhibitions that outline the history of the National Park Service, wildlife preservation, land management, land reclamation, geological survey, and Indian affairs. On display are Indian crafts and artifacts, and turn-of-the-century surveying equipment used to establish western state boundary lines. A recent exhibit showcased the works of 19th-century landscape painter Thomas Moran. ♦ Free. M-F. Photo ID required for adults. 1849 C St NW (at 19th St); disabled access at 18th and E Sts. 208.4743 ᪵ Metro: Farragut West

13 Earth Science Information Center Maps and geological publications are available here. ♦ M-F. 1849 C St NW (at 19th St), Room 2650; disabled access at 18th and E Sts. 208.4047. Metro: Farragut West

13 Indian Craft Shop Native American–made jewelry, baskets, rugs, Navajo and Zuni carvings and other handicrafts are available here. ♦ M-F. 1849 C St NW (at 19th St), Room 1023; disabled access at 18th and E Sts. 208.4056 ᪵ Metro: Farragut West

14 Organization of American States (OAS) Formerly called the **Pan American Union,** this coalition of the United States, Canada, and 33 Latin American and Caribbean nations was formed in 1948. Its headquarters, built in 1910 by **Albert Kelsey** and **Paul Philippe Cret,** is one of the capital's most striking Beaux Arts buildings, rendered in white Georgian marble and black Andean granite. Inside are the **Hall of Heroes and Flags,** where a collection of busts and banners is displayed, and the **Hall of the Americas,** a grand room with barrel-vaulted ceilings, three Tiffany chandeliers, and parquet surfaces, which hosts OAS diplomatic soirees and recitals by artists from the member nations. At the building's center are the **Aztec Gardens,** filled with guavas, banana trees, coffee trees, date plants, breadfruit plants, rubber trees,

cocoa trees, and other exotic plants. The **Peace Tree,** planted by President William Taft in 1910, is a graft of fig and rubber trees, symbolic of the cultural roots of the American continents.

The OAS is the oldest political organization with which the US has been associated, and it hosts lectures and symposia on a variety of inter-American issues. Outside the building's entry, note the statue of Queen Isabella I, a gift from Spain in 1966 and a rare remembrance of the woman who financed Columbus's serendipitous expedition. Tours are available by reservation. ♦ Free. M-F. 17th St and Constitution Ave NW. 458.3751 ᪵ Metro: Farragut West

At the Organization of American States (OAS):

M. STORRINGS

Art Museum of the Americas A statue of the Aztec god of flowers, Xochipilli, overlooks a blue-tile fountain (illustrated above) designed by Gertrude Vanderbilt Whitney. Beyond is a small but excellent collection of modern works. ♦ Free. Tu-Su. 201 18th St NW (at Virginia Ave). 458.6016; www.oas.org ᪵

15 Federal Reserve The ephemeral value of a dollar is set here by "the Fed," a quasi-public institution charged with controlling the national cash flow, setting interest rates, and regulating the pace of the economy. The Fed's board generally meets on Wednesday at 10AM; the meetings are sometimes open to the public. Call 452.3206 for information and the agenda of topics to be discussed. The 45-minute guided tour of the building includes architectural highlights of the Art Deco structure, designed in 1937 by **Paul Philippe Cret,** as well as a 20-minute film, *The Fed: Our Central Bank,* which explains the raison d'être for this vital yet little-understood institution. If such weighty matters overwhelm you, slip into the **Federal Reserve Board Gallery,** which features 19th- and 20th-century painting, sculpture, and works on paper. Tours start at the C Street guard station of the **Eccles Building.** ♦ Free. Gallery: M-F 11AM-2PM. Tours: Th 2:30PM; group tours by appointment. 21st St NW (between

Constitution Ave and C St). Information 452.3000, tour information 452.3326 ♿ Metro: Foggy Bottom/GWU

16 National Academy of Sciences President Abraham Lincoln signed the charter establishing the Academy in 1863, to provide the government with independent, objective, and scientific advice. As the importance of science and technology grew, the institution expanded to include the National Research Council in 1916, the National Academy of Engineering in 1964, and the Institute of Medicine in 1970. The academies and the institute are honorary societies that elect new members to their ranks each year.

To accomplish its work, the institution enlists committees of the nation's top scientists, engineers, and other experts who volunteer their time to study specific concerns. The resulting reports examine a range of issues, from the social impact of AIDS to obesity to science education, nuclear waste, and more. The majority of studies are requested and funded by the federal government.

The academy building was designed in a delightfully understated Greek style by **Bertram Goodhue** in 1924. Note the six window panels: they're two stories high and tell the story of scientific progress from the Greeks to the moderns. The **Great Hall** is also worth a peek. It's an ornate cruciform chamber with a 55-foot-high central dome. In the hall a Foucault pendulum illustrates the earth spinning on its axis. The pendulum, however, is often taken down for receptions (to ensure seeing this phenomenon, visit the **National Museum of American History,** where a pendulum swings perpetually).

Stroll the building's pleasant grounds. Of particular interest is the **Einstein Memorial** (illustrated below), built in 1979 by Robert Berks, in the southwest corner. Children love to climb on the famed physicist's larger-than-life lap, proving the allure of Berks's grandfatherly sculpture.

The academy auditorium, built in 1970 by **Wallace K. Harrison** with an acoustical design by Dr. Cyril Harris, is one of the most acoustically perfect spaces in the city. The chamber walls are composed of a huge curving shell covered with large diamond-shaped facets joined at the edges. Fine art, photography, and other exhibitions occur on a regular basis. Free concerts are held here from fall through spring. ♦ Free. M-F; Sa-Su by appointment. 2101 Constitution Ave NW (at 21st St). 334.2000, concert information 334.2436 ♿ Metro: Foggy Bottom/GWU

17 State Department Founded in 1789, this was the first Cabinet department created. The biggest draw for nondiplomats is the eighth-floor **Diplomatic Reception** rooms, decorated with an outstanding collection of 18th- and 19th-century American art and furniture, much of it historically significant. President Thomas Jefferson's mahogany desk, where some say he drafted portions of the Declaration of Independence, is here. With these surroundings, it's hard to believe you're in a modern office building, but the splendid view of **The Mall** reminds you that you're in Washington. (Visitors who expect to see diplomats in action will be disappointed; this is a fine arts attraction.) Tours fill quickly in the peak season and are by reservation only. ♦ Tours: M-F 9:30AM, 10:30AM, 2:45PM. 2201 C St NW (between 21st and 23rd Sts). 647.3241 ♿ Metro: Foggy Bottom/GWU

M. STORRINGS

National Academy of Sciences

Get Thee to the Greenery

"The city of Washington has never had the praise it deserves from those of us who do not give ourselves altogether to city life. Unlike New York, it makes room for nature in its midst and seems to welcome it." Louis J. Halle wrote these words several decades ago in his classic book *Spring in Washington* (Johns Hopkins University Press, 2d ed, 1988). Surprisingly, despite Washington's staggering growth in the last half century, Halle's words still ring true. Flying into any of DC's airports, travelers are impressed by the overwhelming green space of the city. Parks and other outdoor spaces are the best place to enjoy a lovely spring, summer, or fall day in Washington. They offer a respite from noise, hustle, and people—and refresh you for more adventures in the urban jungle.

With the possible exception of Paris and London, no national capital is as devoted to trees as Washington. The first citywide tree planting on record was Jefferson's promenade of Lombardy poplars from the **White House** to the **Capitol**. But it wasn't until the late 1800s that serious landscape design took hold in the capital. Local politician Alexander "Boss" Shepherd planted 60,000 trees, which along with other civil improvements ran the city coffers $10 million in debt. DC's most famous trees were a gift from Japan in 1912. Today hundreds of Japanese cherry trees flower in the spring around the **Tidal Basin,** causing two weeks of downtown gridlock (so come at dawn for the best viewing). Lady Bird Johnson's national beautification program planted thousands of trees, especially along the **Potomac.** Today Washington is home to over 300 varieties of trees—from Europe, Africa, Asia, and America—which are best described in Melanie Choukas-Bradley and Polly Alexander's *City of Trees—The Complete Field Guide to the Trees of Washington, DC* (Johns Hopkins University Press, 1981). So much greenery makes bird watching very popular in DC. For information on walks and the best viewing spots, contact **The Wild Bird Center** (301/229.9585), **The Audubon Naturalist Society** (301/652.9188), or **The New Columbia Audubon Society** (547.2355).

Aside from **Rock Creek Park,** whose charms and facilities are trumpeted everywhere, hikers will find trails and plenty of wildlife—especially deer, raccoons, and possum—in many parts of the city. West of Rock Creek lies another slice of nonurbanized land, **Glover Archbold Park.** Most of this tract was given to the public in 1924 by Charles C. Glover and Anne Archbold,

Washingtonians who intended the park to be a bird sanctuary and nature refuge for wildlife as well as people. There are occasional picnic tables, but the grounds, which wind for about four miles between Georgetown and Upper Northwest, are intentionally unkempt. A nature trail bordering a small stream runs the length of the park.

Theodore Roosevelt Island and Memorial (285.2598), an 88-acre island in the middle of the **Potomac River,** is a fitting tribute to the 26th President, who was the nation's first "environmental" chief executive. His love of the outdoors, nurtured by his adventures on the frontier, is reflected in the island's wild state; among the only nods to civilization are the 23-foot tall statue of TR, four granite tablets inscribed with some of his epigrams, and a modest nature trail for hikers. In the 18th century the island was owned by a banker who used it for a summer home and raised sheep there. In 1931 the Theodore Roosevelt Memorial Association purchased the land. Access to the island, which is open daily dawn to dusk, is by a causeway connected to Virginia's **George Washington Memorial Parkway,** or by rental canoe from **Thompson's Boat Center** (333.4861) on the DC side of the river.

More challenging hikes are through **Great Falls Park** (9200 Old Dominon Dr, at Georgetown Pike, Great Falls, 703/285.2965) on the Virginia side of the Potomac. Trails are well marked, but warnings must be taken seriously. Every year people are drowned in the dangerous river currents. Children must be especially cautious. From the Beltway, take Exit 13 to Route 193; the park entrance is six miles west.

John F. Kennedy Center for the Performing Arts

18 The John F. Kennedy Center for the Performing Arts When **Edward Durell Stone**'s **Kennedy Center** (acoustically designed by Dr. Cyril Harris) opened in 1971, Washington began to draw the liveliest of national and international arts. Embarking on its 28th season, the center (illustrated above) is host to more than two million people each year.

Entrance to various theaters and restaurants within the complex begin with the center's **Grand Foyer,** where you're greeted by Robert Berks's seven-foot bronze bust of President John Kennedy. The interior space of the foyer is six stories high, with more floor area than two football fields, and is furnished with gifts from nations around the world. Separating the center's six performance spaces spatially and acoustically are the **Hall of States,** a gallery containing the flags of each American state, and the **Hall of Nations,** displaying flags of every nation recognized by the US. Walk-in tours of the center are given daily between 10AM and 1PM; meet in the lobby.

Performances range from huge, long-running theatrical extravaganzas to hundreds of free performances; from the 2,500-voice audience participatory *Messiah Sing-Along* to small Friday evening jazz recitals in the **Foyer.** The center's own programs account for the majority of performances, but local performing arts groups—the **Washington Performing Arts Society, The Washington Opera,** and the **Choral Arts Society of Washington,** to name a few—use hall space to present their own production seasons. Amplifying headsets are available for hearing-impaired persons (a driver's license or major credit card is held as collateral; check at the usher's desk one hour before curtain time). ♦ Free. Daily 10AM-11PM (on performance days). Tours: daily 10AM-1PM. Tour reservations required for groups of 20 or more. New Hampshire Ave NW and Rock Creek and Potomac Pkwy. General information 467.4600, 800/444.1324, tickets 467.4600, tour services 416.8341, hearing-impaired (TTY) 416.8524 ♿ Metro: Foggy Bottom/GWU

Within the Kennedy Center:

18 Concert Hall The 2,750-seat gold-white theater, illuminated by Norwegian chandeliers, presents symphonies, choral groups, dance, and other musical performances. Conductor Leonard Slatkin, the **National Symphony Orchestra**'s music director, has hosted such guest artists as cellist Yo-Yo Ma, violinist Itzhak Perlman, and soprano Jessye Norman.

18 Opera House Three levels of seating face a gold-and-red Japanese-silk stage curtain. Plays, dance performances, operas, and music programs take place here. DC scored a major coup in 1995 when Placido Domingo became artistic director of the **Washington Opera.** He has widened the repertoire to include lesser known works, as well as Latin American operas. He also performs and conducts on occasion. The 1998 season garnered rave reviews for its *Samson et Dalila* opera, and featured musical hits *Fame* and *Annie Get Your Gun* with Bernadette Peters. The theater seats 2,300.

18 Eisenhower Theater Small-scale musicals, dramas, and dance programs fill this 1,200-seat theater. Productions in 1998 included concert versions of *Bells Are Ringing, Where's Charley?,* and *Purlie.*

18 Terrace Theater This 500-seat theater hosts chamber music, poetry readings, and some dramatic productions. In addition to classical music recitals, the 1998 season included Morton Gould's *Tap Dance Concerto for Tap Dance and Orchestral* and chamber music concerts for young people.

18 Theater Lab Experimental works take place in this lab, a black-box space with padded balconies. Within this 399-seat theater, the center's smallest, are young people's shows as well as the long-running comedy whodunit *Shear Madness* that lets the audience play armchair detective.

18 Grand Foyer Home to the **Millennium Stage** since 1997, this unconventional theater space presents free performances daily from 6 to 7PM. Among the many talented acts are a cappella gospel/jazz ensembles, classical pianists, Klezmer groups, and Latino folk musicians.

18 Roof Terrace Restaurant ★$$$ American regional cuisine, such as Maryland crab cakes and broiled Atlantic salmon, is served in opulent surroundings. The atmosphere is better than the food. ♦ American ♦ M-Sa lunch and dinner; Su brunch and dinner; hours may vary with theater schedules. 416.8555 ₺

18 Encore Cafe ★$ Serve yourself, but beware the crush before and after shows. The dining room offers a great view of the Potomac and the city. ♦ American ♦ Daily lunch and dinner. 416.8560 ₺

18 Hors D'Oeuvrerie ★$ This lavish lounge, although frequently crowded, strives for a sedate atmosphere with its mirrored walls and muted colors. Go for a drink and the special shrimp and salmon hors d'oeuvres. ♦ American ♦ Daily lunch and dinner; hours may vary with theater schedules. 416.8555 ₺

19 Watergate Complex This waterfront complex includes apartments with sweeping curves and toothy balustrades. On the lower level of the apartment complex, a mall offers one-stop shopping and amenities, including valet service, a barber shop, a supermarket, a pharmacy, a post office, and a florist. The outwardly unremarkable office building, across from **Howard Johnson's Premier Hotel** (see to the right), is where the bungled burglary of the Democratic Party's National Headquarters, which led to President Richard Nixon's resignation, took place. ♦ New Hampshire and Virginia Aves NW. Metro: Foggy Bottom/GWU

Within the Watergate Complex:

Watergate Shops One of Washington's more prestigious shopping arcades, a half-dozen boutiques circle the exterior of the **Watergate 600 Office Building,** carrying pricey designer fashions. Among the shops are **Valentino, Yves Saint Laurent, Saks-Jandel,** and **Louis Feraud.** ♦ M-Sa. 338.6630 ₺

Watergate Pastry The bakery here is noted for its oven-fresh delicacies, including a variety of mousse cakes, French pastries, and memorable wedding and birthday cakes with unusual fillings. There are also 25 flavors of homemade chocolate, including rum, almond, honey, and orange. ♦ Daily. 2534 Virginia Ave NW. 342.1777 ₺

The Swissôtel Washington-The Watergate $$$$ Formerly **The Watergate,** this hotel's location is perfect if you plan to visit the **Kennedy Center,** Georgetown, the **White House,** or the State Department. Spacious luxury suites blend classic European and Oriental styles with contemporary decor. Most of its 232 rooms have balconies and a view of the Potomac. The lobby boasts a waterfall, marble floor, and fine antiques. Children under 14 stay free. Extras include a health club, concierge and baby-sitting services, plus several restaurants and lounges. The **Potomac Lounge** is tops for tea, cocktails, and piano music. ♦ 2650 Virginia Ave NW. 965.2300, 800/424.2736; fax 337.7915; abaheri@swisswas.mail.att.net; www.swissotel.com ₺

Within The Swissôtel Washington-The Watergate:

Aquarelle ★★$$$$ Chef Robert Wiedmaier, who also oversees the hotel's catering, offers an innovative cuisine at this bistro. Seafood is especially well represented among the appetizers, including a seared salmon with eggplant puree and gâteau of crab. Among the tempting main dishes are rack of lamb, phyllo-wrapped mushroom rolls with squab, and duck with pear-and-turnip puree. Try the hot plum tarragon tart with cinnamon ice cream or the Marquis of chocolate with raspberries for dessert. ♦ Continental/American ♦ Daily breakfast, lunch, and dinner. 298.4455 ₺

20 Howard Johnson's Premier Hotel $$ The 192 spacious rooms at this HoJo's all have refrigerators and many have balconies overlooking the Potomac. Eat at the **America's Best** restaurant, park free in an underground garage, swim in the outdoor pool (weather permitting), and when you check in, ask for the room used by the Watergate burglars. ♦ 2601 Virginia Ave NW (at H St). 965.2700, 800/965.6869; fax 337.5417 ₺ Metro: Foggy Bottom/GWU

21 Doubletree Guest Suites $$$ Each of the 101 suites features a traditional-style living room, dining area, spacious bedroom, large closets, and a fully equipped kitchen. Standard amenities are room service (there's no restaurant on the premises), secretarial and telex services, self-service and valet-service laundry, audiovisual equipment, and temporary memberships in nearby health clubs. This hotel also offers grocery delivery service, a best-seller lending library, and baby-sitters. Children under 18 stay free; pets are allowed for $12 a day. ♦ 801 New Hampshire Ave NW (at H St). 785.2000, 800/424.2900; fax 785.9485. Metro: Foggy Bottom/GWU. Also at: 2500 Pennsylvania Ave NW (at 25th St). 333.8060, 800/424.2900. Metro: Foggy Bottom/GWU

Frank Lloyd Wright called the Corcoran Gallery of Art "the best designed building in Washington."

E.J. Applewhite, *Washington Itself*

Pedal Power

Washington is a bike-friendly city. No American metropolis can rival European capitals like Amsterdam or Copenhagen, where bikes are a mode of transportation, not just recreation. But with 670 miles of paved, off-road multi-use trails, Washington residents and tourists can go most places on two wheels. Cyclists and their bikes are even allowed on **Metrorail** during off-peak hours and weekends (with a special pass).

A few essentials are needed before cyclists take off on a tour of the capital. First, of course, is a bike. Rentals are available from **Thompson's Boat Center** (2900 Virginia Ave NW, at Rock Creek and Potomac Pkwy, 333.4861), **Fletcher's Boat House** (4940 Canal Rd NW, just north of Reservoir Rd, 244.0461), and **City Bikes** (2501 Champlain St NW, at Euclid St, 265.1564) to name a few (see page 9 for other shops). Be sure to rent—and use—a helmet and a strong U-lock.

A good bike map is also a must. An excellent compact guide, small enough to tuck into a back pocket, is Michael Leccese's *Short Bike Rides: Washington, DC* (Globe Pequot Press, 1998). Leccese's snappy prose suggests a variety of rides, many not too strenuous, and the maps are easy to follow. Remember, too, that you're riding in a city, sharing roads with sometimes aggressive drivers. Even off-road lanes are not exclusively for cyclists; joggers, race walkers, in-line skaters, and skateboarders also use the space.

The best rides for tourists are the well-traveled routes along the **Potomac** and **The Mall**. Highly recommended is the 13-mile loop (which takes about 90 minutes at a moderate rate) that starts at **Thompson's Boat Center,** meanders along the river, circles the major monuments, and then retraces your path to **Thompson's.** For families, this route has several advantages: It's scenic, well-traveled, relatively flat, and there are rest rooms and snack bars at the monuments.

If you would rather have a guided tour, **Bike the Sites** (966.8662, www.bikethesites.com) leads small groups around **The Mall** and the **Mount Vernon Trail** (an 18.5-mile path that starts at **Thompson's Boat Center,** crosses the **Potomac,** runs along the Virginia side of the river through **Old Town Alexandria** to **Mount Vernon**). Bike rentals are included in the price. The 4,500-member **Potomac Pedalers Touring Club** (6729 Curran St, just west of Chain Bridge Rd, McLean, Virginia, 202/363.8687) promotes recreational cycling in the Washington area. In addition to weekly rides and tours, it puts out a monthly newsletter called *Pedal Patter.*

22 George Washington University Inn $$
This 95-room hotel was completely renovated in 1996. Half of the rooms have kitchens, the rest come with mini-fridges and microwaves. ♦ 824 New Hampshire Ave NW (between H and I Sts). 337.6620, 800/426.4455; fax 298.7499 ♿ Metro: Foggy Bottom/GWU

Within the George Washington University Inn:

Zuki Moon ★★★$$ This wonderful noodle bar in a casual minimalist setting offers healthy, reasonably priced fare made with locally grown, organic ingredients: noodle soups, chicken salad stir-fry, and grilled salmon to name a few. The tea list is impressive. ♦ Japanese ♦ M-F breakfast, lunch, and dinner; Sa-Su dinner. 333.3312 ♿

23 River Inn $$ A small all-suite hotel that's perfect for longer stays, this inn is within walking distance of the **Kennedy Center,** Georgetown, and the State Department. It has 127 suites and great weekend rates; children under 12 stay free. ♦ 924 25th St NW (between I and K Sts). 337.7600, 800/424.2741; fax 337.6520 ♿ Metro: Foggy Bottom/GWU

Within the River Inn:

Foggy Bottom Café ★$$ Cozy and attractive, this trendy spot serves eclectic fare such as sesame noodles and triple eggs Benedict. It's the perfect spot for pre- or post-**Kennedy Center** dining or for Sunday brunch. ♦ American ♦ M-F lunch and dinner; Sa-Su brunch and dinner. Reservations recommended. 338.8707 ♿

West End

24 Wyndham Bristol Hotel $$$$ With a European ambience and American creature comforts, this 239-room hotel is convenient to Georgetown and the **Kennedy Center.** (Many performers stay here.) Guests can dine at the **Bristol Grill,** relax at the **Bristol Bar,** and watch in-house movies. Parking, 24-hour room service, a fitness center, and valet service are also offered. Children under 18 stay free. ♦ 2430 Pennsylvania Ave NW (between 24th and 25th Sts). 955.6400, 800/996.3426; fax 955.5765 ♿ Metro: Foggy Bottom/GWU

25 Donatello Restaurant ★★$$$ This New York-style Italian bistro—in a renovated town house with exposed brick walls—is just a few steps from Georgetown. A three-pasta combination of *agnolotti,* canelloni, and tortellini or veal chop stuffed with fontina and prosciutto are among the recommended entrées. ♦ Italian ♦ M-F lunch and dinner; Sa-Su dinner. 2514 L St NW (between Pennsylvania Ave and 26th St). 333.1485. Metro: Foggy Bottom/GWU

26 One Step Down Hot jazz sounds emanate from this dark and smoky little hangout. The lineup of local musicians attracts all ages. Live entertainment is featured Monday and Thursday through Sunday nights; call for schedule. Otherwise, the jazz jukebox plays everything from vintage Dixieland to fusion. There is a limited menu comprising sandwiches, pizza, and the like, but no one comes here for the food. ♦ Cover for live performances. Daily; call for performance schedule. 2517 Pennsylvania Ave NW (between L and 26th Sts). 955.7141 ♿ Metro: Foggy Bottom/GWU

WESTIN
HOTELS & RESORTS

27 The Westin Hotel $$$$ Experience Old World elegance in a modern setting, where a recent $6-million renovation made the best even better. Amenities include all-marble bathrooms with extra-deep tubs, in-room minibars, 24-hour concierge and room services, a fitness center, an outdoor pool, the **Promenade Lounge,** and the **Café on M Street** restaurant. Some suites have dining rooms, wood-burning fireplaces, and whirlpools. This 263-room hotel was designed in 1984 by **Skidmore, Owings & Merrill** with the interior by Charles Pfister. Children under 16 stay free. ♦ 2350 M St NW (between 23rd and 24th Sts). 429.0100, 800/848.0016; fax 429.9759 ♿ Metro: Foggy Bottom/GWU

28 Washington Monarch Hotel $$$$ Just across the M Street Bridge from Georgetown, this sparkling 10-story building, designed in 1988 by **Vlastimil Koubek,** has 416 rooms (each with minibar), two restaurants (try the **Colonnade** for fine continental dining), and a state-of-the-art health club—offering a pool, squash and racquetball courts, aerobics classes, and fitness evaluations. Hotel amenities include 24-hour room and concierge services along with on-site parking. Facing an interior garden, a set of glazed arches contains a luxurious bar, lounge, and **The Bistro** restaurant, serving casually upscale pub fare. It's a civilized, airy retreat for a light lunch or drinks. Children under 18 stay free. ♦ 2401 M St NW (at 24th St). 429.2400, 800/228.3000; fax 457.5010 ♿ Metro: Foggy Bottom/GWU

29 1250 24th Street Northwest If you're in the neighborhood, walk by **Don Hisaga**'s elegant office building, designed within preexisting walls. There's a recessed bow front, fully glazed behind a white grid; inside, walkways lead around a sparkling, leafy atrium. ♦ Between M and N Sts. Metro: Foggy Bottom/GWU

30 Park Hyatt Washington $$$$ A spacious 223-room hotel, this place also has 120 suites with fax machines; a health club; 24-hour room and concierge services; special accommodations geared to the physically disabled; and parking (free on Saturday and Sunday). The hotel's restaurant, **Melrose,** serves American cuisine and daily afternoon tea complete with scones and Devonshire cream, plus a fortune-teller to add to the appeal. Children under 12 stay free. ♦ 1201 24th St NW (at M St). 789.1234; fax 457.8823 ♿ Metro: Foggy Bottom/GWU

31 Bread & Chocolate ★$ Quiches and other egg dishes, soups, flaky croissants, rich cakes, and pastries complete the selection. Takeout is available, too. ♦ Cafe ♦ Daily breakfast, lunch, and late-afternoon tea. 2301 M St NW (entrance on 23rd St). 833.8360 ♿ Metro: Foggy Bottom/GWU

32 Asia Nora ★★$$$ Nora Pouillon, the namesake of **Restaurant Nora** in Dupont Circle, runs this jazzy Postmodern joint. Although sometimes noisy and cramped, it's always fun; noodle tasting platters and hearty soups steal the show. ♦ Asian ♦ M-Sa dinner. Reservations recommended. 2213 M St NW (between 22nd and 23rd Sts). 797.4860. Metro: Foggy Bottom/GWU

33 Embassy Suites Hotel $$$ All 318 suites overlook a soaring interior courtyard, picturesque with a garden and duck pond. Service is foremost here: Guests can partake of a complimentary breakfast and Happy Hour, concierge assistance, and room service from 11AM to 11PM, as well as a pool, sauna, and exercise room. The **Panevino Ristorante** serves Northern Italian cuisine. Children under 12 stay free. ♦ 1250 22nd St NW (between M and N Sts). 857.3388, 800/362.2779; fax 293.3173; www.embassy-suites.com ♿ Metros: Foggy Bottom/GWU, Dupont Circle

Child's Play

1 Pick up a starfish and watch the beluga whales eat lunch at the **National Aquarium** in **Baltimore.**

2 Make friends with a computer, learn Morse code, and simulate driving a city bus at the **Capital Children's Museum** near **Union Station.**

3 Pet the animals at **Oxon Hill Farm,** a working replica of a turn-of-the-century farm in suburban Maryland, and at the **Claude Moore Colonial Farm,** an 18th-century farm with a one-room log cabin in Northern Virginia.

4 Listen as authors read their stories at the **Cheshire Cat Children's Bookstore** in Upper Northwest DC and at the **Noyes Children's Library** in **Kensington,** Maryland.

5 Ride the antique carousel in front of the **Arts & Industries Building** on **The Mall.**

6 Visit the **Washington Dolls' House and Toy Museum** for an incredible collection of antique dolls, toys, and dollhouses.

7 Watch a live theatrical performance at the **Discovery Theater** in the **Arts & Industries Building** on **The Mall.**

8 Hike through the wilds of **Rock Creek Park** with a trained naturalist or go in-line skating or bike riding on the park's **Beach Drive** (car-free on weekends).

9 Touch creepy-crawly things from the world of nature at the **Discovery Room** and the **Insect Zoo,** both at the **National Museum of Natural History** on **The Mall.**

10 Take a ride on the European and American trolleys at the **National Capital Trolley Museum,** in suburban Maryland.

---

34 Washington Marriott $$$$ Yet another deluxe choice in this hotel-heavy neighborhood, this 418-room hostelry offers amenities such as an indoor pool, health club, concierge, room service, restaurant (see below), and indoor valet parking. ♦ 1221 22nd St NW (between M and N Sts). 872.1500, 800/228.9290; fax 872.1424; www.marriott.com/marriott/waswe ♿ Metro: Foggy Bottom/GWU

Within the Washington Marriott:

Blackie's House of Beef ★★$$$ It isn't chic, but it delivers what it promises: huge slabs of steak, thick onion soup, and baked potatoes that are a meal in themselves. Skip the fish and the salads—they're an afterthought tagged on for herbivores (a rarity here). ♦ American ♦ M-F lunch and dinner; Sa-Su dinner. 1217 22nd St NW. 333.1100 ♿

> "The Watergate Apartments are a wedding cake and the Kennedy Center is the box it came in."
>
> E.J. Applewhite, *Washington Itself*

Restaurants/Clubs: Red **Hotels:** Blue
Shops/ 🎇 **Outdoors:** Green **Sights/Culture:** Black

35 Sheraton City Centre $$$ Ideal for meetings, this 350-room, 16-suite convention hotel has eight conference rooms and an audiovisual center. Rooms are fitted with work desks, a plus for business travelers. Ask about the **Towers Club,** which includes complimentary breakfast, afternoon tea and cocktails, and concierge service. Government and corporate rates as well as a foreign currency exchange service are all available. A restaurant, lobby/lounge, multilingual staff, health club facilities, and indoor valet parking are other pluses. Children under 18 stay free. ♦ 1143 New Hampshire Ave NW (between 22nd and M Sts). 775.0800, 800/526.7495; fax 331.9491 ♿ Metro: Foggy Bottom/GWU

36 West End Cafe ★★$$ Two spacious dining rooms, one decorated with Yousuf Karsh celebrity portraits, the other outfitted with a bar and grand piano, make this a great place for romantic dinners or quiet luncheons. Popular offerings include Caesar salad, smoked salmon, fried oysters, and informal dishes from pizza to burgers. A pianist performs Tuesday through Saturday. Inquire about free shuttle service to the nearby **Kennedy Center.** ♦ American ♦ Daily breakfast, lunch, and dinner. Reservations recommended. 1 Washington Cir NW (at New Hampshire Ave). 293.5390. Metro: Foggy Bottom/GWU

37 Provence ★★$$$$ Chef Rene Kerdravat, a native of Brittany, re-creates traditional bistro cooking typical of the south of France. ♦ French ♦ M-F lunch and dinner; Sa-Su dinner. Reservations recommended. 2401 Pennsylvania Ave NW (at 24th St). 296.1166 ♿ Metro: Foggy Bottom/GWU

Bests

Carla Cohen
Politics & Prose Bookstore and Coffeehouse

First, it's very important to plan your trip at the best time. Contrary to conventional wisdom, do not come to Washington during cherry blossom time, when it's crowded. Instead, if you come in the spring, come the third week in April when dogwoods and azaleas are in bloom (and tulips and jonquils, and sometimes even lilacs). The best time to visit Washington is in autumn, October and November. It rarely gets cold before the end of November and the leaves are often still on the trees for the first week or so. The air is cool and relatively dry compared to spring, meaning it's fun to walk outside.

- **Start your tour by tourmobile** (operated under the aegis of the **National Park Service**) at **Union Station.** There are not as many trains as when I was a child, and there are no long comfy wooden benches in the waiting room. However, the fun food downstairs and the chic shops more than compensate. And the **Daniel Burnham** building, now nearly 100 years old, is shown to its best advantage. It's still a thrill to stand in that gorgeous waiting room, and it's even more of a thrill to walk out to the **Capitol** dome, right in front of you. Climb on the bus and take off for . . .

- **The Mall:** Not only are there a series of wonderful sites to visit on **The Mall,** but you also need some tips within the buildings. Stop first at the **National Gallery** and, no matter what exhibit is in the **East Wing** (the triangular **I.M. Pei** building) be sure that you allow time for the quiet comfort of the older **John Russell Pope** building, which is really quite grand. I particularly like the Flemish and Dutch galleries, but each period has some remarkable works. And I want to underline, you are likely to have the rooms to yourself.

If you have children with you, you will all enjoy the **Museum of American History** with its views of American interiors through the centuries. The White House dresses used to be my favorite exhibit when I was a little girl.

Do not stand in line for the Washington Monument. The lines are usually long and windows are too small to see anything much.

If you can get tickets to the **Holocaust Museum,** I recommend that you allow time for the movie at the end which is said to be 24 hours of interviews with survivors. It is good to know, at the end of this searing experience, that some fortunate people did survive and make a good life. Their personal recollections are extraordinarily powerful.

Continuing on the bus up to **Capitol Hill,** I highly recommend the **Library of Congress Reading Room.** The **Capitol** is a grand building and the view from the west balcony is a lovely one. The grounds, designed by Frederick Law Olmstead, are gracious and make a great picnic place.

- Slightly off **The Mall,** a short ride on the elegant **Metro** train, is the **National Building Museum.** Once the **Pension Building,** this handsome building was converted into a museum of architecture, but it's the building itself that's worth the visit. Close by is **Chinatown** so you can get a good lunch. Nearby are two other connected museums worth a quick look, the **National Museum of American Art** with its noteworthy **Lincoln Gallery** and the **National Portrait Gallery,** formerly the Patent Office and another excellent 19th-century building.

- **Georgetown** is worth visiting for **Dumbarton Oaks.** This garden is unique: The grounds are beautiful, and fun for adults and children, with intricate landscaping and beautiful garden "rooms." It's only open in the afternoons, but do plan your schedule to go one day. The 17th- and 18th-century houses and narrow streets in Georgetown are attractive, but stay away from the major thoroughfares which are choked with teeny boppers and the shops are merely dull branches of chains.

- **Do not go to the Kennedy Center,** unless there is a special concert or play you want to see. It is embarrassingly run down from the numbers of people who pass through. It's hard to get to, there's no parking, and the food is laughable.

- **Rock Creek Park** and the **National Zoo** are special. The zoo is terrifically well maintained and stocked. The park runs through the city and is used by residents of all classes. I love the area around **Old Pierce Mill** about one mile north of the zoo on **Beach Drive** (the road that runs through the park). There you can visit the mill, the art barn, and picnic and stroll.

- Try to take **a nighttime tour of the city.** The monuments are particularly beautiful at night: **Lincoln** and **Jefferson,** the **Reflecting Pool.**

- Hang around **Dupont Circle** and on **18th Street** in **Adams-Morgan** for a variety of restaurants and a variety of people of all colors and classes. Don't worry about crime. Enjoy the urban experience.

- Come uptown and see some more of the grand neighborhoods. When you get to the 5000 block of **Connecticut Avenue,** stop at **Politics & Prose Bookstore and Coffeehouse,** and we'll give you more tips.

In *Domestic Manners of the Americans* Mrs. Trollope (mother of Anthony) wrote in 1831, "I was delighted with the whole aspect of Washington: light, cheerful and airy, it reminded me of our fashionable watering places . . . The total absence of all sights, sounds, or smells of commerce adds greatly to its charm."

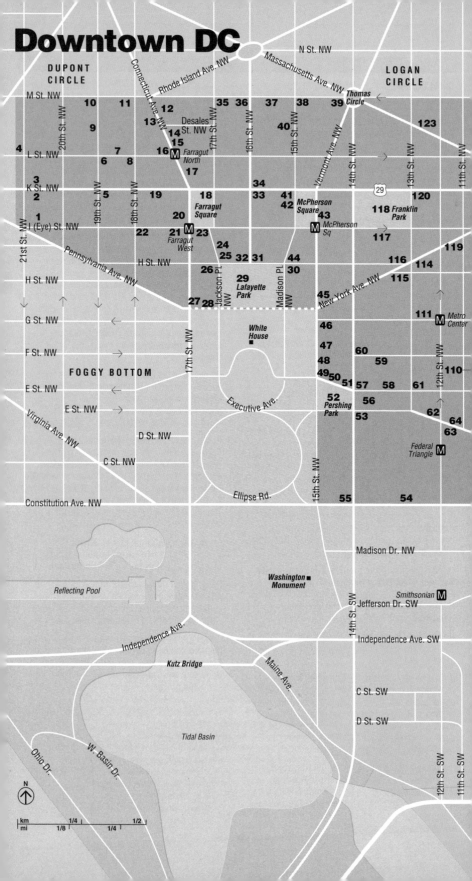

N St. NW

M St. NW   Ⓜ Mt. Vernon Sq/UDC

NORTHEAST

New York Ave. NW

L St. NW

122

121

95 **94**

K St. NW

96

Mount Vernon Square

Massachusetts Ave. NW

I (Eye) St. NW

113

H St. NW

New Jersey Ave. NW

I (Eye) St. NW

93 **92**

90

89 H St. NW

91

88

82

112

8th St. NW

87

G St. NW

97

Ⓜ Gallery Place/Chinatown

G St. NW

84

N Capitol St.

Ⓜ Union Station

98

86

83

Union Station

99

F St. NW

109

108

85

3rd St. NW

4th St. NW

81 **80**

74

79

107

106 105

100

6th St. NW

5th St. NW

E St. NW

75

2nd St. NW

1st St. NW

101

102

Judiciary Square

Ⓜ Judiciary Sq

77

10th St. NW

104 103

73

D St. NW

76

78

65

9th St. NW

72

Pennsylvania Ave. NW

Indiana Ave. NW

7th St. NW

71

C St. NW

70

69

68

Marshall Park

Delaware Ave. NE

66 Ⓜ Archives/Navy Memorial

67

Constitution Ave. NW

Louisiana Ave. NW

The Mall

Reflecting Pool

The Capitol ■

E Capitol St.

4th St. SW

Maryland Ave. SW

SOUTHWEST

C St. SW

1st St. SW

Canal St. SW

New Jersey Ave. SE

Virginia Ave.

S Capitol St.

Ⓜ L'Enfant Plaza

Ⓜ Federal Center SW

Virginia Ave.

10th St. SW

9th St. SW

7th St. SW

E St. SW

E St. SE

Virginia Ave. SE

395 Dwight D. Eisenhower Pkwy.

Downtown DC

The "downtown" area is usually a city's main business district, and it's often where the oldest buildings and most of the shops are located. Originally, during the early 19th century, Washington's main business district was located just west of **Capitol Hill,** on and around **Seventh Street Northwest, Pennsylvania Avenue,** and the **Center Market,** where federal workers from nearby office buildings bought fresh meats, fish, and produce. Washington's first department stores all went up in this part of town. Hotels, serving as temporary lodgings for congressmen, also appeared.

More than a century later, during the 1950s and 1960s, a second downtown business center began emerging a little farther to the west. Boxy office buildings housing the city's burgeoning law firms sprang up along **K** and **M Streets** west of **15th Street,** and a host of restaurants and shops followed. Functional and no-nonsense, the character of this new Downtown is best reflected by the army of business suits walking purposefully along K Street.

Although few of its 19th-century buildings are standing today, Old Downtown is not dominated by boxy office buildings. From the stately Civil War **Pension Building,** which now houses the **National Building Museum,** to the restored **Seventh Street** corridor, it seems better connected to Washington's distant past than any other part of the city.

Where the two sections run together and overlap, they give Downtown something of a split personality. This duality is best appreciated east of 15th Street and **Vermont Avenue,** where old and new stand cheek by jowl: **Ford's Theatre** and the **Hard Rock Cafe;** the historic **F Street** shopping corridor and the trendy **Shops at National Place;** the worn-looking **Chinatown** and the bright, refurbished Seventh Street corridor of galleries, restaurants, and clubs.

Downtown suffered a blow in 1995 when the beloved **Woodward & Lothrop** department store shuttered its doors. Subsequent plans to move the **Washington Opera** to the site were shelved when Placido Domingo opted to stay at the **Kennedy Center.** Though the old "Woodies" is still up for grabs, Downtown DC has received a great boost from the new **MCI Center.** Home to DC's basketball and hockey teams, the sports arena rests atop the Gallery Place/Chinatown Metro stop, and features a sports museum and high-tech, interactive sports entertainment. The complex has energized downtown DC, drawing back visitors who have shunned the area for years.

Hotel Lombardy

1 Hotel Lombardy $$ Ideally located only a few blocks from the **White House,** this classic brick and limestone hotel is one of Washington's best-kept secrets. Originally built in 1929 as private residences, the property's 125 guest rooms (including 38 suites) were renovated in 1994. Most feature comfortable living spaces with oriental rugs and have full kitchens. ♦ 2019 I St NW (between 20th and 21st Sts). 828.2600, 800/424.5486; fax 872.0503. Metro: Foggy Bottom/GWU

Within the Hotel Lombardy:

The Venetian Room ★★$$ After a day of pounding the Washington streets, retreat to Italy. The fare is light—bruschetta, minestrone, and Caesar salad—but the plush banquettes and Venetian-glass chandeliers are rich and soothing. ♦ Italian ♦ Daily breakfast, lunch, and dinner. 828.2600

Café Lombardy

Cafe Lombardy ★★$$ This Italian eatery features such unpretentious fare as tortellini carbonara with smoked tuna, olives, and plum tomatoes; fettuccine Alfredo with sautéed jumbo shrimp; and braised lamb shank with olives, tomatoes, and rosemary. Open-air dining makes this an oasis in warm weather. ♦ Italian ♦ Daily breakfast, lunch, and dinner. 828.2600

1 Arts Club of Washington In 1916 the onetime residence of James Monroe became the permanent home of the **Arts Club,** a local association open to aficionados of 19th- and 20th-century art. Spread over two floors and two buildings (the house next door to the original 1806 structure by architect **Timothy Caldwell** was annexed), ten rooms contain an interesting spectrum of the work, much of which was done by lesser-known artists. Exhibits change every few months. The museum's donated collection of period furniture complement **Caldwell**'s predominantly Georgian design. ♦ Free. Tu-F; Sa 10AM-2PM; Su 1-5PM. 2017 I St NW (between 20th and 21st Sts). 331.7282. Metro: Foggy Bottom/GWU

1 Primi Piatti ★$$$ The trendy, high-style setting is balanced by simple dishes, with an emphasis on pasta and antipasti, as the restaurant's name suggests. But the tables are set too close together, and the din from the omnipresent crowd of young professionals is deafening. ♦ Italian ♦ M-F lunch and dinner; Sa-Su dinner. Reservations recommended. 2013 I St NW (between 20th and 21st Sts). 223.3600 ♿ Metro: Foggy Bottom/GWU

2 Prime Rib ★★★$$$$ The portions are large, the prime rib tops, and the atmosphere formal. Aside from the juicy, two-inch-thick signature entrée, this restaurant does a good crab cake and crab Imperial (jumbo lump crab meat tossed with seasonings and baked in a shell). Soft sounds from the glass-topped grand piano add to the pleasing ambience that includes a leopard-skin carpet, black leather chairs, and lots of flowers. Lunch is a relative bargain. ♦ American ♦ M-F lunch and dinner; Sa dinner. Reservations recommended; jacket and tie required. 2020 K St NW (between 20th and 21st Sts). 466.8811. Metros: Foggy Bottom/GWU, Farragut West, Farragut North

2 Bombay Palace ★★$$ Part of an international chain, this eatery is known for its reliable food. The tandoori chicken, barbecued in a clay oven, and the vegetable *samosas* (stuffed pastries) are among the city's best. The setting is handsome as well, with etched mirrored walls and ornate Indian prints. ♦ Indian ♦ Daily lunch and dinner. Reservations recommended. 2020 K St NW (between 20th and 21st Sts). 331.4200 ♿ Metros: Foggy Bottom/GWU, Farragut West, Farragut North

3 Thai Kingdom ★★$ Still the reigning favorite with many K Street office workers, this place has superb pad thai. Also try the dish called Anna and the King (scallops wrapped in chicken). Because this section of K Street is deserted on weekend evenings, it's the perfect area to avoid the lines typical of Georgetown and Adams-Morgan restaurants. ♦ Thai ♦ Daily lunch and dinner. 2021 K St NW (between 20th and 21st Sts). 835.1700 ♿ Metros: Foggy Bottom/GWU, Farragut West, Farragut North

4 Galileo ★★★★$$$$ The food and interior couldn't be more authentic if you were dining in northern Italy. The simple white walls are hung with pretty prints and watercolors, while terra-cotta floor tiles add still more warmth. The pastas are memorable, especially the meltingly rich risotto and the *agnolotti* (half-moon–shaped ravioli) stuffed with spinach and ricotta. Homemade bread sticks and rolls accompany all the dishes. Besides the main dining room, there are private alcoves along one wall, a covered patio with outdoor tables, and two rooms for private parties, each resembling a dimly lit wine cellar. ♦ Italian ♦ M-F lunch and dinner; Sa-Su dinner. Reservations required. 1110 21st St NW (between L and M Sts). 293.7191 ♿ Metros: Foggy Bottom/GWU, Farragut North

5 International Square This mini-mall includes a variety of shops, and a below-ground food court that offers a variety of fast-food establishments. In nice weather, have your lunch with a view—bring your tray up to the open-air rooftop terrace, which is furnished with tables and chairs. ♦ 1850 K St NW (between 18th and 19th Sts) ♿ Metros: Farragut West, Farragut North

6 Brooks Brothers Setting the tone for the lower Connecticut Avenue area, which contains more lawyers per square foot than anywhere else in America, this traditional menswear store stocks a vast selection of three-piece pin-striped suits. ♦ Daily. 1840 L St NW (at 19th St). 659.4650 ♿ Metros: Farragut West, Farragut North

7 Lincoln Suites $$ You won't get frills like free parking, baby-sitting, or nonsmoking rooms, but you won't pay for them, either. Smack in the heart of the business district and surrounded by some very good restaurants (although it has two dining rooms of its own), this 96-room hotel does provide free access to a health club, room service, and a great weekend rate. Children under 16 stay free. ♦ 1823 L St NW (between 18th and 19th Sts). 223.4320, 800/424.2970; fax 223.8546; www.lincolnhotels.com ♿ Metros: Farragut West, Farragut North

8 Borders Books and Music Two sprawling floors of books and CDs, an extensive magazine stand, foreign newspapers, and a homey espresso bar/cafe with fresh baked goods make this an ideal rest stop. ♦ M-F 8AM-10PM; Sa 9AM-9PM; Su. 1800 L St NW (at 18th St). 466.4999 ♿ Metros: Farragut West, Farragut North

9 Luigi's ★$$ Candlelit, crowded, and casual, this is one of the most reasonable and reliable Italian restaurants in DC. The pizza is crusty, the pasta comes with a variety of sauces, and the house wine is good and cheap. ♦ Italian ♦ Daily lunch and dinner. 1132 19th St NW (between L and M Sts). 331.7574 ♿ Metros: Farragut North, Farragut West

9 Star of Siam ★★$$ Curries are the stars of the menu, but the portions tend to be small, so order appetizers. Try the red curry fish and the crab with curry powder and fresh chilies. ♦ Thai ♦ M-Sa lunch and dinner; Su dinner. 1136 19th St NW (between L and M Sts). 785.2838 ♿ Metros: Farragut North, Farragut West. Also at: 2446 18th St NW (between Belmont and Columbia Rds). 986.4133

10 Rumors On weekends and warm summer evenings, this quintessential "meet market" runs wild. Like all DC bars, this one serves food—burgers, steaks, sandwiches. On Wednesday nights there's a bikini contest . . . honest. ♦ Cover charge F-Sa after 10PM. M-Th, Su 11:30AM-2AM; F-Sa 11:30AM-3AM. 1900 M St NW (at 19th St). 466.7378 ♿ Metro: Dupont Circle

11 Chocolate Moose A great place to buy greeting cards; you'll also find unique jewelry and silly gifts to tweak even the soberest funny bone. Great for unusual DC souvenirs. ♦ M-Sa. 1800 M St NW (at 18th St). 463.0992 ♿ Metro: Farragut North

12 Tiny Jewel Box No longer so tiny, this store has expanded to offer jewelry on the street level, as well as crystal, antique silver, and charming gift items on two upper levels. ♦ M-Sa; closed Saturday Memorial Day–Labor Day. 1147 Connecticut Ave NW (between Desales and M Sts). 393.2747 ♿ Metro: Farragut North

13 Improvisation Don't come here to eat—comedy is the point, the food is almost an afterthought. Tucked away in a basement, the club has established itself as a venue for first-rate comedy, featuring such stand-up artists as Margaret Cho and Robert Schimmel. Bob Becker's hilarious *Defending the Caveman* got its start at the Improv before it went national. Keep well away from the stage unless you're sure you can take a joke; otherwise, it could get a little hairy. ♦ Cover. Showtimes: M-Th, Su 8:30PM; F-Sa 8:30PM, 10:30PM. Reservations recommended. 1140 Connecticut Ave NW (between L and M Sts). 296.7008. Metro: Farragut North

14 Renaissance Mayflower $$$$ Centrally located in the business district, this 660-room hotel has served luminaries and power brokers with style since it opened in 1925. One of the most luxurious lodgings in DC, **Warren & Wetmore**'s yellow brick–and-limestone Beaux Arts building is listed in the National Register of Historic Places. The 475-foot-long lobby is accented with Italian marble, chandeliers, and gilded ceilings. The opulent **Grand Ballroom** is one of the few left in the world, with Wedgwood-like bas-reliefs, terraces, and balconies topped by a 21-foot-high ceiling. Ask for a room with furnishings by Henredon. Some suites have wet bars. The **Café Promenade,** set in a light and airy atrium, serves Mediterranean fare daily; the two eye-catching Italianate murals date back to the hotel's opening. Reservations are recommended for breakfast, lunch, and dinner. The clubby **Town and Country Lounge** offers a buffet lunch and is reputed to serve the best martinis in town. Valet parking, 24-hour room service, health club, concierge service, and nonsmoking rooms all help justify the price tag. Children under 18 stay free. ♦ 1127 Connecticut Ave NW (at Desales St). 347.3000, 800/HOTELS1; fax 466.9082; www.renaissancehotels.com ♿ Metro: Farragut North

15 Connecticut Connection Among the first of a new breed of lunch-crowd malls built at Metro stops, this one, located in the **Farragut North Metro** station, mainly houses several

---

Restaurants/Clubs: Red   **Hotels:** Blue

Shops/🍴 Outdoors: Green   **Sights/Culture:** Black

fast-food establishments beneath the busy street. ♦ 1101 Connecticut Ave NW (at L St) Ġ Metro: Farragut North

16 Rizik's This ritzy fashion salon for women features creations by couture designers such as Valentino, Caroline Herrara, Armani, and Oscar de la Renta. ♦ M-Sa. 1100 Connecticut Ave NW (at L St). 223.4050 Ġ Metro: Farragut North

17 Counter Spy Shop All kinds of James Bond–type gear is sold in this odd little store: night-vision goggles, pepper-spray hand weights, teddy bears with hidden video cameras. The "truth phone" is a vocal lie detector. And the "secret recorder?" It activates when you take a pen out of your shirt pocket. ♦ Hours vary, so call ahead. 1027 Connecticut Ave NW (between K and L Sts). 887.1717 Ġ Metro: Farragut North

18 Admiral David G. Farragut Sculpture A Civil War hero and the first admiral in the US Navy, it was Farragut who said, "Damn the torpedoes, full speed ahead!" Vinnie Ream Hoxie cast this sculpture in 1881 from the metal propeller of the *USS Hartford,* Farragut's flagship. ♦ Farragut Square, 17th and K Sts NW. Metros: Farragut West, Farragut North

19 Barami Sure to spiff up a wardrobe, this New York–based shop purveys chic, exquisitely cut suits and casualwear for women. ♦ M-Sa. 1730 K St NW (between 17th and 18th Sts). 872.3800 Ġ Metros: Farragut North, Farragut West

20 Barr Building **Stanley Simmons** disguised this office building—an unremarkable structure—by encrusting its facade with English High Gothic decorations. It makes a striking contrast to its more utilitarian neighbors. The building is closed to the public. ♦ 910 17th St NW (between I and K Sts). Metro: Farragut West

21 Art Gallery Grille ★$ Modest, fun, stylish—and much hipper than its location near the conservative K Street corridor would suggest—this place serves good, basic, mostly diner-style food. The portions aren't always as generous as they could be, but the bustling atmosphere provides a lively break from the business-as-usual lunch spots. ♦ American ♦ M-F breakfast, lunch, and

dinner. 1712 I St NW (between 17th and 18th Sts). 298.6658 Ġ Metro: Farragut West

22 Taberna del Alabardero ★★★$$$$ Exquisite decor—Spanish painting and tapestries, romantic lighting, and couches set around walls—as well as wonderful service and splendid Spanish cuisine can all be found here. The paella is a sure bet, as are the seafood and vegetable specials, but leave room for such delicious desserts as flan or custard with honeydew melon. The lunch menu offers good food at good value. ♦ Spanish ♦ M-F lunch and dinner; Sa dinner. Reservations recommended. 1776 I St NW (entrance on 18th St). 429.2200 Ġ Metro: Farragut West

23 Map Store You'll always know where you're going if you come here first. This place stocks maps of every area in the world as well as travel guides. ♦ M-Sa. 1636 I St NW (between Connecticut Ave and 17th St). 628.2608 Ġ Metro: Farragut West

24 Bombay Club ★★★★$$$$ A favorite of the Clintons, the most elegant Indian restaurant in the city offers superb service and inspired fare. Start with an appetizer of *sev puri* (thin, fried noodles and potato with tamarind and mint chutney). Move on to tandoor-cooked salmon marinated with yogurt, or a delicate vegetable curry. There's live piano music nightly. ♦ Indian ♦ M-F lunch and dinner; Sa dinner; Su brunch and dinner. Reservations recommended; jacket and tie required. 815 Connecticut Ave NW (between H and I Sts). 659.3727 Ġ Metro: Farragut West

25 US Chamber of Commerce Building Another of DC's innumerable Roman temples, this structure by architect **Cass Gilbert,** is trimmed with a wall of Ionic columns that harmonize with the nearby **Treasury Building.** It is closed to the public. ♦ 1615 H St NW (at Connecticut Ave). 659.6000. Metro: Farragut West

Washington's first apartment building (all rentals) was built in 1880. Called Portland Flats, it was located at Thomas Circle and had a public dining room, a drug store, and a full staff. However, few of the apartments had kitchens as residents were expected to pay extra for their meals in the dining room.

Renwick Gallery

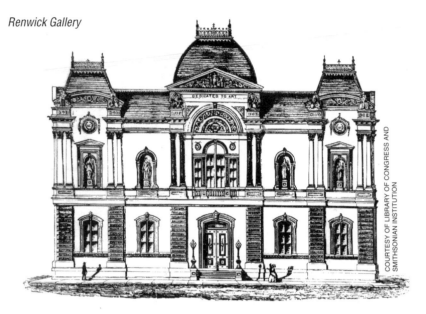

COURTESY OF LIBRARY OF CONGRESS AND SMITHSONIAN INSTITUTION

26 Decatur House Commodore Stephen Decatur, a brave and reckless naval hero (best known for having once uttered the toast "Our Country! In her intercourse with foreign nations may she always be in the right; but our country, right or wrong!"), lived in this house, which many say was built with proceeds from government-sanctioned privateering. Its simple exterior and formal interiors—especially the splendid second-floor ballroom—represent the best of the Late Federal style, as interpreted by architect **Benjamin Latrobe** in 1818. ♦ Admission. Tu-F 10AM-3PM; Sa-Su and holidays noon-4PM; tours every 30 minutes. 748 Jackson Pl NW (at H St). 842.0920; www.decatur_house@nthp.org & Metro: Farragut West

27 Renwick Gallery James Renwick designed this Second Empire mansion (illustrated above) in 1859 to display the private art collection of banker William Wilson Corcoran (who later moved his holdings to more spacious digs at the **Corcoran Museum**). A branch of the Smithsonian Institution's **National Museum of American Art** (see page 91), this museum focuses on American crafts and decorative art. Past shows have included Louis Comfort Tiffany masterworks, New American furniture, quilts from the antebellum South, and George Ohr pottery. Climb the large staircase to the marvelous Grand Salon on the second floor. Furnished in 1870s style, the room contains overstuffed Louis XV sofas where visitors can rest and admire the 19th-century paintings and incredibly ornate moldings. The gift shop features books, glass, fiber, ceramic, metal, and wood objects by contemporary artists.

Group tours can be arranged by appointment. ♦ Free. Daily. Pennsylvania Ave NW and 17th St. 357.2700; www.nmaa.si.edu/renwick & Metro: Farragut West

28 Blair House (Blair-Lee Houses) Actually four town houses built in 1824, these used to accommodate visiting foreign dignitaries. Harry Truman stayed here while the **White House** was being renovated. They are not open to the public. ♦ 1651 Pennsylvania Ave NW (between Jackson Pl and 17th St). Metro: Farragut West

M. STORRINGS

29 Lafayette Park Designed by **Pierre-Charles L'Enfant,** as part of **President's Park,** this area was made public land by Thomas Jefferson. It was here that laborers camped and bricks were dried during **White House** construction. First called **Jackson Square,** it was renamed for Revolutionary War hero Major General Marquis de Lafayette at a reception held during his last US visit. At Yorktown, Virginia, he had successfully led colonial troops against the British. At the park's center towers Clark Mills's statue of Andrew Jackson, depicted riding a spirited horse as he reviews troops before the Battle of New Orleans (illustration on page 76). In the park's corners are more statues: Major General Comte de Rochambeau, another Frenchman who distinguished himself in the Revolutionary War, stands in the southwest corner; Brigadier General Thaddeus Kosciuszko, Polish-born hero of Saratoga, stands at the northeast corner; Baron von Steuben, Prussian native and leader at Valley Forge, stands in the northwest corner; and Lafayette, pleading with the French people to support America's revolutionary cause, stands in the southeast corner.

During the turbulent 1960s, the park was often the scene of demonstrations. Today, lunchtime brown-baggers and tourists outnumber the few dedicated protesters camped on the sidewalk, hoping to catch the president's eye. For security reasons, the Pennsylvania Avenue side of the park has been closed to vehicular traffic since 1996. ♦ Bounded by Pennsylvania Ave NW and H St, and Madison and Jackson Pls NW. Metros: McPherson Sq, Farragut West

30 Dolley Madison House Now part of the **Claims Court** complex, this was the house where the widowed former First Lady lived until her death in 1849. So many power seekers and members of the social elite flocked here in the 1840s that the Lafayette Square house earned a reputation as the *real* lobby of the **White House.** Today, it's closed to the public. ♦ H St NW and Madison Pl. Metro: McPherson Sq

31 St. John's Church and Parish House This Episcopalian church has been nicknamed the "Church of Presidents," because every man who has held that office—beginning with James Madison—has occupied **Pew 54** at least once since the building was completed. Architect **Benjamin Latrobe** followed a simple Greek Cross plan, to which **James Renwick** later (in 1883) added the portico, extended nave, steeple, Palladian windows, and enlarged seating. The nearby **Parish House** is a French Second Empire opus—elegant even in its scaled-down form. ♦ 1525 H St NW (at 16th St). 347.8766 & Metros: Farragut West, McPherson Sq

32 Hay-Adams Hotel $$$$ The former site of John Hay's and Henry Adams's homes is now one of the city's most exclusive hotels, with 140 Edwardian and Georgian rooms and 25 suites, many of which overlook **Lafayette**

Park and the **White House.** (Back in the 1980s, Oliver North and his pals wooed potential contributors to their private Contra fund in the hotel's bar and restaurants.) Amenities include full concierge service, 24-hour maid and butler service, valet parking, and three restaurants, including **Lafayette,** which offers excellent New American cuisine and a fancy afternoon tea. ♦ 800 16th St NW (at H St). 638.6600, 800/424.5054; fax 638.2716 & Metros: Farragut West, McPherson Sq

33 The Carlton $$$$ This elegant hotel features 200 rooms and 17 suites, with butler service on every floor, as well as a restaurant and bar. Go to the **Crystal Room** at 8AM on any given weekday and you're likely to spot a DC journalist going one-on-one with a political bigwig. These early-morning interviews are locally known as "Sperling Breakfasts," after *Christian Science Monitor* reporter Godfrey Sperling. ♦ 923 16th St NW (at K St). 638.2626, 800/325.3535; fax 638.4231 & Metros: Farragut West, McPherson Sq

Within The Carlton:

Lespinasse ★★★$$$$ This Washington outpost of the New York original is dressed up in a royal-blue–and-gold setting with opulent trimmings—Limoges china, Riedel crystal, and a hand-stenciled ceiling. New French-trained chef Sandro Gamba offers a superb shellfish ragout and cream of chestnut soup. Excellent main dishes include risotto with asparagus and tiny mushrooms, four variations of lamb presented in one dish, and a salmon-and-tuna platter. Save room for lemon gâteau or rice pudding. The six-course chef's menu is a good value. ♦ French ♦ M-F lunch and dinner; Sa dinner. Reservations required; jacket and tie recommended. 879.6900 &

34 Capital Hilton $$$$ Centrally located, this 525-room hotel has been extensively refurbished since it was the **Statler Hilton.** It has several unexceptional restaurants, plus gift, flower, and candy shops in the lobby. Ask for a corner room for extra windows and a doubly good view. Amenities include 24-hour room service, a multilingual staff, baby-sitting, a health club, and concierge service. Children 12 and under stay free. ♦ 1001 16th St NW (at K St). 393.1000, 800/HILTONS; fax 639.5784; www.hilton.com & Metros: Farragut West, McPherson Sq

The longest parade in Pennsylvania Avenue's history took place at the end of the Civil War, when 200,000 Union troops marched down the avenue, up to 60 abreast, for two days.

A Civil War Salute

To protect the capital city, which straddles the line that divided North and South during the Civil War, the Union erected 68 forts and batteries. The only battle actually fought within District lines took place on 11 July 1864 at **Fort Stevens** (Piney Branch Rd NW and 13th St, 576.6851), where President Lincoln came to observe and, oblivious to the bullets whizzing by, nearly lost his life. Remains of other fortifications can be found in city parks—including **Fort Reno** (near Fessenden St NW and Reno Rd, 673.7660), the highest point of the city, now a site for summer concerts and soccer games; and **Battery Kemble** (Chain Bridge Rd NW, between MacArthur Blvd and Loughboro Rd, 426.6829), now a favorite spot for sledding and dog-walking.

Washington's Civil War–era landmarks also include stops on the underground railroad. Fugitive slaves received help from Georgetown's first African-American church, **Mount Zion United Methodist Church** (1334 29th St NW, between Dumbarton and O Sts, 234.0148). Note the tin ceiling's West African influence and the pews carved by African-American craftsmen. Just a few blocks away is **Mount Zion cemetery** (at Q and 27th Sts NW)—the area's oldest black burial ground—which served as a hiding place for runaway slaves.

Throughout many of DC's neighborhoods, you're likely to find a Civil War hero at the center of famous circles, by a square, or in a park. **Sheridan Circle** features an impressive equestrian statue honoring General Philip H. Sheridan. The fountain gracing **Dupont Circle** is a memorial to Rear Admiral Samuel Francis Dupont, the first naval hero of the Civil War.

Not far from Thomas Circle, the **Metropolitan AME Church** (1518 M St NW, between 15th and 16th Sts, 331.1426) served as yet another temporary safe haven for fugitives on the underground railroad. Farther up Vermont Avenue, at U Street, the newly unveiled **African-American Civil War Memorial** commemorates the sacrifices made by black soldiers who served the Union during the war.

Heading downtown, you'll find bronze horsemen honoring heroes at **Farragut Square** (17th St NW, between I and K Sts) and **McPherson Square** (15th St NW, between I and K Sts). A 14-foot-tall General William Tecumseh Sherman towers over the intersection of 15th Street Northwest and Pennsylvania Avenue, where he is said to have reviewed his troops in 1865.

Those seeking memorials to our Civil War–era president can start with *Abe Lincoln, Rail Joiner,* which stands in the courtyard of the Department of the Interior (C and 19th Sts NW). Of course, an even grander tribute to the man who sought to preserve the Union is the **Lincoln Memorial** (23rd St, between Independence Ave SW and Constitution Ave NW, 426.6895), designed by **Henry Bacon** and completed in 1922. Recognized around the world, Daniel Chester's marble statue—a seated figure of President Lincoln—touches everyone with the majesty of his pose and the warmth and wisdom of his face.

Those wishing to retrace Abraham Lincoln's steps should visit the cottage at the **Old Soldiers' Home** (3700 N Capitol St, between Irving St NW and Harewood Rd NW, 722.3000). The relatively remote site is where Lincoln wrote the Emancipation Proclamation (in July 1862). Three years later he was shot at **Ford's Theatre** (511 10th St NW, between E and F Sts, 426.6924) and then carried across the street to the home of William Petersen. (516 10th St NW, 426.6830). The assassination conspirators, led by John Wilkes Booth, met at Mary Surratt's boardinghouse (604 H St NW, between Sixth and Seventh Sts), now **Go-Lo's Restaurant** in the heart of Chinatown. All were caught, tried, and hung—although to this day Mrs. Surratt's guilt remains in question.

On your way to DC's fourth and final Lincoln statue, you'll come upon a massive sculpture at the east end of **The Mall**—the **General Ulysses S. Grant Memorial.** The result of a design competition won by unknown New Yorker Henry Shrady, Grant is shown on horseback surrounded by artillery, infantry, and cavalry. Farther east in Lincoln Park (E Capitol St, between 13th and 11th Sts) stands the *Emancipation Monument* depicting Lincoln with the Emancipation Proclamation in his hand and a slave, newly free, his chains cast off to the side. The $18,000 necessary to erect the monument, dedicated on 14 April 1876, was contributed by freed slaves. Before that document was delivered, however, many runaway slaves were taking refuge at the **Ebenezer United Methodist Church** (Fourth and D Sts SE, 544.1415). One of these fugitives, Frederick Douglass, escaped north and started the abolitionist *North Star* newspaper. From 1877 until his death in 1895, the great orator and statesman lived at **Cedar Hill** (1411 W St SE, between 16th and 14th Sts, 426.5960), a 15-acre estate overlooking the **Potomac.**

Farther afield, you may want to visit the home of Clara Barton (5801 Oxford Rd, south of MacArthur Blvd, Glen Echo, Maryland, 301/492.6245), supervisor of nurses during the Civil War and founder of the **US Red Cross.** Across the river in **Alexandria** is the **Boyhood Home of Robert E. Lee,** a Federal-style house at 607 Oronoco Street (between N St Asaph and N Washington Sts, 703/548.8454). The Confederate general attended **Christ Church** (118 N Washington St, between King and Cameron Sts, Alexandria, 703/549.1450. For 30 years General Lee and his wife Mary Custis lived at **Arlington House** (Arlington National Cemetery, Memorial Dr and Jefferson Davis Hwy, Arlington, 557.0613), a Greek-revival mansion on a hilltop overlooking the cemetery, the Potomac, and DC. Northern Virginia is home to 29 other notable Civil War sites, including **Manassas** and **Forts Ward** and **C.F. Smith.** For more information, call the **Virginia Civil War Trails** project (888/CIVILWAR).

NATIONAL GEOGRAPHIC SOCIETY

35 National Geographic Society The society has been funding worldwide exploration and publishing its monthly travelogue since 1888. **Edward Durell Stone** designed this modern structure in 1964 to serve as the society's headquarters. The first of his many Washington buildings, it may also be his best—balanced and restrained. The ground floor houses **Explorers Hall,** a low-key museum that can be experienced in an hour's time. Probably the hall's best-known object is the giant (11 feet tall), hand-painted, freestanding globe, which has become the symbol of the society. The hall's permanent installation is **Geographica,** an interactive geography center with touch-screen modules that chronicle undersea explorations, display up-to-the-minute weather information, delve into human evolution, and explore the solar system. Visitors can stick their hand into a swirling "tornado," inspect an ancient Olmec stone head, or walk under a flying dinosaur. At **Earth Station One,** a 72-seat amphitheater that simulates an orbital flight 23,000 miles above earth, visitors answer geography questions posed by the pilot/narrator (really a computer) by pushing buttons next to their seats; the answers then appear on a large screen. The well-stocked shop offers an excellent collection of National Geographic maps, atlases, videos, and lavish photography books. *Marabar,* a monumental 1984 environmental sculpture by Elyn Zimmerman, sits on the plaza between the 17th Street and M Street buildings. It consists of a dozen large pieces of granite quarried in South Dakota. Some of the surfaces have been left in their natural state, while others have been sheared clean and polished to reflect a small pool. **Skidmore, Owings, & Merrill** designed the society's M Street building in 1984. Resembling a terraced ziggurat, it contains offices and the **Gilbert H. Grosvenor Auditorium.** ♦ Free. Daily. 1145 17th St NW (at M St). Information 857.7588, tours and groups 857.7689 ♿ Metro: Farragut North

36 Hubbard Memorial Hall Hornblower & Marshall designed this simple, massive Italianate building in 1902, with enormous Romanesque windows lighting the second story. It was the original headquarters of the **National Geographic Society** (see above), which eventually outgrew the space and moved; now the society inhabits only a part of the complex, which is not open to the public. ♦ 16th and M Sts NW. Metro: Farragut North

37 Metropolitan AME Church The national church of African Methodism was once a stop on the Underground Railroad. Members of its congregation used to hide escaped slaves behind the structure's broad Gothic revival facade, and funeral services for Frederick Douglass were held here. Its influential black congregation has been active in the civil rights struggle ever since. **Samuel T. Morsell** designed the church in the mid-1800s; of particular architectural interest are the two-foot-thick brick-bearing walls on the first floor, which support the vast second-story sanctuary. ♦ 1518 M St NW (between 15th and 16th Sts). 331.1426 ♿ Metros: Farragut North, McPherson Sq

38 Madison Hotel $$$$ The classiest of Washington's older hotels is accustomed to dealing with the whims of visiting heads of state—it even features a top-security floor. The 353-room hostelry includes 24-hour room service, a multilingual staff, valet parking, several cafes and bars, nonsmoking rooms, and health club access. Be sure to take a peek at the gorgeous antiques in the lobby. ♦ 1177 15th St NW (at M St). 862.1600, 800/424.8577; fax 785.1255; www.dcmadisonhotel.com. Metros: Farragut North, McPherson Sq

39 The Wyndham Hotel $$$$ Formerly the **Westin Washington,** this modern luxury hotel features 380 rooms and 20 **Guest Offices** (rooms catering to business travelers) set around a soaring atrium. Amenities include 24-hour room service, complimentary weekday newspaper delivery, valet parking, a bar, and a sauna and fitness center. The executive floors (11 and 12) have a private lounge. The elegant **Verandah Restaurant** serves breakfast, lunch, and dinner; while the **Bake Shop** offers sweet-tooth–satisfying treats. ♦ 1400 M St NW (at Thomas Cir). 429.1700, 800/VISTA.DC; fax 785.0786; www.wyndham.com ♿ Metro: McPherson Sq

40 The Washington Post One of the nation's most influential newspapers, it was started in 1877 and immediately began to flounder. In 1933 Eugene Meyer, a Wall Street tycoon and former governor of the Federal Reserve Board, bought the paper at a bankruptcy auction. *The Post* gained recognition under Meyer and later under his son-in-law, Philip Graham, although critics accused Graham of using the paper as his own personal soapbox.

But under the leadership of former editor Ben Bradlee and former publisher Katharine Graham, who took over after the death of her husband, Philip, the paper became a national force, ushering in a renaissance in American journalism that started with the publication of the Pentagon Papers (a classified study of US involvement in Vietnam) in 1971 and reached its apogee with the relentless investigative reporting of the Watergate scandal and its aftermath. In 1974—two years before Robert Redford and Dustin Hoffman played *Post* reporters Woodward and Bernstein in the movie *All the President's Men*—the power of the press impressed enough young people to cause a 15-percent jump in journalism school enrollment over the previous year.

But it hasn't been all glory days; the paper has experienced its share of hard times, too. In 1975 a journalists' strike over modernization erupted into violence. Janet Cooke won and then returned a Pulitzer Prize for a series of articles about a child heroin addict because the subject, as it turned out, was a fictional composite, not a real person. More recently, the debut issue of a revamped Sunday magazine section drew fire from the African-American community for its emphasis on crime in the community.

Individuals at least 11 years old and groups of up to 40 can take a 45-minute tour of the newsroom, pressroom, and on-site museum. ♦ Tours: M 10AM-3PM. Reservations required. 1150 15th St NW (between L and M Sts). 334.7969. Metro: McPherson Sq

41 Chapters Literary Bookstore This general bookstore specializes in literary criticism, literary biography, and poetry. Evening and Saturday afternoon readings attract national and local talent. ♦ M-Sa. 1512 K St NW (between 15th and 16th Sts). 347.5495 ♿ Metro: McPherson Sq

In 1800 Abigail Adams wrote to her daughter about her occupation of the new President's House: "The house is made habitable but there is not a single apartment finished . . . We have not the least fence, yard, or other convenience, without, and the great unfinished audience-room (the East Room) I make a drying room of, to hang up the clothes in."

The Architecture of Washington, American Institute of Architects

Mary Surratt, executed for her involvement in Lincoln's assassination, ran a boarding house at 604 H Street Northwest, in what is now Chinatown.

42 Georgia Brown's ★★★$$ Updated Southern recipes are the specialty of this down-home restaurant with curved wood walls and an open kitchen. After a bowl of she-crab soup, try shrimp with grits, Charleston *perlau* (Carolina red rice, shrimp, and sausage), or frogmore stew (a seafood broth of shrimp, fresh fish, oysters, scallops, and clams over potatoes). In the Southern tradition, end your meal with pecan pie. This place draws as diverse a clientele of young and old, black and white as any restaurant in the city. ♦ Southern ♦ M-F lunch and dinner; Sa dinner; Su brunch and dinner. 950 15th St NW (between I and K Sts). 393.4499 ♿ Metro: McPherson Sq

43 Gerard's Place ★★★$$$$ Come here for food as refreshingly simple and modest as the decor. Chef Gerard Pangaud—the youngest ever to earn two stars from the Michelin guide—excels in preparing honest, good French dishes stripped of pretentious presentations and esoteric ingredients. Highly recommended are the veal with prosciutto, artichokes, and mushrooms; lobster poached in ginger; and lamb wrapped in eggplant. The pistachio soufflé with fresh cherries is a grand finale. ♦ French ♦ M-F lunch and dinner; Sa dinner. Reservations recommended. 915 15th St NW (between I and K Sts). 737.4445 ♿ Metro: McPherson Sq

44 Southern Building In designing this 1912 structure, architect **Daniel Burnham** reined in his characteristic flamboyance, using clean lines and balanced proportions to make it fit in gracefully with its neighbors. Architect **Moshe Safdie** raised the commercial office building to the height called for in its original specifications, since **Burnham** had shaved off a few floors in his execution. Although it's open to the public, there isn't much reason to go inside. ♦ 805 15th St NW (between H and I Sts) ♿ Metro: McPherson Sq

45 National Savings and Trust Company Constructed in 1880, the remodeled **National Savings Building** is part of the Bankers' Classic Group, which includes three other Roman-temple structures: **American Security and Trust Company** (15th St NW and Pennsylvania Ave); **Riggs National Bank** (1503 Pennsylvania Ave NW, at 15th St); and the **Union Trust Building** (15th and H Sts NW). **James Windrim**'s design, which employs whimsical turrets and an unusual mixture of Victorian ornamentation, stands in direct juxtaposition to the other three, whose massive exterior columns recall the **Treasury Building.** The intention was to give Washington's financial area an imposing face, a concept fashionable among bankers of the era. You can walk into the ground-floor branch of **Crestar Bank,** if you like, to check out the impressive interior with its original marble fixtures. ♦ 15th St NW and New York Ave. Metro: McPherson Sq

46 Political Americana Two blocks from the **White House**, this shop sells mugs, T-shirts, hats, ties, and other items that proudly indicate Democratic or Republican (or Socks and Buddy, the First Pets) allegiance. It's the place to go for a Teddy Roosevelt button or a "Wee Publican" baby bib. ♦ Daily. 685 15th St NW (at G St). 547.1871 ♿ Metros: McPherson Sq, Metro Center

46 Old Ebbitt Grill ★★$$ This bustling, Victorian-style saloon is loaded with old-time Washington charm. Etched glass panels, velvet banquettes, and a mahogany bar add to the mood. Along with splendid raw oysters, the menu offers trout parmesan, London broil, pastas, and luscious desserts. But the place is best known for its burgers. ♦ American ♦ Daily breakfast, lunch, and dinner. Reservations recommended. 675 15th St NW (between Pennsylvania Ave and G St). 347.4801 ♿ Metros: McPherson Sq, Metro Center

47 Metropolitan Square When the facade of the **National Metropolitan Bank** was incorporated into this mixed-use office/retail complex, preservationists weren't the only ones who complained: The Secret Service said the upper floors offered a far too clear view of the **White House.** A compromise was reached; the roof deck, used during summer for social functions, cannot be used after 6PM without the Secret Service being notified. On the 15th Street side, clear panels allow for camera shots but block the more dangerous kind. Shops here include **Fahrney's Pens** (628.9525) and **Galt Bros.** jewelry (347.1034). ♦ 607 15th St NW (between Pennsylvania Ave and G St). 628.0655 ♿ Metros: McPherson Sq, Metro Center

48 Hotel Washington $$$ This refurbished Italian Renaissance–style hotel, with 364 rooms, boasts of being Washington's oldest continuously operating hotel (it was built in 1918). Nearly every 20th-century US president, as well as countless national and international dignitaries, has lodged here. There are three restaurants and a workout room; complimentary afternoon tea and hors d'oeuvres are served daily in the lobby to hotel guests. Two nonsmoking floors are available; children under 14 stay free. ♦ 515 15th St NW (between Pennsylvania Ave and G St). 638.5900; fax 638.4275;

www.hotelwashington.com ♿ Metros: McPherson Sq, Metro Center

Within the Hotel Washington:

Sky Room/Sky Terrace ★$ The fare is standard burgers and sandwiches, but this rooftop bar and restaurant has a panoramic view of the **White House, Treasury Building,** and **The Mall,** which at night may just be one of the highlights of your trip. ♦ American ♦ Daily lunch and dinner mid-May–mid-Oct. 638.5900 ♿

49 Occidental Grill ★★$$ Papered from floor to ceiling with glossies of famous Washingtonians, this lively, salon-style restaurant scores with a menu that ranges from burgers to grilled swordfish and onion rings. Excellent American wines are available by the glass. ♦ American ♦ Daily lunch and dinner. Reservations recommended. 1475 Pennsylvania Ave NW (between 14th and 15th Sts). 783.1475 ♿ Metros: McPherson Sq, Metro Center

50 Willard Collection Shops Rodeo Drive meets Pennsylvania Avenue at this shopping center, featuring **Chanel, Harriet Kassman,** and other chic shops. **Jackie Chalkley** peddles one-of-a-kind jewelry, handmade knits, and other pricey items. ♦ M-Sa. 1455 Pennsylvania Ave NW (between 14th and 15th Sts) ♿ Metros: McPherson Sq, Metro Center

In 1861 a major fire at the old Willard Hotel was extinguished by the New York Fire Zouaves, who dressed like the French Zouaves who served in the Crimean War. The Willard Brothers handsomely rewarded them for saving the hotel.

Pierre-Charles L'Enfant's bill for the design of the federal city totaled $95,000; his invoice was rejected. After eight years of silence, he finally was paid a total of $1,394.20. Unfortunately, most of the money went to his numerous creditors. When he died in 1825, he had a net worth of $45 and a remote Maryland grave marked only by a cedar tree. Recognized as a visionary 80 years after his death, he was reinterred in Arlington Cemetery.

Restaurants/Clubs: Red   Hotels: Blue
Shops/♦Outdoors: Green   **Sights/Culture:** Black

51 Willard Inter-Continental Hotel $$$$
During its various incarnations, this building
designed by **Henry J. Hardenbergh** has
served as temporary home for 10 presidents-
elect, including Lincoln, Harding, and Pierce,
and as a temporary White House for Calvin
Coolidge in 1923. The term "lobbyist" was
coined for the men who skulked in this lobby,
waiting for a word with the powerful. During
the mid-1980s, **The Oliver Carr Company**
with help from consulting architect **Vlastimil
Koubek** renovated the imposing turn-of-the-
century Beaux Arts marble building (drawing
below), which had been abandoned in the
1960s, to its previous glory. The former front
desk, now a concierge station, is a petal-
shaped wonder of marble, glass, and polished
wood. Highlights of the 340-room hotel
include the **Peacock Alley, Round Robin,** and
Nest bars, the **Café Expresso** coffee shop, 24-
hour room service, and nonsmoking rooms.
Children under 14 stay free. ♦ 1401
Pennsylvania Ave NW (at 14th St). 628.9100,
800/327.0200; fax 637.7326;
www.interconti.com & Metro: Metro Center

Within the Willard Inter-Continental Hotel:

Willard Room ★★$$$$ Opulent Edwardian
decor and secluded banquettes set the stage
for formal dining on such New American dishes
as roast rack of lamb, venison, and squab.
The rich oak-paneled room with its elegant
appointments is a consistent winner in polls
for Washington's best restaurant decor.
♦ American/French ♦ M-F breakfast, lunch,
and dinner; Sa dinner. Reservations
suggested; jacket and tie
recommended. 637.7440 &

52 Pershing Park This little
swatch of turf offers a
shimmering decorative
pool; a thicket of trees; a
refreshment kiosk selling
beer, soft drinks, and
snacks; a skating rink in
winter; and tables and
chairs, a striking
contrast to the
stark—some
might say
soulless—
Freedom Plaza
(see page 83).
♦ Pennsylvania
Ave NW (between
14th and 15th
Sts). Metros:
Metro Center,
Federal Triangle

**53 National
Aquarium**
Resembling a rec
room one might
find in a friend's

basement, this is a handy refuge from the
summer heat, if not much of an aquarium.
Established by the federal government in 1873
and spread out over a variety of locations, the
now-centralized aquarium went private in
1982. It's the nation's oldest aquarium, and it
has been showing its age for some time now:
You may be disappointed by the slim pickings
and lackluster maintenance. Seventy tanks
display fresh- and saltwater marine
specimens. There are also slide presentations,
a touch tank for children to handle live critters,
and a gift shop. ♦ Nominal admission. Daily.
Commerce Bldg, 14th St NW and Constitution
Ave. 482.2826, recorded information
482.2825 & Metro: Federal Triangle

54 Departmental Auditorium Arthur Brown,
Jr.'s dynamic sculpture in the exterior
pediments hints at the opulence within. The
Neo-Classical/Beaux Arts theater style was
used liberally in movie houses nationwide at
the time; this one was completed in 1935, but
it's one of the few theaters where all the gold,
marble, and crystal you see are the real thing.
The 1,300-seat auditorium is used mainly for
ceremonial events, both public and private.
♦ 1301 Constitution Ave NW (between 12th
and 14th Sts). Metro: Federal Triangle

Willard Inter-Continental Hotel

55 District Building Once reviled as a monstrosity, this overblown 1908 Beaux Arts edifice eventually won fans. The building is headquarters for much of DC's city government, but its infrastructure is deteriorating badly. And given the uncertain state of the District's finances, its future remains hazy indeed. It isn't open to the public. ♦ 1350 Pennsylvania Ave NW (at 14th St). Metro: Federal Triangle

56 Freedom Plaza Venturi, Rauch and Scott Brown intended the open, block-long plaza (also known as "Western Plaza") to be a witty re-creation of the disrupted axis between the Capitol and the White House, but their plan was compromised when local censors eliminated its vertical elements, leaving only a broad concrete plaza, devoid of trees, statues, or anything else that might engage the eye. All that remains is the inlaid map of L'Enfant's city plan. It's used occasionally for outdoor concerts. ♦ Pennsylvania Ave NW (between 13th and 14th Sts). Metros: Federal Triangle, Metro Center

57 J.W. Marriott $$$$ Conveniently located between the National Theatre (see below), the National Press Building, which houses reporters' offices, and the Shops at National Place (see below), this 773-room hotel is the flagship of the locally based chain. Guests—many of them conventioneers—have access to nonsmoking rooms, 24-hour room service, valet parking, a health club, and a choice of two restaurants and two lounges. Children under 18 stay free. ♦ 1331 Pennsylvania Ave NW (at 14th St). 393.2000, 800/228.9290; fax 626.6991 ♿ Metros: Metro Center, Federal Triangle

58 National Theatre Established in 1835 and restored to its former glory in 1983, the 1,672-seat theater specializes in Broadway-bound productions and road shows. Recent performances have included *Chicago*, *Rent*, and *Ragtime*. Its production schedule is sporadic, so call ahead for information. ♦ Box office during performance weeks: M 10AM-6PM; Tu-Sa 10AM-9PM; Su noon-9PM. 1321 E St NW (between 13th and 14th Sts). Information 628.6161, telecharge 800/233.3123 ♿ Metros: Metro Center, Federal Triangle

59 Shops at National Place Another Downtown impulse mall, this one contains 125,000 square feet of retail shopping temptations—more than 80 boutiques and restaurants, including Filene's Basement and Easy Spirit Shoes. The terra-cotta tile-and-brass interior opens to the lobby of the J.W. Marriott hotel (see above) and extends to the National Press Building at the east end of the block. ♦ Stores M-Sa; Su noon-5PM. F St NW (between 13th and 14th Sts). 662.1250 ♿ Metro: Metro Center

60 Red Sage ★★$$$$ Here the whimsical interior (complete with barbed wire and cowhide seats) looks as if it cost a million bucks, and it did—several times over. Though the Southwestern-style food doesn't always hit the bullseye, it's a fun ride. Try the wood-roasted chicken and black-bean and chorizo sauce, and the exotic double pecan–chili lamb chop with smoked lamb sausage. The more expensive section downstairs has a broader menu. ♦ American ♦ M-Sa lunch and dinner; Su dinner. Reservations recommended. 605 14th St NW (between F and G Sts). 638.4444 ♿ Metro: Metro Center

60 Red Sage Bakery This small offshoot of the adjacent restaurant sells homemade cakes, cookies, and brownies, as well as a few Southwestern hot sauces. ♦ M-F. 1335 F St NW (between 13th and 14th Sts). 638.3276 ♿ Metro: Metro Center

W A R N E R 🛡 T H E A T R E

61 Warner Theatre Opened in 1924 as the Earle, a vaudeville house, this 2,000-seat theater later flourished as a movie house, and then a concert hall. Subsequent renovations have it looking much like its former self: Crystal chandeliers hang from the gilded ceiling, the walls are done in shades of red and green, with various ornamentation. It's now used for film premieres, road shows, and a variety of performances: Dance troupes under the direction of Mikhail Baryshnikov and Twyla Tharp, the gospel musical *I Know I've Been Changed,* and jazz vocalist Cassandra Wilson, have graced the stage in recent years. ♦ Box office: M-F; Sa noon-3PM. 13th and E Sts NW. 783.4000 ♿ Metros: Metro Center, Federal Triangle

62 Les Halles ★★$$$ Inspired by Parisian brasseries, this restaurant's specialty is beef—try the *côte de boeuf* (a sumptuous prime rib for two)—but the kitchen also does justice to lamb and chicken. And pork lovers must try the rich pork loin with buttered potato puree. The large room has high tin ceilings, wood floors, burgundy leather banquettes, and plenty of greenery. Opt for terrace dining in fair weather. An upstairs area is designated for cigar smoking, but the ventilation system keeps the fumes well confined. ♦ French ♦ Daily lunch and dinner. 1201 Pennsylvania Ave NW (at 12th St). 347.6848 ♿ Metros: Federal Triangle, Metro Center

---

An article in the *Washington Post* said that the FBI Building "would make a perfect stage set for a dramatization of George Orwell's *1984*."

Pavilion at the Old Post Office

M. STORRINGS

63 Pavilion at the Old Post Office This Romanesque Revival chateau (illustrated above), which once served as the **Old Post Office,** was threatened by demolition in the 1970s, but was saved as a result of a fight led by the late Nancy Hanks, head of the National Endowment for the Arts from 1969 to 1977. Sponsored by the Evans Development Company and restored during the 1980s by **Arthur Cotton Moore,** it's a bold example of urban revitalization: It took the 1976 Cooperative Use Act to open up this government building to commercial use. Today, government offices occupy the upper seven floors, while the indoor mall below attempts to pump life into the staid, bureaucratic Federal Triangle area.

The mall's atrium is stylishly decked out with Victorian brass fittings, red oak woodwork, and frosted glass. A dozen or so specialty shops (with plenty of T-shirts and souvenirs for the kids), several restaurants and cafes, and a wide assortment of fast-food establishments serving tacos, curries, crepes, ice cream, and the like now fill the restaurant arcade. The mall's interior focal point is the stage, where free entertainment—dancers, musicians, magicians—offers a pleasant diversion for afternoon shoppers pausing for a fast lunch. Free tours of the building's 315-foot-high clocktower (DC's second-tallest structure, after the **Washington Monument**) leave from the stage level every five to seven minutes daily between 8AM and 10:45PM from the first Sunday in April until Labor Day, and daily between 10AM and 5:45PM the rest

of the year. An eastern annex containing yet more food outlets and stores opened in the early 1990s. ♦ Stores: Daily. 1100 Pennsylvania Ave NW (at 11th St). 289.4224 ♿ Metro: Federal Triangle

64 Planet Hollywood ★$ The movie lover's analogue of the **Hard Rock Cafe,** this place features motion picture memorabilia, continuous film clips running on TV screens, and dressed-up junk food bearing celebrity names. Sample the apple strudel; rumor has it that the recipe comes from co-owner Arnold Schwarzenegger's mom. The gift shop is a must, if only for browsing. ♦ American ♦ Daily lunch and dinner. 1101 Pennsylvania Ave NW (at 11th St). 783.7827 ♿ Metro: Metro Center

65 J. Edgar Hoover FBI Building Within this unlovely beige concrete building, our national police force keeps track of "Most Wanted" criminals and expands the science of criminology. It was Teddy Roosevelt who created the Federal Bureau of Investigation in 1908, seeking to fight political corruption. You'll learn more about the bureau in an introductory video presentation; then tour the high-tech labs and exhibits tracing the FBI's history, from the gangster era through the Cold War decade of espionage to its current, more scientific crime-fighting techniques. The tour ends with the ever-popular firearms demonstration performed by a special agent. ♦ Free. Tours M-F. Reservations recommended for large groups. E St NW (between Ninth and 10th Sts). 324.3000 & Metros: Metro Center, Gallery Pl/Chinatown, Federal Triangle, Archives/Navy Memorial

66 National Archives About 60 years ago—after the documents that serve as the foundation of the federal government were variously lost, mistaken for worthless paper, threatened by advancing armies, and left to crumble in dark vaults—a suitable home was finally created for the Declaration of Independence, the Bill of Rights, and the US Constitution. The archives are the nation's 21-floor safe-deposit box: Treaties, laws, maps, land claims, bills of sale, sound recordings, and other important documents fill 250,000 four-drawer filing cabinets.

The seemingly infinite amount of memorabilia here includes Richard Nixon's letter of resignation, the Emancipation Proclamation, the surrender documents of Japan's World War II government, a copy of the Magna Carta, and even a letter from the King of Siam to Abraham Lincoln expounding the efficiency of elephant labor.

The archives' main attractions, though, are the Declaration of Independence, the Constitution, and the Bill of Rights, all on permanent display in the domed **Rotunda,** accessible via the Constitution Avenue entrance. They are sealed in helium to guard against aging, and lowered into deep vaults at night for added security. Barry Faulkner's massive murals depicting the forging of these papers encircle the display. In the **Exhibition Hall** around the **Rotunda** are rotating exhibitions, most of them thematic, celebrating the American genius for invention, or a single remarkable person. Many of the exhibitions rely on photographs and engravings. Spanning the history of photography, the collection includes many historical works, such as Mathew Brady's Civil War photos. Motion pictures—140,000 reels—and literally miles of sound recordings, from FDR's "Fireside Chats" to Tokyo Rose's propaganda messages, are also on file.

The archives is more than a museum, however: Access to important records and research assistance is offered for genealogical searches. Immigration records; ships' logs; slave transit and ownership records; treaties with Native-American tribes; and volumes of information on taxes, military service, births, and deaths help families rediscover their heritage. (One story researched here was Alex Haley's *Roots*.)

The building that houses so much American minutiae has a shimmering white exterior trimmed with Corinthian columns, evidence of architect **John Russell Pope**'s facility with classical forms. Ninety-minute behind-the-scenes tours are offered. Make reservations by calling at least two weeks in advance. The gift shop sells document facsimiles, cards, and books.

In 1993, the **National Archives** opened a branch in suburban Maryland, for public use as a research facility; at the **New Archives** (its informal name) you can listen to the legendary Watergate Tapes. Call the Washington or Maryland number with your research request, and you'll be directed to the right location. Note that researchers must be at least 16 years old; evening and weekend researchers should call ahead to ensure that the records in question will be available. ♦ Free. Rotunda and Exhibition Hall: daily Jan-Mar, Sept-Dec; daily 8:45AM-9PM Apr-Aug. Tours: M-F 10:15AM, 1:15PM. Research areas: M-Sa. Constitution Ave NW (between Seventh and Ninth Sts). Information 501.5000, tours 501.5205, genealogical information 501.5400 & Metro: Archives/Navy Memorial. Also at: 8601 Adelphi Rd (between University Blvd and Metzerott Rd), College Park, Maryland. 301/713.6800 &

67 Mellon Fountain Sidney Waugh's elegant fountain comprises three concentric bronze basins; the outermost is the largest ever cast. From the center gushes a 20-foot-high plume of water. ♦ Sixth St NW (between Constitution and Pennsylvania Aves). Metro: Archives/Navy Memorial

COURTESY OF THE CANADIAN EMBASSY, WASHINGTON, DC

68 Canadian Embassy This massive marble building (pictured above) includes a 175-seat theater, a library, and an art gallery, plus a three-story rotunda and waterfall set in a titanic courtyard. The views of the **Capitol** and the eastern end of **The Mall** from the courtyard are worth a photo or two. ♦ Gallery: M-F. Library: by appointment. 501 Pennsylvania Ave NW (between Constitution Ave and Sixth St). 682.1740 & Metro: Archives/Navy Memorial

69 Capital Grille ★★$$$$ Subdued lighting and dark wood paneling help give this classic New York–style steak house a comfortable clubby feel. "Dry-aged" steaks and fresh seafood flown in daily from New England stand out among the entrées. There is a separate smoking section, and the restaurant keeps a collection of cigars for diners who enjoy topping off their meal with a stogie. ◆ Steak house ◆ M-F lunch and dinner; Sa-Su dinner. Reservations suggested. 601 Pennsylvania Ave NW (at Sixth St). 737.6200 ♿ Metro: Archives/Navy Memorial

70 Temperance Fountain In the late 19th century, eccentric California dentist Henry Cogswell used to donate these fountains—on which his name was always prominently inscribed—to any city that would accept one, hoping that pedestrians would slake their thirst with cool water rather than booze. The city long ago stopped maintaining the fountain's obsolete cooling system—which means that although the citizenry may not be dry, Cogswell's fountain is. ◆ Pennsylvania Ave NW and Seventh St. Metro: Archives/Navy Memorial

71 Market Square This two-tower complex includes 210 apartments, a visitors' center, restaurants, offices, shops, and an open-air park. ◆ 701-801 Pennsylvania Ave NW (between Seventh and Ninth Sts). ♿ Metro: Archives/Navy Memorial

Within Market Square:

Navy Memorial Conklin Rossant's circular plaza, 100 feet in diameter, features four shimmering waterfalls and Stanley Bleifeld's *Lone Sailor,* a bronze sculpture that stands on the world's largest grid map. Free military band concerts take place here in the summer. The adjacent visitors' center has a small museum, a gift shop, and daily screenings of the 36-minute film *At Sea* in its IMAX theater. ◆ Nominal admission. 737.2300 ♿

701 ★★$$ Contemporary American cuisine—seafood pastas, roasted chicken, fresh fish—is served here in formal surroundings: Floor-to-ceiling windows flood the dining area; light, thick carpeting and plush tablecloths provide hushed elegance; and widely spaced tables afford privacy. Lobbyists, lawyers, businesspeople with expense accounts, and the pre-theater crowd like its convenient location—the impressive list of caviar and vodka may also have something to do with it. ◆ American ◆ M-F lunch and dinner; Sa-Su dinner. 393.0701 ♿

72 Dutch Mill Deli ★$ Serve yourself cafeteria-style at this deli, which specializes in gigantic sandwiches and platters, as well as decent soups. Its proximity to surrounding museums is a plus. ◆ American ◆ M-Sa breakfast and lunch. 639 Indiana Ave NW (between Sixth and Seventh Sts). 347.3665 ♿ Metro: Archives/Navy Memorial

M. STORRINGS

73 Darlington Fountain Friends of Joseph Darlington—an esteemed member of the bar—dedicated this Art Deco sculpture to his memory after his death in 1920. The naked nymph standing beside a fawn created quite a stir among the barrister's Baptist coreligionists when it was erected. Sculptor Carl Jennewin's pointed reply was that the nymph arrived "direct from the hands of God instead of from the hands of a dressmaker." ◆ Judiciary Square, Fifth and D Sts NW. Metro: Judiciary Sq

73 Old City Hall Built by **George Hadfield,** English architect and protégé of Benjamin West, this is one of the earliest Greek Revival buildings in the city. The east wing was completed in 1826, the west in 1849. It was DC's city hall until 1873, when the title passed from the district to the federal government. Now, it houses Superior District Court offices, which are not open to the public. ◆ 451 Indiana Ave NW (at Fifth St). Metro: Judiciary Sq

74 National Law Enforcement Officers' Memorial The walled plaza, dedicated in late 1991, honors federal, state, and local law enforcement officers who have died in the line of duty, dating as far back as 1794. The memorial's pathways, encircling a terraced pool, are guarded on each side by majestic bronze lions. A staffed information kiosk is open daily. ◆ E St NW (between Fourth and Fifth Sts). 737.3400. Metro: Judiciary Sq

---

Restaurants/Clubs: Red **Hotels:** Blue
Shops/ 🍴 Outdoors: Green **Sights/Culture:** Black

75 US Tax Court Built in 1974 by **Victor Lundy,** this is a showpiece of engineering: Granite and bronze-tinted glass sheath the exterior, while the third-floor court chambers are suspended from the ceiling by more than 100 three-inch-thick steel cables. The building was designed to span the nearby freeway; though that plan was abandoned, its form still reflects the original intent. Concrete and teak lend texture to the interior surfaces, which you won't be able to see unless you have a matter of unpaid back taxes to settle with Uncle Sam. ◆ Third St NW (between D and E Sts). Metro: Judiciary Sq

76 Hyatt Regency Capitol Hill $$$$ Not in danger of being upstaged by its ponderous neighbors, this elegant hotel offers an exquisite lobby and extensive gift shop in addition to 834 rooms, 20 meeting and banquet rooms, a health club, an indoor pool, and a variety of restaurants and lounges in cafelike settings. Indoor parking and nonsmoking floors are available. Children under 15 stay free. ◆ 400 New Jersey Ave NW (at D St). 737.1234, 800/233.1234; fax 737.5773 ♿ Metro: Union Station

77 Holiday Inn on the Hill $$ The 341 spacious rooms here (some nonsmoking) offer free HBO movies. Amenities include an outdoor pool, health club, and a tour bus to historic sites. Indoor parking is available for a fee. The **Senator's Sports Restaurant and Bar** serves American cuisine. Children under 18 stay free. ◆ 415 New Jersey Ave NW (between D and E Sts). 638.1616, 800/228.5151; fax 638.0707 ♿ Metro: Union Station

78 La Colline ★★★$$ This elegant brasserie a block from **Union Station** offers good French food at bargain prices. Try one of the prix-fixe selections, or go à la carte with rack of lamb, chateaubriand, or fresh fish. Entrées change with the season, however, and may not always be available. Leave room to sample something from the dessert carts. Also investigate the wine list—the selection of wines available by the glass changes weekly. ◆ French ◆ M-F breakfast, lunch, and dinner; Sa dinner. Reservations recommended. 400 N Capitol St (at D St NW). 737.0400 ♿ Metro: Union Station

The Hotel
GEORGE

79 Hotel George $$$ Formerly the **Hotel Bellevue,** this 139-room property is one of the growing number of small, contemporary hotels with a distinct personality. Chic and elegant, the spacious guest rooms feature classic (from the 1940s on) and contemporary touches, including granite-topped desks and marble-and-black-granite

bathrooms. Complimentary daily newspapers, overnight shoe-shine service, and a fitness center with mens' and ladies' steam rooms are among the amenities. New York pop artist Steve Kaufman, a former apprentice to Andy Warhol, painted the portrait of George Washington in the lobby. ◆ 15 E St NW (between N Capitol St and New Jersey Ave). 347.4200; fax 347.4213 ♿ Metro: Union Station

Within the Hotel George:

Bis ★★★★$$$$ Rave reviews accompanied the opening of winning chef Jeff Buben's modern, new bistro, where a glass-fronted balcony overlooks the bar and the kitchen is visible through a wall of slightly rippled glass. Buben's limited menu has a classic French accent, with such dishes as country-style rabbit, ravioli stuffed with braised beef over chard, striped bass Provençal, and risotto with prawns done to perfection. Leave room for the *tarte tatin*. ◆ French ◆ M-F breakfast, lunch, and dinner; Sa-Su brunch and dinner. Reservations recommended. 661.2700

80 Phoenix Park Hotel $$$$ Once small, this property with a Dublin accent attracted so many guests that an ambitious $12-million addition was constructed in 1995, adding a ballroom, meeting rooms, and effectively doubling the number of units to 149. Modernized deluxe rooms and penthouse suites include voice mail, in-room movies, mini-bars, and computer hookups. There's a health club, concierge service, and room service from 6AM to midnight. Children under 12 stay free. The weekend rates are great. ◆ 520 N Capitol St (at F St NW). 638.6900, 800/824.5419; fax 393.3236 ♿ Metro: Union Station

Within the Phoenix Park Hotel:

The Dubliner At this traditional Irish pub, pints of Guinness follow shots of Jameson and Paddy's, and each night Celtic bands encourage customer sing-alongs and plenty of blarney. ◆ Daily 11AM-2AM. 737.3773 ♿

81 The Irish Times ★$ Housed in what looks to be a Chinese restaurant—check out the pagoda-style roof—this boisterous pub caters to a regular crowd of **Capitol Hill** staffers and embassy employees. (Ronald Reagan used to come here on St. Patrick's Day.) Generous portions of stewed chili and fish-and-chips are favorites during the busy lunch hour. The jukebox plays Irish hits nonstop, from *Molly Malone* to U2. There's live entertainment Wednesday through Saturday, beginning after 9PM and lasting into the wee hours. ♦ Irish ♦ Daily lunch and dinner. 14 F St NW (between N Capitol St and New Jersey Ave). 543.5433 ♿ Metro: Union Station

82 Government Printing Office and Bookstore A mecca for information mavens, the center publishes 1.4 billion volumes a year. It's one of the world's largest in-house printing operations (employing some 5,000 workers), using enough paper yearly to fill 25 miles of train cars. Its most important publications are the *Congressional Record* and the *Federal Register,* the government's daily trade paper. Thousands of consumer-information books and booklets are published here. Its all-time best-seller, *Infant Care,* has sold more than 17 million copies since its first printing in 1914. The bookstore stocks more than 3,000 titles and offers 17,000 more in its catalog, plus NASA and National Park Service posters, how-to books, government guides, histories, and most government publications. The main building is a massive Romanesque Revival edifice composed entirely of handmade brick. ♦ Bookstore M-F. 710 N Capitol St (between G and H Sts NW). 512.0132 ♿ Metro: Union Station. A second bookstore is at: 1510 H St NW (at 15th St). 653.5075. Metro: McPherson Sq

83 Georgetown University Law Center Designed at the same time (in 1971) as the **Kennedy Center for the Performing Arts** and by the same architect, **Edward Durell Stone,** the law center has been widely criticized as an inhospitable mass of brick. Although it's open to the public, there isn't much of anything worth going in to see. ♦ 600 New Jersey Ave NW (at F St). 662.9000 ♿ Metro: Union Station

84 Jewish Historical Society of Greater Washington Officially named the **Lillian and Albert Small Jewish Museum,** it is set within **Adas Israel,** DC's oldest synagogue. The building—a modest, redbrick structure—is a National Historic Shrine. Within the museum, the society keeps records and oral histories of the community's Jewish heritage and mounts special exhibitions of Judaica. ♦ Free. M-Th, Su, or by appointment. 701 Third St NW (between E St and Massachusetts Ave). 789.0900; www.jewishhistoricalsoc.com ♿ Metro: Gallery Pl/Chinatown

85 Holy Rosary Church Built in 1913 by early Italian immigrants, this simple Catholic church is at the heart of what used to be Washington's Little Italy. From behind the altar a massive, recently refurbished *Madonna and Child*

reaches up to the arched, coffered ceiling. Also note the jewel-like mosaic stations of the cross. Services are still conducted in English and Italian, and the modern **Casa Italiana,** a recent addition, accommodates post-Mass cappuccino, special functions, and a language school. ♦ Third and F Sts NW. 638.0165; fax 638.0793; casaital@erols.com; www.holyrosarychurch.org. Metro: Judiciary Sq

COURTESY OF THE NATIONAL BUILDING MUSEUM

86 National Building Museum (NBM) For years, this low-budget Victorian version of the Palazzo Farnese in Italy was ridiculed as a white elephant. Its offices held 1,500 clerks processing pension payments for pre–World War I veterans and their families; during a period of 40-odd years, they doled out $8 billion. In the middle of this century the building (illustrated above) was threatened with destruction, then happily rediscovered. In 1980 it became the home of this museum, which is dedicated to documenting and explaining the US's vital building trade, from the craft of hard hats to the role of architects.

Along with exhibitions, the museum highlights controversial architectural issues with film and video. It has compiled an archive/data bank of thousands of models, drawings, blueprints, and other documents. The permanent exhibit *Washington: Symbol and City* explores the capital's architecture, including its monuments. Visitors are asked to choose their favorite among the designs originally submitted for the **Washington Monument.**

The building's most stunning display, though, is itself. Its central court—once the city's largest indoor space—is as long as a football field and about 16 stories high. Four tiers of balconies—some supporting ornate iron grillwork—climb its interior walls. In the center are the eight largest Corinthian columns in the world, measuring 76 feet high and 25 feet in diameter; each required 70,000 bricks to build.

Army Quartermaster General **Montgomery C. Meigs,** engineer of the **White House** dome, is responsible for the inspired design of this building, whose offices radiate from the central court and its balconies. One architect remarked that only a thunderstorm or an inaugural ball could fill the vast space. In fact, the inaugural celebrations of Cleveland, Harrison, FDR, Nixon, Carter, Reagan, Bush, and Clinton were held here. Hundreds of windows let in natural light and ventilation without the heat of a conventional skylight.

The gift shop, the best among the city's museums, sells unique, well-designed merchandise. ♦ M-Sa; Su noon-4PM. Tours: M-F 12:30PM; Sa-Su 12:30PM, 1:30PM; groups by appointment. 401 F St NW (at Fourth St). 272.2448 ⚅ at G St entrance. Metros: Judiciary Sq, Gallery Pl/Chinatown

87 Mr. Yung's Restaurant ★★$ Delicious dim sum and other Chinese delicacies are served in this Chinatown standby. The decor is nothing to speak of, but the service is attentive. ♦ Chinese ♦ Daily lunch and dinner. 740 Sixth St NW (between G and H Sts). 628.1098 ⚅ Metro: Gallery Pl/Chinatown

87 Burma Restaurant ★★$ Sample the cuisine of Burma—now Myanmar—including such sure bets as mango pork (permeated with red chili pepper) and tamarind fish (grilled and rubbed with chili spice). The vegetarian entrées and noodle dishes are superb examples of Chinatown's most exotic cuisine. ♦ Burmese ♦ M-Sa lunch and dinner; Su dinner. Reservations recommended. No credit cards accepted. 740 Sixth St NW (between G and H Sts), Second floor. 638.1280. Metro: Gallery Pl/Chinatown

88 Red Roof Inn $ This hotel (formerly a **Comfort Inn**) offers 197 simple rooms just four blocks from the **Washington Convention Center** (see page **95**). Amenities include nonsmoking rooms, valet service, a fitness room, laundry facilities, and whirlpools in some units. Dine at the **Café Express** coffee shop. Children under 18 stay free. ♦ 500 H St NW (at Fifth St). 289.5959, 800/843.7663; fax 682.9152 ⚅ Metro: Gallery Pl/Chinatown

89 Full Kee ★$ This is the late-night gathering spot for chefs seeking authentic Chinese food—all for the cost of a sandwich. Bowls of broth and plates of noodles are topped with your choice of garnishes. If you can read Chinese, order one of the daily specials. ♦ Chinese ♦ Daily lunch and dinner. No credit cards accepted. 509 H St NW (between Fifth and Sixth Sts). 371.2233 ⚅ Metro: Gallery Pl/Chinatown

90 Szechuan Gallery ★$$ Enlist your waiter's help in choosing from the vast menu of often fiery appetizers and main courses. Some of the best dishes are on the Taiwanese menu. ♦ Szechuan/Hunan/Taiwanese ♦ M-F lunch and dinner; Sa-Su dinner. 617 H St NW (between Sixth and Seventh Sts). 898.1180 ⚅ Metro: Gallery Pl/Chinatown

90 Tony Cheng's Mongolian Restaurant ★★$$ This is fun food: Pick raw ingredients from the buffet, and the chefs will stir-fry it before your eyes on a massive Mongolian griddle. Upstairs, try **Tony Cheng's Seafood Restaurant** for fresh fish, Cantonese-style. ♦ Mongolian/Cantonese ♦ Daily lunch and dinner. 619 H St NW (between Sixth and Seventh Sts). Ground floor dining room 842.8669; upstairs dining room 371.8669 ⚅ Metro: Gallery Pl/Chinatown

90 Da Hua Food A one-stop shop for Asian chefs, head here for fresh meat and fish, produce, Pan-Asian staples, and cookbooks. It's short on decor but—more important—long on authentic ingredients. Check the second floor for china, cookware, shoes, games, and other imported specialties. ♦ Daily 10AM-7:30PM. 623 H St NW (between Sixth and Seventh Sts). 371.8888 ⚅ Metro: Gallery Pl/Chinatown

91 Hunan Chinatown ★★$$ White tablecloths, attentive service, and well-prepared Northern Chinese favorites make this a consistent winner. Boiled dumplings in chili sauce, tea-smoked duck, and two-flavored lobster are all excellent choices. ♦ Szechuan/Hunan ♦ Daily lunch and dinner. 624 H St NW (between Sixth and Seventh Sts). 783.5858 ⚅ Metro: Gallery Pl/Chinatown

92 Coco Loco ★★$$ Sample Mexican tapas in a cafe setting in the front; or pig out on a Brazilian buffet in the rear, with fabulous salad and vegetable bars and mixed-grill meats carved at your table, right off giant skewers. In warm weather, sample selections from either menu in the walled courtyard. At 11PM Friday and Saturday, the dance floor fills with diners working off the calories to a Latin beat. Joining the fun late Saturday night are exotic Brazilian dancers. ♦ Mexican/Brazilian ♦ M-F lunch and dinner; Sa-Su dinner. Reservations recommended. 810 Seventh St NW (between H and I Sts). 289.2626 ⚅ Metro: Gallery Pl/Chinatown

Washington, DC was greatly moved by the death of Abraham Lincoln. At D Street Northwest, between Fourth and Fifth Streets, is the first public monument to the President, dedicated on 15 April 1868, the third anniversary of his death.

Fade to Washington

It may not enjoy the year-round mild climate of Los Angeles or come close to having the soaring skyline of New York, but Washington has served Hollywood well as a setting (or a model) for films ranging from political thrillers to, well, political comedies.

Advise and Consent (1962) Allen Drury's hot-button novel of Capitol Hill maneuvering over a Cabinet nomination gets a respectful adaptation by director Otto Preminger. It features a superb cast, headed by Henry Fonda, Walter Pidgeon, Gene Tierney, and, in his last movie, Charles Laughton.

All the President's Men (1976) This film about the unraveling of the Watergate scandal stars Robert Redford and Dustin Hoffman as Woodward and Bernstein, Oscar winner Jason Robards as Ben Bradlee, and Hal Holbrook as Deep Throat, the mysterious man in the parking garage. The **Main Reading Room** of the **Library of Congress** is the scene for the film's most amazing shot.

An American President (1995) Rob Reiner directed this romantic froth about a widowed president (Michael Douglas) who falls for a feisty lobbyist (Annette Bening). The **Oval Office** was uncannily replicated in the film's Hollywood set. Co-stars Michael J. Fox.

Being There (1980) A quiet man named Chauncy Gardener becomes the toast of Washington, dispensing simple statements that are taken as sage observations. In this masterful satire, based on Jerzy Kosinski's novel, Peter Sellers gives one of his best (and last) performances; Oscar winner Melvyn Douglas and Shirley MacLaine play his benefactors.

Born Yesterday (1950) This classic comedy about a tycoon in Washington who hires an intellectual to "educate" his ditsy mistress stars Broderick Crawford, William Holden, and the sublime Judy Holliday. The lukewarm 1993 remake features John Goodman, Don Johnson, and Melanie Griffith.

Dave (1993) Perhaps the best presidential comedy stars Kevin Kline as the president's body double. He manages to turn the **White House** upside down, and romance First Lady Sigourney Weaver, when he's "filling in." Directed by Ivan Reitman, the film also stars Charles Grodin.

The Day the Earth Stood Still (1951) One of the few 1950s sci-fi adventures that holds up as more than just kitsch, this literate and gripping story has an alien ship landing on the **Ellipse.** Its pilot, trying to convey a message of peace, is misunderstood and treated as a threat to our national security. Patricia Neal and Michael Rennie star.

Dr. Strangelove or: How I Learned to Stop Worrying and Love the Bomb (1964) Director Stanley Kubrick's wicked satire, about a nutty general trying to launch atomic war against the Soviets, still hits the bull's-eye. Peter Sellers gives a knockout performance playing three different roles. The outstanding cast includes Sterling Hayden,

George C. Scott, Keenan Wynn, and James Earl Jones.

Enemy of the State (1998) When attorney Robert Clayton Dean (Will Smith) unwittingly receives a tape that the National Security Agency is after, Gene Hackman's rogue surveillance expert steps in to help. Plenty of action and DC area scenes; however, **Adams-Morgan** and **Dupont Circle** are, in reality, more than a block apart.

The Exorcist (1973) The horror tale of a girl possessed, adapted from the best-selling novel, ushered in a new era in graphic special effects. Linda Blair, Ellen Burstyn, and Max von Sydow star. The house, on **Georgetown**'s **Prospect Street,** and the adjacent stairs leading down to M Street, are still Washington's biggest movie-based tourist attractions.

A Few Good Men (1993) This court-martial drama has a young defense attorney (Tom Cruise) butting heads with the military establishment represented by a harder-than-nails Jack Nicholson. Demi Moore and Kevin Bacon also star. Many exterior shots were filmed in Washington and suburban Virginia.

Heartburn (1986) Nora Ephron's revenge on her philandering husband, Washington journalist Carl Bernstein, was to write a thinly disguised novel about the breakup of their marriage. Meryl Streep plays Ephron opposite a randy Jack Nicholson.

In the Line of Fire (1993) This cat-and-mouse thriller stars Clint Eastwood as an aging Secret Service agent trying to erase bad memories of 1963 Dallas by trying to prevent a crazed assassin (John Malkovich) from getting to the current president. Good rooftop chase filmed on Capitol Hill.

Independence Day (1996) This sci-fi sleeper hit the box office jackpot. A bevy of spaceships attacks the earth, and blows up the **White House** in the process. Bill Pullman portrays the president; Will Smith and Jeff Goldblum round out the cast.

The Last Detail (1973) A profane and often hilarious story of a pair of Navy "lifers" (Jack Nicholson, Otis Young) who are escorting a sad-sack seaman (Randy Quaid) from Norfolk, Virginia, to a New Hampshire prison. Their stopover in Washington is one of the film's many highlights.

Mr. Smith Goes to Washington (1939) A naïve new senator (James Stewart) stands up for honesty in a corrupt Senate. One of Frank Capra's most well-known films, it co-stars the one-and-only Jean Arthur. Though most of the Washington scenes were shot in Hollywood, Stewart's visit to the **Lincoln Memorial** was filmed on location.

No Way Out (1987) Kevin Costner stars in this sensational thriller about a naval officer caught in a compromising situation involving the dead mistress of a Cabinet official. Gene Hackman and Sean Young costar.

93 Chop Steak ★$ One of Chinatown's funkier spots—the name suggests a burger emporium until you get the pun—it offers standard Cantonese fare to a local clientele. ◆ Cantonese ◆ Daily lunch and dinner. 719 H St NW (between Seventh and Eighth Sts). 898.1886 & Metro: Gallery Pl/Chinatown

94 A.V. Ristorante Italiano ★★$$ This simple family restaurant has been serving a rich variety of Central and Southern Italian fare for about half a century. Everything from pizza to pasta to veal in all its permutations is offered here. ◆ Italian ◆ M-F lunch and dinner; Sa dinner. 607 New York Ave NW (at Sixth St). 737.0550 & Metro: Mt. Vernon Sq/UDC

94 Marrakesh ★$$ The exotic Moroccan setting—pillows strewn on low sofas, and waiters outfitted in traditional dress—is enhanced by the belly dancers who perform nightly. In keeping with the place's sensual nature, diners eat with their hands (which the staff washes and dries before the meal). More an event than a meal, the seven-course prix-fixe dinner lasts for several hours. Dishes include chicken with lemon and olives, lamb shish kebab with honey, and couscous with vegetables. Top off the experience with baklava and mint tea. ◆ Moroccan ◆ Daily dinner. Reservations required. No credit cards accepted. 617 New York Ave NW (between Sixth and Seventh Sts). 393.9393 & Metro: Mt. Vernon Sq/UDC

95 Rupperts ★★★★$$$$ On a perfectly nondescript block in a former storefront is this unpretentious but marvelous find. You'll be greeted like an old friend and served simple yet satisfying food from an American menu that changes daily, depending on the availability of the freshest meats, fish, and produce. Make sure to order a side dish of gorgonzola mashed potatoes with whatever you're having. It will take a concerted effort, however, not to spoil your appetite with the fabulous breads. ◆ American ◆ Tu-W, F-Sa dinner; Th lunch and dinner. Reservations recommended. 1017 Seventh St NW (between New York Ave and L St). 783.0699 & Metro: Mt. Vernon Sq/UDC

96 Mount Vernon Square Built in 1903 by **Ackerman and Ross** as the **Carnegie Library,** this splendid marble Beaux Arts building has been restored for use by the Mount Vernon campus of the **University of the District of Columbia.** The engineering and architecture departments are housed here, and it is not open to the public with the exception of the **Carnegie Foyer,** which is available for rental; call 274.5119. ◆ K St NW (between Seventh and Ninth Sts). Metros: Mt. Vernon Sq/UDC, Gallery Pl/Chinatown

97 Martin Luther King Jr. Library The main branch of Washington's public library system, designed in 1972 by **Ludwig Mies van der Rohe,** is more than just a repository of books. Besides sponsoring a citywide arts program, the library features a permanent collection of paintings, sculpture, and photographs on display in the **Anteroom Gallery** and throughout the building. In addition, children's programs, poetry readings, theatrical performances, and concerts all take place here. The **Washingtoniana Room** contains probably the world's largest collection of DC-related information (books, registers, photos, etc.) dating from the early 19th century, and the **Star Library** contains masses of information from the old *Washington Star* newspaper. The building's simple, black steel–and–glass box design was one of the architect's last works and is the epitome of his style. Underground parking is available. ◆ M, W, F-Sa; Tu, Th 10AM-9PM; Su 1-5PM. 901 G St NW (at Ninth St). 727.1111 & Metros: Gallery Pl/Chinatown, Metro Center

NATIONAL MUSEUM OF AMERICAN ART

98 National Museum of American Art (NMAA) At press time, the NMAA was closed for extensive renovations and scheduled to reopen in 2002. During its 92-year stint as the US Patent Office, this building held archives of American ingenuity. Now the arched and pillared marble hallways that **Robert Mills** designed in the mid-1800s contain a wealth of American artistic talent. The building (illustrated on page 92) is a century-old replica of the Parthenon rendered in Virginia freestone. During the Civil War, it served as a temporary barracks, hospital, and morgue. Clara Barton and Walt Whitman ministered to the wounded here.

On the building's north side, the **NMAA** celebrates more than two centuries of native talent. Its installations enable visitors to trace the development of native styles and movements. The country's oldest art collection, it includes more than 35,000 pieces, including works by Edward Hopper, Andrew Wyeth, Winslow Homer, Mary Cassatt, Jacob Lawrence, and Benjamin West. There are selections of Hiram Powers's sculpture, oils by Albert Pinkham Ryder, and the country's largest collection of New Deal art.

The artwork leads visitors through America's past and present: wild landscapes and frontier lifestyle depicted by Thomas Moran and Albert Bierstadt; and portraits of Americans, both common and uncommon, painted by Cecilia Beaux and Charles Willson Peale. The third-

National Museum of American Art

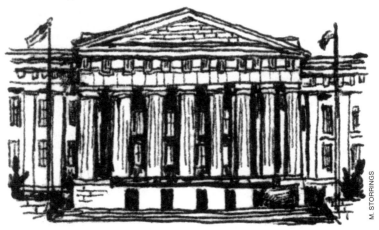

M. STORRINGS

floor **Lincoln Gallery,** site of its namesake's second inaugural reception, evokes the energy of the 20th century as captured in the works of Franz Kline, Isamu Noguchi, Robert Rauschenberg, and Helen Frankenthaler. The hallways of **NMAA** connect with the **National Portrait Gallery** (see below), so visiting both is easy.

The museum also has folk art, a large collection of miniatures, an 80,000-volume library, and a collection of daguerreotypes and photos dating back to 1839. The **Archives of American Art** (open to researchers) also serves the National Portrait Gallery. Besides permanent and rotating exhibitions, it hosts lectures and film series. One of the museum's more unusual displays, right as you walk in the door, is the *Throne of the Third Heaven of the Nations' Millennium General Assembly,* so named by its creator, James Hampton, who crafted a throne, altar, pulpits, and offertory tables entirely of aluminum and gold foil, light bulbs, and cardboard. A branch of the museum, the **Renwick Gallery** (see page 76), located in a separate building diagonally across from the **White House,** exhibits American crafts and decorative arts.

In fair weather, you can sit at tables beneath the elms in the courtyard that separates the two great museums. At lunchtime, bring a snack and picnic here, or eat at the building's pleasant **Patent Pending** cafeteria. ♦ Free. Daily. Tours: M-F noon; Sa-Su 2PM. G St NW (between Seventh and Ninth Sts). Information 357.2700, lecture and film information 357.3095 & Metro: Gallery Pl/Chinatown

98 National Portrait Gallery At press time, this gallery was also closed for extensive renovations and scheduled to reopen in 2002. Most visitors to this gallery find it both humbling and inspiring to stand face-to-face with so much greatness. It's filled with the

images of George Washington that many Americans first see on their schoolroom walls, as well as portraits of explorers, military heroes, Hollywood moguls, composers, and prizefighters. Among the colorful figures immortalized on canvas are Babe Ruth, Butch Cassidy, and the Sundance Kid. The federal government unintentionally began this collection in 1857 when it commissioned a series of presidential portraits. The permanent collection now totals more than 11,000 objects, including paintings, sculptures, etchings, photographs, and drawings. Works by John Singleton Copley, John Singer Sargent, Thomas Sully, Augustus Saint-Gaudens, and Charles Willson Peale, among other artists, can be found here. Call for information on special exhibits and lectures. ♦ Free. Daily. Tours: M-F 10AM-2PM; Sa-Su 11AM-2PM. F St NW (between Seventh and Ninth Sts). Information 357.2700, special events 357.2920 & Metro: Gallery Pl/Chinatown

99 MCI Center This sports and entertainment complex, which opened to great fanfare in 1997, is home to the **Washington Capitals** (NHL), **Wizards** (nee **Bullets;** NBA), and **Mystics** (WNBA). The modern center also hosts hundreds of events, including concerts and conventions, throughout the year. With only 400 parking spaces to serve the 20,000-seat arena, fans are encouraged to take the **Metro**—not only environmentally smart, the setup also seems to make for more jovial crowds arriving and leaving events. Though some grumble that this new addition has made **Seventh Street** too chic, most welcome the much-needed economic shot in the arm.

♦ 601 F St NW (at Sixth St). Tickets 432.7328 ⚭ Metro: Gallery Pl/Chinatown

Within the MCI Center:

Discovery Channel This three-level multimedia store explores the oceans, land, and sky. You don't have to buy anything to be fascinated by the electronics that make this environment possible. ♦ M-Sa 10AM-9PM; Su. 639.0908

MCI National Sports Gallery Celebrating American sports, exhibits and memorabilia include Babe Ruth's bat, Magic Johnson's jersey, and Oksana Baiul's skating costume. Plus 35 interactive video games let you compete with the pros. ♦ Admission; free with ticket to sports event. Daily noon-6PM, until 10PM on game days. 661.5133

100 The District Chophouse & Brewery ★★ $$ This new brewpub serves gargantuan platters of "jock food"—porterhouse, New York strip, and stout Delmonico steaks—plus bottomless salads to game-goers as well as a lively lunch crowd. ♦ American ♦ M-F lunch and dinner; Sa-Su dinner. 509 Seventh St NW (between E and F Sts). 347.3434 ⚭ Metro: Gallery Pl/Chinatown

100 Miya Gallery This tiny gallery is worth seeking out for ethnic art—in the form of carved wooden statues, baskets, and straw hats—that you're unlikely to find anywhere else in the city. ♦ M–F noon-7PM; Sa 1-5PM. 629 E St NW (at F St). 347.6330; nsagi@interchange.org. Metro: Gallery Pl/Chinatown

101 Jaleo ★★$$ By day, this stylish tapas bar is a businessperson's lunch place and by night it's a gathering spot for the young and the hip, as well as the theater crowd. Especially good are the *gambas al ajillo* (garlic shrimp) and *tortilla española* (Spanish omelette). The restaurant's bar is a perfect spot to nurse a beer or drink coffee. Two live dancers perform the *Sevillana* on Wednesday nights. ♦ Spanish ♦ Daily lunch and dinner. 480 Seventh St NW (at E St). 628.7949 ⚭ Metros: Archives/Navy Memorial, Gallery Pl/Chinatown

102 Shakespeare Theatre Originally located at the **Folger Shakespeare Library** on **Capitol Hill,** the theater company moved to these larger, more modern digs in 1992. This space lacks the character and charm of the **Folger,** but, on the plus side, there's not a single obstructed view in the 449-seat, horseshoe-shaped house. A selection of Shakespearean works and classical plays are performed from October through June; call ahead for current offerings. ♦ Box office: M-Sa; Su noon-6PM. 450 Seventh St NW (between D and E Sts) 547.1122 ⚭ Metros: Archives/Navy Memorial, Gallery Pl/Chinatown

103 Zenith Gallery Contemporary fine art, crafts, and neon fill this art space. ♦ M-F; Sa noon-7PM; Su noon-5PM. 413 Seventh St NW (between D and E Sts). 783.2963 ⚭ Metros: Archives/Navy Memorial, Gallery Pl/Chinatown

103 The Mark ★★$$$ Chef Alison Swope's ever-changing, eclectic menu is influenced by the American South, Italy, and Spain. Recent hits served in the minimalist dining room have included baklava with portobello mushrooms and feta, salmon with fiddlehead ferns, and lemon mascarpone. This eatery may not always reach the mark, but the innovative menu draws its share of fans. ♦ American/Continental ♦ M-Sa lunch and dinner; Su brunch and dinner. 401 Seventh St NW (at D St). 783.3133 ⚭ Metro: Archives/Navy Memorial

104 406 Group Located just down the street from the Smithsonian art museum–gallery complex, this building is a bonus for the visitor with time to spare: Three first-rate art galleries occupy its three floors, adding richness to the Seventh Street arts corridor. ♦ 406 Seventh St NW (between D and E Sts). Metros: Archives/Navy Memorial, Gallery Pl/Chinatown

Within the 406 Group:

104 David Adamson Gallery Local and international painters, sculptors, and graphic artists such as Kevin MacDonald and Michael Clark are showcased here. ♦ Tu-Sa. 628.0257

105 Ritz Nightclub Each of the five dance floors on these four stories moves to a different beat: reggae, soca, progressive R&B, live jazz, and Top 40. The upscale, predominantly black crowd is dressed to the nines. ♦ Cover. W, Su 10PM-3AM; Th 5PM-2AM; F 5PM-3AM; Sa

9PM-4AM. 919 E St NW (between Ninth and 10th Sts). 638.2582. Metros: Gallery Pl/Chinatown, Metro Center

106 Federal Election Commission (FEC) You may have a hard time finding the agency that monitors campaign financing and that's probably just the way most elected officials like it. The **FEC** doesn't get prime office space, and it's easy to walk by the agency without even noticing it. But its helpful and knowledgeable staff make the computerized records available to the public. So stop by and get a printout of your congressperson's records, and discover which political action committees are supporting his or her campaign. It's easy, and you'll probably learn more about the way the federal government works here than on a tour of the **Capitol.** ♦ M-F. 999 E St NW (at 10th St). 694.1220, 800/424.9530 ♿ Metros: Metro Center, Gallery Pl/Chinatown

106 Hard Rock Cafe ★$ Yet another link in the wildly successful international chain, this one displays such relics as Bo Diddley's first handmade guitar, the bodice Marilyn Monroe wore in *Gentlemen Prefer Blondes,* and the Best New Artist of the Year Grammy awarded to the Beatles in 1964. The decent burger and such fare is obviously not the point. ♦ American ♦ Daily lunch and dinner. 999 E St NW (at 10th St). 737.7625 ♿ Metros: Metro Center, Gallery Pl/Chinatown

107 Ford's Theatre Here, on 14 April 1865, during a performance of *Our American Cousin,* Abraham Lincoln was assassinated. Afterward, more than 100 years would elapse before the unlucky theater would open its doors again. A small basement contains mementos connected with both the president and his assassin, including the clothing Lincoln was wearing, the derringer pistol John Wilkes Booth used, and the diary in which he recorded his resolve to perform the deed. Upstairs, you can see the flag-draped box in which Lincoln was seated when Booth crept up behind him. The 699-seat theater built in 1863 by **James J. Gifford,** is now a venue for productions of contemporary plays and musicals, such as *Twilight in Los Angeles: 1982* and *Magnificent Yankee.* The National Park Service maintains the theater, as well as the **Petersen House**—where Lincoln died—across the street (see below). The theater offers tours daily except during matinees (on Thursday, Saturday, and

Sunday) or during rehearsals, so call ahead before you go. All tours are free and self-guided. ♦ Daily. 511 10th St NW (between E and F Sts). Information 426.6924, box office 347.4833 ♿ Metros: Gallery Pl/Chinatown, Metro Center

108 Riggs Bank Built in 1891 by **James G. Hill,** this is one of the few Chicago School buildings to have gone up in a city that has always preferred European Beaux Arts styles to the uncluttered boldness of American Midwestern design. ♦ Ninth and F Sts NW. Metros: Gallery Pl/Chinatown, Metro Center

109 The Bank This three-story dance hall, formerly called **Fifth Column,** has deejays spinning techno, house, Hi NRG, funk, and acid jazz. Be warned that the neighborhood is home to some aggressive panhandlers. ♦ Cover. M, W-Sa 10PM-2AM. 915 F St NW (between Ninth and 10th Sts). 737.3250 ♿ Metros: Gallery Pl/Chinatown, Metro Center

COURTESY OF THE NATIONAL PARK SERVICE

110 Petersen House Located across the street from **Ford's Theatre** (see above), this former boarding house is where Abraham Lincoln was carried after being shot on that fateful night in 1865. On view and outfitted with period furnishings are the front parlor where Mary Todd Lincoln and her son Robert Todd waited through the night; the back parlor; and the bedroom where Lincoln died the next morning. On display is Lincoln's bloodstained pillowcase. ♦ Free. Self-guided tours daily. 516 10th St NW (between E and F Sts). 426.6830 ♿ Metros: Gallery Pl/Chinatown, Metro Center

111 Hecht's Metro Center The main store of the local chain emphasizes mid-priced clothing, kitchenware, and linens. The **Metro Fare** snack bar is a fine place to grab a quick bite between errands. ♦ M-Sa 10AM-8PM; Su noon-6PM. 1201 G St NW (at 12th St). 628.6661 ♿ Metro: Metro Center

112 Grand Hyatt $$$$ This hotel offers 947 rooms, including 58 suites—three of which have saunas. Check out the hotel's 12-story atrium, which has a 7,000-square-foot lagoon, the **Grand Slam** sports bar, and three restaurants: **Zephyr's** for New York–style deli, the **Grand Cafe** coffee shop, and **Via Pacifica,**

for Italian and Asian cuisine. Other amenities include parking, valet services, an indoor pool, a fitness center, and nonsmoking rooms. Children under 17 stay free. ♦ 1000 H St NW (at 10th St). 582.1234, 800/223.1234; fax 637.4781 ⑤ Metros: Metro Center, Gallery Pl/Chinatown

113 Washington Convention Center Since its opening in 1983, this center has hosted more than 1,000 events—car and boat exhibitions; antiques, flower, and travel trade shows; political rallies; and high school graduation ceremonies. All told, the center has been credited with bringing more than $1 billion into the area. The convention center has about 380,000 square feet of exhibition space, 40 meeting rooms, and state-of-the-art facilities offering everything from audiovisual support to language translation and satellite conferencing. Note that the neighborhood is a bit dicey—don't go off exploring by foot after dark. In response to increasing demands for more space, construction has begun on another convention center (a supplement, not a replacement) at nearby **Mount Vernon Square**. ♦ 900 Ninth St NW (between H St and New York Ave). 789.1600; www.dcconvention.com ⑤ Metro: Gallery Pl/Chinatown

114 National Museum of Women in the Arts Collector Wilhelmina Holladay founded this museum in 1981 to examine and celebrate the work of female artists; in 1987 the collection and library moved to this 1907 Renaissance Revival building, which was originally a Masonic temple. The collection contains more than 500 works—paintings, drawings, sculpture, and other media from the 16th century to the present. International in scope, the museum displays works by Mary Cassatt, Frida Kahlo, Berthe Morisot, and Camille Claudel. There's an excellent library devoted to women artists and a gift shop. ♦ Donation. M-Sa; Su noon-5PM. Group tours by appointment. 1250 New York Ave NW (at 13th St). 783.5000; www.nmwa.org ⑤ Metro: Metro Center

115 Inter-American Development Bank Building This huge structure, designed by **Skidmore, Owings & Merrill** in 1985, is a modern salute to the old office buildings surrounding it. Heavy columns, Roman barrel vaults, and a limestone facade lend it a Baroque flair, although its sheer mass (12 stories, 1.2 million square feet of space, and more than 1,200 windows) puts it squarely in the 20th century. Inside, more than a quarter-acre of Greek and Italian tile paves the **Grand Court**, and a waterfall plunges down from the skylight seven stories overhead. This is turned off when an exhibit is installed in the court. Although the rest of the building is not open to the public, you're welcome to come to the

atrium during business hours. ♦ 1300 New York Ave NW (at 13th St). 623.1000 ⑤ Metro: Metro Center

Mozart CAFÉ

116 Café Mozart ★$$ Classic home cooking of Valkyrian proportions—*landjaeger* sausage, sauerbraten, and sauerkraut—is the specialty here. There's a carry-out delicatessen on the premises, and free parking is available. ♦ Austrian/German ♦ Daily breakfast, lunch, and dinner. 1331 H St NW (between 13th and 14th Sts). 347.5732 ⑤ Metros: McPherson Sq, Metro Center

117 Tuscana West ★★$$ Across the street from **Franklin Park** (see below), one of Downtown's loveliest squares, is this Northern Italian restaurant, with faux-marble walls, cherrywood booths, a brick oven for pizza, and an open kitchen. It sounds terminally trendy, but good *pomodoro* (tomato) soup and a wide selection of pastas, modest prices, and attentive, enthusiastic service combine to make it a winner. ♦ Italian ♦ M-F lunch and dinner; Sa dinner. 1350 I St NW (between 13th and 14th Sts). 289.7300 ⑤ Metro: McPherson Sq

118 Franklin Park One of Downtown's most spacious open spaces and its surrounding neighborhood, formerly home to an "adult" strip, have been resuscitated by nearby office building developments. Gently sloping walkways, a central fountain, lush green trees, and plenty of shaded benches make it a perfect lunch spot. ♦ Bounded by I and K Sts NW, and 13th and 14th Sts NW. Metro: McPherson Sq

119 Capitol City Brewing Company ★$$ The appeal of this Washington brew pub is its super-fresh beer. The availability of beers changes nightly, so check the massive bulletin board to get a description of what's on tap. If you're not sure what to try, order a sampler—it's well worth the money. The food here is nothing fancy—mostly meat dishes, with a couple of fish choices thrown in—but it's generally well prepared, and the portions are generous. But be forewarned: If you're looking to have a quiet dinner, avoid the after-work rush, when lawyers, lobbyists, and other Washington types jam the place. ♦ American ♦ Daily lunch and dinner. 1100 New York Ave (at 11th St). 628.CCBC ⑤ Metro: Metro Center. Also at: 2 Massachusetts Ave NE (at N Capitol St). 842.BEER. Metro: Union Station

Growing Up First

By the time they are elected, most American presidents have grown families. But several of the children who have occupied the **White House** have managed to fascinate and entertain us. Here's how some of them went about doing it.

Thomas (Tad) Lincoln was only seven when his father was elected president. Nicknamed Tadpole—and affectionately called Tad—he was the youngest of Lincoln's sons and his father's favorite. Though hampered by a speech impediment and slow to read and write, mischievous Tad was clever enough to figure out how to make all the **White House** bells ring at once—testing the patience of many a staff member.

Probably the most boisterous clan to occupy the Executive Manse were the **Roosevelt Children.** The brood of six included **Alice,** Teddy's daughter by his first wife. Declaring herself "allergic to discipline," Alice and her teenage antics provided much fodder for the tabloids. She smoked on the **White House** roof, drank publicly, and was immortalized in the popular song *Alice Blue-Gown.* The younger children were scarcely more manageable: **TR Junior** once fired a rifle into the ceiling of the presidential dressing room (with his father's blessing) just to make sure it worked; **Quentin,** who had a high-spirited group of friends called "The White House Gang," transported his pony, Algonquin, to his brother **Archie**'s room on the **White House** elevator.

Margaret Truman was hardly a child when her father was president, but she lived with her parents throughout their **White House** years. An only child of older parents, Margaret was doted on by her father. In her twenties she launched a singing career and gave a concert at **Constitution Hall** in 1950. A bad review by *Washington Post* critic Paul Hume prompted the president to write a stinging rebuke, part of which read: "Some day I hope to meet you. When that happens you'll need a new nose, a lot of beefsteak for black eyes, and perhaps a supporter below!" The *Post* printed Truman's letter, in full, on the front page.

When the Kennedy family moved into the **White House, John Jr** was only a newborn and **Caroline,** three years old. Caroline's pony, Macaroni, roamed freely on the **White House** grounds, while inside she attended pre-school (formed by her mother) with the children of several Kennedy friends. John Jr delivered one of the most poignant moments at JFK's funeral when he saluted his father's casket.

Both Lyndon Johnson and Richard Nixon brought teenage daughters to the presidential mansion. **Lynda Johnson** married Charles Robb (who was later elected US Senator from Virginia) in 1967, becoming the first **White House** bride since Woodrow Wilson's daughter, Eleanor. **Julie Nixon** married David Eisenhower, President Eisenhower's grandson, completing a family dynasty.

Amy Carter, who moved into the **White House** when she was nine, had three grown brothers. Her mother once said, "It is almost as though she has had four fathers, and we have had to stand in line to spoil her." Known to read books during state dinners, Amy was one of the only Presidential children to attend DC's public schools.

Despite the multiple scandals that plagued her father, **Chelsea Clinton** was successfully shielded from the public for much of her tenure in the **White House**. The Clintons were so protective of their only child that initially many Americans didn't know they had a daughter. Chelsea attended **Sidwell Friends School** in northwest Washington and, at 17, went to Stanford University. Ironically, in her sophomore year the daughter of prosecutor Kenneth Starr (who led the investigation of President Clinton) joined her at Stanford.

---

120 Franklin School Building The ornate brickwork, mansard roof, and Italianate window arches of this building designed in 1868 by **Adolph Cluss,** brought new prestige to public schoolhouses and influenced their design citywide. The children of presidents Andrew Johnson and Chester Arthur studied here, and Alexander Graham Bell made his first light-transmitted wireless telephone call from the building. The original bell towers, dormers, cornices, and other exterior features have since been replicated. ♦ 13th and K Sts NW ⅙ Metro: McPherson Sq

121 Henley Park Hotel $$$$ Fashioned after England's fine hostelries, this refurbished former apartment building seems truly royal. Catch an afternoon tea in the **Wilkes Room** off the hotel's parlor. Full meals can be had at the **Coeur de Lion,** which serves American cuisine infused with regional influences. The stiff tariff of this 96-room establishment is justified by such amenities as baby-sitting, limousine service, 24-hour room service, a concierge, and a multi-lingual staff; children under 16 stay free. ♦ 926 Massachusetts Ave NW (between Ninth and 10th Sts). 638.5200, 800/222.8474; fax 638.6740. Metros: Mt. Vernon Sq/UDC, Metro Center

Restaurants/Clubs: Red	**Hotels:** Blue
Shops/ ♠ **Outdoors:** Green	**Sights/Culture:** Black

Morrison-Clark

Historic Inn & Restaurant

122 Morrison-Clark Inn $$$ Washington's first historic inn (it opened in 1987) occupies the former **Soldiers, Sailors, Marines, and Airmens Club.** The 54 rooms are furnished with 19th-century antiques, Neo-Classical, or French pieces. Original red-mahogany and gold-leaf pier mirrors and carved marble fireplaces decorate its bar and restaurant (see below). Complimentary continental breakfast, a fitness center, valet parking, and concierge service complete the picture. ♦ 1015 L St NW (between 10th and 11th Sts). 898.1200, 800/332.7898; fax 289.8576 ♿ Metro: Metro Center

Within the Morrison-Clark Inn:

Morrison-Clark Restaurant ★★★★
$$$$ The Southern menu varies with the season at this pretty Victorian, where four large pier mirrors overlook marble fireplaces and circular cabbage-rose banquettes. Three of chef Susan Lindeborg's more popular entrées are rabbit loin stuffed with pecan cornbread and topped with Maker's Mark bourbon sauce; seared chicken breast with country ham, wide noodles, and tarragon; and superb soft-shell crabs. Be sure to save room for one of the delicious desserts. ♦ American ♦ M-F lunch and dinner; Sa dinner; Su brunch and dinner. Reservations recommended. 898.1200 ♿

123 Church of the Ascension and St. Agnes The exterior is a good example of High Victorian Gothic design, while the interior features cast-iron columns, walnut pews, a gold- and silver-leaf mural, and abstract designs in the nave windows. ♦ 1217 Massachusetts Ave NW (between 12th and 13th Sts). 347.8161 ♿ Metros: McPherson Sq, Mt. Vernon Sq/UDC

Bests

Geoffrey Dawson
Co-owner and Builder, Buffalo Billiards, Bedrock Billiards, Atomic Billiards, CarPool, Aroma Lounge

Sunset cocktails at the rooftop bar of the **Hotel Washington** (15th St and Pennsylvania Ave NW) overlooking the **White House** and the **Washington Monument.** This is a local favorite. Wait for a table by the railing; it is worth it. Great on a hot, rainy night.

Any show at the **930 Club** at 815 V Street NW (at Ninth St); easy access by cab, **Metro,** or car. This new venue for an old club is great. National acts (Dylan, Bodeans, Lou Reed) as well as local bands. Holds 900 people, so everyone is close to the stage.

Biking or Roller Blading on the **Crescent Trail** between **Georgetown** and **Bethesda.** This runs next to the **Potomac River** and connects two great eating and shopping areas. Smooth and well-maintained asphalt make it the best place in the area for these sports.

Canoeing and rowing at **Fletcher's Boat House** (244.0461). Fletcher's has been there forever, almost, and so have the boats. Canal access as well as to the Potomac River where locals go to fish. 4940 Canal Road NW (just north of Reservoir Rd) or take the Crescent Trail about three miles out of Georgetown.

Sunday runs with **Fleet Feet** (387.3888). Phil and Jan have been operating this great **Adams-Morgan** runners' store for over a decade. They have a devoted local following and go for great runs on Sundays. They know everything about the running scene in DC and will be glad to share it.

Cleveland Park and the **Uptown Theater** offer lots for evening entertainment. **Red** line **Metro** to **Cleveland Park.** The **Uptown Theater** is among the finest in the country, old style with huge screen and balcony. Lots of restaurants and bars nearby. Really safe neighborhood.

Adams-Morgan for congestion and wild nightlife. Lack of parking and lots of traffic make this a great place to walk or taxi to. Close to **Downtown** and loaded with restaurants and bars. You can't miss finding a place that fits.

Rock Creek Park. The park police close **Beach Drive** on Saturday and Sunday. This runs through the heart of the city and is a great place to run, bike, or blade. The **National Park Service** has all the info on special events. Follow **Rock Creek Parkway** north from Downtown to Beach Drive.

Dr. Joe Goldblatt
Founding Director, The Event Management Program, George Washington University

The **Smithsonian's Folk Life Festival** brings a world of culture to Washington, DC each summer. Hundreds of performers and craftspeople (as well as ethnic chefs) fill the hall with the sites, sounds, and tastes of a kaleidoscope of cultures. This is just one of hundreds of free events offered throughout the year.

> Bad politics cause poverty more often than bad business.
>
> Hugh Thomas, *A History of the World*

Logan Circle/ Howard University

North of Downtown DC, away from most of the monuments and museums, the glitzy stores and hip galleries, are the quiet neighborhoods of Logan Circle and Howard University. They're as rich in history as any Washington enclave, much of it preserved in their ornate mansions, apartment buildings, and churches.

The area's western border is **16th Street Northwest**, whose dramatic lineup of churches, temples, and shrines makes it a required walking tour for even the most casual admirer of architecture. Mary Henderson, wife of US Senator John Henderson, was instrumental in developing the street in the late 19th and early 20th centuries. Her crowning achievement was **Meridian Hill Park**, a gently terraced series of waterfalls and fountains.

Head east and you'll come to Logan Circle, named after notable Civil War general and Illinois senator John A. Logan. Many of the city's most elegant mansions are located in this area, where residents, eager to renovate and preserve these Victorian homes, have banded together to quell encroaching criminal activity. The nearby **14th Street** corridor, the site of riots after the assassination of Martin Luther King Jr. in 1968, has been rejuvenated after years of neglect. In the mid-1980s, the city erected the **Frank D. Reeves Municipal Center** at 14th and **U Streets**, and a group of cafes, craft shops, and clubs known as the "New U" soon sprang up around it. The Metro's **Green Line** serves the neighborhood, making it easily accessible to the rest of the city.

To the northeast is the **Howard University** campus, since 1867 a bastion of African-American higher education. The campus sits atop a hill overlooking the city and the huge **McMillan Reservoir;** the university hospital occupies the site of the old **Griffith Stadium**, home for many years to Washington's former **American League** baseball team—the **Senators.** South of Howard is **Le Droit Park;** in the early years of this century some of the city's leading black citizens resided in these mansions. In recognition of that fact, and of its splendid examples of Revival period design, **Le Droit Park** is listed on the National Registry of Historic Places.

1 Scott Circle General Winfield Scott, whose likeness was sculpted in 1874 by Henry Kirk Brown, rides through the circle, and a statue of Daniel Webster, sculpted in 1900 by Gaetano Trentanove, stands in the small triangular park just to the west. At 1 Scott Circle are the **General Scott Apartments,** designed in 1942 by **Robert O. Scholz.** One of the city's last and best Art Moderne buildings, it also was the first to have central air-conditioning. Also of interest, at the end of Embassy Row, in front of the country's bland modern embassy (1601 Massachusetts Ave NW), note the stylized bronze kangaroo and the emu holding the Australian seal. ♦ Metro: Farragut North, Dupont Circle

2 Doubletree Hotel Park Terrace $$ Located only six blocks from the **White House,** this attractively remodeled hotel offers the traveler 189 rooms, 33 apartments, free parking, and meeting rooms. Children under 16 stay free. ♦ 1515 Rhode Island Ave NW (between 15th St and Scott Cir). 232.7000; fax 332.7152; www.doubletreehotels.com. Metro: Farragut North, Dupont Circle

Within the Doubletree Hotel Park Terrace:

Chardonnay ★★$$$ As the name might suggest, this restaurant's claim to fame is a superb wine list, which showcases American varietals at reasonable prices. The regional American dishes can be a little uneven; stick with simple grilled dishes and the irresistible homemade desserts. The real bonus: large portions. ♦ American ♦ Daily breakfast, lunch, and dinner. Reservations recommended. 232.7000 &

3 Grace Reformed Church Teddy Roosevelt laid the cornerstone for this church, designed in 1903 by **Abner Ritcher.** Presidents Eisenhower and Nixon worshiped here as well. ♦ 1405 15th St NW (between Rhode Island Ave and P St). 387.3131 & Metro: Dupont Circle

4 National City Christian Church The larger-than-life scale of this colonial-style church, designed by **John Russell Pope,** is heightened by its position atop a small knoll. Its perch, coupled with the elegant steeple, makes the church one of the highest buildings in town. Presidents James Garfield and Lyndon Johnson prayed here. ♦ 5 Thomas Cir (between 14th St and Massachusetts Ave). 232.0323 ♿ Metro: McPherson Sq

5 Thomas Circle In the center of this busy roundabout stands a sculpture of Major General George H. Thomas, created in 1879 by John Quincy Adams Ward. The statue of the man known as the "Rock of Chickamauga" surveys Downtown DC to the south. ♦ Metro: McPherson Sq

6 Luther Place Memorial Church This Civil War–era house of worship designed by architect **Judson York** is a soaring Neo-Gothic structure of red sandstone that provides a fitting balance to the **National City Christian Church** (see page 97) nearby. ♦ 1226 Vermont Ave NW (between Thomas Cir and N St). 667.1377 ♿ Metro: McPherson Sq

7 Mary McLeod Bethune Council House Born in South Carolina in 1875, Mary McLeod Bethune was the 15th of 17 siblings, whose parents were freed slaves. She rose to prominence in the field of education as a founder of Bethune-Cookman College in Daytona Beach, Florida. Under Calvin Coolidge and Herbert Hoover, she worked for the National Child Welfare Commission. In 1935 Bethune came to Washington as special adviser on minority affairs to the Roosevelt administration and as director of the Division of Negro Affairs in the National Youth Administration. She organized African-American officials into the "Black Cabinet," which lobbied for a fair share in New Deal programs, and founded the National Council of Negro Women. This Victorian town house, which served as the council's headquarters from 1943 to 1966, is now a center for black women's history and a National Historic Site. ♦ Free. M-F. 1318 Vermont Ave NW (between N St and Logan Cir). 673.2402. Metro: McPherson Sq, Mt. Vernon Sq/UDC

The area south of Howard University, Le Droit Park, became an elite African-American community in the late 1800s. Prominent members of the neighborhood included poet Paul Laurence Dunbar; educator Dr. Anna Cooper; educator Robert Terrell and activist Mary Church Terrell; Washington's first mayor, Walter Washington; as well as many lawyers, educators, writers, and members of the Howard University faculty. Today, Le Droit Park is a designated historic district prized for its Victorian homes.

8 Logan Circle The Victorian and Richardsonian town houses built here between 1875 and 1900 made Logan Circle one of DC's most fashionable addresses. During the 1920s and 1930s, the area's racial makeup shifted, and by 1940 the city's most prominent black politicians and other social leaders were living here. Neglect, in the decades that followed, took its toll on the neighborhood, but determined preservationists have restored many of the circle's buildings. The area still has some problems, so it may be best to visit during the daytime. ♦ Metro: Mt. Vernon Sq/UDC, Shaw/Howard Univ

9 Studio Theatre Five professional productions a year draw on classic and contemporary works, including such recent hits as *Gross Indecency: The Three Trials of Oscar Wilde* and *The Vagina Monologues,* written and performed by Eve Ensler. ♦ Box office M-F; Sa-Su noon-6PM (to 9PM on performance nights). 1333 P St NW (at 14th St). Information 232.7267, box office 332.3300 ♿ Metro: Dupont Circle, Shaw/Howard Univ

10 Woolly Mammoth Theater The repertory season invariably includes some of DC's most audacious productions, such as Nicki Silver's *Raised In Captivity;* Bill Corbett's *The Big Slam;* and Sara Felder's *June Bride,* an autobiographical show about a lesbian juggler who wants a traditional Jewish wedding. ♦ Box office daily noon-6PM. 1401 Church St NW (at 14th St). 393.3939 ♿ Metro: Dupont Circle

11 Temple of the Scottish Rite In designing this temple, architect **John Russell Pope** was inspired by the Tomb of Mausolus at Halicarnassus in Greece, one of the Seven Wonders of the World. He based the proportions of the 1915 building on numbers significant to Masonic mysticism, and it reflects an array of styles, from Egyptian to Roman. The two huge sphinxes that guard the entrance to the shrine, each cut from a solid block of limestone, were sculpted by Alexander Weinman. The temple is now the headquarters of the Supreme Council of the Southern Jurisdiction of the 33rd Degree of the Ancient and Accepted Scottish Rite of Freemasonry. ♦ M-F; closed holidays; groups of 25 or more by special arrangement. 1733 16th St NW (at S St). 232.3579. Metro: Dupont Circle

12 Source Theatre A force in Washington's experimental theater community, this theater offers classics and new plays, as well as late-night comedies. It's also the venue for the Washington Theater Festival, a four-week showcase of new plays that runs every July and August. ♦ Box office: M-F; Sa noon-6PM. 1835 14th St NW (between S and T Sts). 462.1073 ♿ Metro: U St/Cardozo

U Street in Its Heyday

During the early to mid-1900s, the U Street corridor—an area just north of **Downtown**, bounded by **North Capitol Street** and **15th Street Northwest**, and **M Street Northwest** and **Florida Avenue Northwest**—emerged as a vibrant city neighborhood, a cultural destination, and a magnet for successful black businessmen. The proximity to **Howard University** attracted writers, artists, and scholarly types who found congenial surroundings where they could take up residence. Sadly, the riots of 1968 devastated the area, and nearly two decades passed before it underwent an economic revival. Today, a stroll around the neighborhood evokes memories of days gone by and, happily, reveals many new signs of the area's most recent renaissance.

The magnificent **Howard Theatre** (Seventh and T Sts NW) opened in 1910 and attracted large audiences to its concert hall, renowned for its superb acoustics. After decades of deterioration, plans are now underway for the **Howard**'s restoration. With the opening of the **Lincoln Theatre** (1215 U St NW, between 12th and 13th Sts, 328.6000) in 1922, the area became known as "Black Broadway." The annual President's Birthday Balls were held at the **Lincoln** during the Roosevelt and Truman administrations. First Lady Eleanor Roosevelt once attended with Lucille Ball and Red Skelton by her side. U Street was the place to see and be seen. Thousands came to the neighborhood to hear the likes of Pearl Bailey, Ethel Waters, Nat King Cole, Lena Horne, Ella Fitzgerald, Harry Belafonte, Leontyne Price, Sidney Poitier, and Sammy Davis, Jr.

Jelly Roll Morton opened a club nearby at 1211 U Street Northwest. Duke Ellington lived one block away at 1212 T Street Northwest, and his "Washingtonians" performed on U Street before moving on to Harlem's Cotton Club. The first internationally acclaimed African-American opera singer, Lillian Evans Tibbs, known as Madame Evanti, lived at 1910 Vermont Avenue Northwest (at 10th St), a town house that has remained in the Tibbs family for five generations.

Poets who made their home in the area include Sterling Brown (2464 Sixth St NW, between Howard Pl and Fairmont St), Paul Laurence Dunbar (321 U St NW, between Third and Fourth Sts), and Langston Hughes, who lived at the 12th Street YMCA (1816 12th St NW, between S and T Sts). Jean Toomer wrote his novel *Cane* while residing at 1341 U Street Northwest (between 13th and 14th Sts). Other literati drawn to the area included novelist Zora Neale Hurston, historian and publisher Carter G. Woodson, and **Howard University** philosophy professor Alain Locke.

Robert Terrell, a lawyer and community leader, and his wife Mary Church Terrell, civil and women's rights activist, lived at 1323 T Street Northwest (between 13th and 14th Sts) and at 1615 S Street Northwest (between 16th and 17th Sts). **US Supreme Court** Justice Thurgood Marshall once made his home in an apartment at the **Whitelaw Hotel** at 1839 13th Street Northwest (between S and T Sts). Congressman and clergyman Adam Clayton Powell resided at 8 Logan Circle Northwest. Dr. Charles Drew, a professor and the head of surgery at **Howard University Medical School**, whose plasma discoveries led to the development of blood banks, lived at 328 College Street Northwest (at Fourth St).

Mary McLeod Bethune, educator and presidential advisor to FDR, resided at 1318 Vermont Avenue Northwest (between N St and Logan Cir). The Victorian row house, now a small museum, is open to the public. The National Archives for Black Women's History, also housed here, includes Bethune's papers and those of the National Council of Negro Women (of which Bethune was both founder and president), and are available by appointment (673.2402).

In recent years, the **U Street/Cardozo Metro** stop, built in 1991, has increased accessibility to the U Street corridor. New restaurants and clubs, like **U-topia** (1418 U St NW, between 14th and 15th Sts, 483.7669), the **930 Club** (815 V St NW, at Ninth St, 393.0930), and **State of the Union** (1357 U St NW, between 13th and 14th Sts, 588.8810) have breathed new life back into the area. The **Whitelaw Hotel**, designed by **Isaiah T. Hatton,** one of the first African-American architects, was restored in 1991 as an apartment building. The increasingly popular **Ben's Chili Bowl** (1213 U St NW, between 12th and 13th Sts, 667.0909), in the building that once housed the Minniehaha silent-movie theater and later a pool hall, has become a neighborhood meeting spot and city landmark. Next door, the restored **Lincoln Theatre** once again opened its doors to the public in 1994 and now draws theatergoers to the area. As the song goes, here on U Street, almost a century later, "everything old is new again."

13 U-topia ★$$ It's more the atmosphere than the food that makes this stalwart of the new U Street scene worth trying. Live music accompanies an eclectic menu that ranges from lamb couscous to New York sirloin. Another draw: unbeatable martinis.
♦ International ♦ Daily lunch and dinner. 1418 U St NW (between 14th and 15th Sts). 483.7669 ♿ Metro: U St/Cardozo

ATTICUS
Used Books & Music

14 Atticus Exuding plenty of idiosyncratic charm, this store stocks used books, CDs, records, Malcolm X paraphernalia, unusual T-shirts, and more. Even if you're not looking for anything in particular, stop in for some inspiring browsing and a chat with local author and owner Richard Peabody. ♦ M-Sa; Su noon-6PM. 1508 U St NW (between 15th and 16th Sts). 667.8148; www.atticusbooks.com. Metro: U St/Cardozo

15 Millennium Flamingo lamps, 1950s toasters, spiffy vinyl furniture—this two-floor rummage shop is delightfully stuck in a time warp. The first floor has lots of vintage clothing. ♦ M 3:30-7PM; Th-F, Su noon-7PM. 1528 U St NW (between 15th and 16th Sts). 483.1218 ♿ Metro: U St/Cardozo

16 State of the Union Celebrate the end of the Cold War at this funky music club, decorated with what look like leftover signs from a May Day parade in Moscow. There are live bands, deejays, some art shows, and even a bit of theater. The bar menu has a Russian accent.
♦ Hours vary; call ahead. 1357 U St NW (between 13th and 14th Sts). 588.8810. Metro: U St/Cardozo

17 Lincoln Theatre Following the example set by the **Warner Theatre** located Downtown, this veteran venue for theater, stage shows, and movies has been restored to its original luster. Back in the 1920s, the theater was an important cultural magnet for the area's flourishing African-American community. Over the years, however, it fell into disrepair, and it finally was shuttered in the 1970s. Today, concerts by the **Count Basie Orchestra,** gospel musicals, and mini–film festivals have transformed the theater into the showplace it originally was intended to be.
♦ 1215 U St NW (between 12th and 13th Sts). Box office 328.6000, tickets 432.SEAT ♿ Metro: U St/Cardozo

Ben's Chili Bowl

17 Ben's Chili Bowl ★$ Check out this hole-in-the-wall cafe, a long-favored (and late-night) hangout of **Howard University** students, civil rights leaders, and musicians. Bill Cosby has been known to stop by when he's in town. The chili dogs are world famous and the chili ranges from reasonably mild to eye-tearingly hot and spicy. ♦ American ♦ M-Sa breakfast, lunch, and dinner; Su lunch. No credit cards accepted. 1213 U St NW (between 12th and 13th Sts). 667.0909. Metro: U St/Cardozo

18 African-American Civil War Memorial (Spirit of Freedom) Dedicated in 1998, this memorial honors the 201,943 black soldiers and their 7,000 white officers who served the Union during the Civil War. The Ed Hamilton sculpture features a bronze statue of black soldiers before three low semicircular granite walls that bear stainless-steel plaques with the names of all soldiers in the 166 regiments of the US Colored Troops. The $2.6-million monument stands in a small park in the Shaw neighborhood, which is named for Robert Gould Shaw, the white commander of the all-black 54th Massachusetts regiment (made famous by the 1989 film *Glory* starring Morgan Freeman and Denzel Washington). Eventually, the memorial will also include a heritage center in the nearby **Masonic Temple Lodge** on U Street. ♦ Vermont Ave NW and U St. 667.2667; www.afroamcivilwarmemorial.org ♿ Metro: U St/Cardozo

19 930 Club Named for its original location at 930 F Street, DC's pioneer live music club during the punk era now features top local and national bands—from grunge to glam—including Natalie Merchant, the Roots, and They Might Be Giants. ♦ Cover. Hours vary; call ahead. 815 V St NW (at Ninth St). 393.0930 ♿ Metro: U St/Cardozo

Ladies First

While the nation's attention generally focuses on the chief of state, several first ladies have captured their fair share of both press headlines and the public's imagination. Whether owing to a striking fashion sense or a radical political stance—or even just for speaking up when women generally didn't—the White House wives have left their individual marks on both the capital and the country.

1797-1801 Wife of one president and mother of another, **Abigail Smith Adams** rarely stifled a political opinion, freely discussing current events with her typically male dinner guests. Despite her keen intellect, Abigail remains best known for stringing clotheslines through a vacant room in the White House.

1809-17 While journalists continually tried to rename her Dorothea, **Mrs. James Madison** insisted her name was just plain Dolley. She furthered the Adams style of drawing-room diplomacy well past her days as first lady, for her White House successors—as well as their husbands—sought her social and political opinions until her death in 1849. Always a style-setter, Dolley's trademark was a turban decorated with flowers and feathers.

1845-49 At 41, the popular **Sarah Childress Polk** took her religion and her new role as first lady seriously, gaining great respect for her conservative standards. The Polks banned dancing and drinking at the White House—the first considered frivolous, the second somewhat sinful. On inauguration night, when the Polks arrived for the celebration, the dancing came to a halt. Following the first couple's two-hour stay, the music and dancing resumed.

1877-81 The first president's wife with a college degree, **Lucy Webb Hayes** was an alumna of Wesleyan Female College in Cincinnati, Ohio. Referred to as "Lemonade Lucy" because she forbade even wine to be served at the White House, she brought the Easter Egg Roll to the White House grounds when children were banned from the Capitol lawns.

1885-89 and 1893-97 The only first lady to be married in the White House was **Frances Folsom Cleveland.** The president insisted on a small private ceremony inside, but crowds were allowed to peek through the windows.

1889-93 While replacing a china closet, **Caroline Lavinia Scott Harrison** became interested in the bits and pieces of dinnerware she found, and began a White House collection of past presidents' china. She also was elected the first president-general of the newly formed Daughters of the American Revolution in 1891.

1909-13 Not a woman to hide in her husband's shadow, **Helen Herron Taft** set a precedent by riding beside the president in the inaugural procession down Pennsylvania Avenue to the White House. She ignored other conventions as well—allowing her cow, named Mooly-Wholly, to graze the White House lawn, and introducing musicales at state dinners. She also suggested placing cherry trees around the Tidal Basin.

1915-21 The second wife of President Woodrow Wilson, **Edith Bolling Galt Wilson** proved invaluable to him and to the nation when his health was failing. She allowed few to bother Wilson during his illness, serving as a de facto president, sending news and policy decisions from him to his administration.

1933-45 Often criticized and always controversial, **Anna Eleanor Roosevelt** traveled 38,000 miles in her initial year as first lady and kept up the pace throughout her tenure. Known as the "First Lady of the World," Eleanor Roosevelt spoke her mind freely in her syndicated column "My Day," on radio broadcasts, and in special press conferences for women reporters.

1961-63 Setting the fashion trends for the 1960s, **Jacqueline Bouvier Kennedy** was the first of the first ladies to appoint a personal dress designer. Women all over the world wore copies of her suit dresses and pillbox hats. Jackie Kennedy also brought culture to the mansion by inviting distinguished guests to perform and be honored.

1974-77 Known for speaking out on social issues, **Betty Ford** brought new candor to her office. She helped open up the issues of breast cancer and chemical dependency for public discussion.

1981-89 The only first lady to hold the office after a film career, **Nancy Reagan** decided to do something with her influence halfway through her husband's administration. She began a personal campaign to educate the country's youth about the dangers of drug abuse, making frequent television appearances and imploring youngsters to "Just Say No" to drugs. Her opinionated nature caused friction between herself and Raisa Gorbachev during a visit to Russia, when she criticized her Soviet counterpart for discounting the religious content of several paintings during a tour.

1989-93 Known even before her arrival at the White House as the "Silver Fox," **Barbara Bush** impressed many detractors by demonstrating a self-mocking sense of humor during her first address as first lady. Criticized before the election for her dowdy style—fake pearls and matronly dresses—she paused during her speech to model her latest unremarkable outfit. During George Bush's presidency, she established her own cause: improving the quality of education in America.

1993-2001 Though other first ladies throughout history may have been equally powerful, only lawyer and activist **Hillary Rodham Clinton** was handed the massive—and daunting—job of trying to reform the national health care system (because of federal nepotism laws, a volunteer position). Following—and despite—the debacle, the first lady focused her energies on the running of the White House. In fact, it was at her urging that smoking was officially banned there.

20 Le Droit Park In the 1870s architect **James McGill** designed 64 homes in the picturesque Romantic Revival style, with patterned slate roofs. Fifty or so remain, most of them on the 400 block of U Street and the 500 block of T Street. By 1920 **Le Droit Park** had become the premier address for middle-class African-Americans and a center for their businesses and culture. The neighborhood is now a historic district. ♦ Bounded by Second, Sixth, Fifth, U, and Elm Sts NW and Rhode Island and Florida Aves NW. Metro: Shaw/Howard Univ

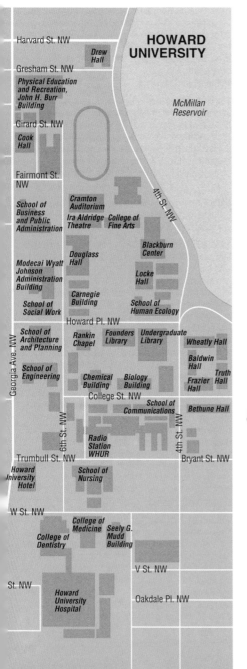

21 Howard University Founded in 1867 by General Oliver O. Howard, head of the Freedmen's Bureau and an outspoken champion of civil rights, it is one of the more prestigious universities in the nation, with 12,000-plus students in 18 schools that include medicine, law, and theology. Among the school's alumni are the late Supreme Court Justice Thurgood Marshall, former Atlanta mayor Andrew Young, and the late Patricia Roberts Harris, former secretary of the Department of Health and Human Services. The **Founders Library** (806.7250) on the south side of the quadrangle contains black history exhibitions and the **Moorland-Spingarn Research Center** (806.7239), the largest collection of black literature in the country. ♦ M-F 10AM-3PM. Tours: by appointment. 2400 Sixth St NW (at Howard Pl NW). Information 806.6100, tours 806.2900 ♿ Metro: Shaw/Howard Univ

Within Howard University:

Howard University Gallery Renowned for its dedication to the arts, this gallery holds Italian Renaissance paintings from the **Kress Collections** and a permanent display of African art, as well as works by outstanding African-American artists. Special exhibitions change regularly. ♦ M-F. College of Fine Arts, 2455 Sixth St NW. 806.7070 ♿

22 Florida Avenue Grill ★★$ Down-home Southern cooking is served in this old-style diner. For breakfast, try the scrapple (a Philadelphia specialty), home fries, grits, and biscuits. For lunch or dinner, recommended dishes include the pan-fried chicken, spareribs, or ham hocks, all served with greens or cabbage, sweet potatoes, and beans or rice. The homemade corn muffins can't be beat. ♦ Southern ♦ Tu-Sa breakfast, lunch, and dinner. No credit cards accepted. 1100 Florida Ave NW (at 11th St). 265.1586 ♿ Metro: U St/Cardozo

23 Meridian Hill Park (Malcolm X Park) The southern end of this 12-acre green space is a spectacular sight during warm months. Built in 1930, "a water staircase," formed by 13 terraced waterfalls, flows down to a large pool; nearby, an even larger lily pond surrounded by benches beckons. Though neighbors have been largely successful in ridding the park of undesirable characters, it's still best to visit during the day. ♦ Bounded by 15th and 16th Sts NW, and W and Euclid Sts NW. Metro: U St/Cardozo

24 All Souls Unitarian Church James Gibbs's design for London's St. Martin-in-the-Fields (on Trafalgar Square) has been much copied, but seldom as successfully. Hailed by critics as one of the best re-creations, this church was built in 1924 by the architectural firm **Coolidge and Shattuck**.

Following the Unitarian tradition, its simple interior is devoid of religious icons. ◆ 2835 16th St NW (at Harvard St). 332.5266 & Metro: U St/Cardozo

25 Old Soldiers' Home The oldest military retirement facility in the country features a Norman-style fortress (constructed in the mid-1800s) complete with crenellated battlements. It reportedly was built with ransom money that General Winfield Scott exacted from Mexico City during the Mexican-American War in the 1840s. ◆ 3700 N Capitol St (between Irving St NW and Harewood Rd NW). Metro: Fort Totten

26 Rock Creek Cemetery The city's oldest cemetery is filled with historic graves, including the famous *Adams Memorial,* a haunting statue of a woman sculpted in 1890 by Augustus Saint-Gaudens. Commonly called *Grief,* the memorial was commissioned by writer Henry Adams in honor of his wife, Clover, who committed suicide by drinking her photographic chemicals. **Stanford White** designed the memorial's setting. Other local notables interred here are Julius Garfinckel, Henry Lansburg, and Montgomery Blair. ◆ Webster St NW (between Rock Creek Church Rd and Third St). 829.0585. Metro: Fort Totten

Within Rock Creek Cemetery:

St. Paul's Episcopal Church The first church in the area was built on this spot in 1775, 63 years after the congregation had first convened here. Of the **Delos H. Smith** original, only the brick walls remain, owing to a 1921 fire. The Federal splendor of the church—now reconstructed—is best exemplified by several excellent stained-glass windows. ◆ 726.2080 &

27 Walter Reed Army Medical Center The hospital facilities here are located within a huge seven-story square. Especially worth noting is the headquarters of the **Armed Forces Institute of Pathology,** built in the late 1940s as a prototype for the "atomic bomb–proof" buildings intended to be the standard for Downtown's architecture. But the development of the hydrogen bomb in the early 1950s rendered that vision—and this windowless building—almost immediately obsolete. ◆ 6825 16th St NW (between Aspen St and Alaska Ave). 782.3501 & Metro: Takoma

On the grounds of Walter Reed Army Medical Center:

National Museum of Health and Medicine This facility was founded in 1862 to research medical conditions that arose during the Civil War. (Most soldiers died from diarrhea or dysentery.) Amputation was the most common treatment for wounds, hence the museum's grisly photographs of amputations and collection of severed limbs—not a sight for the squeamish. Also on view are models of battle evacuation methods and rescue efforts, such as mule-drawn litters, trains, and horse-drawn ambulances. On permanent display is *Living in a World with AIDS,* a multimedia exhibition addressing the medical, cultural, and historical impact of AIDS. ◆ Free. Daily. Bldg 54. 782.2200 &

Otis Historical Archives These rooms house about one-half mile of documents, photographs, and glass-plate negatives on the subject of military medicine and pathology. The collection includes about 1,500 photographs of wounded Civil War soldiers. ◆ Free. By appointment only. Bldg 54. 782.2212 &

Ann Greer
Theater Critic, America Online's Digital City Washington

Not all the theatrics in Washington take place on **Capitol Hill**—in addition to the **Kennedy Center,** which presents touring shows and free early evening performances, there are several top-notch resident theaters, including **Arena Stage** for the American cannon, **Studio Theatre** for an eclectic mix of offerings, **Shakespeare Theatre** for the Bard and the classics, and **Woolly Mammoth** for wacky looks at life. Visit **TICKETplace** in the **Old Post Office** building (at 12th St and Pennsylvania Ave), for half-price, day-of-performance bargains.

And not all museums are on **The Mall**—the **National Gallery** and **Smithsonian** museums are wonderful, but also try the **Phillips Collection** with its fabulous Bonnards in the **Dupont Circle** neighborhood, the

Corcoran Gallery near the **White House,** and the **National Museum of Women in the Arts,** the only museum of its type in the world.

On Capitol Hill, check out two incredible libraries, both of which have ongoing exhibitions: the **Library of Congress,** the largest library in the world with its spectacular **Jefferson Building,** and the **Folger Shakespeare Library,** the repository of the world's largest collection of materials on the Bard's plays.

Before you leave the southern part of the city, visit **Hains Point** on the **Potomac** and "The Awakening," a sculpture of a sleepy giant emerging from the ground. Then head up **Rock Creek Parkway,** Washington's lush urban greensward, to the **Washington National Cathedral.** This Gothic stone structure complete with buttresses and gargoyles has a great view of the city, and its grounds include an herb cottage, a greenhouse, and a lovely English-style garden.

Dupont Circle/ Adams-Morgan

A frequent criticism hurled at the nation's capital is that it lacks "real" neighborhoods—areas of ethnic and economic diversity with friendly cafes, restaurants, bookstores, markets, galleries, and clubs grouped within convenient walking distance. Although that characterization may be somewhat true, there is an area that *does* fit that description: Dupont Circle/Adams-Morgan.

East of **Rock Creek Park**, between **Columbia Road** (to the north) and **M Street** (to the south), the urban hiker will discover a section of DC where gleaming office towers give way to rows of brick town houses and stately pre-war buildings. Elegant restaurants drawing the power elite sit next to low-rent cafes and funky bars. Vibrant art galleries line leafy **R Street** and a variety of bookstores (some with cozy cafes) cater to all kinds of tastes.

During the 1950s and 1960s, the fountain at Dupont Circle was the center of much "hanging out," which occasionally included people demonstrating against society's various ills. Today, the circle, with its benches and chessboard tables, attracts an eclectic—if less politically minded—crowd from suited corporate types to Spandexed bike messengers.

Adams-Morgan (north of Dupont Circle) was also once the scene of political activity, but of a different sort. Once known as **Lanier Heights**, the neighborhood gained its current name in the 1950s: After the Supreme Court voted to integrate public schools in *Brown v. The Board of Education,* two elementary schools, Adams (white) and Morgan (black), were merged as a symbol of hope. This auspicious union set the tone for what is now the only truly integrated neighborhood in DC.

The gentrification of Adams-Morgan began in the 1970s, when urban pioneers, seeking to buy cheap and renovate, took advantage of the incredibly low prices of the area's historic homes. Although many of its black residents moved out around this time, the neighborhood was saved from homogeneity by successive waves of immigration—especially from South American and African countries. During the 1970s and 1980s, the neighborhood also experienced an influx of gay residents, who helped fuel the local club scene. Due to this rich cultural mix, Adams-Morgan's restaurants, clubs, and shops reflect a diversity unmatched by any other Washington neighborhood, making it a popular weekend destination for tourists and Washingtonians alike.

Unfortunately, the transit system planners didn't anticipate the area's popularity, and it is a bit of a hike to and from the closest **Metro** stations, **Dupont Circle** and **Woodley Park/Zoo.** Parking can be a major problem here, too. But despite transportation woes, most people consider these the city's cutting-edge neighborhoods—and Washington's most authentic neighborhood experience.

1 Dupont Circle A bronze statue of Civil War Admiral Samuel Francis Dupont used to adorn the circle, but the Dupont family whisked the statue away to Delaware and replaced it with this graceful marble fountain. The figures below its basin represent the wind, the sea, and the stars. Dupont Circle's benches and lawn are popular venues for political demonstrations, chess matches, and just hanging out. ◆ Metro: Dupont Circle

2 Doyle Washington Hotel $$$$ The former **Dupont Plaza** has adopted an Art Deco look with an elegant Irish accent. The 314-room property's new, stone-framed lobby features sculptures imported from Ireland and Celtic-style lattice work. All guest rooms have been refurbished and come with wet bars and refrigerators; two-bedroom presidential suites offer galley kitchens, sitting areas, and incredible views of Dupont Circle and Downtown. Along with Irish hospitality at its best, the hotel offers indoor parking, baby-sitting, valet service, laundry and dry-cleaning services, and nonsmoking rooms. **Claddagh's** restaurant, open daily for breakfast and dinner, serves both American and traditional Irish fare (shepherd's pie and black-and-white pudding). **Biddy Mulligan's** bar serves much of the same for lunch. Children under 17 stay free. ♦ 1500 New Hampshire Ave NW (at Dupont Cir). 483.6000; fax 362.3265; www.doyle-hotel.ie & Metro: Dupont Circle

3 Super Crown Granted, this chain mega-bookstore isn't exactly quaint. But it has a terrific selection of books, both in print and on cassette, as well as magazines and videos. Relax at the little espresso bar while you read your purchases. ♦ Daily 9AM-11PM. 11 Dupont Cir NW (between P St and New Hampshire Ave). 319.1374 & Metro: Dupont Circle. Also at: Numerous locations throughout the suburbs

3 Washington Club (Patterson House) Designed by **Stanford White** in 1902, this wedge-shaped building fronts Dupont Circle. A gleaming-white Italian palazzo, it now houses a women's club and is not open to the public. ♦ 15 Dupont Cir NW (between P St and New Hampshire Ave). 483.9200. Metro: Dupont Circle

4 National Trust for Historic Preservation (McCormick Building) The **McCormick Building** (illustrated below) was once the most opulent apartment house in DC. Each of its five floors contained one 11,000-square-foot apartment, in which notables, among them Andrew Mellon, dwelled. Designed by **Jules Henri de Sibour** and considered the best of his many DC works (which include the former **Canadian Chancery** nearby), the building lends a Parisian flair to the neighborhood. It is now the headquarters for the nonprofit National Trust, which labors hard to save other special buildings. ♦ M-F. 1785 Massachusetts Ave NW (between 17th and 18th Sts). 588.6000 & Metro: Dupont Circle

5 Jefferson Hotel $$$$ With the feel of an elegant British estate, this hostelry offers 69 rooms and 35 suites. Original documents signed by Thomas Jefferson are on view in the lobby and reading room. Rooms are outfitted with antiques and reproduction furniture; some have canopy beds and fireplaces. Amenities include a restaurant (see below), concierge and valet services, 24-hour room service, and valet parking. Children under five stay free. ♦ 1200 16th St NW (at M St). 347.2200, 800/368.5966; fax 331.7982; www.slh.com/slh & Metros: Farragut North, Farragut West

Within the Jefferson Hotel:

Jefferson Restaurant ★★★$$$ A wood-burning fireplace, Federal-period furnishings, and lots of nooks and crannies make this a cozy spot. The kitchen here is far more adventurous than most hotel restaurants, with such dishes as Chilean bass with mushroom puree, smoked tomato, and ricotta gnocchi; and pan-roasted sturgeon with lentils. ♦ American ♦ Daily breakfast, lunch, and dinner. Reservations advised; jacket and tie recommended. 347.2200

6 Sumner School Museum and Archives Built in 1872 by **Adolph Cluss,** and named for

McCormick Building

M. STORRINGS

abolitionist **Charles Sumner,** this historic, redbrick building served as DC's first school for black children. It has since been renovated and now houses the archives of all of DC's public schools, plus revolving exhibitions on local history and culture. ♦ Free. M-F Sept-June. 1201 17th St NW (at M St). 727.3419 ♿ Metros: Farragut North, Farragut West

7 B'nai B'rith Klutznick Museum Two thousand years of history, with emphasis on early Jewish-American settlements, are brought to life by more than 500 objects, making the permanent collection here one of the largest of its kind in the US. Thousand-year-old coins and a 16th-century Torah wrapper help illuminate the history of the Jewish people. A series of annual exhibitions covers a broad range of subjects, from archaeology to modern art. Free films are scheduled year-round, and nationally known columnists and speakers hold lectures on a weekly basis. Group and multilingual tours can be arranged in advance. The museum's library is closed to the public. ♦ Donation. M-F, Su; closed Jewish holidays. 1640 Rhode Island Ave NW (between Scott Cir and 17th St). 857.6583 ♿ Metros: Farragut North, Farragut West

8 Canterbury $$$ Comfortable and elegant, each of the 99 junior suites features a sitting area, kitchenette, and wet bar. A complimentary continental breakfast greets you every morning. The renovated basement dining room, **Brighton-on-N,** serves New American cuisine. Nonsmoking rooms are available, and children under 12 stay free. ♦ 1733 N St NW (between 17th and 18th Sts). 393.3000, 800/424.2950; fax 785.9581 ♿ Metro: Dupont Circle

8 Tabard Inn $$ A haven for Anglophiles, this friendly bed-and-breakfast might be mistaken for a place right out of the English countryside, thanks to its rustic but comfy furnishings and dark paneled walls. It has 42 rooms, many with fireplaces (and at least one boasting an upright piano), and a restaurant (see below). Guests often congregate in the large first-floor parlor and cocktail lounge. Most of the staff has been here for many years, adding to the inn's familial air. ♦ 1739 N St NW (between 17th and 18th Sts). 785.1277; fax 785.6173 ♿ Metro: Dupont Circle

Within the Tabard Inn:

Tabard Inn Restaurant ★★$$ The casual, bustling dining room, decorated with folk art, is a local favorite for Sunday brunch. It features a menu of healthful, inventive dishes: lavish salads, fish with crisp vegetable garnishes, and pasta. Save room for the homemade desserts. There's garden dining in warm weather. The adjoining bar—more like a living room, really—is a romantic place for a drink in the winter, when the fireplace blazes. ♦ American ♦ M-Sa breakfast, lunch, and dinner; Su brunch and dinner. Reservations recommended. 833.2668 ♿

9 St. Matthew's Cathedral John F. Kennedy worshiped in this late 19th-century church, and his funeral mass was said here; an inscription marks the spot of the casket. The dome, reminiscent of Florence, Italy's Cathedral of Santa Maria del Fiore, and the simple brick geometries of the exterior give no hint of the florid interior, with its fine mosaic work. The architectural firm **Heins and Lafarge** is responsible for its design. ♦ 1725 Rhode Island Ave NW (between 17th St and Connecticut Ave). 347.3215 ♿ Metro: Farragut North

9 Longfellow Building DC's first modern "glass-box" structure, it was built in 1940-41 by **William Lescaza,** who also designed the Swiss Embassy. ♦ 1741 Rhode Island Ave NW (between 17th St and Connecticut Ave). Metro: Farragut North

10 Betsy Fisher A standout among Washington's often staid clothiers, this small boutique carries the creations of young American designers from across the country. ♦ M-Sa. 1224 Connecticut Ave NW (between Jefferson Pl and N St). 785.1975 ♿ Metro: Dupont Circle

11 Bacchus ★★$$ With a new tentlike decor—bolts of striped fabric are draped across the ceiling—as fresh as its food, this Middle Eastern dining spot serves excellent goodies in a charming little dining room. The *baba ganooj* is perfection, and the phyllo stuffed with meat or cheese are a delight. ♦ Middle Eastern ♦ M-F lunch and dinner; Sa dinner. Reservations recommended. 1827 Jefferson Pl NW (between Connecticut Ave and 19th St). 785.0734. Metro: Dupont Circle

---

When the 14-story Cairo apartment building (still standing on Q Street Northwest, near 17th Street) was built in 1894, it exceeded the reach of Washington's municipal firefighting equipment. It also exceeded the height of the Capitol building. Soon after, Congress passed a law that no building would exceed 130 feet, abolishing the city's skyscraper potential.

Wandering Washington's Literary Lanes

Washington's primary concern may be government, but its literary dimension—past and present—also holds a place of prominence. Book lovers can enjoy a truly capital experience by following the footsteps of legendary writers where they worked and played. Some sites have since been replaced or are still private residences, leaving your imagination to create images from the past. Other sites, like the **Library of Congress** and the **Hay-Adams Hotel**, invite you in for a novel experience.

Among the literary greats who resided in upper northwest Washington was Randall Jarrell, who lived at 3916 Jenifer Street Northwest (between 39th St and Reno Rd) while poetry consultant to the **Library of Congress** from 1956 to 1958. Some in the neighborhood gained a reputation for hosting literary salons or throwing grand bashes. Classical scholar Edith Hamilton, author of *The Greek Way,* entertained in grand style at 2448 Massachusetts Avenue Northwest (between Sheridan Cir and Waterside Dr). The renowned columnist and founder of *The New Republic* magazine, Walter Lippmann, held an annual New Year's Eve party at 3525 Woodley Road Northwest (between 35th and 36th Sts).

No Washington neighborhood is richer in literary history than **Georgetown.** Francis Scott Key, author of the *Star Spangled Banner,* lived at 3518 M Street, but his home was torn down to make way for the **Key Bridge** (named in his honor). Louisa May Alcott resided at 30th and M Streets (now a gas station) while working at the Union Hotel Hospital during the Civil War. She moved away after contracting a case of typhoid and pneumonia, but not before acquiring the material for *Hospital Sketches.* Sinclair Lewis, Nobel Prize winner and author of many satirical novels, including *Main Street* and *Babbitt,* lived at 3028 Q Street (between 30th and 31st Sts). Nearby 3106 P Street (between 31st St and Wisconsin Ave) was home to Pulitzer Prize winner Katherine Anne Porter, author of acclaimed short stories and the novel *Ship of Fools.* Poet and librarian of Congress, Archibald MacLeish, resided at 1520 33rd Street (between P St and Volta Pl); and columnist Drew Pearson, whose daily column was titled "Washington Merry-Go-Round," made his home at 2820 Dumbarton Street (between 28th and 29th Sts).

Not every writer's footsteps can be traced to Georgetown, however. Clare Boothe Luce—playwright, magazine editor (for *Vogue* and *Vanity Fair*), and congresswoman—lived first at the grand Wardman Park apartment building, now part of the **Marriott Wardman Park Hotel** (2660 Woodley Rd NW, between Connecticut Ave and 29th St) and then at **The Watergate Hotel** (2650 Virginia Ave NW, between New Hampshire Ave and Rock Creek and Potomac Pkwy).

In the early 1960s Tom Wolfe, author of *Bonfire of the Vanities* and *A Man in Full,* paid $85 a month for a one-bedroom apartment at 1343 Connecticut Avenue Northwest (between N St and Dupont Cir). Frances Hodgson Burnett, beloved children's book author of *Little Lord Fauntleroy* and *The Secret Garden,* gained a reputation as a scintillating hostess of literary salons in her mansion at 1770 Massachusetts Avenue Northwest (between 17th and 18th Sts). Her husband, Dr. Swan Burnett, operated on James Thurber after he suffered an eye injury. (James Thurber was the writer and *New Yorker* cartoonist who immortalized the secret life of Walter Mitty.) The Thurbers spent their winters at 2031 I Street Northwest (between 20th and 21st Sts), on the same street where the poet Stephen Vincent Benet was born.

Among the African-American writers who took up residence near **Howard University** are Paul Laurence Dunbar (at 321 U St NW, between Third and Fourth Sts), Jean Toomer (at 1341 U St NW, between 13th and 14th Sts), and Langston Hughes at the 12th St YMCA (1816 12th St NW, between S and T Sts). One of the world's best African-American collections is at the **Moorland-Spingarn Research Center** (806.7239) at **Howard University.**

Walt Whitman came to Washington during the Civil War to care for his brother and wounded soldiers. He took a room downtown at 1407 L Street Northwest (between 14th St and Vermont Ave) and then at 1205 M Street Northwest (between 12th and 13th Sts). He was fired from his job at the Department of the Interior after his supervisor discovered *Leaves of Grass* in his desk drawer.

Every literary tour of Washington should include a stop at the **Hay-Adams Hotel** (800 16th St NW, at H St, 638.6600), once home to America's greatest man of letters, Henry Adams, author of *The Education of Henry Adams.* He and good friend John Hay—also an author, President Lincoln's private secretary, and secretary of state to Presidents McKinley and Roosevelt—built adjoining houses across from **Lafayette Square.** The twin houses were taken down in 1927 and replaced by the elegant hotel now standing (see page 77). The **Willard Hotel** (14th St NW and Pennsylvania Ave, 628.9100) also has its place in literary history. Julia Ward Howe wrote *The Battle Hymn of the Republic* as a guest. Nathaniel Hawthorne took up residence while reporting on the Civil War for *Atlantic Monthly.* Mark Twain dined there and Emily Dickinson visited.

Neighboring **Chinatown** is home to DC's main public library. An austere building of steel and glass, the **Martin Luther King Jr. Library** (901 G St NW, at Ninth St, 727.1111) was designed by **Mies van der Rohe.**

To the northeast Marjorie Kinnan Rawlings, author of the children's classic, *The Yearling,* grew up at 1221 Newton Street Northeast (between 13th and 12th Sts) and attended Western High School (now Duke Ellington).

12 Sam & Harry's ★★★$$$ This steak house is giving **Morton's of Chicago** in Georgetown a run for its money. The beef is superb, and the chicken, fish, and other dishes are more than adequate. The service is outstanding, and the dining room—outfitted in dark wood and brass—manages to be comfortable and classy. Another plus: It has one of the nicest bars around. ♦ Steak house ♦ M-F lunch and dinner; Sa dinner. 1200 19th St NW (at M St). 296.4333 ᵭ Metro: Dupont Circle

12 Georgetown Seafood Grill ★★$$$ A Georgetown original, this classic seafood spot moved here in 1998. Along with some of the best crab cakes in the city, it serves an excellent catch of the day—like yellowfin tuna with lemon-thyme butter or grilled Atlantic salmon with hot scallion and sesame sauce. ♦ Seafood ♦ M-F lunch and dinner; Sa-Su dinner. 1200 19th St NW (at M St). 530.4430 ᵭ Metro: Dupont Circle

13 The Palm ★★$$$$ Regular patrons, including high-powered lobbyists and sports figures, prize this institution's clubhouse atmosphere and steak-and-potatoes fare. The lobster is also superb. Caricatures of famous personages, scribbled by artist Jame Hille, dominate the walls. ♦ American ♦ M-F lunch and dinner; Sa-Su dinner. Reservations required. 1225 19th St NW (at Jefferson Pl). 293.9091 ᵭ Metro: Dupont Circle

13 C.F. Folks This is perhaps the city's best carryout joint; its menu ranges from Mexican to French and its clientele is a bipartisan blend of messengers and lobbyists. Arrive either early or late to avoid the worst of the lunch crush. If the few sidewalk tables are occupied, take your lunch to Dupont Circle and watch the people parade. ♦ M-F 11:45AM-2:30PM. 1225 19th St NW (at Jefferson Pl). 293.0162 ᵭ Metro: Dupont Circle

14 i Ricchi ★★$$$$ Though critics have charged that the authentic Tuscan fare here has stumbled in recent years, the eatery's high ceilings, large columns, and golden, mural-decorated stucco walls help create an enchanting dining experience. Rabbit cooked with rosemary and sage and garnished with fried polenta is one of its most often requested specials. The homemade Florentine almond and hazelnut cookies are perfect for dunking. ♦ Italian ♦ M-F lunch and dinner; Sa dinner. Reservations recommended. 1220 19th St NW (between M and N Sts). 835.0459 ᵭ Metro: Dupont Circle

15 Olsson's Books & Records One of DC's best haunts for bibliophiles, this top-flight, full-service shop also offers a wide selection of pop, jazz, country, blues, and classical CDs and cassettes. ♦ M-Sa 10AM-9PM; Su noon-6PM. 1307 19th St NW (between N St and Dupont Cir). 785.1133 ᵭ Metro: Dupont Circle. Also at: Numerous locations throughout the area

16 Lawson's Gourmet Shop here for great finds in take-out food, from salads and breads to pastries and wines. Catering and delivery services also are offered. ♦ M-Sa. 1350 Connecticut Ave NW (at Dupont Cir). 775.0400 ᵭ Metro: Dupont Circle. Also at: 1350 I St NW (between 13th and 14th Sts). 789.0800. Metro: McPherson Sq

16 Proper Topper All kinds of hats—from berets and fedoras to dress hats and straw boaters—fill this chic shop. There are toppers for men, women, and children. ♦ M-Sa; Su noon-6PM. 1350 Connecticut Ave NW (at Dupont Cir). 842.3055. Metro: Dupont Circle. Also at: Union Station, 50 Massachusetts Ave NE (at First St), West Hall. 371.0639. Metro: Union Station

17 Vertigo Books Left-of-center politics are the dominant theme at this funky, friendly store, housed in a former bank. Check out the immense vault door leading to a back storeroom. ♦ M-Sa; Su noon-5PM. 1337 Connecticut Ave NW (between N St and Dupont Cir). 429.9272. Metro: Dupont Circle

---

Restaurants/Clubs: Red   **Hotels:** Blue

Shops/ 🍴 Outdoors: Green   **Sights/Culture:** Black

17 Mr. Eagan's ★$ One of the few true dives in Washington, it's dark, cheap, and filled with regulars. There's plenty of bar food if you're hungry, but basically this is just a good, old-fashioned watering hole. ♦ American ♦ Daily lunch and dinner. 1343 Connecticut Ave NW (between N St and Dupont Cir). 331.9768 ♿ Metro: Dupont Circle

17 The Big Hunt ★$ There's nothing particularly fancy about this bar/restaurant, but the food is better than at most such places. The service is casual but prompt, the jukebox outstanding. There's a private room for parties. ♦ American ♦ Daily dinner. 1345 Connecticut Ave NW (between N St and Dupont Cir). 785.2333 ♿ Metro: Dupont Circle

18 Euram Building Designed in 1971 by **Hartman-Cox,** this is one of Washington's more imaginative contemporary buildings. Its eight slick stories of brick, glass, and prestressed concrete surround an inner courtyard. ♦ 21 Dupont Cir NW (between 19th St and New Hampshire Ave) ♿ Metro: Dupont Circle

19 Historical Society of Washington, DC (Heurich Mansion) Christian Heurich was a German immigrant who achieved tremendous wealth in the beer industry during the 19th century. His legacy to Washington is this turreted, 31-room Romanesque Revival mansion. With much of its opulent interior left intact, the building gives modern-day visitors an accurate picture of the life of the upper class around the late 1890s. The building also houses the city's historical society, whose wonderful library includes books, clippings, detailed journals, photos, and other artifacts limning Washington over the years. In summer, pack a lunch and picnic in the lovely garden. ♦ Admission. W-Sa. Group tours by appointment. 1307 New Hampshire Ave NW (between 20th St and Dupont Cir). 785.2068; www.hswdc.org ♿ Metro: Dupont Circle

20 Hampshire Hotel $$ Although not as lavishly decorated as others in the neighborhood, this hotel has 92 comfortable rooms and a warm, responsive staff. The suites are spacious, with stocked wet bars and sitting rooms. There is a dining room; however, the hotel's location puts guests within walking distance of Georgetown's many fine restaurants. Two floors of nonsmoking rooms are available, and children under 12 stay free. ♦ 1310 New Hampshire Ave NW (at 20th St). 296.7600, 800/368.5691; fax 293.2476 ♿ Metro: Dupont Circle

21 Embassy Square Suites Hotel $$$ An air of Washington elegance is apparent in the lobby's oil portraits, fine woods, and high ceilings. The 250 suites are available in three sizes: junior, one-bedroom, and two-bedroom; ask for one overlooking the garden courtyard (which features a swimming pool). Other pluses: a multilingual staff, underground parking, and a restaurant and nightclub, as well as a stocked kitchen and minibar in every suite. Nonsmoking rooms are available, and children under 16 stay free. Ask about weekend specials. ♦ 2000 N St NW (at 20th St). 659.9000, 800/424.2999; fax 429.9546; www.staydc.com ♿ Metro: Dupont Circle

22 Marston Luce Eighteenth- and 19th-century American folk art—weather vanes, antique garden furniture, decoys, carvings, signs, and paintings—are sold here. ♦ M-Sa. 1314 21st St NW (between N and O Sts). 775.9460 ♿ Metro: Dupont Circle

23 Second Story Books DC's leading source for used books is lined with floor-to-ceiling shelves of old, rare, and out-of-print editions—all at reasonable prices. A search service and appraisals are also available. ♦ Daily 10AM-10PM. 2000 P St NW (at 20th St). 659.8884 ♿ Metro: Dupont Circle. Also at: 4836 Bethesda Ave (between Woodmont Ave and Arlington Rd), Bethesda, Maryland. 301/656.0170. Metro: Bethesda; 12160 Parklawn Dr (at Wilkins Ave), Rockville, Maryland. 301/770.0477

23 12" Dance Records If you're having trouble finding this place, follow your ears: On weekends you can hear dance music booming out of the club's second-story windows. This is where Washington's deejays come to scope out new material. ♦ M-Th, Sa noon-9PM; F noon-midnight; Su 2-7PM. 2010 P St NW (between 20th and Hopkins Sts). 659.2010 ♿ Metro: Dupont Circle

23 Al Tiramisù ★★$$ Though the food is quite good, the real charm here is the ebullient, familial atmosphere enhanced by chef Luigi Diotaiuti. As testimony to his skill, Diotaiuti is routinely asked to cater Italian Cultural Society functions. Try homemade gnocchi, grilled portobello mushrooms,

carpaccio, or spinach-ricotta *agnolotti.*
♦ Italian ♦ Daily lunch and dinner. 2014 P St
NW (between 20th and Hopkins Sts).
467.4466. Metro: Dupont Circle

23 Pesce ★★$$$ In a town filled with steak
houses, this small, casual seafood spot is a
welcome alternative. The colorful
Mediterranean menu changes daily, but
always features tastefully presented fish
dishes. Pan-seared baby flounder is a sure
bet. There's also a well-stocked market on the
premises. ♦ Seafood ♦ Daily lunch and dinner.
2016 P St NW (at Hopkins St). 466.FISH &
Metro: Dupont Circle

23 Sala Thai ★★$ Splendidly authentic Thai
food, right down to the ultrasweet iced tea, is
served in a cool, neon-lit basement room. You
won't go wrong with the pad thai. This place is
a gem, particularly at lunchtime, when the
service is more consistently attentive and the
noise level more bearable. ♦ Thai ♦ Daily
lunch and dinner. 2016 P St NW (at Hopkins
St). 872.1144 & Metro: Dupont Circle

24 Pan Asian Noodles and Grill ★★$ A real
find, this kitchen turns out the best noodles in
town. Try the "drunken noodles" (a plate of
steamed flat noodles topped with a stir-fry of
minced chicken in a spicy basil sauce). The
servings are remarkably large, given the low
prices. ♦ Chinese ♦ M-Sa lunch and dinner; Su
dinner. Reservations recommended. 2020 P St
NW (between Hopkins and 21st Sts).
872.8889. Metro: Dupont Circle

24 Cafe Japone ★$$ If you've never tried
sumo-video sushi, or sushi pizza, this is the
place to do so. But beware the lackluster
service. ♦ Japanese ♦ Daily dinner.
Reservations recommended. 2032 P St NW
(between Hopkins and 21st Sts). 223.1573.
Metro: Dupont Circle

25 Obelisk ★★★$$$$ This Italian dining
room serves innovative fare as starkly elegant
as the setting. The real gems include ravioli
with eggplant in a light tomato sauce, grilled
veal medaillons served with morels, and duck
breast served in a simple thyme–duck stock.
The well-selected wine list is reasonable
and the waiters, extremely knowledgeable.
♦ Italian ♦ Tu-Sa dinner. Reservations
recommended. 2029 P St NW (between 20th
and 21st Sts). 872.1180. Metro: Dupont Circle

25 Pizzeria Paradiso ★★$$ Although it
shares **Obelisk**'s address, this place is miles
apart in ambience. Gourmet pizza is what this
place does and does well. It isn't cheap—a
12-inch cheese pizza runs about $12—but the
crusts are remarkably flavorful, the toppings
fresh and abundant. Be warned, though: Long
lines form here on weekends. ♦ Italian ♦ Daily
lunch and dinner. 2029 P St NW (between
20th and 21st Sts). 223.1245. Metro: Dupont
Circle

26 Backstage Performing arts–related books,
scripts, sheet music, and other publications
can be found here. Ready-made and custom
theatrical costumes are sold and rented;
dancewear and stage makeup are available as
well. ♦ M-W, F-Sa; Th 10AM-8PM. 2101 P St
NW (at 21st St). 775.1488 & Metro: Dupont
Circle

26 Radisson Barcelo Hotel $$$ This hotel's
best feature is its lovely location, west of
Dupont Circle on the verge of **Rock Creek
Park.** An outdoor pool, a sauna, an exercise
room, and valet and concierge services are
among the amenities. Nonsmoking
accommodations are available among its 297
rooms. The **Gabriel** restaurant has upscale,
night-club decor and an inventive
Southwestern American menu. ♦ 2121 P St
NW (between 21st and 22nd Sts). 293.3100,
800/843.6664; fax 857.0134;
www.radisson.com & Metro: Dupont Circle

27 Brickskeller ★$ Beer mavens worldwide
rave about this place because it gives them
exactly what they want: hundreds of brands of
beer in a basement pub conducive to heavy
drinking. The food, however, is unremarkable.
♦ American ♦ M-F lunch and dinner; Sa-Su
dinner. 1523 22nd St NW (between P and Q
Sts). 293.1885 & Metro: Dupont Circle

28 Buffalo Bridge Spanning **Rock Creek Park,**
this impressive structure, open to cars and
pedestrians alike, sports aqueductlike arches
and four handsome buffaloes sculpted by A.
Phimister Proctor. From Rock Creek Parkway,
you can see the Indian heads (in full war
bonnet) that support the arches. The bridge
was designed in 1914 by **Glenn** and **Bedford
Brown.** ♦ 23rd and Q Sts NW. Metro: Dupont
Circle

29 Sheridan Circle The statues of Union
general Philip H. Sheridan and his favorite
horse, Rienzi, were sculpted in 1909 by
Gutzon Borglum, creator of Mount Rushmore.
Along the outside curb in the southeast
quadrant sits a small memorial to Chilean
ambassador Orlando Letelier and aide Ronni
Karpen Moffitt, who were killed here in 1976
when a remote-controlled bomb blew up their
car—a crime for which Chilean secret police
and army officials were eventually held
responsible. ♦ Metro: Dupont Circle

30 Addison/Ripley Gallery Ltd. Works by
contemporary American painters and
sculptors, including local artists Edith Kuhnle,

Rebecca Cross, and Greg Hannan, grace these walls. ♦ Tu-Sa. 9 Hillyer Ct NW (just east of Florida Ave). 328.2332 ♿ Metro: Dupont Circle

31 Cosmos Club (Townsend Mansion) A railway baron's wife commissioned this palace, designed at the turn of the century by the architectural firm **Carrère and Hastings.** Its facade is the city's most ostentatious. Today, it's the home of a private club for achievers in the arts, politics, and science. A good-ol'-boy holdout, the club finally got around to admitting female members in 1988. ♦ 2121 Massachusetts Ave NW (between Q St and Florida Ave). 387.7783 ♿ Metro: Dupont Circle

The **Phillips** Collection
America's first museum of modern art

32 Phillips Collection In 1921, when Duncan and Marjorie Phillips opened two rooms of their four-story brownstone to the public, they created the first American museum of modern art. Duncan had already amassed an exemplary collection, starting with American Impressionists and expanding into the French Impressionists and Post-Impressionists. Eventually, the Phillipses' holdings spanned not only European and American Modernism but also precursors of Modernism, such as Goya, El Greco, and Delacroix. Today, this jewel of a museum preserves a private-home atmosphere, and art lovers can stroll through the rooms or take advantage of the many couches and chairs to rest and admire the paintings. Art students posted in each room can answer any questions.

Works by such artists as Degas, Monet, Van Gogh, Cézanne, Bonnard, Klee, Matisse, Braque, Rothko, and Renoir fill most of the Phillipses' original home and an adjoining building (added in 1960). Following the Phillipses' wishes, the museum sponsors publications, loans to other museums, and special exhibitions. The museum's most well-known painting is Renoir's *Luncheon of the Boating Party.* The restored **Goh Annex,** which doubled the facility's exhibition space, allows the permanent collection to remain on view during temporary shows. The firm **Hornblower & Marshall** designed the original building in 1897. It was remodeled in 1915 by **McKim, Mead, and White,** and restored in 1984 by **Arthur Cotton Moore Associates.**

Gallery talks take place at 12:30PM the first and third Thursday of each month. Free Sunday-afternoon concerts are given at 5PM September through May. A gift shop and cafe are on the premises. ♦ Donation Tu-F;

admission Sa-Su. Tu-W, F-Sa; Th 10AM-8:30PM; Su noon-7PM. Tours: W, Sa 2PM; call to arrange group tours a month in advance. 1600 21st St NW (at Q St). Information 387.2151 ♿ Metro: Dupont Circle

33 Anderson House/Society of the Cincinnati In 1783, a group of US Revolutionary War officers facing demobilization proposed forming an elite organization (the Society of the Cincinnati) to preserve their camaraderie. The group survived, though at the time it was regarded as undemocratic, even potentially conspiratorial. George Washington's membership, however, helped withstand such attacks. The name derives from Lucius Quinctius Cincinnatus, a Roman leader whose life Washington's paralleled. (The city of Cincinnati, Ohio, was named by a member of the society.) Membership is limited to male descendants—usually first-born—of those original officers, with a few exceptions; even the French have a chapter, due to the role they played in the Revolution.

Behind the stately Palladian facade of the society's headquarters is one of the city's finest town houses, whose opulent interiors contain artistic treasures from the US, Europe, and Asia, including society portraits by such famous American painters as Gilbert Stuart, John Trumbull, Daniel Huntington, and Cecilia Beaux. The **Harold Leonard Stuart Memorial Library** of reference works on the American Revolution is open to the public. Walk-in self-guided tours are available; guided tours are provided for groups of 20 or more. ♦ Free. Tu-Sa 1-4PM. 2118 Massachusetts Ave NW (at Q St). 785.2040 ♿ Metro: Dupont Circle

34 The Westin Fairfax Washington, DC $$$$ Despite several name changes in recent years—from **Ritz-Carlton** to **Luxury Collection** to **Westin**—this property has remained a constant class act. (It was also the childhood home of Vice President Al Gore during the 1950s, when his father was a US senator.) American antiques and reproductions decorate these 230 rooms: Such niceties as hand-carved mahogany headboards and embroidered English chintz bedspreads are the norm. Valet parking, a multilingual staff, secretarial assistance, and 24-hour room service are among the hotel's many extras. The marvelously intimate alcoves in the **Fairfax Bar** are perfect venues for cocktails, light lunches, and afternoon tea. A formal dining room (see below) serves three meals daily. Nonsmoking rooms are available, and children under 12 stay free. ♦ 2100 Massachusetts Ave NW (at 21st St). 293.2100, 800/325.3589; fax 736.1420 ♿ Metro: Dupont Circle

Within The Westin Fairfax Washington, DC:

Jockey Club ★★$$$$ Private-club elegance, a staff schooled in the grand old manner, and a refined continental menu characterize this dining room. The soft-shell crabs and sautéed John Dory with asparagus and fresh truffles are winners. This was a bipartisan favorite of both Jacqueline Kennedy and Nancy Reagan. ♦ Continental ♦ Daily breakfast, lunch, and dinner. Reservations recommended; jacket and tie required. 835.2100 &

35 Blaine Mansion A three-time presidential hopeful during the late 1800s, James Blaine used to occupy this Victorian fortress (now used as office space), designed by **John Fraser** in 1881. ♦ 2000 Massachusetts Ave NW (at 20th St). Metro: Dupont Circle

36 Starbucks While the coffee drinks are excellent and the beans for sale fresh and aromatic, the atmosphere is little better than an upscale McDonald's; there's virtually nowhere to sit. ♦ M-F 6:30AM-10PM; Sa-Su 7AM-10PM. 1501 Connecticut Ave NW (at Dupont Cir). 588.1280 & Metro: Dupont Circle. Also at: Numerous locations throughout the city

36 Beadazzled Besides affordable jewelry, this friendly store sells glass, plastic, ceramic, and metal beads in all shapes and sizes; jewelry-making tools; stringing materials; and books on how to put it all together to make a masterpiece. ♦ M-Sa; Su noon-6PM. 1507 Connecticut Ave NW (between Dupont Cir and Q St). 265.2323 & Metro: Dupont Circle

36 Kramerbooks & afterwords, A café ★ $$ This institution specializes in hardcovers and paperbacks, a little quiche, and a split of wine. The extensive selection of books fills two rooms that are connected to a cozy cafe on one side, and a live music venue, **afterwords,** on the other. Known as a pick-up joint for the literati, it's open 24 hours on weekends, and live music is performed Wednesday through Saturday evenings. ♦ American ♦ Daily breakfast, lunch, and dinner. 1517 Connecticut Ave NW (between Dupont Cir and Q St). Bookstore 387.1400; cafe 387.3825 & Metro: Dupont Circle

37 Raku ★★$ This self-proclaimed Asian diner serves mainly Japanese and Chinese fusion fare with fast service. Especially good for lunch, it turns out a fine yakatori. ♦ Asian

♦ Daily lunch and dinner. 1900 Q St NW (at 19th St). 265.7258 & Metro: Dupont Circle. Also at: 7240 Woodmont Ave (between Bethesda Ave and Elm St), Bethesda, Maryland. 301/718.8680. Metro: Bethesda

38 Kathleen Ewing Gallery Specializing in 19th- and 20th-century masterwork photography, this gallery holds monthly exhibitions and represents more than two dozen American and European photographers. ♦ W-Sa. 1609 Connecticut Ave NW (between Q and 20th Sts). 328.0955. Metro: Dupont Circle

38 Melody Record Shop A welcome relief from the chains, this connoisseur's shop stocks all manner of CDs and tapes, from rock, blues, and jazz to reggae and vocals. ♦ Daily. 1623 Connecticut Ave NW (between Q and 20th Sts). 232.4002 & Metro: Dupont Circle

38 Lambda Rising One of the best gay-lesbian bookstores in the country, this place offers a large selection of nonfiction and fiction titles. Check out the creative window displays. ♦ Daily 10AM-midnight. 1625 Connecticut Ave NW (between Q and 20th Sts). 462.6969 & Metro: Dupont Circle

39 Sostanza ★$$ Formerly **Trattoria "al Sole,"** this new Italian restaurant is known for its pasta dishes and such Florentine specialties as thick steak seared over a wood fire. However, the excellent bread and side dishes, like fried zucchini, often outstrip the steaks. ♦ Italian ♦ M-F lunch and dinner; Sa dinner. Reservations recommended. 1606 20th St NW (between Q St and Hillyer Pl). 667.0047 & Metro: Dupont Circle

The Columbia Heights neighborhood near Adams-Morgan originally had streets named for major universities: Yale, Harvard, Princeton, Columbia, and Dartmouth. In the early 1900s, when the city began alphabetizing streets, Yale was changed to Fairmont, Princeton to Girard, and Dartmouth to Lamont. Harvard fit into the grid and was retained, Princeton was changed from street to place, and Columbia Street became Columbia Road, a major thoroughfare.

39 Childe Harold ★$$ Country star Emmylou Harris performed at this local bar and DC institution before hitting the big time. Although they no longer feature live music, you can get burgers downstairs and more formal fare upstairs. The patio is pleasant in warm weather, and there's a private room for parties. But no matter where you sit, the waiters have a tendency to vanish mysteriously. ♦ American ♦ M-F lunch and dinner; Sa-Su brunch and dinner. 1610 20th St NW (between Q St and Hillyer Pl). 483.6702 & Metro: Dupont Circle

40 Xando ★★$ Whether you read it "Zando" or "Ex and Oh," (management's playing coy), this funky coffee bar is packed on weekends with Gen-Xers. Besides coffee, light fare and alcohol also are served here. Ever popular here are s'mores: graham crackers, chocolate, and marshmallows, which you roast over a miniature flame pot. ♦ American ♦ Daily 6AM-1AM. 1647 20th St NW (at R St). 332.6364 & Metro: Dupont Circle. Also at: 1350 Connecticut Ave NW (at Dupont Circle). 296.9341 & Metro: Dupont Circle

41 La Tomate ★$$ Indulge in fresh, well-prepared Italian food at reasonable prices. The huge windows are ideal for people watching, and tables are set outdoors for alfresco summer dining. ♦ Italian ♦ Daily lunch and dinner. 1701 Connecticut Ave NW (at R St). 667.5505 & Metro: Dupont Circle

41 Mystery Books The perfect place to pick up fun vacation reading, this place exemplifies what a bookstore *should* be: The staff knows its stuff, they let you browse for as long as you want, and they most probably have what you want in stock. The shop hosts readings and book signings; a free mail-order catalog is also available. ♦ M-Sa; Su noon-5PM. 1715 Connecticut Ave NW (between R and S Sts). 483.1600, 800/955.2279 & Metro: Dupont Circle

When he was called a "two-faced man" in a debate with Stephen A. Douglas, future president Abraham Lincoln replied, "If I had another face, do you think I would wear this one?"

42 Ginza Futons, kimonos, shoji screens, lamps, jewelry, porcelain, and other typically graceful Japanese crafts are sold here. ♦ M-Sa; Su noon-6PM. 1721 Connecticut Ave NW (between R and S Sts). 331.7991 & Metro: Dupont Circle

42 City Lights of China ★★★$ Although it looks unassuming—its light green walls are bare save for one framed celebrity-patron photo (of the Rolling Stones!)—this place just may be the best Chinese eatery in town. The ingredients are always fresh, the portions large, and the preparation (especially of shrimp and scallops) expert. The always perfect Peking duck, eggplant with garlic, and salt-baked shrimp, are standouts on a huge menu. ♦ Chinese ♦ M-F lunch and dinner; Sa-Su dinner. Reservations recommended. 1731 Connecticut Ave NW (between R and S Sts). 265.6688. Metro: Dupont Circle

43 Kulturas Books and Records Most bibliophiles love secondhand stores, and this is one of the neighborhood's best, specializing in books on the humanities. ♦ Daily 11AM-8PM. 1741 Connecticut Ave NW (between R and S Sts). 462.2541 & Metro: Dupont Circle

The Newsroom

43 News Room In a town of diplomats, politicians, and media junkies, this shop's comprehensive collection of out-of-town and foreign newspapers and magazines is a local necessity. ♦ M-F 7AM-10PM; Sa 7AM-11PM; Su 7AM-9PM. 1753 Connecticut Ave NW (at S St). 332.1489 & Metro: Dupont Circle

44 Ruth's Chris Steakhouse ★★$$$ Carnivore heaven, this dining room gives its chief rivals—**The Palm** and **Morton's of Chicago**—some serious competition. The prices here are a bit more reasonable; the atmosphere, less exclusive and clubby. ♦ Steak house ♦ Daily lunch and dinner. 1801 Connecticut Ave NW (at S St). 797.0033 & Metro: Dupont Circle. Also at: 2231 Crystal Dr (at S 23rd St), Arlington. 703/979.7275 & Metro: Crystal City

45 Friends Meeting of Washington Designed in 1930 by **Walter H. Price,** this simple, slate-roofed stone building, reminiscent of a country cottage, eloquently embodies the Quakers' disdain for ostentation. President Herbert Hoover and his wife worshiped here. ♦ 2111 Florida Ave NW (between Decatur and Phelps Pls). 483.3310 ♿ Metro: Dupont Circle

46 Geoffrey Diner Gallery This is one of the city's top showcases for furniture and artwork in the American and English Arts and Crafts style, which was popular at the turn of the century. You might find an exhibit of exquisite Tiffany lamps or furnishings by the famous California designers Greene & Greene. ♦ By appointment only. 1730 21st St NW (between R St and Florida Ave). 483.5005. Metro: Dupont Circle

47 Odéon ★$$ The portions are large, and the pasta is well prepared at this funky restaurant. The drawback is that the tables are too close together. On weekends, when the restaurant gets crowded, you may be an unwilling eavesdropper on the dinner conversations around you. ♦ Italian ♦ M-F lunch and dinner; Sa-Su dinner. 1714 Connecticut Ave NW (between R and S Sts). 328.6228 ♿ Metro: Dupont Circle

47 Teaism ★$ Stark, yet serene, this two-level teahouse serves all types of teas—black, oolong, green, and more. The iced mint tea is a bracing refresher on a hot day. Also available are Japanese bento box assortments, kabobs, hamburgers, stir-fry dishes, and desserts. ♦ International ♦ Daily. 2009 R St NW (at Connecticut Ave). 667.3827. Metro: Dupont Circle

48 Gallery K Contemporary European and American paintings, sculptures, and drawings, as well as American folk art and Native American works, are collected here. ♦ Tu-Sa. 2010 R St NW (between Connecticut Ave and 21st St). 234.0339. Metro: Dupont Circle

48 Gallery Affrica Traditional African art—masks, figures, pottery, textiles, and beadwork—is the focus of this gallery. ♦ W-Sa noon-6PM. 2010½ R St NW (between Connecticut Ave and 21st St). 745.7272. Metro: Dupont Circle

48 Marsha Mateyka Gallery L.C. Armstrong, Aline Feldman, Robert Motherwell, and William T. Wiley are some of the artists

represented in this space, where contemporary American and European paintings, sculpture, and works on paper are on display. ♦ W-Sa, and by appointment. 2012 R St NW (between Connecticut Ave and 21st St). 328.0088. Metro: Dupont Circle

49 Anton Gallery Owners Gail Enns and John Figura feature works by Washington artists such as Bob Barnard, Tom Nakashima, Mary Annella Frank, and Reid McIntyre. ♦ W-Su noon-5PM. 2108 R St NW (between 21st St and Florida Ave). 328.0828. Metro: Dupont Circle

49 Fondo del Sol Visual Arts and Media Center This center showcases works by Latin American, Native American, Caribbean, and African-American artists. Video presentations accompany the exhibits. ♦ W-Sa 12:30-5:30PM. 2112 R St NW (between 21st St and Florida Ave). 483.2777 ♿ Metro: Dupont Circle

50 Restaurant Nora ★★★$$$$ High-quality American cuisine—homegrown herbs, organic vegetables, and additive-free meats—is served in a lovely, country-style dining room and a glass-enclosed courtyard. Try the rockfish with lobster mashed potatoes or pork with cumin. Although it's a favorite among the famous, from *The Washington Post*'s Ben Bradlee to President Clinton, the atmosphere and service remain decidedly democratic with a small "d." ♦ American ♦ Daily dinner. Reservations recommended. 2132 Florida Ave NW (at R St). 462.5143. Metro: Dupont Circle

51 Decatur Terrace Marking the terminus of 22nd Street is a delightful staircase and fountain. ♦ Decatur Pl NW (between Florida and Massachusetts Aves). Metro: Dupont Circle

THE TEXTILE MUSEUM

52 Textile Museum In 1896, George H. Myers purchased an Oriental rug for his college room and began a lifelong fascination with the art of textiles. In 1925, he turned his home and rich collection—now more than 14,000 textiles and 1,300 rugs—into this privately endowed showcase. The articles on display come from all over the world—the Mediterranean, North Africa, the Near and Far East, and Central and South America. His collection is now housed in this building designed in 1916 by **John Russell Pope.** The museum's 7,000-book resource library on textiles is open from 10AM until 2PM Wednesday through Saturday. By appointment, museum curators will analyze and appraise your textiles. The gift shop, housed in Myers's old library, offers textiles, publications, and more. Call for information on special exhibitions, lectures, and workshops. ♦ Donation. M-Sa; Su 1-5PM. 2320 S St NW (between Phelps Pl and 24th St). 667.0441 & Metro: Dupont Circle

53 Woodrow Wilson House This National Historic Landmark in Wilson's onetime home commemorates our 28th president, who created the Federal Reserve Board and participated in the establishment of the League of Nations. Wilson's distinguished career—as author of nine books, college professor, president of Princeton University, and governor of New Jersey—is covered in exhibitions and photographs. The museum sponsors special events, including walking tours of the surrounding Kalorama neighborhood, a Christmas open house 1920s style, and Veterans Day services. The house was built in 1915 by **Waddy B. Wood.** ♦ Admission. Tu-Su. 2340 S St NW (between Phelps Pl and 24th St). 387.4062 & Metro: Dupont Circle

54 Japanese Embassy With its iron gates and austere courtyard, the original chancery building, built in 1932, manages to look at once Neo-Georgian and Japanese. Although the embassy isn't open to the public, a branch of it, the **Japan Information and Cultural Center** (1155 21st St NW, between L and M Sts, 939.6949), hosts art shows as well as a lecture series. ♦ 2520 Massachusetts Ave NW (between Sheridan Cir and Waterside Dr). Metro: Dupont Circle

55 Islamic Center A collaborative effort by the various Islamic nations that maintain embassies in Washington, this cultural and religious center is one of the most interesting sights in town. The white limestone building is filled with fine craft works by Middle Eastern artisans, including an ebony pulpit inlaid with ivory; stained glass windows; and Persian carpets. The mosque, in the center of a courtyard, faces Mecca, and a 160-foot minaret rises above the complex. Among the most active in the country, the congregation comprises Moslems from more than 40 countries. The center publishes informative literature and conducts lectures; a bookstore is on the premises. Tours may be arranged by request. ♦ 2551 Massachusetts Ave NW (at Belmont Rd). 332.8343 & Metro: Dupont Circle

56 The Lindens Designed in 1754 by **Robert Hooper,** this New England–style Georgian house is, in fact, the oldest in Washington. But it didn't have a DC address until 1934, when it was disassembled and moved from its original spot in Danvers, Massachusetts. So, according to how you phrase it, the runner-up, Georgetown's **Old Stone House,** could get

the title on a technicality. ♦ 2401 Kalorama Rd NW (at Kalorama Cir). Metro: Dupont Circle

57 Taft Bridge Inn $ This Georgian-style bed-and-breakfast is a charming alternative to cookie-cutter grand hotels. Each of the 13 guest rooms is individually decorated with antiques of a particular period or style—Victorian, Colonial, French Provincial. Four rooms have private baths, six have fireplaces. Guests also have use of a paneled drawing room, porticoed porch, and garden. Amenities include laundry and housekeeping services, parking, and complimentary breakfast. ♦ 2007 Wyoming Ave NW (between 20th St and Connecticut Ave). 387.2007; fax 387.5019. Metros: Dupont Circle, Woodley Park/Zoo

58 Normandy Inn $$ Visiting French officials appreciate the charm of this 75-room hotel, with its chic tearoom and patio and Tuesday evening wine-and-cheese receptions. The hotel was remodeled in 1993, but there is no restaurant. Nonsmoking rooms are available, and children under 12 stay free. ♦ 2118 Wyoming Ave NW (between Connecticut Ave and 23rd St). 483.1350, 800/424.3729; fax 387.8241 & Metro: Dupont Circle

59 Sofitel Hotel $$$$ This large hotel offers 145 rooms, all with sitting areas and mini-bars. Other niceties here include the bistro-style **Trocadero Cafe,** overnight parking, 24-hour room service, a health club, valet and baby-sitting services, and a multilingual staff. Moreover, nonsmoking rooms are available, and children under 14 stay free. ♦ 1914 Connecticut Ave NW (between Leroy Pl and California St). 797.2000, 800/424.2464; fax 462.0944. Metro: Dupont Circle

59 Washington Courtyard by Marriott $$ Here the lobby sports an old English look with dark woods and chandeliers. This well-situated hotel offers 147 rooms, room service, an outdoor swimming pool, a health club, off-street parking, and a dining room. ♦ 1900 Connecticut Ave NW (at Leroy Pl). 332.9300, 800/842.4211; fax 328.7039 & Metro: Dupont Circle

60 Cubi XI Abstract sculptor David Smith used steel, nickel, and chrome to fashion this powerful and startling work. Standing 11 feet tall, these squares and rectangles of gleaming metal—perched above a reflecting pool—seem to hold the force of gravity at bay. ♦ Universal North Bldg, 1875 Connecticut Ave NW (between Florida Ave and T St). Metro: Dupont Circle

Washington Hilton and Towers

61 Washington Hilton and Towers $$$$
Still remembered primarily as the place where
John Hinckley shot Ronald Reagan in 1981,
this huge property is always filled with
conventioneers. A multilingual staff, three
restaurants, a jogging course, and exercise
rooms are among the amenities offered here.
The lighted tennis courts and Olympic-size
outdoor pool are open to hotel guests and
health club members. Nonsmoking rooms are
available, and children under 18 stay free.
♦ 1919 Connecticut Ave NW (at Columbia
Rd). 483.3000, 800/HILTONS; fax 232.0438;
www.washington-hilton.com. Metro: Dupont
Circle

62 Kalorama Guest House $$ For budget-
minded travelers, these four Victorian town
houses (three at Adams-Morgan, one in
Woodley Park) are a fine choice. The rooms
are charmingly outfitted with such details as
brass beds, thick comforters, and late-
Victorian antiques. A continental breakfast
and Sherry in the evening, use of the laundry
room, and local telephone calls all are
included in the low rate. Only 24 of the 50
rooms have private baths, however, and
there's no restaurant. ♦ 1854 Mintwood Pl
NW (between Columbia Rd and 19th St).
667.6369. Metro: Woodley Park/Zoo. Also at:
2700 Cathedral Ave NW (at 27th St).
328.0860. Metro: Woodley Park/Zoo

63 Grill from Ipanema ★★$$ There's a lot
to enjoy about this popular restaurant. The
Brazilian fish dishes are excellently prepared;
try the fresh seafood stews, marinated grilled
fish, or *feijoada* (black-bean stew). The
tropical drinks taste great, but they pack quite
a punch; stand forewarned or you might find it
difficult to stand at all. After 11PM, this spot is
jumpin'. ♦ Brazilian ♦ M-Tu dinner; W-Su
lunch and dinner. 1858 Columbia Rd NW (at
Kalorama Rd). 986.0757. Metro: Woodley
Park/Zoo

64 Bedrock Billiards Several years ago, this
was one of the only decent pool halls in
Washington. It's got more competition now,
and with only eight tables available there's
often a wait, but it has terrific atmosphere,
beer, munchies—and board games like
Scrabble and Battleship to divert you. ♦ M-Th
4PM-1AM; F-Sa 2PM-2AM; Su noon-
midnight. 1841 Columbia Rd NW (between
Mintwood Pl and Biltmore St). 667.7665.
Metro: Woodley Park/Zoo

64 Fleet Feet If you're craving exercise while
vacationing but left your gear at home, this
place is for you. A neighborhood institution

(formerly across the street), the little store
carries all kinds of athletic shoes and workout
wear, and has a knowledgeable staff. ♦ M-F
10AM-8PM; Sa 10AM-7PM; Su noon-4PM.
1841 Columbia Rd NW (between Mintwood Pl
and Biltmore St). 387.3888 ♿ Metro: Woodley
Park/Zoo

65 Cashion's Eat Place ★★★$$$ At this
casual, New American eatery, owner/chef Ann
Cashion takes success personally: She
handwrites the frequently changing menu,
adorns the walls with personal photos, and
injects her impeccable taste into the culinary
selections. Always fresh and adventurous, her
specialty dishes might include lamb seared
with eggplant and garlic, or duck breast with
sour cherries. ♦ American ♦ Daily dinner.
1819 Columbia Rd NW (between Mintwood Pl
and Biltmore St). 797.1819. Metro: Woodley
Park/Zoo

65 Perry's ★★$$ Brightly colored and
imaginatively arranged sushi is served here,
along with other tempting offerings. The
atmosphere is stylish, and the rooftop deck
commands perhaps the best view of any
restaurant in the city. But for the privilege of
sitting outside, you'll have to buy $10 worth
of food per person, drinks not included.
♦ Japanese/American ♦ Daily dinner. 1811
Columbia Rd NW (between Mintwood Pl and
Biltmore St). 234.6218. Metro: Woodley
Park/Zoo

66 Miss Pixie's Resembling a favorite aunt's
attic, this wonderful little antiques shop is run
by Pixie Windsor, who often bakes cookies for
her customers. Furniture, books, glassware,
oddball art, and other reasonably priced
goods fill one-and-a-half stories. ♦ Th-Su
noon-7PM. 1810 Adams Mill Rd NW
(between Columbia Rd and Calvert St).
232.8171. Metro: Woodley Park/Zoo

67 Mama Ayesha's Restaurant Room ★★
$ Formerly called the **Calvert Cafe**, this
inexpensive Middle Eastern spot was renamed
and renovated after the death of its long-time
proprietor. Mama Ayesha's family—still at the
helm and serving such veterans as *baba
ganooj*, hummus, and stuffed grape leaves—
has added an outdoor cafe. For a real bargain,
make a meal out of appetizers. ♦ Middle

Eastern ♦ Daily lunch and dinner. 1967 Calvert St NW (between Adams Mill Rd and Woodley Pl). 232.5431 ♿ Metro: Woodley Park/Zoo

68 Chief Ike's Mambo Room ★$ Popular with the 20-something crowd, this casual bar/restaurant features live blues and alternative rock bands during the week and dancing on weekends. Belly up to the bar and try the Jell-O shooters. ♦ American ♦ M-Sa dinner; Su lunch and dinner. 1725 Columbia Rd NW (between Quarry and Ontario Rds). 332.2211 ♿ Metro: Woodley Park/Zoo

69 City Bikes Two former bicycle messengers founded this impressive store, which rents and sells all-terrain Miyatas, Giants, and Terry Precision Bicycles. The service is great, too. ♦ M-W, F-Sa; Th 10AM-9PM; Su noon-5PM. 2501 Champlain St NW (at Euclid St). 265.1564 ♿ Metro: Woodley Park/Zoo

70 Mixtec ★★$ Ebullient owner Pepe Montesinos offers spit-roasted chicken and freshly squeezed fruit drinks on his extensive menu of Mexican specialties—grilled pork, soft tacos, burritos, and the like. The food—always fresh—is an excellent value. ♦ Mexican ♦ Daily lunch and dinner. 1792 Columbia Rd NW (at 18th St). 332.1011. Metro: Woodley Park/Zoo

70 Red Sea ★★$$ The first, though no longer the best, of Adams-Morgan's many Ethiopian restaurants, this place serves up satisfyingly spicy meat-and-vegetable stews, and other delectables, that are scooped up with *injera* (spongy bread). ♦ Ethiopian ♦ Daily lunch and dinner. 2463 18th St NW (between Kalorama and Columbia Rds). 483.5000 ♿ Metro: Woodley Park/Zoo

70 Tryst ★★★$$ This wonderful new coffee bar attracts a mix of 20-somethings, students, politicos, and writers. The furniture—circa 1950—is arranged living room–style, and in warm weather, French doors open to the street. Beyond superb coffee, light and homey fare—including bowls of cereal, muffins, and cakes—plus beer and wine are served. ♦ American ♦ M-F 7AM-2AM; Sa 7AM-3AM; Su 8AM-midnight. 2459 18th St NW (between

Kalorama and Columbia Rds). 232.5500; fax 232.5508 ♿ Metro: Woodley Park/Zoo

71 Millie & Al's ★$ The quintessential neighborhood tavern, it offers casual conversation, a golden-oldies jukebox, dim lighting, and cheesy pizza. ♦ Pizza ♦ M-Th dinner; F-Su lunch and dinner. No credit cards accepted. 2440 18th St NW (between Belmont and Columbia Rds). 387.8131 ♿ Metro: Woodley Park/Zoo

71 I Matti ★★$$ With the broadest repertoire of any Italian restaurant in the area, this place offers everything from singularly excellent pizzas to such unusual concoctions as *spiedini alla carlone* (rabbit cutlets with sausage, pancetta, veal, sage, and onions). All dishes are carefully prepared and served in a congenial setting. ♦ Italian ♦ M-Sa lunch and dinner; Su dinner. Reservations recommended. 2436 18th St NW (between Belmont and Columbia Rds). 462.8844 ♿ Metro: Woodley Park/Zoo

71 Meskerem ★★$$ Sit at a woven-straw table and dine on specialties such as *kitfo* (a spicy steak tartare) and shrimp *wat* (shrimp cooked in fiery spices). When the balcony is open, diners sit Ethiopian style—atop leather cushions on the floor. ♦ Ethiopian ♦ Daily lunch and dinner. Reservations recommended on weekends. 2434 18th St NW (between Belmont and Columbia Rds). 462.4100 ♿ Metro: Woodley Park/Zoo

72 Betty Such elegant and beautifully made clothing is usually reserved for small boutiques in New York. But this shop, where many of the owners' formal creations as well as pieces by Jil Sander and other, lesser-known designers are displayed, is worth a side trip to Adams-Morgan. Accessories include jewelry, handbags, and hair ornaments. A seamstress is on the premises. ♦ M, W-Su noon-9PM. 2439 18th St NW (between Kalorama and Columbia Rds). 234.2389. Metro: Woodley Park/Zoo

72 Café Lautrec ★$$ Live jazz and decent French food make this small, noisy, and smoky room one of the most popular destinations in Adams-Morgan. If you arrive after 8PM on a weekend evening, you're sure to have a wait—and a quiet meal is out of the question. ♦ French ♦ Daily dinner. 2431 18th St NW (between Kalorama and Columbia Rds). 265.6436 ♿ Metro: Woodley Park/Zoo

72 La Fourchette ★★$$ Graced with tasteful floor-to-ceiling murals of French cafe scenes, this bistro serves such daily specials as bouillabaisse, duck, rabbit, and lobster with beurre blanc and a julienne of vegetables. ♦ French ♦ M-F lunch and dinner; Sa-Su dinner. 2429 18th St NW (between Kalorama and Columbia Rds). 332.3077 ♿ Metro: Woodley Park/Zoo

73 Cities ★★$$$ Though this eatery used to change its decor and menu periodically to reflect different cities around the world, it's now decided on a more stable Continental theme—at least as far as the decor is concerned. The still-evolving menu features such stalwarts as Dover sole, halibut with leeks, bouillabaisse, and mixed grill. Try to come on a warm, sunny day, when the French doors are thrown open to the Adams-Morgan street scene. ♦ International ♦ M-Sa dinner; Su brunch and dinner. Reservations recommended. 2424 18th St NW (between Belmont and Columbia Rds). 328.7194. Metro: Woodley Park/Zoo

73 Felix Restaurant and Bar ★★★$$ Chef David Scribner's hopping establishment combines a cool dancing bar with a traditional comfort-food restaurant. Surprisingly, this split personality is rather endearing. Scribner's specialties include a wonderful matzoh ball soup and beef brisket, but the grilled pork chop and fettuccine with mushrooms, tomato, and shaved parmesan are also good bets. Save room for a brownie with ice cream and whipped cream, or grilled banana with caramel. Then burn it off with late evening dancing. ♦ American ♦ M-Sa dinner; Su brunch and dinner. 2406 18th St NW (between Belmont and Columbia Rds). 483.3549. Metro: Woodley Park/Zoo

73 Belmont Kitchen ★★$$ It's worth suffering the trendiness for the upside-down Chicago-style pizzas, fresh grilled salmon or tuna, and such home-style desserts as flourless chocolate cake and Key lime pie. ♦ American ♦ Daily lunch and dinner. Reservations recommended. 2400 18th St NW (at Belmont Rd). 667.1200 ♿ Metro: Woodley Park/Zoo

74 Little Fountain Café ★★$ A pleasant escape from the mobbed sidewalks of Adams-Morgan, this European-style bistro of tile floors and stucco walls has a soothing, burbly fountain. New Zealand lamb chops, chicken *en croute* (in puff pastry), and vegetarian lasagna are good bets, but save room for the homemade desserts. ♦ International ♦ Daily

dinner. 2339 18th St NW (between Kalorama and Columbia Rds). 462.8100. Metro: Woodley Park/Zoo

74 Tom Tom ★$ Even in Adams-Morgan this art studio/bar/restaurant is unique. Sip some sangria or munch on pizza or tapas while watching an artist paint, draw, or even weave. There's a large draft beer selection and Thursday nights bring live jazz. Stargazers will love the roof deck. ♦ American ♦ Daily lunch and dinner. 2333 18th St NW (between Kalorama and Columbia Rds). 588.1300. Metro: Woodley Park/Zoo

75 Shake Your Booty This chic shop blends high fashion with superb craftsmanship in its unique selection of shoes, bags, and jewelry. European imports and cutting-edge American styles round out the stock. ♦ M, W–Su noon-8PM. 2324 18th St NW (between Kalorama and Belmont Rds). 518.8205. Metro: Woodley Park/Zoo

76 Roxannes ★$ Homemade smashed potatoes (with skins), fried calamari, barbecued shrimp, fajitas, and 34 kinds of tequila are some of the ways this trendy place pulls in a crowd. A metal lizard and stenciled walls add whimsy to the top level; downstairs is the **Peyote Cafe,** with a less extensive menu. Rooftop seating is a plus in warm weather. ♦ Southwestern ♦ M-Sa dinner; Su brunch and dinner. 2319 18th St NW (between Kalorama and Columbia Rds). 462.8330. Metro: Woodley Park/Zoo

76 Brass Knob Architectural Antiques Architectural leftovers from old American homes fill this two-story shop. Among the minute details are a wide assortment of doorknobs, house letters, and mailboxes; but it's the chandeliers—from Victorian to 1950s models—that shine here. ♦ M-Sa; Su noon-5PM. 2311 18th St NW (between Kalorama and Columbia Rds). 332.3370. Metro: Woodley Park/Zoo

The Whitehurst Freeway, the elevated roadway that provides a canopy over K Street along Georgetown's waterfront, was completed in 1949. The firm that handled the job, Alexander and Repass, was unusual for the time, because Alexander was black and Repass white, and Washington was very much a segregated city. The men had been friends since 1910 when they were teammates on the University of Iowa football team. Their company also completed the Tidal Basin project.

Fabulous Freebies

A bonanza for the budget-conscious, Washington's **Smithsonian** museums (14 in all) and the **National Zoo** offer free admission. As if that weren't enough, the city abounds with free cultural entertainment. If you have time, here are more options—all on the house.

The **Library of Congress** (707.5502; see page 22) gives free classical recitals from October through May, with top-notch participants, including the Juilliard String Quartet. Free tickets are released 90 minutes before the concerts.

Most Monday nights in fall and spring, the **National Theatre** (783.3372; see page 50) presents free one-act plays, local bands, and other musical performances. Children's entertainment usually appears Saturday mornings.

From October through June, the **National Gallery of Art** (see page 48) holds free Sunday evening concerts (842.6941, 737.4215), some commemorating exhibits, in the **West Garden Court.** Admission is first come, first served. All year long, the museum presents free classic films (842.6799) most Saturdays at 2:30PM and Sundays at 6PM in its large, plush theater in the **East Building.**

DC satisfies even the most hardcore film buff. Free classic feature films are shown most weekday evenings at 7PM at the **Library of Congress**'s **Mary Pickford Theater** (707.5677; see page 22) in the **James Madison Memorial Building.** The movies are first-rate.

The **National Archives** (501.5000; see page 85) screens free revival films, short documentaries, and archival footage at its 217-seat theater.

From September to June, the **Hirshhorn Museum** (357.2700; see page 83) shows free independent films most Thursdays and Fridays at 8PM. Art documentaries are shown Thursdays at noon and Saturdays at 1PM, children's films are Saturdays at 11AM.

Su 11:30AM-7PM. 2122 18th St NW (at Wyoming Ave). 797.7160 & Metros: Dupont Circle, Woodley Park/Zoo

77 Yawa This well-kept bookshop stocks fiction, nonfiction, and children's books by African and African-American writers. Other items include greeting cards, incense, woven bags, and wood carvings. ♦ M-Sa 11AM-9PM; Su noon-6PM. 2206 18th St NW (between Wyoming Ave and Kalorama Rd). 483.6805. Metros: Dupont Circle, Woodley Park/Zoo

77 Addisu Gebeya Wander in here for a taste of Ethiopia. Exotic spices, such as *awaze, mitmita,* and *berbere,* as well as the popular *injera* (foamy-textured round bread) are sold here. Books, tapes, and records are also available. ♦ Daily 9AM-10PM. 2202 18th St NW (between Wyoming Ave and Kalorama Rd). 986.6013. Metros: Dupont Circle, Woodley Park/Zoo

78 Skynear and Company Find here a collection of hand-painted furniture pieces, elaborate birdcages, leopard-print chairs and sculptures, animal statues, and other assorted household furnishings in a variety of funky, ornate, even Neo-Classical styles. Some of the stuff's really weird; some of it, truly beautiful. ♦ Tu-Th 11AM-7:30PM; F-Sa 11AM-8:30PM;

79 El Tamarindo ★$ There's nothing fancy here, just good, cheap Mexican and Salvadoran food, cold beer, and tables that can seat large parties. Not on the tourist circuit, this spot attracts a local crowd. ♦ Mexican/Salvadoran ♦ Daily lunch and dinner. 1785 Florida Ave NW (between U and California Sts). 328.3660 & Metro: Dupont Circle. Also at: 7331 Georgia Ave NW (at Geranium St). 291.0525 & Metro: Takoma

80 Straits of Malaya ★★$$ Dishes from Malaysia and Singapore are served in an attractive and relaxing setting. Try the *poh pia* (shredded leeks, bean sprouts, and chicken stir fried and served on pancakes) or the curried Chinese eggplant, served either vegetarian style or with meat. The rooftop deck and sidewalk cafe are wonderful in good weather. ♦ Malaysian ♦ M-F lunch and dinner; Sa-Su dinner. Reservations recommended. 1836 18th St NW (between Swann and T Sts). 483.1483 & Metro: Dupont Circle

81 Lauriol Plaza ★★$$ The Spanish fare at this modern, airy—if sometimes noisy—cafe is taking on something of a Tex-Mex accent.

The fajitas are wonderful, but don't overlook some of the best Spanish offerings, including roast pork and garlic chicken. When it's warm, dine on the terrace. ♦ Spanish/Tex-Mex ♦ Daily lunch and dinner. Reservations recommended. 1801 18th St NW (at S St). 387.0035 ὁ Metro: Dupont Circle

National Museum of American Jewish Military History

82 National Museum of American Jewish Military History It shouldn't come as any surprise, in a city with so many statues, memorials, and museums dedicated to the military, to find this specialized (but thoroughly fascinating) institution. World War II is understandably emphasized, although exhibits on other fronts have been about Desert Storm and the role of Jewish women in the military. ♦ Free. M-F; Su 1-5PM. 1811 R St NW (between 18th and 19th Sts). 265.6280. Metro: Dupont Circle

83 Belmont House (Eastern Star Temple) Architect **Ernest Sanson** was imported from France specifically for this undertaking (American architect **Horace Trumbauer** was the project manager); the resulting 1908 building exudes Gallic Romanticism, the wedge-shaped lot dictating the structure's shape. Its opulent interiors, complete with Louis Tiffany glass, brought the total construction cost to $1.5 million. Much of the original owner's art collection remains in the house, though it now belongs to the Order of the Eastern Star, a fraternal organization, which bought it in 1935 for a paltry $100,000. The building is closed to the public. ♦ 1618 New Hampshire Ave NW (between Corcoran and R Sts). 667.4737. Metro: Dupont Circle

84 First Baptist Church Designed in 1955 by **Harold E. Wagoner,** the massing of this Neo-Gothic church, reminiscent of the work of **Frank Lloyd Wright,** playfully leads the eye upward toward a steeple that isn't there. ♦ 1328 16th St NW (entrance on O St). 387.2206 ὁ Metro: Dupont Circle

85 Foundry United Methodist Church Built in 1904 by **Appleton P. Clark,** it has fan vaults of rusticated gray granite that are characteristic of High Gothic Revival; the low dome contributes to this building's renowned acoustics. The church is named for Georgetown foundry owner Henry Foxhall, who established it. ♦ 1500 16th St NW (at P St). 332.4010 ὁ Metro: Dupont Circle

86 Cafe Luna ★$ A pleasant, casual atmosphere reigns in this basement restaurant, which serves excellent sandwiches, pasta, and pizza. ♦ American/Italian ♦ M-F breakfast, lunch, and dinner; Sa-Su brunch and dinner. 1633 P St NW (between 16th and 17th Sts). 387.4005 ὁ Metro: Dupont Circle

86 Skewers ★★$$ Exotically decorated with Middle Eastern fabric hanging from the ceiling, and walls painted in peacock blue, mint green, and red, this place is located directly upstairs from **Cafe Luna** (see above). Order any of the delicious kabobs—all served with saffron rice or homemade pasta and a skewer of fresh vegetables crowned with almonds and raisins. ♦ Middle Eastern ♦ M-Sa lunch and dinner; Su dinner. Reservations recommended. 1633 P St NW (between 16th and 17th Sts). 387.7400 ὁ Metro: Dupont Circle

86 Bua ★★$$ Delicious Thai food, a comfortable setting, and a caliber of service usually found at more expensive restaurants combine to make a pleasurable dining experience. ♦ Thai ♦ Daily lunch and dinner. Reservations recommended. 1635 P St NW (between 16th and 17th Sts). 265.0828 ὁ Metro: Dupont Circle

86 Il Radicchio ★★$ Have spaghetti your way: a bottomless bowl with a choice of sauces, all at prices that are straight out of Dubuque. Needless to say, it's very popular with the neighborhood's younger denizens. ♦ Italian ♦ Daily lunch and dinner. 1509 17th St NW (between P and Q Sts). 986.BOBS ὁ Metro: Dupont Circle. Also at: 1211 Wisconsin Ave NW (between M and N Sts). 337.2627

87 J.R.'s A lively gay crowd gathers at this bar, thanks in large part to the deejays, who are continuously pumping out popular dance tunes. Snack food is available and there's never a cover charge. ♦ M-Th 2PM-2AM; F-Sa 2PM-3AM. 1519 17th St NW (between P and Q Sts). 328.0090. Metro: Dupont Circle

88 Fox & Hounds Lounge Don't let the fancy word "lounge" fool you: This is a basic, no-frills neighborhood bar serving generous drinks at good prices. It's connected to **Trio Restaurant** next door (see below), the kitchen of which supplies the bar food. ♦ M-F 11AM-1:30AM; Sa-Su 10AM-2:30AM. 1533 17th St NW (between P and Q Sts). 232.6307 ὁ Metro: Dupont Circle

88 Trio Restaurant ★$ Long before 17th Street became Restaurant Row, this comfortable dive was a local favorite for meat loaf, waffles, and other hearty, diner-style fare. Eat on the outdoor patio in fair weather. ♦ American ♦ Daily breakfast, lunch, and dinner. 1537 17th St NW (at Q St). 232.6305 ♿ Metro: Dupont Circle

89 Universal Gear Style-conscious men shop here for clothes and accessories—socks, belts, and watches. ♦ M-Th, Su 11AM-10PM; F-Sa 11AM-midnight. 1601 17th St NW (at Q St). 319.1157 ♿ Metro: Dupont Circle

90 Reincarnations Opulent accessories for the home, including well-crafted furniture and a wild array of shower curtains, occupy this four-story town house. Despite the tony location, prices here are reasonable. ♦ Daily 11AM-8PM. 1606 17th St NW (between Q and Corcoran Sts). 319.1606. Metro: Dupont Circle. Also at: 917 King St (between N Alfred and N Patrick Sts), Alexandria. 703/838.9217. Metro: King Street

91 Julio's Rooftop Pizza ★$ Respectable pizza, an irresistible all-you-can-eat Sunday brunch, and a nice view from the roof deck add up to a popular neighborhood spot. ♦ Italian ♦ Daily lunch and dinner. 1604 U St NW (at New Hampshire Ave). 483.8500. Metros: Dupont Circle, U St/Cardozo

91 Stetson's ★$ The closest thing in DC to a real live Texas bar, this local hangout is the place for burgers, enchiladas, and the like. There's a pool table upstairs. ♦ Tex-Mex ♦ Daily dinner. 1610 U St NW (between New Hampshire Ave and 17th St). 667.6295. Metros: Dupont Circle, U St/Cardozo

92 Meridian House John Russell Pope built this limestone-faced, Louis XVI–style town house for Irwin Boyle Laughlin, a former ambassador to Spain and member of the Pittsburgh steel family. The entrance hall, loggia, and dining room are particularly impressive. Since 1961, the mansion has been home to Meridian House International, a nonprofit foundation that promotes international understanding through exhibits, concerts, and other cultural events, as well as tours and seminars for thousands of visitors to the US each year. ♦ Free. W-Su 2-5PM. 1630 Crescent Pl NW (between 16th and 17th Sts). 667.6800 ♿ Metro: U St/Cardozo

Next door to the Meridian House:

White-Meyer House Another John Russell Pope creation, this Georgian-style mansion was constructed in 1912 for Ambassador Henry White, an American diplomat; Meridian House International (see above) annexed it in 1987. Together, this and the Meridian House form a blocklong international campus. ♦ 1624 Crescent Pl NW

93 Inter-American Defense Board This 1906 building by George Oakley Totten, Jr. is also known as the "Pink Palace." It's a Gothic version of Venice, Italy's Ducal Palace (note the windows), but the massing is somewhat awkward. ♦ 2600 16th St NW (at Euclid St). Metros: Woodley Park/Zoo, U St/Cardozo

94 Gala Hispanic Theater Within a school located in Mount Pleasant, a residential area to the north of Adams-Morgan, this professional, 100-seat theater produces contemporary Latin American works in both Spanish and English. ♦ Shows: F-Sa 8PM; Su 4PM. Box office: M-F; Sa 9AM-1PM and 7:30-8PM. 1625 Park Rd NW (between 16th and 17th Sts). 234.7174 ♿ Metro: Cleveland Park

95 Fio's ★★$ A sentimental favorite, this Italian cafe within Woodner Apartments is straight out of the 1950s, with Leatherette booths, a menu leaning heavily to red sauce and fried calamari, bargain prices, and family-style service. ♦ Italian ♦ Tu-Su dinner. 3636 16th St NW (between Oak St and Piney Branch Pkwy), Lobby level. 667.3040 ♿

Bests

Richard Peabody
Poet/Editor/Teacher/Bookshop Co-Owner, Atticus Books

DC was meant to be seen from the **Potomac River.** Take a cruise out of **Old Town Alexandria** and watch the white marble monuments line up on the horizon.

The area has numerous bike paths, but I recommend biking to **Mount Vernon** along the Potomac when the fall leaves are turning.

Buy fresh seafood or shellfish on the wharf at the **Washington Harbour.**

Catch an up-and-coming local act or indie tour at the **Black Cat Club** in the trendy **U Street corridor.** The big national acts end up a few blocks down the street at the **930 Club.** People come from all over the country to buy retro furnishings from **Millennium.** If you want antique chairs or tables try **Good Wood.** The refurbished **Lincoln Theater** is an amazing place for a show or concert. And all of U Street comes alive after dark.

Watch a **Caps** hockey or **Wizards** basketball game at the new **MCI Center.** And DC is also home to the Women's NBA **Mystics** and the two-time championship-winning national soccer team, the **DC United.**

Rent a rowboat or canoe at **Fletcher's Boat House** and take a closer look at **Great Falls** or **Georgetown.**

Arlington, Virginia, is becoming a happening night spot. Check out a poetry reading or singer/songwriter at the **Iota** or trendy band at **Galaxy Hut.** Eat Vietnamese at **Cafe DaLat** or the **Queen Bee.**

Great sushi specials in **Rosslyn** at **Appetizer Plus.**

Get lost in the gothic corridors of the **Washington National Cathedral**—a great place to catch the 4th of July fireworks. And their **Herb Cottage** and gardens are wonderful to stroll in the summer. You can watch the bell ringers and even take a workshop in stone carving.

Sit in the **Rotunda** of the **Library of Congress Reading Room** on a rainy day and peruse a book you've always wanted to read but could never find anywhere.

Don't miss the bonsai gardens at the **National Arboretum.**

Catch a rarely seen film at the **AFI (American Film Institute)** or visit the huge **IMAX screen** at the **Air and Space Museum.**

Visit the Pre-Columbian art collection at **Dumbarton Oaks** and stroll the formal gardens.

The **Signature Theater** has been winning awards for their ambitious productions, particularly musicals. They're located in **Shirlington,** Virginia.

Dawdle in the **Whistler Room** at the **Freer Gallery** (a DC treasure) and spend time with the changing exhibits of Asian art.

The **National Museum of Women in the Arts** is housed in an imposing space. They have a permanent collection but the traveling shows are wonderful.

Avant-garde tastes for art or performance are quenched at the **DC Arts Center** in **Adams-Morgan.** Parking is nearly impossible in the restaurant-heavy area. So cab it or walk from **Dupont Circle** and explore all the shops.

Swing dance in the **Spanish Ballroom** or see what the resident artists are doing in their yurt studios at **Glen Echo Park.**

Jazz buffs have to go to **Blues Alley** in **Georgetown** to pay homage to the greats. Another spot nearby is **One Step Down.**

Spring in DC is the best. Rent a bike and peddle around the cherry blossoms at the **Tidal Basin.**

DC has a folk music mecca in nearby **Alexandria— The Birchmere.** Not to be missed.

Take a writing class or attend a function at the **Writer's Center** in **Bethesda,** Maryland.

Listen to live chamber music in the enclosed courtyard of the **National Gallery of Art**.

Have lunch at the **Phillips Collection** cafe and admire this special house of art.

Fly a kite in March at the **Washington Monument.**

Eat a romantic dinner at the **Old Angler's Inn** nestled beside the **C&O Canal** almost to **Potomac,** Maryland.

Meditate at F. Scott and Zelda Fitzgerald's grave at **St. Mary's Church** in **Rockville.**

Lonesome Dove author Larry McMurtry co-owns a DC book shop—**Booked Up** in Georgetown. Many other shops have grown up around his as well. Try them all.

Nostalgia buffs can ride European and American trolleys on the weekend at the **Trolley Museum** in **Silver Spring.**

It's almost impossible to get a ticket, but if you can, you must watch the **Washington Redskins** play football in the beautiful new **Jack Kent Cooke Stadium** in **Landover,** Maryland. Nothing else brings the disparate DC area together like the **Redskins.** Accessible by **Metro,** but a trek. After the game (or if you can't snag tickets), hang out at **Colonel Brooks' Tavern** for a burger and beer in **Brookland** near **Catholic University. Dance Place** is a few blocks away for those who would rather watch the human body run through different sort of paces.

Allan Stypeck

President, Second Story Books, Inc. and Senior Member, American Society of Appraisers

---

Take in the mosaics and murals with literary themes and domed reading room inside the **Library of Congress**'s recently restored rococo **Jefferson Building**. Just one block up on First Street, enjoy a good lunch and great desserts in the **US Supreme Court**'s public dining area.

Detour off the beaten path to the **Mexican Cultural Center** (adjacent to the embassy on 16th Street) for murals, paintings, and sculptures set in a beautiful interior.

For exquisite textiles from everywhere in the world other than North America and Western Europe, visit the **Textile Museum** on S Street NW (great gift shop). It is located in **Kalorama,** a neighborhood dotted with majestic embassy residences and great for quiet strolls. Just east on S Street are steps leading down the hill past a secluded lion's head fountain. Around the corner is the **Phillips Collection** of Impressionist Art (cozy lunch room in basement), and directly across **Massachusetts Avenue** is the **Anderson House** museum and library. This imposing mansion is an impressive repository of military history with special emphasis on the Revolutionary War. Take a moment to contemplate the tranquil, if out-of-place, Buddhist garden in the back.

In upper **Georgetown,** visit the **Museum of Pre-Columbian Art** adjacent to the manicured gardens of **Dumbarton Oaks.** Nearby on **Wisconsin Avenue, Germaine's** has great Vietnamese food.

Canoe or kayak on the **Potomac,** change into clean clothes and walk across **MacArthur Boulevard** for a memorable, yet pricey, lunch or dinner on the patio of **Old Angler's Inn.**

Georgetown

Next to **Capitol Hill**, Georgetown is Washington's best-known neighborhood; after **Dupont Circle/Adams-Morgan**, it's DC's hippest, and is certainly among the city's wealthiest. Georgetown's popularity is not hard to understand—its tree-lined streets and historic town houses give it a fetching elegance, while the country's oldest Catholic institution of higher learning lends it the zesty atmosphere of a college town.

Georgetown was founded in 1751, forty years before DC; due to its choice location on the **Potomac River**, it briefly prospered as a major international port. There's little evidence of that now, however; the waterfront, which once contained warehouses and ramshackle docks, is marred by an elevated freeway, the **Whitehurst**, which carries commuters to and from suburban Maryland and Virginia. Although Georgetown was the terminus of the **Chesapeake & Ohio Canal**, the area failed to catch on with real estate speculators. When the B&O railroad put the canal out of business, Georgetown fared even worse. It became part of the District of Columbia in 1871; in reality, it functioned as a poor stepchild to Washington.

In the early 20th century, Georgetown was rediscovered. Urban pioneers were looking for cheap housing, of which there was plenty in crumbling Georgetown. By the 1950s, when Congressman John F. Kennedy set up house

in the area (at 3217 P St) to prepare for a run at larger quarters down **Pennsylvania Avenue**, Georgetown's Cinderella-like transformation was complete. The prices of modest 19th-century homes had already skyrocketed into the six figures, with larger ones exceeding the million-dollar mark.

During the Kennedy and Johnson years, and even into the Nixon era, no Washington neighborhood was hotter for shopping, dining, and club-hopping. Along Georgetown's two main arteries, **M Street** and **Wisconsin Avenue**, establishments sprang up, flourished, and often disappeared, to be quickly replaced by others eager for a fashionable address.

Today, Georgetown still boasts some of the best shopping in town, thanks in part to the Neo-Victorian shopping mall, **Shops at Georgetown Park.** Eateries are plentiful, and due to the large college student population, most of them are quite affordable. Since it's a 15-minute walk from the nearest **Metro** stop **(Foggy Bottom/GWU)**, finding a parking spot is virtually impossible (garage rates are very steep, too). Exploring by foot may be the best option—and there's no better way to savor the quaint cobblestone streets. Try not to miss the **Washington Harbour** complex, with its restaurants, shops, and lovely waterfront promenade. It allows visitors a chance to sit and observe the tranquil yet powerful Potomac River.

FOUR SEASONS HOTEL

1 The Four Seasons Hotel $$$$ Luxurious, elegant, and relaxed, this is a favorite resort of celebrities, including Tom Hanks, James Taylor, Bonnie Raitt, and Boyz-II-Men. Many of the 196 rooms overlook the historic **C&O Canal** or **Rock Creek Park**. Amenities include an elegant dining room (see below), a multilingual staff, 24-hour room service, complimentary weekday limo service, a pool, a health club, and valet parking. The **Garden Terrace** bar overlooking Rock Creek, with its soft flowered sofas, piano, and profusion of greenery, is one of the city's best cocktail-hour rendezvous spots; a pleasureful afternoon tea is served here daily; the Sunday Jazz brunch is a local favorite; and a light menu is available throughout the day. Children under 16 stay free. ♦ 2800 Pennsylvania Ave NW (between Rock Creek and Potomac Pkwy and M St). 342.0444, 800/332.3442; fax 944.2076; www.fourseasons.com

Within The Four Seasons Hotel:

Seasons ★★★$$$$ The hotel's ultraposh dining room, with its floor-to-ceiling windows and slate floors, offers stylish fare in a stunning setting. Superb choices include soft-shell crabs, roast chicken with stuffing under the skin, and risotto. Ask to see the wine list, which has won awards from both *Wine Spectator* and *Wine Enthusiast* magazines. Top the meal off with a piece of "Mile High Lemon Merengue Pie" or a homemade berry sorbet. ♦ American ♦ M-F breakfast, lunch, and dinner; Sa-Su breakfast and dinner. Reservations recommended. 944.2000 &

Lorenzo This boutique carries men's designer clothing (and a few women's items) direct from Italy—at prices that have so many zeros tacked on they seem to be quoted in lire. ♦ M-Sa 10:30AM-7:30PM; Su noon-5PM. 2812 Pennsylvania Ave NW. 965.6149

1 Animation Sensations Original cartoon art—sketches, paintings, and animation cels—from *The Jungle Book, Pinocchio, Yellow Submarine,* "The Roadrunner," and "The Flintstones," and hundreds of other productions can be found here. A host of studios, including Disney, Warner Brothers, and Hanna Barbera, are represented. ♦ M-Sa; Su noon-5PM. 2820 Pennsylvania Ave (between Rock Creek and Potomac Pkwy and M St). 337.5024

2 Enriqueta's ★★$$ Known as Washington's original Mexican restaurant, this dependable spot features the varied cuisine of the country's provinces—from pork in fruit sauce to chicken mole—prepared so well you'll swear off tacos forever. And the Tex-Mex staples (especially the enchiladas) are delicious, too. ♦ Mexican ♦ M-F lunch and dinner; Sa-Su dinner. 2811 M St NW (between 28th and 29th Sts). 338.7772 &

3 Janis Aldridge Gallery Seventeenth-through 20th-century architectural and botanical prints and paintings set off by exquisite French mats, glow softly on the walls of this little shop. Decoupage screens, antique china, and decorative accessories worthy of a Georgetown manse are available as well. ◆ Tu-Sa. 2900 M St NW (at 29th St). 338.7710

3 American Hand Plus This store showcases works by contemporary American ceramists and jewelers, as well as elegant housewares. Just call it Wedding Gift Central. ◆ M-Sa; Su 1-5PM. 2906 M St NW (between 29th and 30th Sts). 965.3273 &

4 Vietnam Georgetown ★★$ One of the pioneers among Washington-area Vietnamese restaurants, it's still a great place for a quick, cheap meal. Try the spring rolls or the fragrant beef noodle soup; in warm weather ask for a table on the patio. ◆ Vietnamese ◆ Daily lunch and dinner. 2934 M St NW (between 29th and 30th Sts). 337.4536 &

5 Music City Roadhouse ★$ Hankerin' for down-home Southern cookin'? Look no farther than this spot in trendy Georgetown. Its family-style all-you-can-eat meals have insanely low prices. Kids under six eat free, under 12 half-price. There's a Sunday brunch with live gospel music, too. ◆ American ◆ M-Sa dinner; Su brunch and dinner. 1050 30th St NW (between K St and the Chesapeake & Ohio Canal). 337.4444 &

6 The Latham Hotel $$$ An offshoot of the Philadelphia original, this hotel offers 143 rooms, a rooftop pool, genuine elegance, and a prime location. Many of the rooms have great views of the C&O Canal. ◆ 3000 M St NW (at 30th St). 726.5000, 800/Latham.1; fax 337.4250 &

Within The Latham Hotel:

Citronelle ★★★$$$$ One of Washington's finest restaurants brings a little bit of LA to the capital city; the "French, California style" cuisine is both creative and aesthetically pleasing, and the open kitchen allows diners to watch the chef at work. The menu changes frequently, but when available, the rack of lamb or Greek swordfish are musts. The restaurant's design is nearly as fine as its food: A lounge overlooks the sunken dining area, which is studded with plants and artwork. Besides the main room, there are two smaller dining rooms—one lined with glassed-in wine racks and the other, an indoor garden. ◆ American ◆ Daily breakfast, lunch, and dinner. Reservations recommended. 625.2150 &

The first known play produced in Washington was held in Georgetown in 1790. McGrath's Company of Comedians presented *The Beggar's Opera*.

7 Garrett's ★$$ Upstairs in the dining room, the fare is pretty standard—burgers, pasta—but the downstairs bar is a popular neighborhood pub. On summer nights, there can be a lengthy wait to get in on either floor. ◆ American ◆ Daily lunch and dinner. 3003 M St NW (between 30th and 31st Sts). 333.1033

8 Loughboro-Patterson House An authentic Federal-period restoration, it is made more interesting by a single delicate dormer in the roofline. The house was built in 1806 and restored by **Macomber & Peter** 58 years later. It is now a private residence. ◆ 3039-41 M St NW (between 30th and 31st Sts)

8 Old Stone House This little cottage is believed to be the only surviving pre-Revolutionary structure built in DC. The house, a National Park Service Historic Site, is furnished in 18th-century style, and its old-fashioned gardens with fruit trees and masses of blooms are a welcome respite from the bustle of M Street. ◆ Free. W-Su. 3051 M St NW (between 30th and 31st Sts). 426.6851

8 Miss Saigon ★★$ Noodle soup with roasted quail, crisp egg rolls, and caramel salmon with black pepper are some of the exotic specialties at this pretty pink-and-green restaurant, decorated with potted trees. The place is often packed. In warm months there's intimate seating on the adjacent patio. ◆ Vietnamese ◆ Daily lunch and dinner. Reservations recommended on weekends. 3057 M St NW (between 30th and 31st Sts). 333.5545

8 Efx The finest beauty, bath, and hair products (from Aveda to Kiehl) are sold in this whimsical boutique. Patrons can sit at luxurious vanity tables and dab away with makeup samples. ◆ M-Sa 10AM-9PM; Su noon-6PM. 3059 M St NW (between 30th and 31st Sts). 965.1300. Also at: 1745 Connecticut Ave NW (between R and S Sts). 462.1300. Metro: Dupont Circle

9 The Washington Post Office, Georgetown Branch In 1857 **Ammi Young** designed this timelessly simple composition of heavy plain stone walls, acclaimed as one of the best Italianate Federal buildings ever built. Stunningly renovated in 1997, it's worth a look. ◆ 1215 31st St NW (between M and N Sts) &

10 Paper Moon ★$$ The neon-lit, sleek-style dining room is often noisy with a young international bar crowd who want to see and be seen in the wide-open dining room. The menu features good pasta served in enormous bowls, plus pizzas and salads. ◆ Italian ◆ Daily lunch and dinner. Reservations recommended. 1073 31st St NW (between the Chesapeake & Ohio Canal and M St). 965.6666 &

11 Chesapeake & Ohio Canal Historically, this is one of the last and best preserved of the great canals that helped move goods westward in the late 18th and early 19th centuries. An engineering marvel, the canal employs 74 locks and the 3,100-footlong **Paw Taw Tunnel** carved through the stone mountains of western Maryland. The **C&O** extends just over 184 miles, from Georgetown to Cumberland, Maryland, where the Allegheny Mountains interrupted its intended meeting with the Ohio River.

The precursor of the **C&O,** the **Potowmack Canal** was the brainchild of George Washington: He invested $10,000 in the Potowmack Canal Company—stocks that were eventually left to endow **George Washington University**—and supervised much of the work. John Quincy Adams broke ground for the larger canal on 4 July 1828, and for several decades mule-drawn canal clippers slowly carried lumber, coal, whiskey, and grain from the West along the **C&O.** By the end of the 19th century, the railroad had stolen most of the canal's customers, and by 1924, the **C&O** was obsolete. The best-preserved portion of the canal is the 22-mile stretch from Georgetown to Seneca, Maryland, although you can hike or bike the old **Towpath** for the canal's entire length.

The National Park Service sponsors guided hikes and maintains campsites. The timberland nestled along the waterway and its rich wildlife make it an idyllic spot for outdoor activities, such as rock climbing (by permit) on its rugged overhangs, canoeing, boating, and, in winter, ice-skating. There are even some old gold mines, battle sites, and cabins along the route.

From April through October, catch the *Georgetown* at the dock at 30th Street in Georgetown (653.5190) or the *Canal Clipper* at the famous **Great Falls Tavern** in Potomac, Maryland (301/299.3613). Both are mule-drawn canal boat replicas, run by operators in full period attire. Canoes and rowboats can be rented at **Fletcher's Boat House,** 4940 Canal Road Northwest (just north of Reservoir Rd), three miles west of Georgetown (244.0461); **Jack's Boats,** 3500 K Street Northwest, at Francis Scott Key Bridge (337.9642); **Swain's Lock** on River Road, 2.5 miles west of Potomac

Village, Maryland (301/299.9006); or **Thompson's Boat Center,** 2900 Virginia Avenue Northwest, at Rock Creek and Potomac Parkway (333.9543, 333.4861). ◆ Admission for park and boat rides. *Georgetown* and *Canal Clipper* departures W-Su; schedule times vary; call ahead. C&O Headquarters: 16500 Shepherds Town Pike (at James Rumsey Bridge), Sharpsburg, Maryland. 301/739.4200, recording 301/299.2026

12 Café La Ruche ★★★$$ A sophisticated renovation has given this cafe, a favorite among French nationals in Washington, a much sleeker look. Moss-green banquettes, late–18th century framed French posters, and Parisian street signs only add to the appeal. Renowned for its fresh-fruit tarts, chocolate mousse, and luscious cakes, this restaurant balances the sweet stuff with huge salads, rich slices of zucchini pie and quiche, and low-priced daily specials, such as mussels, grilled chicken with garlic, and trout amandine. There's outdoor dining in warm weather. ◆ French ◆ M-F lunch and dinner. 1039 31st St NW (between K St and the Chesapeake & Ohio Canal). 965.2684 &

13 Chelsea's DC's large Latino community has long come here to dance to the latest salsa from live bands. The club also offers live Ethiopian, Arabic, and Persian music and weekend performances of satirical cabaret by the Capitol Steps, a bunch of current and former congressional aides who get their revenge onstage. ◆ Cover F-Sa. Live Ethiopian music M 9:30PM-2AM. Arab music W 9:30PM-2AM. Latin bands Th 9:30PM-2AM; F-Sa 10PM-4AM. Capitol Steps F 8PM; Sa 7:30PM. Persian music Su 9:30PM-2AM. Box office M-F. 1055 Thomas Jefferson St NW (between K St and the Chesapeake & Ohio Canal). 298.8222 &

14 Washington Harbour After a cement factory occupied this riverfront site for years, the Fine Arts Commission recommended that a park be built to replace it. Instead **Arthur Cotton Moore**'s bombastic mixed-use development was built in 1986. Though some may criticize its somewhat clunky flamboyance, it redeems itself by providing a boardwalk promenade with panoramic views of the river, a popular spot in fine weather. Also here are indoor and outdoor restaurants, a few shops, and an office complex. Boats docked at the boardwalk are available for sight-seeing tours down river to **The Mall** and back. ◆ 3000 K St NW (at 30th St). 944.4140 &

At Washington Harbour:

Sequoia ★★$$ The terrace tables of this harborside restaurant are arguably among the best places in town to catch the sunset on a warm evening. An immense interior dining room is for the see-and-be-seen crowd, although the view is difficult to upstage. The extensive menu of contemporary American cuisine includes such dishes as a sirloin tenderloin peppercorn salad with lentils and spicy greens in a roasted-garlic vinaigrette; shrimp and wild mushroom linguine in a black peppercorn and garlic butter sauce; Maryland crab cakes; and honey-marinated pork tenderloin, topped with "Virginia Gentleman Whiskey Sauce" and served with smashed potatoes (mashed with skins on) and greens. ♦ American ♦ Daily lunch and dinner. 944.4200 ♿

Harbour Cafe ★★$ Enjoy a well-seasoned salad or an enormous deli sandwich on homemade bread in the little cafe area. For a great riverside picnic, get your feast to go. ♦ Deli ♦ M-F lunch and dinner. 944.4330 ♿

Tony and Joe's Seafood Place ★$$ Fish it is, served simply and fresh in a casual and comfortable dining room. ♦ Seafood ♦ Daily lunch and dinner. 944.4545 ♿

Hisago ★★$$$$ Handsome traditional decor, meticulous service, and authentic Japanese cuisine—sushi, sashimi, tempura—render this place very appetizing indeed, but without an expense account the Tokyo-style prices may be a little hard to swallow. ♦ Japanese ♦ M-F lunch and dinner; Sa-Su dinner. Reservations recommended. 3050 K St NW. 944.4181 ♿

15 Hibiscus Cafe ★★$$ It's off the beaten path, tucked beneath the west end of the Whitehurst Freeway, but this hot spot serves delicious nouvelle Island cuisine in a brightly colored setting to its legion of devoted fans. ♦ Caribbean ♦ Reservations recommended. Tu-Sa dinner. 3401 K St NW (between Potomac St and the Francis Scott Key Bridge). 965.7170 ♿

16 Grace Episcopal Church This early Gothic Revival stone church was established in 1866 as a mission to the boaters on the **Chesapeake & Ohio Canal** (see page 129). ♦ 1041 Wisconsin Ave NW (between South St and the Chesapeake & Ohio Canal) ♿

17 Pirjo An unusual selection of casual but somehow very elegant clothing and jewelry for women is featured at this boutique. Envision Chairman Mao meets Calvin Klein. ♦ M-W, F-Sa; Th 11AM-8PM; Su noon-5PM. 1044 Wisconsin Ave NW (between K St and the Chesapeake & Ohio Canal). 337.1390 ♿

Patisserie Cafe Didier

17 Patisserie Cafe Didier ★★★$ Located on a small street that's easy to miss, this place is worth searching out. Light meals—soufflés, quiches, salads, and gourmet pizzas—can be topped off with the most divine pastries offered anywhere. ♦ French ♦ Daily breakfast and lunch. 3206 Grace St NW (just west of Wisconsin Ave). 342.9083 ♿

18 Filomena's ★$$ A huge and noisy basement-level space with a tiled floor and lots of hanging greenery, this restaurant is filled with trendy types gobbling up pasta and veal, seafood, and chicken dishes. ♦ Italian ♦ Daily lunch and dinner. Reservations recommended. 1063 Wisconsin Ave NW (between the Chesapeake & Ohio Canal and M St). 338.8800

18 Pleasure Place Racy lingerie, blue movies, and adults-only toys are available here for those who wouldn't dare venture into (or can't find) one of the dwindling number of "adult" bookstores Downtown. ♦ M-Tu 10AM-10PM; W-Sa 10AM-midnight; Su noon-7PM. 1063 Wisconsin Ave NW (between the Chesapeake & Ohio Canal and M St). 333.8570 ♿ Also at: 1710 Connecticut Ave NW (between R and S Sts). 483.3297. Metro: Dupont Circle

18 Houston's ★$ The line outside the door is there for a reason. Although the Texas-style menu of burgers, ribs, seafood, salads, and grilled chicken may not seem remarkable, this casual pub pulls off the formula with consistency and value. ♦ American ♦ Daily lunch and dinner. 1065 Wisconsin Ave NW (between the Chesapeake & Ohio Canal and M St). 338.7760 ♿

Blues Alley

18 Blues Alley ★$$ Jazz fans come to this intimate night spot to hear such stars as Wynton Marsalis, Lou Rawls, Eartha Kitt, and Nancy Wilson. To complement the music, there's a menu of New Orleans–style dishes as well as seafood and steaks. Dinner guests are given preferential seating during the shows. Those who want to enjoy the music and the candlelit ambience without eating will have to pay a cover charge. The club is set on a small alley officially named in its honor in 1982. ♦ Southern ♦ Cover. Dinner. Shows: M-Th, Su 8PM, 10PM; F-Sa 8PM, 10PM, midnight. Box office: daily noon-10:30PM. Reservations recommended; required for certain shows. 1073 Wisconsin Ave NW (between the Chesapeake & Ohio Canal and M St). Main entrance on Blues Alley. 337.4141

19 Nathan's ★★$$$ Pin-striped politicos, lobbyists, and business people gravitate toward this clubby bar that has a quality view of the passing sidewalk crowd. In addition to a lively bar scene, this place has surprisingly good food: handmade pasta, fresh seafood, and veal dishes. For brunch, try one of the 10 versions of eggs Benedict. ♦ American ♦ M-F lunch and dinner; Sa-Su brunch and dinner. Reservations recommended. 3150 M St NW (at Wisconsin Ave). 338.2000 &

19 Georgetown Tobacco Native Washingtonian David Berkebile has supplied the city with smokes since 1964—ever popular with celebrities and politicians, including Anwar Sadat who used to stock up on the store's special-blend pipe tobacco. ♦ M-Sa 10AM-9PM; Su noon-8PM. 3144 M St NW (between 31st St and Wisconsin Ave). 338.5100 & Also at: Tyson's Corner Center, 1961 Chain Bridge Rd (between I-495 and International Dr), McLean, Virginia. 703/893.3366

20 Bistro Français ★★★$$ Francophiles will delight in the authentic bistro fare prepared in a romantic wood- and mirror-paneled restaurant. This cafe is great for after the theater and it stays open to the wee hours. ♦ French ♦ Daily lunch, dinner, and late-night meals. 3128 M St NW (between 31st St and Wisconsin Ave). 338.3830 &

21 Mr. Smith's ★$ Fresh fruit daiquiris and the garden patio are the big advertised draws for this casual restaurant, but the piano bar in the front room also packs them in. Good burgers and sandwiches round out the fun. ♦ American ♦ Daily lunch and dinner. 3104 M St NW (between 31st St and Wisconsin Ave). 333.3104 &

22 Booked Up Up an iron stairway, this antiquarian bookstore, owned by Larry McMurtry, author of *Lonesome Dove* and *The Last Picture Show,* features a broad collection ranging from first editions of *The Maltese Falcon* to 15th-century incunabula. ♦ M-F 11AM-3PM; Sa 10AM-12:30PM. 1204 31st St NW (between M and N Sts). 965.3244

22 Urban Outfitters This is the source for dorm-room furnishings, Girbaud and Generra casual clothing, wacky postcards, and just about every other necessity for the Georgetown University set. ♦ M-Th 10AM-10PM; F-Sa 10AM-11PM; Su noon-8PM. 3111 M St NW (between 31st St and Wisconsin Ave). 342.1012 &

23 Old Glory All American Barbecue ★$$ Reveling in the flag, Elvis, Patsy Cline, and everything else that makes our country unique, this place has a noisy downstairs bar with TVs blaring the day's big sporting event and an upstairs dining room that is a little calmer. There's a choice of several sauces for your ribs. It's not as good as mamma's home cookin', though. ♦ Barbecue ♦ Daily lunch and dinner. 3139 M St NW (between 31st St and Wisconsin Ave). 337.3406

24 J. Paul's ★$$ The under-30 preppy crowd bellies up to the bar, while the dining room features decent bar food such as fresh seafood, pasta, burgers, chicken, and ribs. Check out the "meet market" at the bar through the large picture windows. ♦ American ♦ M-F lunch and dinner; Sa-Su brunch and dinner. 3218 M St NW (between Wisconsin Ave and Warehouse Pl). 333.3450 &

24 The Shops at Georgetown Park With more than a hundred stores, boutiques, and shops, this $100-million shopping complex is impressive by any standards. Billed as the world's first shopping park, it is the only such commercial venture that overlaps a national park—the historic **C&O Canal** (see page 129), which has supported Georgetown trade since 1831. It was certainly the first DC shopping mall to capture the attention of well-heeled shoppers and reverse the retail traffic pattern back into Northwest Washington. And it may be the first shopping mall anywhere to be included on group-tour itineraries.

Built in 1981 behind a preserved and reconstructed century-old facade in the heart of commercial Georgetown, the mall boasts a magnificent Victorian interior. Its three levels of brass-and-iron-railed mezzanine shopping encircle a grand atrium and an indoor garden that flourishes under the skylight roof. All the details, from the brass-and-glass elevators to regular performances of classical music, give **Georgetown Park** an aura of sophistication (the prices do, too). This is not a bargain-hunter's paradise. Sale signs are small, unobtrusive—and rare. Buzzwords such as "European-tailored," "chic," and "unique" aren't exaggerations. This is snob shopping at its best.

Among the mall's tony fashion boutiques are **Polo Ralph Lauren** (965.0904) for men and **Cache** (342.0146) and **Bebe** (965.2323) for women's apparel. For gifts and furniture, try the **Bombay Company** (333.0852), and for fine toys, there's **FAO Schwarz** (965.7000). The **Chesapeake Knife and Tool Co.** (338.5700) carries an international selection of cutlery, hunting and collectors' knives, and accessories. Visit **Godiva Chocolatier** (342.2232) for the most delectable calories; **Waldenbooks** (333.8033) for paperback best-sellers as well as fine art, literature, and history books; and **Victoria's Secret** (965.5457) for lingerie, from modest to racy. The **Canal Walk Cafes** offer a variety of light items that won't bog you down during your shopping expedition. Shoppers get up to two hours free parking with a $10 purchase, validated at the concierge center. ♦ Mall: M-Sa 9AM-9PM; Su noon-6PM. Individual store hours may vary. 3222 M St NW (between Wisconsin Ave and Warehouse Pl). 298.5577

25 The Body Shop Stop in for quality (and environmentally correct) skin lotions, shampoos, soaps, and other personal grooming items. ♦ M-Sa 10AM-9:30PM; Su noon-7PM. 3207 M St NW (between Wisconsin Ave and Potomac St). 298.7353 &

26 Clyde's ★★$$ Over 30 years old and nicely renovated in 1996, this archetypal fern bar has matured nicely, thank you. It's the place's classics that bring people back: the quintessential cozy-pub decor, good thick burgers, excellent crab cakes, and brunch—still among the best omelettes and Bloody Marys around. ♦ American ♦ M-F lunch and dinner; Sa-Su brunch and dinner. 3236 M St NW (between Wisconsin Ave and Warehouse Pl). 333.9180 &

27 Dean & DeLuca Georgetown New York's acclaimed food market has a Washington outpost in the heart of Georgetown, right next door to **The Shops at Georgetown Park** (see page 131). Shopping here is a twofold experience: First your eyes pop at the vast selection of coffees, fresh pastas, deli items, fresh fish and meats, and gourmet nibblings; then your eyes pop again at the price of such quality. Careful shopping does yield some relative bargains. ♦ M-Th, Sa-Su 10AM-8PM; F 10AM-9PM. 3276 M St NW (between Warehouse Pl and 33rd St). 342.2500 &

Within Dean & Deluca Georgetown:

Dean & DeLuca Cafe ★★★$$ Take a load off with a cup of espresso or a sandwich. As with the food emporium, if you order carefully, the bill won't dent your wallet too severely. ♦ Cafe ♦ Daily breakfast, lunch, and dinner. 342.2500 & Also at: 1299 Pennsylvania Ave NW (at 13th St). 628.8155 & Metros: Federal Triangle, Metro Center

27 April Cornell Try warming up a room with the richly ornate, hand-printed tablecloths, placemats, comforters, and duvets for sale here. The patterns really are exquisite. Vintage-style women's clothing and pottery are also sold. ♦ Daily. 3278 M St NW (between Warehouse Pl and 33rd St). 625.7887

28 Aditi ★★★$$ This may not be the plushest Indian restaurant in town, but it's certainly one of the best, with complex curries, tandoori chicken, stir-fried lamb, and vegetarian selections that are just as satisfying as the meat dishes. ♦ Indian ♦ Daily lunch and dinner. 3299 M St NW (at 33rd St). 625.6825 &

Zed's

INDESCRIBABLY DELICIOUS

29 Zed's Ethiopian Cuisine ★★$$ Excellent *wats* and *alechas* (spicy sweet stews) and the best *injera* (a soft bread used in place of utensils) in DC can be found here. ♦ Ethiopian ♦ Daily lunch and dinner. Reservations recommended for six people or more. 3318 M St NW (between 33rd St and the Francis Scott Key Bridge). 333.4710 &

30 Stoddert House This large, rangy, and ornate Federal town house was built in 1787 by owner and architect **Benjamin Stoddert**, who called it **Halcyon House**. Although the north facade has been completely redesigned, the south side and garden of this private residence remain as they were two centuries ago. ♦ 3400 Prospect St NW (at 34th St)

31 Quality Hill The entire neighborhood may once have been called Quality Hill after its many fine homes; somehow, this 18th-century house by **John Thomson Mason** was the sole inheritor of the nickname. It is now a private residence. ♦ 3425 Prospect St NW (between 34th and 35th Sts)

32 Prospect House The view (or prospect) of the Potomac commanded from this sharply detailed Federal house by **James M. Lingan** is the basis for the name. Built in 1788, the house is now a private residence. ♦ 3508 Prospect St NW (between 35th and 37th Sts)

33 3600 Prospect Street Northwest Scenes in *The Exorcist* were filmed at this redbrick building owned by **Georgetown University.** It was modified for the movie, but you can still walk down the steep steps (to M St) where the title character met his fate. ♦ Between 35th and 37th Sts

34 1789 ★★★★$$$$ Tucked in a town house, this restaurant offers impeccable service and a lavishly intimate Federal-style decor. Limoges china, oil lamps, and a blazing fireplace in winter add to the enchanting mood. The menu is American, with chef Ris Lacoste often focusing on seafood. Crab cakes are a good starter, followed by the excellent rack of lamb in Merlot sauce. A pre-theater menu is served from 6PM to 6:45PM. There's free valet parking. ♦ American ♦ Daily dinner. Reservations recommended; jacket required. 1226 36th St NW (at Prospect St). 965.1789 ♿

35 Georgetown University Founded by John Carroll in 1789, the country's first Roman Catholic university has always been open to "students of every religious profession" and today its students hail from 110 countries around the world. But even if you haven't come for an education, its shady cobblestoned streets also make for a pleasant walk.

The **Old North Building** was the original structure, finished in 1792. The fortresslike **Healy Building,** built in 1879 by **Smithmeyer and Pelz,** is a grim German Gothic affair topped with an amazing spire. (The best view of the school's famous spires is to be had across the river in Arlington.) The building was named for the Reverend Patrick Healy, the country's first black person to earn a doctorate.

The university's highly regarded School of Medicine sponsors a 535-bed hospital. Other colleges include schools of arts and sciences, nursing, business administration, and language, as well as the country's most applied-to law school. **GU**'s location in the nation's capital is one reason it includes the country's first and largest foreign service program.

Campus tours can be arranged by calling the undergraduate admissions office three weeks in advance. ♦ 37th St NW (between Prospect and P Sts). Information 687.5055, admissions and tours 687.3600 ♿

36 Cox's Row Built in 1817 by **John Cox,** this is often acclaimed as the finest series of Federal row houses in Georgetown. Some of the middle houses were remodeled during the Victorian era; the end houses remain as they were originally built. All are private residences now. ♦ 3327-39 N St NW (between 33rd and 34th Sts)

37 Smith Row These five Federal houses, side by side, are nearly identical in construction. Built in 1815 by **Walter** and **Clement Smith,** all are now private residences. ♦ 3255-63 N St NW (between Potomac and 33rd Sts)

38 Booeymonger ★★$ Huge sandwiches to eat in or take out are the specialty at this small cafe. Also try its locally famous cinnamon coffee. ♦ American ♦ Daily breakfast, lunch, and dinner. 3265 Prospect St NW (at Potomac St). 333.4810 ♿

39 Morton's of Chicago ★★★$$$$ A favorite of Capitol Hill powerbrokers, this macho steak house makes a show of parading its raw beef before customers to demonstrate its quality and freshness. In truth, the steak and prime rib, which are shipped in from Chicago, are widely considered the best around. Be prepared, however, to pay dearly: These magnificent slabs of meat command hefty prices. ♦ Steak house ♦ Daily dinner. Reservations recommended. 3251 Prospect St NW (between Wisconsin Ave and Potomac St). 342.6258 ♿ Also at: 8075 Leesburg Pike (at Old Gallows Rd), Tyson's Corner, Virginia. 703/883.0800 ♿

39 Cafe Milano ★★$$$ Haute cuisine and haute couture combine to make this cafe a people watchers paradise. The "show" is good, and the fare is fresh and delicate; good choices include *vitello tonnato* (veal in a creamy tomato sauce) and any of the enormous salads with shaved parmesan. ♦ Italian ♦ Daily lunch and dinner. 3251 Prospect St NW (between Wisconsin Ave and Potomac St). 333.6183 ♿

Restaurants/Clubs: Red   **Hotels:** Blue

Shops/ ♥ Outdoors: Green   **Sights/Culture:** Black

39 Georgetown Billiards There are 25 pool tables here, but something about the place isn't quite right—it lacks a heart. Still, if you're in the mood for a game of eight ball, this is the place. ◆ M-Th 11AM-midnight; F-Sa 11AM-2AM. 3251 Prospect St NW (between Wisconsin Ave and Potomac St). 965.POOL ᕟ

40 Restoration Hardware This California-based outlet is not your father's hardware store. Occupying the old **Key Theater** (pictures of the much-loved **Key** hang in the windows), this shop carries furniture, housewares, hardware, and offbeat items that invoke an earlier era—including the Slinky, rubber gardening boots, and cocktail shakers. ◆ M-Sa 10AM-9PM; Su noon-6PM. 1222 Wisconsin Ave NW (between M and Prospect Sts). 625.2771; www.restorationhardware.com ᕟ

41 Olsson's Books & Records The staff is knowledgeable and will special-order books; the classical-recordings section is tops. Famous authors appear now and then to autograph their latest offerings. ◆ M-Th 10AM-10:45PM; F-Sa 10AM-midnight; Su noon-7PM. 1239 Wisconsin Ave NW (between M and N Sts). 338.9544 ᕟ Also at: numerous locations throughout the area

42 Britches of Georgetowne This is the uncontested headquarters for young professionals seeking a distinctively trendy look. **Britches Great Outdoors** (333.3666) is down the block at No. 1225. You can shop at several locations throughout the DC metropolitan area. ◆ M, W, F-Sa; Tu, Th 10AM-9PM; Su noon-6PM. 1247 Wisconsin Ave NW (between M and N Sts). 338.3330 ᕟ Also at: numerous locations throughout the city

42 Diesel This outrageous Italian jeans company has staked its claim on the neighborhood's young shoppers, male and female. Mod tops and accessories can also be found here. ◆ M-Th 10AM-8PM; F-Sa 10AM-9PM; Su 11:30AM-7PM. 1249 Wisconsin Ave NW (between M and N Sts). 625.2780 ᕟ

43 Martin's Tavern ★★$$ The oldest tavern in Georgetown is warm, classy, and quieter than most other Irish pubs. Tiffany lamps and gold-framed paintings give the place a clubby feeling. The conservative clientele comes for the Virginia crab cakes or the excellent lamb chops. Especially charming around Christmas, the dining room is overtaken with extravagant decorations and holly, and a big red bow wraps the facade. ◆ Irish/American ◆ M-F breakfast, lunch, and dinner; Sa-Su brunch and dinner. 1264 Wisconsin Ave NW (at N St). 333.7370 ᕟ

44 Martin's A fine selection of high-quality china, crystal, porcelain, and silver is offered here. ◆ M-Sa. 1304 Wisconsin Ave NW (between N and O Sts). 338.6144 ᕟ

44 The Georgetown Inn $$$ This 95-room hotel, one in a series of restored 18th-century buildings, features traditional decor and fine antiques throughout. Amenities include a restaurant (see below), small health club, room service, and valet parking. ◆ 1310 Wisconsin Ave NW (between N and O Sts). 333.8900, 800/424.2979; fax 625.1744 ᕟ

Within The Georgetown Inn:

Daily Grill ★★$$ Harking back to American grills of the 1920s, this casual eatery sports simple black booths, burnished wood, and black-and-white photos of Georgetown. Best bets from the enormous menu include Manhattan clam chowder, blackened chicken sandwich, Cobb salad, and strawberry shortcake. ◆ American ◆ M-Sa lunch and dinner; Su brunch and dinner. 337.4900 ᕟ

45 Susquehanna Antiques American and English antiques of the 18th and 19th centuries, plus some 19th- and 20th-century paintings, can be found here. ◆ M-Sa. 3216 O St (between Wisconsin Ave and Potomac St). 333.5843 ᕟ

45 St. John's Episcopal Church, Georgetown Parish The second-oldest Episcopal church in DC was built in 1809 by **Dr. William Thornton** and renovated in 1870 by **Starkweather & Plowman.** Like **Thornton**'s design for the **Capitol,** this Georgian edifice was drastically altered in the renovation. ◆ M-Th 9AM-3:30PM. Services: Su 8:30AM, 10AM. 3240 O St NW (at Potomac St). 338.1796 ᕟ

46 Commander Salamander The source for all things fabulous: myriad articles of black clothing, sequins, rhinestone sunglasses, and the latest in hairspray colors. The funky-punky clientele alone is worth seeing. ♦ M-Th 10AM-10PM; F-Sa 10AM-11PM; Su noon-8PM. 1420 Wisconsin Ave NW (between O and P Sts). 337.2265 ⚹

47 Just Paper/Georgetown Paint and Paper Handmade gift wrap, faux-finishing supplies, tea in bulk, unusual pens, and creative cards are just some of the wonderful miscellany that fill this shop. ♦ M-Sa; Su noon-4PM. 3232 P St NW (at Wisconsin Ave). 333.9141

48 Au Pied de Cochon ★$ A bustling, affable round-the-clock bistro, it serves hearty French fare: omelettes, crepes, quiches, pigs' feet, and ratatouille. The black bean soup is great, but the best buy is the lobster, when it's available. During colder months, the glass-enclosed patio is a cozy place to drink mugs of coffee; let it snow. ♦ French ♦ Daily 24 hours. 1335 Wisconsin Ave NW (at Dumbarton St). 337.6400 ⚹

BETSEY JOHNSON

48 Betsey Johnson A bevy of zebra skirts, crushed-velvet dresses, fleecy coats with that destroyed-by-the-dry-cleaner look, and plaid everything is displayed in this ultra hip shop. If this is your thing (and your wallet allows), go ahead and pounce. ♦ M-F; Sa 11AM-8PM; Su noon-6PM. 1319 Wisconsin Ave NW (between N and Dumbarton Sts). 338.4090

49 Paolo's ★★$ Hugely popular, this bar/restaurant fills the narrow site with a pleasing sense of space and style. The service here is both brisk and friendly, and the pasta, salads, and fish of the day stand out on the modern menu. ♦ Italian ♦ Daily lunch and dinner. 1303 Wisconsin Ave NW (between N and Dumbarton Sts). 333.7353 ⚹

50 Laird Mansion (Laird/Dunlop Lovering House) Built in 1799 by **William Lovering,** this was originally the home of tobacco merchant John Laird. Robert Todd Lincoln, son of the 16th president, also once owned this Federal-period mansion, now a private residence. ♦ 3014 N St NW (between 30th and 31st Sts)

51 Decatur House After Commodore Stephen Decatur, the dashing naval hero of the War of 1812, was killed in a duel, his widow moved to this stately Federal-style house. Built in 1813 by **John Stull Williams,** it is now a private residence. ♦ 2812 N St NW (between 28th and 29th Sts)

52 Christ Church, Georgetown Built in 1886 by **Henry Law,** this scaled-down Gothic cathedral features an unusual gabled tower.

Although it's too small to be really awe-inspiring, it fits neatly into the neighborhood. This is actually the third building on the site; the parish was founded in 1817. The chapel and its garden, adjacent to the west of the church, were added in 1968. The chapel was designed by **Philip Ives,** and the garden landscape design was by Peter G. Rolland. Francis Scott Key was a member of the Episcopal congregation. ♦ Services: M-F noon, 6PM; Su 8AM, 9AM, 11AM. 31st and O Sts NW. 333.6677 ⚹

53 Miller House This New England clapboard–style house is set in the midst of the city's original neighborhood. The portico hints at the Greek Revival styles that gained popularity soon after it was built in 1840. It's now a private residence. ♦ 1524 28th St NW (between P and Q Sts)

54 Reuben Daw's Fence Made in the 1860s of musket barrels from the 1848 Mexican-American War, this fence encloses three houses on P Street and a pair on 28th Street. ♦ 2803 P St NW (at 28th St)

55 Appalachian Spring Fine country-style American crafts, including pottery, quilts, and jewelry, are sold here. ♦ M-Sa; Su noon-6PM. 1415 Wisconsin Ave NW (between O and P Sts). 337.5780 ⚹ Also at: Union Station, 50 Massachusetts Ave NE (at First St), East Hall. 682.0505 ⚹ Metro: Union Station; Reston Town Center, New Dominion Pkwy (off Reston Pkwy), Reston, Virginia. 703/478.2218 ⚹

55 Little Caledonia This treasure trove of furnishings for Anglophiles has kitchenware, fabrics, furniture, lamps, and one of the best Christmas-card selections going. ♦ M-Sa. 1419 Wisconsin Ave NW (between O and P Sts). 333.4700 ⚹

55 Opportunity Shop of the Christ Child Society A consignment and thrift shop like you've never seen. Downstairs is the conventional thrift shop; upstairs is a treasure trove of silver, furniture, and china culled from some of the finest homes in Washington. ♦ Tu-Sa 10AM-3:45PM. 1427 Wisconsin Ave NW (at P St). 333.6635

Thomas Twining, writing in 1795, describes Georgetown as "a small but neat town . . . the road from Virginia and the Southern States, crossing the Potomac here, already gives an air of prosperity to this little town, and assures its future importance, whatever may be the fate of the projected metropolis."

The Architecture of Washington, American Institute of Architects

55 Thomas Sweet Ice Cream *Bon Appetit* named this old-fashioned ice-cream parlor "among the ten best in America." Fine coffee, bagels, soup, and homemade sandwiches are also in the offering. ♦ M-Sa 8AM-midnight; Su 9AM-midnight. 3214 P St NW (at Wisconsin Ave). 337.0616

56 Hugo Boss Elegant men's suits, casual sportswear, accessories, and other items by the German designer fill this shop. ♦ M-Sa 11AM-8PM; Su noon-6PM. 1517 Wisconsin Ave NW (between P and Q Sts). 625.BOSS

57 The Phoenix This boutique offers a quality collection of hand-crafted items from Mexico: wedding dresses, contemporary silver jewelry, women's clothing, candelabras, and pottery. ♦ M-Sa; Su 1-6PM. 1514 Wisconsin Ave NW (between P St and Volta Pl). 338.4404 ♿

57 Secondhand Rose Shop here for contemporary women's clothing in almost-new condition at good prices, with many designer names and cocktail dresses. The really cheap stuff is in the bathroom. ♦ M-Sa Jan-June, Sept-Dec; Tu-Sa July-Aug. 1516 Wisconsin Ave NW (between P St and Volta Pl). 337.3378

58 Pomander Walk Renovation in the 1950s changed this from a blighted alley to a charming set of private residences.

59 Volta Bureau Built in 1893 by **Peabody & Stearns,** this strange amalgam of early Roman temple and institution is home to the Alexander Graham Bell Association for the Deaf. Bell funded the building with money he received from his work on improving the phonograph, and there's a small monument to him inside. ♦ M-F. 3417 Volta Pl NW (at 35th St). 337.5220 ♿

Mount Zion United Methodist Church at 1334 29th Street Northwest is reportedly the oldest black congregation in the District of Columbia, with records that go back to 1830. Before the Civil War it was a station on the Underground Railroad.

The highest-ranking KGB agent to defect from the Soviet Union, Vitaly Yurchenko, did so after dining at the venerable Au Pied de Cochon. Soon after, the Georgetown restaurant introduced the "Yurchenko shooter," a drink of Stolichnaya and Grand Marnier.

60 Convent of the Visitation After a near-disastrous fire in 1993 destroyed much of Visitation School, the convent and school were rebuilt and expanded. The convent's three buildings—an 1820 Federal-style chapel, a Gothic monastery, and an ornate Victorian school building dating from 1872—represent a merry pastiche of 19th-century tastes. ♦ 35th St NW (between P St and Reservoir Rd)

61 Mackall-Worthington House Built in 1820 by **Leonard Mackall,** this large, Federal-style house was once the focal point of the neighborhood it occupies. The incongruous mansard roof was added later. A private residence, it is not open to the public. ♦ 1686 34th St NW (between Reservoir Rd and R St)

62 A Mano Glimmers of Provence and Tuscany suffuse this shop where majolica and faience tableware and garden pots, fine linens, and imported silver abound. ♦ M–Sa; Su noon–5PM. 1677 Wisconsin Ave NW (between Q and R Sts). 298.7200

63 Patisserie Poupon Simply the best and most artistic pastries and chocolate in the city are created at this authentic Parisian patisserie. Whether for tea or lunch, customers are tempted by sweets, salad platters, huge baguette sandwiches, and superb coffee. ♦ Tu-Su. 1645 Wisconsin Ave NW (between Q and R Sts). 342.3248

64 Tudor Place Martha Washington's granddaughter, Martha Parke Custis, and her husband, Thomas Peter, were the original occupants of this house, completed in 1816 by architect **Dr. William Thornton.** Their descendants lived here until 1983. Between 1805 and 1816, wings were added to the original pavilion; the entire structure is now open to the public as a historic house, with period furnishings and formal gardens. Breathtaking candlelit tours are given during the Christmas season. ♦ Voluntary contribution. Tours: Tu-F 10AM, 11:30AM, 1PM, 2:30PM; Sa 10AM-3PM, on the hour. Reservations required. 1644 31st St NW (between Q and R Sts). 965.0400

Dumbarton House

65 Cooke's Row Although Georgetown is perhaps best known for its Federal-style buildings, these mid-Victorian charmers offer a welcome twist on the row-house theme. Built in 1868 by **Starkweather & Plowman,** each of the four villas has more than 4,000 square feet of space and its own side yard. The exterior details—bay windows, dormers, porches—give each building its own character: The outer two are in the Second Empire style; the middle two are Italianate. Inside, however, these four private residences have exactly the same floor plan. ♦ 3009-29 Q St NW (between 30th and 31st Sts)

66 Dumbarton House Known until 1932 as **Bellevue,** this is a typical early 19th-century Georgian home complete with oval rooms, ornate mantels, and breezy hallways (see above). **Benjamin Latrobe** installed the rear bays. The house is now owned by the National Society of the Colonial Dames of America, which has maintained the Federal furnishings, including Hepplewhite and Sheraton pieces, and fine collections of silver and china. Tours available; call for times. ♦ Tu-Sa 9:30AM-noon. 2715 Q St NW (between 27th and 28th Sts). 337.2288 ♿

67 Evermay In 1801, when it was built by **King and Hedges,** this was considered the most elegant house in the city—and that was back when opulence was the neighborhood norm. Now a private residence, it has been restored to its former extravagance, and features a garden of Southern favorites such as azaleas, magnolias, and boxwood. ♦ 1623 28th St NW (between Q and R Sts)

68 Beall House George Washington's great-nephew, Colonel George Corbin Washington, and his bride, Elizabeth Beall, were given this house as a wedding gift by her father. The original Georgian structure, built in 1784, has been much altered. The building is now a private residence. ♦ R St NW (between 28th and 32nd Sts)

68 Oak Hill Cemetery Such notables as John Howard Paine (author of *Home, Sweet Home*); statesmen Edwin M. Stanton, James G. Blaine, and Dean Acheson; and socialite Peggy O'Neil are buried in this cemetery, given to the city by William Wilson Corcoran. The **1849 Gatehouse** and the simple Gothic Revival chapel, built in 1850 by **James Renwick,** are architecturally noteworthy. ♦ M-F. 3001 R St NW (between 28th and 32nd Sts). 337.2835

69 Montrose Park This small, quiet woodland-hugging park has tennis courts, a playground, picnic areas, and walking trails. **Lovers Lane,** a cobblestone walking path, forms the western border, separating Montrose and **Dumbarton Oaks** estate (see below). Tennis courts are available on a first-come, first-served basis. ♦ R St NW (between 28th and 32nd Sts). 426.6827 ♿

One of the most distinctive elements of Washington Harbour's Postmodern architecture is a series of large lampposts that line the property's riverfront. The "lampposts" are actually pylons supporting an electronic floodgate that can be raised when the Potomac threatens.

Restaurants/Clubs: Red	Hotels: Blue
Shops/♀Outdoors: Green	Sights/Culture: Black

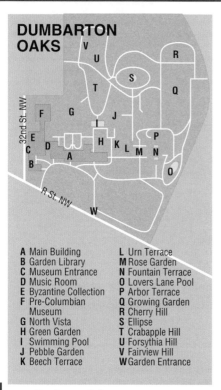

DUMBARTON OAKS

A Main Building
B Garden Library
C Museum Entrance
D Music Room
E Byzantine Collection
F Pre-Columbian Museum
G North Vista
H Green Garden
I Swimming Pool
J Pebble Garden
K Beech Terrace
L Urn Terrace
M Rose Garden
N Fountain Terrace
O Lovers Lane Pool
P Arbor Terrace
Q Growing Garden
R Cherry Hill
S Ellipse
T Crabapple Hill
U Forsythia Hill
V Fairview Hill
W Garden Entrance

Several libraries house books reserved for scholars, although the **Rare Books Room** is sometimes open for viewing. The libraries hold more than 100,000 books on landscape gardening and Byzantine and pre-Columbian art.

The 10 acres of formal gardens designed by Beatrix Farrand and Mrs. Bliss are a wonderland of manicured walkways, terraces, arbors, and pools. A favorite spot is the Pebble Garden Fountain, an expanse of intricately patterned pebble mosaics that sparkle through a thin layer of water in spring and summer. A graceful Italianate fountain features a pair of putti romping on seahorses while water springs from the hands of a third. ◆ Admission Apr-Oct; free Nov-Mar. Museum: Tu-Su 2-5PM. Gardens: Daily 2-6PM Apr-Oct; 2-5PM Nov-Mar. 1703 32nd St NW (between R and S Sts). Information 339.6401, tours for groups of 12 or more 339.6400

71 Dumbarton Oaks Park These 27 acres of natural woodlands are particularly well known for their profusion of spring wildflowers. The fact that they are only accessible by foot—via **Lovers Lane** off 31st and R Streets—helps keep them unspoiled. The land was given to the city by Robert and Mildred Bliss, who once lived next door at Dumbarton Oaks. No picnicking or pets are allowed on the grounds.

70 Dumbarton Oaks Famous for its enchanting gardens and world-class museums of Byzantine and Pre-Columbian art, this estate was originally part of the Port of Georgetown land grant made by Queen Anne in 1702. Former ambassador Robert Woods Bliss purchased the property in 1920, and he and his wife, Mildred, began assembling the present museum collection. In 1963 **Philip Johnson** designed a small museum (a group of nine domed glass cylinders) to house the **Pre-Columbian Collection.** The intricate objects designed by Aztecs, Mayans, and other peoples include gold necklaces and jade figurines. The adjacent **Byzantine Collection** displays mosaics, sculpture, ivories, and other medieval items. The restored 1801 mansion is filled with European art and architectural treasures; the **Music Room,** where the Blisses entertained such noted friends as composer Igor Stravinsky, contains El Greco's *The Visitation.*

72 Japan Inn ★★★$$$ Sit at a communal table in the **Teppan-Yaki Room** and have your steak, chicken, or shrimp cooked on a stainless-steel grill right before your eyes. If you want a more private experience, reserve a tatami room upstairs, where you'll sit at a low table and sup on sukiyaki and *shabu shabu* (sliced beef and vegetables cooked in a pot of hot broth) prepared by a kimonoed waitress at your table. If you have a big appetite, order a full dinner of sashimi, sushi, or tempura. ◆ Japanese ◆ M-F lunch and dinner; Sa-Su dinner. Reservations recommended. 1715 Wisconsin Ave NW (between R and S Sts). 337.3400 &

73 Miller and Arney Antiques, Inc. Eighteenth- and 19th-century American and European antiques, as well as lamps, rugs, and accessories, can be found here. ◆ M-Sa. 1737 Wisconsin Ave NW (at S St). 338.2369 &

Bests

Erich Parker
Senior Vice President-Communications, Association & Issues Management

The best cappuccino in town can be found at **Casa Italiana,** the social hall connected to **Holy Rosary Church** (595 Third St NW, at F St). After every mass on Sunday, you can queue up to one table to pay for your libation (half of Starbucks' take) and then wait

on another line to turn in the little slip of paper you've just been given in exchange for your reward. So Italian. And so worth the wait.

Café La Ruche is aptly named. A beehive of activity it is, in the best tradition of a neighborhood bistro. The neighborhood is **Georgetown**—not so tony as it once was—which makes the stroll to **La Ruche** all the more appealing. Owner/chef Jean-Claude Cauderlier will treat you like family and charge you like family. The prices can't be beat. The tuna steaks make me crazy, and the pastries, made on the premises, will simply change your life.

Washington, DC is often touted as the fourth-largest theater town in the country. All well and good, but it's theater troupes like **Washington Shakespeare Company** (actually located just across the **Potomac** in **Arlington,** Virginia) that make Washington an *exciting* theater town. Heavy on the Bard, but you're just as likely to see Brecht, Strindberg, or Stoppard. They take risks; they assume you've got a brain in your head.

The overpass on the **Washington Beltway (I-495)** that you approach (traveling south toward Maryland) just as the towering spires of the **Mormon Temple** come into view always brings a smile. No matter what. There, just as the temple appears above the tree line, gleaming and otherworldly, you see the work of a graffiti artist/wag who's painted "Surrender Dorothy" on the elevated roadway. Of course, the authorities paint over it, and weeks later the Wicked Witch's admonition appears again. Like magic.

You'll pinch yourself, thinking you've walked through the looking glass and into an Italian villa or perhaps a grand public space on The Continent. But you haven't; you're in the **Great Hall** of the **Jefferson Building** of the **Library of Congress.** Breathtaking marble staircases, statuary, and frescoes (painted in the 19th century by Brumidi), all on a scale that makes this one of the exalted indoor sights of the city.

If you're in town on a Sunday and like to treasure hunt, you can't beat the **Georgetown Flea Market.** It's been a staple of Washington life for countless years. Over 150 stalls in a public school parking lot offer up the furniture, china, books, rugs, silver, artwork, vintage clothing, jewelry, and assorted unclassifiable stuff that Washington's cliff dwellers and transient diplomatic community have collected or hoarded or simply acquired along the way. It's all about patina, dust, stunning lines, aggressively bad taste, memories and, yes, sometimes amazing buys. How about a hand-carved, wooden corner bracket from mid-1800s China or a mahogany chair from the floor of the House of Representatives? Both recent flea market finds!

When I'm trying to impress an out-of-towner, I'll always casually, even offhandedly, suggest meeting at the **Whistler Room** in the **Freer Gallery,** "a pleasant spot from which to head to lunch or visit one of the museums that line the Mall." Pleasant indeed. Try exquisite or shimmering or ravishing. Suffice to say, we usually linger there so long that our luncheon menu boasts a vendor hot dog, and our luncheon conversation examines my newfound gift for understatement.

Remember those sing-alongs around the campfire? Well, drop by **Xando** coffee bar near **Dupont Circle** (1647 20th St NW, at R St) for a scouting jamboree flashback. Yes, they've got s'mores on the menu. And just like camp, you make your own. The graham crackers, chocolate bars, and marshmallows are served around a sterno pot that looks like it came from a Polynesian restaurant equipment closeout. It's funky fondue for baby boomers. You can almost smell the Clearasil.

Nora Pouillon
Executive Chef/Owner, Restaurant Nora and Asia Nora

Attending the Sunday morning farmers' market at **Dupont Circle**—wonderful farmers selling fresh, seasonal produce—a great "village" atmosphere right in the heart of DC.

Going to the **East Wing** of the **National Gallery of Art,** where there are always interesting exhibits.

Also, the **Museum of Natural History, Freer Gallery,** and **Holocaust Museum,** along with so many of the other great museums in DC.

Bicycle riding along the paths of the canal.

Dinner at **Nora**'s—of course!

Roller Blading skating and biking along **Beach Drive** when it is closed.

Visiting **the memorials at night**—the **Lincoln, Vietnam Wall** in particular—and sitting on the steps of the **Jefferson** overlooking the **Tidal Basin** across to the **White House.**

If spring, definitely check out the fantastic cherry blossoms around the Tidal Basin and drive through the dogwood trees and azaleas in the **Kenwood** neighborhood of **Bethesda,** Maryland.

Check out what is on at the **Kennedy Center.**

Take tea at **The Four Seasons Hotel** in **Georgetown.**

For night life, go to **BET** or the **930 Club,** where there are always good bands/music.

Shop in **Georgetown Park**—stop at **Dean & DeLuca** for coffee or lunch and don't forget to wander around the store and enjoy their fantastic selection of produce.

Rent a boat on the **Potomac** and go across to **Roosevelt Island.**

Step back into history and visit **Mount Vernon.**

Scour the antiques shops on **Wisconsin Avenue.**

Visit the **Washington National Cathedral.**

Go for a drink at the top of the **Hotel Washington** on 15th Street.

Ice skating in front of the **Willard Hotel.**

Dining at **Asia Nora** too!

Driving out to the **Eastern Shore** and visit **St. Michael's** and **Tillman's Island**—perfect for antiquing.

The only two American presidents to be buried in Arlington Cemetery are John F. Kennedy and William Howard Taft.

Upper Northwest

Woodley Park, Tenleytown, Cleveland Park, Spring Valley, Friendship Heights, and **Chevy Chase/DC** are all mini-neighborhoods in the triangle-shaped area known as Upper Northwest. Possessing a definite suburban feel, this is where many of Washington's loveliest homes and some of its finest shops can be found. **American University** is here, as is the **US Naval Observatory**, site of the vice president's residence. Nearby, on one of Washington's highest elevations, sits the magnificent **National Cathedral.** The area's two main commercial thoroughfares, **Wisconsin** and **Connecticut Avenues,** are lined with some of the city's finest historic apartment buildings, particularly along Connecticut north of the **National Zoo.** Upper Northwest's third "Main Street," **Massachusetts Avenue,** is lined with embassies both magnificent and modest. Adding to the refined atmosphere is the Cleveland Park area, between the **Cathedral** and Connecticut Avenue. Cleveland Park takes its name from President Grover Cleveland who, in the late 19th century, led an exodus of Washingtonians here to escape downtown's steamy summer humidity, which was especially suffocating in the low-lying **Mall** area near the **Potomac.** The higher ground and leafy shade trees in this area provided respite and a site for luxurious mansions, one of which—**Hillwood,** owned by cereal heiress Marjorie Merriweather Post—now serves as a museum.

Washington's most far-flung neighborhood, Upper Northwest offers the quiet of suburbia within city limits and rewards the casual stroller with yet another view of our multifaceted national home. But unless you're driving, reaching certain spots in this tranquil refuge can be time-consuming: As some places are far from any **Metrorail** stop, the slower **Metrobus** is your only option.

From 1941 until he became President in 1945 Harry Truman, with wife Bess and daughter Margaret, lived at 4701 Connecticut Avenue Northwest, No. 209. After FDR's death, the Trumans moved from the apartment to Blair House (to allow Mrs. Roosevelt time to leave the White House) and then to 1600 Pennsylvania Avenue.

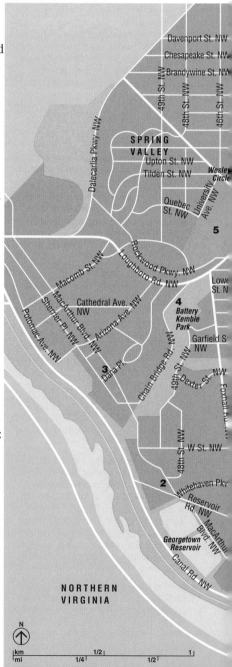

1 Embassy of the Federal Republic of Germany This construction cleverly fit a lot of working space into a narrow, sloping site. A white steel trellis lightens the bulk of the structure, built in 1964 by **Egon Eiermann,** and makes it compatible with the residential neighborhood. The cool, sophisticated design is vastly more imaginative than most Washington embassies. ♦ M-F 9AM-noon. 4645 Reservoir Rd NW (between Foxhall Rd and 47th St). 298.4000

2 Once Is Not Enough Some of the secondhand clothing in this second-floor shop has never been worn—many items still have the original price tags. Well-to-do area residents bring their high-fashion Valentino, Ungaro, Chanel, and Donna Karan designer fashions here for consignment. ♦ M-Sa. 4830 MacArthur Blvd NW (between Reservoir Rd and W St). 337.3072 &

3 Listrani's ★$ This neighborhood cafe features good pizzas and pasta and offers free home delivery within a limited area. Pizza is

served every day until midnight, except Sunday, when it's served until 9PM. ♦ Italian ♦ Daily lunch and dinner. 5100 MacArthur Blvd NW (at Dana Pl). 363.0619

4 Battery Kemble Park Named after Governor Kemble, a former president of West Point Foundry in Cold Spring, New York, this pocket of green is the ideal spot for summer picnics and Frisbee tosses. In winter, when there's enough snow, it turns into great sledding territory. The south end of the jogging path connects to the **C&O Canal Towpath.** A small cannon battery, which was once part of the capital's chain of Civil War defenses, is preserved by the National Park Service. ♦ Chain Bridge Rd NW (between MacArthur Blvd and Loughboro Rd). 426.6829

5 American University (AU) This Methodist-affiliated university is one of the area's leading educational and cultural forces. Among the colleges attended by the university's 11,000 students are arts and sciences, law, nursing, public affairs, and international service. FM radio station **WAMU** broadcasts National Public Radio, bluegrass, and locally produced public-affairs programs. **Hurst Hall,** the oldest building on the 77-acre campus, dates back to 1896. The public is welcome to movies at the **Wechsler Theater,** literary readings in **Gray Hall,** and music and sports events in **Bender Arena. Watkins Art Gallery** hosts undergraduate and graduate exhibitions. Call for more information. ♦ Guided campus tours by appointment. 4400 Massachusetts Ave NW (between Ward and Wesley Cirs). 885.1000, tours 885.6000 ♿ Metro: Tenleytown/AU

6 Foxhall Square Mall This indoor mall features two dozen small shops, including a drug store and (244.3500). ♦ 3301 New Mexico Ave NW (between Cathedral Ave and Embassy Park Dr). 363.0027. Metro: Tenleytown/AU

For generations, the work of Italian and Italian-American stone carvers has adorned Washington's most famous buildings, with the National Cathedral being perhaps their most impressive. Though they usually re-created figures from sculptors' plastic models, the carvers were given free reign with some of the gargoyles and grotesques found in the niches of the Cathedral. With binoculars, a careful viewer can see cats, an owl, a beast with four arms, the head of a horse, a hoofed beast with bells (symbolic of the Cathedral bell ringers), and a drunk stone carver, chisel and mallet in hand.

Restaurants/Clubs: Red **Hotels:** Blue
Shops/ ♟ Outdoors: Green **Sights/Culture:** Black

7 Sutton Place Gourmet This comprehensive, gourmet food store has prime meats (the aged fillets are unmatched), freshly baked pastries, over 50 different breads, produce from around the world, 400 varieties of cheese, fresh seafood (including superb salmon), nearly 100 oils, wines, and prepared entrées ready to take home and serve. It's not cheap, but the quality is generally worth the price. ♦ M-Sa 8AM-9PM; Su 8AM-8PM. 3201 New Mexico Ave NW (between Cathedral Ave and Embassy Park Dr). 363.5800 ♿ Metro: Tenleytown/AU. Also at: Numerous locations throughout the area

SUTTON PLACE GOURMET

Sushi-Ko
JAPANESE RESTAURANT

8 Sushi-Ko ★★★★$$ DC's first sushi bar is still its best. Now sporting a coppery-red exterior, this great place is even better with the re-hire of local favorite chef Tetsuro Takanashi. His kitchen prepares a vast range of top-quality fresh fish and seafood, as well as tempura and a few broiled dishes. The adventurous can try grilled baby octopus with mango and daikon salad. ♦ Japanese ♦ M dinner; Tu-Su lunch and dinner. 2309 Wisconsin Ave NW (between Observatory La and Calvert St). 333.4187 ♿

9 Busara ★★$$ Here you'll find Thai food filtered through a California sensibility: less heat, more vegetable dishes, less frying. Try the pad thai, *larb gai* (minced chicken with lime and pepper), or shrimp bikini (fried shrimp spring roll). ♦ Thai ♦ Daily lunch and dinner. 2340 Wisconsin Avenue NW (between Hall Pl and Calvert St). 337.2340 ♿

9 Faccia Luna ★★$ This pizzeria wins the prize for the best pie in town, thanks to its thin, chewy crust and spicy sauce. Also recommended are unusual subs and the grilled-chicken sandwich with walnut-garlic sauce. ♦ Italian ♦ M-Sa lunch and dinner; Su dinner. 2400 Wisconsin Ave NW (between Hall Pl and Calvert St). 337.3132 ♿

9 Austin Grill ★★★$ This jaunty restaurant is serious about the food; no fewer than three salsas are set on the table. A casual young crowd lines up here for the fajitas, enchiladas, grilled pork chops, and some of the best chili in DC. Afterward, cool off with a margarita. ◆ Tex-Mex ◆ Tu-Su lunch and dinner; M dinner. 2404 Wisconsin Ave NW (between Hall Pl and Calvert St). 337.8080

9 Grog & Tankard Big with a very young (20-something) crowd, this nightclub/bar features ear-splitting live rock music every night, with an emphasis on local bands. ◆ M-Th, Su 5PM-1:30AM; F-Sa 5PM-2:30AM; showtime 9PM. 2408 Wisconsin Ave NW (between Hall Pl and Calvert St). 333.3114 &

9 Rocklands ★★★$ Vegetarians beware: This barbecue joint may turn you into carnivores. Pork, chicken, and fish are grilled over red oak and hickory, and come with such tasty sides as tart potato salad, apple compote, minted cucumber salad, and mustard greens. The teal blue and red diner decor, complete with stools along the counter, grows on you. ◆ Barbecue ◆ Daily lunch and dinner. 2418 Wisconsin Ave NW (between Hall Pl and Calvert St). 333.2558; www.rocklands.com. Also at: 4000 Fairfax Dr (at N Quincy St), Arlington. 703/528.WOOD. Metro: Virginia Square

10 Savoy Suites $$ Located right across the street from the **Russian Embassy,** this 150-room establishment has a floor of nonsmoking rooms. There is a restaurant as well as an outdoor cafe, and some rooms include kitchens or Jacuzzis. Children under 18 stay free. ◆ 2505 Wisconsin Ave NW (between Calvert and Davis Sts). 337.9700; fax 337.3644 &

COURTESY UNITED STATES NAVAL OBSERVATORY

11 Naval Observatory This was originally the **Depot of Charts and Instruments,** located in Foggy Bottom and charged with keeping navigational charts. The first astronomical involvement was for the testing of ship chronometers. **Observatory Circle** was created to distance the delicate instruments from the rumblings of city traffic. Collections include atomic clocks and a refractor telescope that was used in the 1877 discovery of the Martian moons. Free 90-minute observatory tours are offered every Monday evening, except federal holidays. Tours are limited to the first 90 visitors. Group tour reservations must be made in advance. ◆ Free. Tours: M 8:30PM (gates open around 8PM). Valid ID required for entrance; parking outside grounds on Observatory Cir; enter at South Gate across from the New Zealand Embassy. Observatory Cir NW (off Massachusetts Ave). Recording 762.1467, tour reservations 762.1438 &

On the grounds of the Naval Observatory:

Vice President's House In the early 1970s, Congress decided that too much money was being spent on security measures for the homes of US vice presidents. So in 1975, over protests by the Navy, it co-opted this house, which for decades had been home to naval admirals. Despite the fact that it is located on a navy post, which makes it easy to defend, this large, sunny Victorian home with acres of lawn doesn't seem like a fortress at all. The residence is not open to the public.

12 British Embassy Edward Luytens's grandiose classicism glorified the British Raj in Delhi; here, he created a country house in the style of Christopher Wren for HMG representatives. Back in the 1930s, they received hardship pay for enduring the rigors of Washington summers—but at least the building and its ample lawns reminded them of home. William McVey's statue of Winston Churchill seems to be trying to hail a cab in front of the embassy. He hasn't had any luck in the 20-odd years he's been standing here; neither will you. The 1997 death of Princess Diana had the Embassy flooded with mourners and its steps laden with bouquets. ◆ 3100 Massachusetts Ave NW (between Whitehaven St and Observatory Cir). 462.1340 &

13 Kahlil Gibran Memorial Garden Directly across the street from the **British Embassy** (see above), this landscaped garden is dedicated not to a politician or military figure, but to the Lebanese-born poet and philosopher best known for his book *The Prophet.* A bronze bust of Gibran overlooks a small marble pool facing the street. Behind it, set in a grove of trees, is a fountain surrounded by a circle of stone benches inscribed with quotes from Gibran's inspirational writings, such as: "We live only to discover beauty. All else is a form of waiting." ◆ Massachusetts Ave NW (between 30th and 34th Sts)

14 Saint Sophia Greek Orthodox Cathedral DC's Greek Orthodox congregation meets in this magnificent Byzantine-inspired building, which was designed in 1956 by **Archie Protopappas.** The mosaics are definitely worth seeing. ◆ M-F; services: Su 9:30AM. Tours: by appointment. 36th St NW and Massachusetts Ave. 333.4730

One of the most coveted Washington invitations is the June Garden Party, held annually at the British Embassy in honor of the Queen's birthday.

**WASHINGTON
NATIONAL
CATHEDRAL**

15 Washington National Cathedral If
America were to have an official national
cathedral, this would certainly be the one. No
federal money was used in its creation, but
citizens from every part of the country have
contributed funds. Over the years, it has been
the site for the burial services of presidents
Wilson and Eisenhower and generals Bradley
and MacArthur. Services for the men and
women killed in Vietnam were held here, as
were prayer services for the Iranian hostages
and a memorial service for Commerce
Secretary Ron Brown. Although the cathedral
is the seat of the Washington Episcopal
Diocese, it has maintained the ecumenical
stance of its founders. It has no standing
congregation but opens its doors to
worshipers of all denominations.

In 1893 Congress created the Protestant
Episcopal Cathedral Foundation, and Henry
Yates Satterlee—Washington's first bishop—
began securing the land and raising funds, a
mission that would last a lifetime. Two
architects were hired, **George Bodley** of
Britain, and **Henry Vaughn,** an American.

Although they had to exchange drawings
across the Atlantic, the design was completed
in only 13 months. No less important was the
hiring of the George A. Fuller Company as
chief contractor, which it remained until 1980.
Over the years the company maintained a staff
of technicians able to build with limestone in
the stone-on-stone Gothic style of the 14th
century. For most of this century (it was
begun in 1907; construction was completed in
1990), the cathedral has grown slowly in size
and splendor until the limestone towers of this
Gothic cathedral (formally the **Cathedral
Church of St. Peter and St. Paul**) rose high on
Mount Saint Alban, above the treetops of
Upper Northwest.

In 1907, Teddy Roosevelt officiated at
groundbreaking ceremonies for the cathedral,
using the silver trowel George Washington
used when laying the cornerstone of the **US
Capitol.** Architect **Philip Frohman** took over
the project in 1919, refining the design and
supervising every facet of construction for the
next 40 years. The church is built in the shape
of a cross (see illustration below), with twin
towers in the west and a **Gloria in Excelsis
Tower** in the center. (Its top marks the highest
point in Washington.) Ninety-six angels, each
with a different face, pose in a frieze around
the tower, which holds a 10-bell peal and a
53-bell carillon.

As you tour the cathedral, remember that in
Gothic architecture, structure and symbol
merge. The design must communicate as
much as the hymnals, but often without

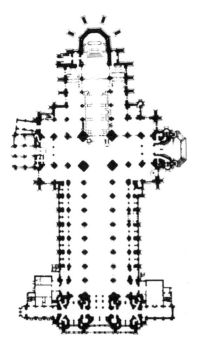

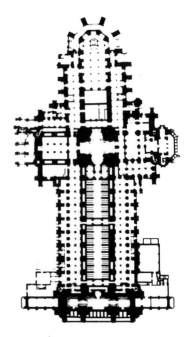

words, so look closely for the narratives and references in the intricate carvings and luminous windows. Enter the cathedral at the north or south transept, or through the doors at the west end. When entering from the west you will find yourself in the narthex (enclosed porch). Inlaid into the mosaic floor are the 50 state seals.

In the nave above the **Warren Bay** is the **Space Window,** which commemorates the scientists and astronauts of *Apollo XI.* (Moon rock retrieved on that mission is embedded in the glass.) Farther down is **Wilson Bay,** containing the tomb of Woodrow Wilson, the only president buried in the District of Columbia. A crusader's sword on the sarcophagus symbolizes Wilson's quest for peace through the League of Nations. Look for a thistle (representing his Scottish heritage) and for the seal of Princeton University (Wilson was once its president).

A few steps toward the center of the cathedral should place you in the crossing, a magnificent space where the transepts bisect the nave. Four massive stone piers soar 98 feet to meet the vaulted ceiling. The pulpit is made of stones from Canterbury Cathedral. It was here that Martin Luther King Jr. delivered his last Sunday sermon before his assassination in Memphis, Tennessee. Don't miss the charming **Children's Chapel,** where everything is scaled down, designed to delight a child. The windows tell the stories of Samuel and David as boys, and the kneelers are embroidered with all manner of baby animals—pets as well as wild beasts.

N.C. Wyeth, the father of Andrew Wyeth, painted the altar panel in the **Holy Spirit Chapel,** where golden-haloed angels sing the praises of God on a piercing field of blue.

If you've been walking along the aisles, now might be a good time to step closer to the center and admire the nave. Part of the genius of Gothic architecture was the flying buttress, which, by taking the weight of the roof from the walls, allowed the walls to be opened with stained-glass windows. Scores of windows on either side of the nave depict biblical themes as well as artists who have glorified God in their works: Dante, Milton, Bach, and Christopher Wren.

Turn toward the western end of the cathedral to view the dazzling **West Rose Window,** designed by Rowan LeCompte. The fiery wheel (25 feet, 11 inches in diameter) burns with kaleidoscopic color, particularly as it catches the last rays of a setting sun.

On the lower floor, or crypt, are four more chapels, burial vaults, a gift shop/bookstore (with excellent cathedral guides), and a visitors' lounge.

Before leaving, you might want to take the elevator at the west end of the main level to the **Pilgrim Observation Gallery.** Located in the twin towers, the gallery's 70 windows command a panoramic view of Washington, Maryland, and Virginia, as well as a bird's-eye look at some of the cathedral's exterior carvings.

The cathedral's close (grounds) is a 57-acre plot that includes three schools, a college of preachers, and some delightful gardens. A stroll here can be a restful way to end an afternoon of sight-seeing. Leave the building from the south transept or west doors and go to the **Herb Cottage,** where sachets, herbs, honeys, and herb vinegars are for sale. Outside, a small garden is redolent with the scent of rosemary, mint, and other herbs. Continue south through a Norman arch to enter one of the city's loveliest garden spaces, the **Bishop's Garden.** Actually several gardens, it includes a rose garden, a medieval herb garden, boxwood, magnolias, and the **Shadow House,** a small medieval stone gazebo that's cool in the summer and dry in the rain—a perfect resting spot.

A bit farther down the hill is Herbert Hazeltine's statue of George Washington, a bronze of the young lieutenant general astride a graceful, well-muscled horse—according to rumor, the spitting image of the famous racehorse Man O' War. In the style of the ancient Egyptians, the horse's eyes are made of glass.

You might also take a walk on the **Woodland Path,** maintained by local garden clubs. It starts at a Japanese footbridge and makes its way up a wooded hill planted with wildflowers. The **Cathedral Greenhouse** southeast of the church raises rare herbs; if you're interested, be sure to request a catalog of the ones on sale.

The Summer Festival is a series of free outdoor concerts featuring multifaith music ranging in style from choral to gospel and bluegrass. The dramatic Christmas Eve service, complete with a pageant and balloons, clowns, and mimes, draws crowds, especially when the first family is in attendance. The carillon is played every Saturday afternoon, and organ recitals follow Evensong on Sunday; call for more information.

The cathedral is served by most of the Massachusetts Avenue and Wisconsin Avenue buses. A $2 donation is requested for tours, which take about 30 to 45 minutes and leave continuously from the west entrance except during services. ♦ Donation. Cathedral: daily Labor Day–Apr; M-F 10AM-9PM, Sa-Su May–Labor Day. Services: M-F 7:30AM, noon, 4PM; Su 8AM, 9AM, 10AM, 11AM, 4PM; no

10AM service during July and August. Chapel of the Good Shepherd: daily 6AM-10PM. Pilgrim Observation Gallery: daily 10AM-3:30PM. Tours: M-F 10AM-3:15PM; Su 12:30-2:45PM. Wisconsin Ave NW (between Massachusetts Ave and Woodley Rd). Information 537.6200, 24-hour recording 364.6616 &

16 Cafe Deluxe ★★★$$ A hit since it opened its French doors in 1995, this brasserie and bar offers surprisingly good fare: tuna burger with ginger mayo, Greek feta cheese salad, ever-popular meat loaf, and excellent daily soups. A victim of its own success, there's often an hour-plus wait on weekends—especially for the outdoor patio. ◆ American ◆ M-Sa lunch and dinner; Su brunch and dinner. 3228 Wisconsin Ave NW (between Woodley Rd and Macomb St). 686.2233 & Metro: Cleveland Park

17 Cactus Cantina ★★$ A long wait for a table at dinnertime is always a possibility, but you can while the time away with a margarita at the bar and whet your appetite for the delicious grilled quail, spareribs, or beef fajitas to come. The portions are generous. ◆ Tex-Mex ◆ Daily lunch and dinner. 3300 Wisconsin Ave NW (at Macomb St). 686.7222 & Metro: Cleveland Park

18 Cleveland Park Bookshop A respite from the oversized chain stores, this quiet neighborhood book shop stocks a solid variety of books in all categories. The staff will help you find just the right gift for a serious reader. ◆ M-Sa 10AM-10PM; Su. 3416 Wisconsin Ave NW (between Newark St and Idaho Ave). 363.1112 & Metro: Cleveland Park

CLEVE-LAND PARK BOOK SHOP

The first movie at the Uptown Theater on Connecticut Avenue Northwest was *Cain and Mabel*, with Marion Davies and Clark Gable. The Uptown still hosts Washington premieres with Hollywood stars at the openings. Locals know to look for the crisscrossed spotlights that illuminate the night sky—and the stretch limos that block the avenue.

---

19 Rosedale This genteel and breezy 18th-century clapboard house was built by **Uriah Forrest** as a country home before the city grew to surround it. It's now affiliated with Youth for Understanding, an international exchange program for high school students. Grounds are open to the public and are popular for ad hoc soccer games and dog walkers. ◆ 3501 Newark St NW (between 34th Pl and 36th St). Metro: Cleveland Park

20 Winthrop Faulkner Houses Three mid–20th-century houses by **Winthrop Faulkner** fit into their surroundings by using the vernacular of their older neighbors. All are now private residences. ◆ 3530 Ordway St NW (between 34th Pl and 36th St). Metro: Cleveland Park

21 Sidwell Friends School Administration Building (The Highlands) Built as a country home, this 1822 stone Georgian house features unorthodox but handsome square columns that were not part of **Charles J. Nourse**'s original design. You'll have to view this place from afar, however; the grounds are private. In 1997, President Clinton delivered the commencement address here for Chelsea's graduating class. ◆ 3825 Wisconsin Ave NW (between Quebec and Upton Sts). Metro: Tenleytown/AU

22 Café Olé ★★★$$ *Mezze* (small portions) of French, Italian, North African, and other cuisines are the specialty at this simple, modern eatery. The vast menu offers round-the-world tasting with such superb dishes as chicken Provençal, *polenta tartufo* (grilled mushrooms mixed with caramelized onions and garlic), and Casablanca (cured salmon with grilled fennel, barley, peppers, jicama, and curry aioli). Year-round outdoor dining is available on the enclosed patio. ◆ International ◆ Daily lunch and dinner. 4000 Wisconsin Ave NW (between Rodman and Van Ness Sts). 244.1330 & Metro: Tenleytown/AU

23 Glover Archbold Park When you tire of the bustle around the monuments and museums, this is the perfect escape: 183 acres of deliciously unkempt park and a sanctuary for local wildlife. Paths wind through the park, crossing Foundry Beach Creek. The 3.6-mile nature trail is smooth enough for jogging. ◆ Van Ness St NW (between Wisconsin and Nebraska Aves). 426.6829. Metro: Tenleytown/AU

24 Travel Books and Language Center This unusual bookstore is totally devoted to maps, travel literature, guidebooks, international cookbooks—and everything else the traveler or armchair traveler might need. Readings by prominent travel writers are held here regularly. ♦ M-Sa 10AM-10PM; Su noon-7PM. 4437 Wisconsin Avenue NW (between Tenley Cir and Albemarle St). 237.1322; travelbks@aol.com ♿ Metro: Tenleytown

25 Dancing Crab ★$$ Crabs are the order of the day. Grab a mallet and a pitcher of beer, and go to it. Dress in keeping with the casual atmosphere—the tablecloths are brown paper; the napkins, paper towels. ♦ Seafood ♦ Daily lunch and dinner. Reservations recommended. 4611 Wisconsin Ave NW (between 41st and Davenport Sts). 244.1882. Metro: Tenleytown/AU

26 Krupin's ★★$$ Appearing like a mirage to homesick New Yorkers, this deli doles out potato pancakes, blintzes, lox and bagels, and matzoh ball soup. ♦ Jewish ♦ Daily 8AM-10PM. 4620 Wisconsin Ave NW (between Brandywine and Chesapeake Sts). 686.1989 ♿ Metro: Tenleytown/AU

27 Yosaku ★$$ Sushi, tempura, and other Japanese favorites are served in an airy dining room and sidewalk cafe. ♦ Japanese ♦ M-F lunch and dinner; Sa-Su dinner. 4712 Wisconsin Ave NW (between Chesapeake and 42nd Sts). 363.4453 ♿ Metro: Tenleytown/AU

28 El Tamarindo ★$ The atmosphere is nothing to speak of, but this restaurant serves hearty Salvadoran-Mexican food—enchiladas, tacos, and variations on the usual themes—at rock-bottom prices. ♦ Salvadoran/Mexican ♦ Daily lunch and dinner. 4910 Wisconsin Ave NW (between Ellicott and Fessenden Sts). 244.8888 ♿ Metros: Tenleytown/AU, Friendship Heights. Also at: 1785 Florida Ave NW (between U and California Sts). 328.3660 ♿ Metros: U St/Cardozo, Dupont Circle; 7331 Georgia Ave NW (at Geranium St). 291.0525 ♿ Metro: Takoma

28 Booeymonger ★★$ Overstuffed sandwiches—from a Reuben to the Veggie Special—are the forte of this casual restaurant. The brownies are divine. ♦ American ♦ Daily breakfast, lunch, and dinner. 5252 Wisconsin Ave (between Harrison and Jenifer Sts). 686.5805 ♿ Metro: Friendship Heights

28 Mazza Gallerie Neiman-Marcus anchors this high-fashion mall. Among the more than 50 other stores are **Filene's Basement**

(966.0208) for budget shopping; **Williams-Sonoma** (244.4800) for fine housewares; and **Kron Chocolatier** (966.4946). A recent, massive renovation converted the entire third floor into a multiplex cinema. ♦ M-F 10AM-8PM; Sa; Su noon-5PM. 5300 Wisconsin Ave NW (at Jenifer St). 966.6114 ♿ Metro: Friendship Heights

28 Washington Dolls' House and Toy Museum Antique dollhouses, dolls, and toys make up the collection in one of the city's more unusual museums. ♦ Admission. Tu-Sa; Su noon-5PM. 5236 44th St NW (between Harrison and Jenifer Sts). 244.0024. Metro: Friendship Heights

28 Lord & Taylor The DC branch of the traditional New York department store carries high-quality women's and men's clothing, shoes, linens, china, and accessories. There's free two-hour parking for customers. ♦ M-F 10AM-9PM; Sa-Su. 5255 Western Ave NW (between 45th and Jenifer Sts). 362.9600 ♿ Metro: Friendship Heights. Also at: Fair Oaks Mall, Hwy 50 and I-66, Fairfax, Virginia. 703/691.0100 ♿; White Flint Mall, Rockville Pike (between Strathmore Ave and Nicholson La), North Bethesda, Maryland. 301/770.9000 ♿ Metro: White Flint

29 Roche Bobois Extremely elegant (and expensive) European furniture is sold at this shrine to interior decoration. ♦ Tu-Sa; Su noon-5PM. 5301 Wisconsin Ave NW (at Jenifer St). 686.5667 ♿ Metro: Friendship Heights

29 Chevy Chase Pavilion More subdued and low-key than most malls, this one has fifty stores and restaurants on three levels that surround a skylit atrium; the whole place is decorated in cool green, gold, and cream. Giant faux palm trees line the requisite fast-food establishments on the bottom floor. Stores include **Koala Blue** (244.9732) and **Country Road Australia** (342.7361), for fashions from Down Under; and the **Pottery Barn** (244.9330) for housewares. ♦ M-F 10AM-8PM; Sa; Su noon-5PM. 5345 Wisconsin Ave NW (between Jenifer St and Western Ave). 686.5335. Metro: Friendship Heights

Within Chevy Chase Pavilion:

The Cheesecake Factory ★$$ This bustling California import specializes in cheesecakes, of course (35 flavors in all). Before you indulge in dessert, peruse the extensive menu, which offers a dizzying variety of entrées. You may want to share the huge portions. Good bets are the crab cakes, Szechuan dumplings, and fried calamari. Long waits for a table are common. ♦ American ♦ M-Sa lunch and dinner; Su brunch and dinner. 364.0500 &

California Pizza Kitchen ★$ Not quite as ubiquitous as MacDonald's—yet—but an amazing number of these trendy pizzerias have opened in Washington. Unusual toppings are the specialty here, but you can get old favorites like pepperoni, too. ♦ American ♦ Daily lunch and dinner. 363.6650 & Also at: Numerous other locations throughout the city

29 Embassy Suites Hotel at Chevy Chase Pavilion $$$ Located right above **Chevy Chase Pavilion** (see above), this all-suite hotel offers 198 suites with kitchenettes; a health club with an indoor pool, sauna, and Jacuzzi; meeting rooms; and **Cafe Cino**, serving a breakfast buffet, lunch, and dinner. All rates include complimentary breakfast and cocktails. Children under 17 stay free. ♦ 4300 Military Rd NW (at 43rd St). 362.9300, 800/EMBASSY; fax 686.3405 & Metro: Friendship Heights

30 American City Diner 2 ★$ This re-creation of a 1950s diner is authentic down to the Coke machine, tabletop jukeboxes, and the menu, which includes the inevitable burgers, chili dogs, and milk shakes. Unfortunately, the food is overpriced and served in skimpy portions. ♦ American ♦ M-Th, Su breakfast, lunch, and dinner; F-Sa 24 hours. 5532 Connecticut Ave NW (at Morrison St). 244.1949 & Metro: Friendship Heights

30 Bread & Chocolate ★$ There's a tearoom featuring soups, salads, and French-influenced entrées, as well as a carryout bakery. Both are good for after-movie Sacher torte binges. ♦ French-American ♦ Daily breakfast, lunch, and dinner. 5542 Connecticut Ave NW (between Morrison and McKinley Sts). 966.7413 & Metro: Friendship Heights. Also at: 4200 Wisconsin Ave NW (at Van Ness St). 363.3744 & Metro: Tenleytown/AU; 666 Pennsylvania Ave SE (at Seventh St). 547.2875 & Metro: Eastern Market

30 Magruder's This gourmet food store, part of a local chain, is famous for its produce. Though not as roomy as suburban locations, it offers a better selection than most grocers in the area. There's parking in the rear. ♦ M-Tu 8AM-8PM; W-Sa 9AM-9PM. 5626 Connecticut Ave NW (at Northampton St). 244.7800 & Metro: Friendship Heights. Also at: Bradlick Shopping Center, 6936 Braddock Rd (at Backlick Rd), Annandale,

Virginia. 703/941.8864 &; Congressional Plaza, 170 Halpine Rd (between Rockville Pike and E Jefferson St), Rockville, Maryland. 301/881.1181 & Metro: Twinbrook; 205 N Washington St (at Beall Ave), Rockville, Maryland. 301/424.1098 & Metro: Rockville

31 Politics & Prose This full-service bookstore specializes in, but isn't limited to, the books and interests of local authors, be they public policy or fiction. Great book-signing parties are held here. Comfortable furniture for browsers is a nice touch. A pleasant coffee bar addition in the lower level serves pastries and light lunches. Parking in the rear. ♦ M-Th, Su 9AM-10PM; F-Sa 9AM-midnight. 5015 Connecticut Ave NW (between Fessenden St and Nebraska Ave). 364.1919 & Metro: Tenleytown/AU

31 Marvelous Market With the best bread south of New York, this bakery also offers sandwiches and the usual assortment of coffees and light snack foods. ♦ M-Sa 7:30AM-8PM; Su. 5035 Connecticut Ave NW (between Fessenden St and Nebraska Ave). 686.4040 & Metro: Tenleytown/AU. Also at: 1514 Connecticut Avenue NW (between Dupont Cir and Q St). 986.2222 & Metro: Dupont Circle; 4832 Bethesda Avenue (between Woodmont Ave and Arlington Rd), Bethesda, Maryland. 301/986.0555 & Metro: Bethesda

32 University of the District of Columbia (UDC) Formed in 1976 by the merger of three colleges, **UDC** is a commuter school: More than two-thirds of its 14,000 students attend part-time. The 10-building complex at the urban **Van Ness** campus houses the colleges of liberal arts, engineering, and life sciences, as well as a 1,000-seat auditorium, a physical activities center, outdoor tennis courts, an FM radio station **(WDCU),** and an athletic field. ♦ 4200 Connecticut Ave NW (at Van Ness St). 274.5000 & Metro: Van Ness/UDC

33 The Intelsat Building A silvery spaceship, improbably located on a bustling commercial strip, houses the United Nations of satellite communications. Octagonal office "pods," protected from the sun by louvers of photogray glass, and cylindrical stair towers faced in glass brick are clustered around four top-lit atria. **John Andrews** laid out the complex with the local architectural firm of **VVKF** to create an energy-efficient working environment. Existing trees were preserved, but the building makes no attempt to hide itself from public gaze. ♦ Information tours about Intelsat (not of the building itself) are available by appointment; call a week in advance. 3400 International Dr NW (at Van Ness St). Information 944.7500 ♿ Metro: Van Ness/UDC

34 Kuwaiti Embassy, Cultural Division This gracefully balanced cube artfully plays with the Islamic motif of rotated squares. Note how the square tinted windows are cut diagonally by steel tubes. It was designed in 1982 by the architectural firm **Skidmore, Owings & Merrill.** ♦ 3500 International Dr NW (just south of Van Ness St). 364.2100. Metro: Van Ness/UDC

35 Brazilian-American Cultural Institute For the authentic Carioca spirit, or a taste of Bahia, this is the place: live music, the best new artists, films, and samba, plus a library and language lessons can all be found here. ♦ M-F 9AM-9PM. 4103 Connecticut Ave NW (at Upton St). 362.8334. Metro: Van Ness/UDC

36 Hillwood There are plenty of good reasons to visit the estate of the late Marjorie Merriweather Post, cereal heiress and longtime cornerstone of DC—and American—society. A recent renovation here improved climate conditions for art preservation, returned the gardens to their 1950s (during Mrs. Post's lifetime) appearance, and added a new visitors' center that includes a theater, reservations office, and museum shop. The house, a 40-room redbrick Georgian mansion designed by **John M. Deibert** dates from 1926, when it was a showpiece of Gatsby-esque formality. The estate was purchased by Post in 1955, and under her direction it surpassed its earlier opulence. A two-year renovation by **Alexander McIlvaine** included the addition of a third story to the structure. The heiress's staff included a

chef, a butler, a footman, and a resident curator. The last is a clue to the estate's raison d'être: Every bit a museum even while it was a residence, the place displayed an excellent and eccentric collection of French and Imperial Russian art. Included are gilded icons and ecclesiastical vestments, portraiture and folk art, Fabergé eggs, gold and silver crafts, and fine porcelain, including the royal service of Catherine the Great. (Post had traveled with one of her husbands, the first ambassador to the Soviet Union following the Revolution.) Fine French furniture and tapestries fill the house.

Outside, on the 25-acre estate, are formal Japanese and French gardens, a one-room Russian dacha (summerhouse), and a **Rose Garden.** The gardens, created by Perry Wheeler (who also designed the famous Rose Garden at the White House), exhibit more than 3,500 varieties of flora. Within the greenhouse alone flourish more than 5,000 kinds of orchids. Finally, to the southeast, over the treetops of **Rock Creek Park** (see page 151), is a stunning view of the **Washington Monument.** A two-hour tour is offered, featuring a film on the history of Hillwood narrated by Post's daughter, Dina Merrill. Reservations must be made several weeks in advance, and children under 12 are not allowed on the tour; only the grounds may be visited without reservations. An on-the-premises cafe serves light fare and a proper tea with scones. ♦ Admission. Tours: Tu-Sa 9AM, 10:30AM, noon, 1:30PM, 3PM; reservations required several weeks in advance. Grounds: Tu-Sa 11AM-3PM. Cafe: Tu-Sa. 4155 Linnean Ave NW (just south of Upton St). 686.5807. Metro: Van Ness/UDC

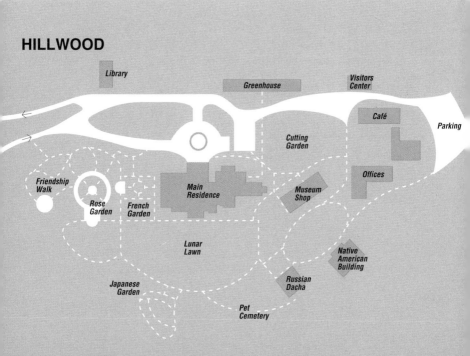

HILLWOOD

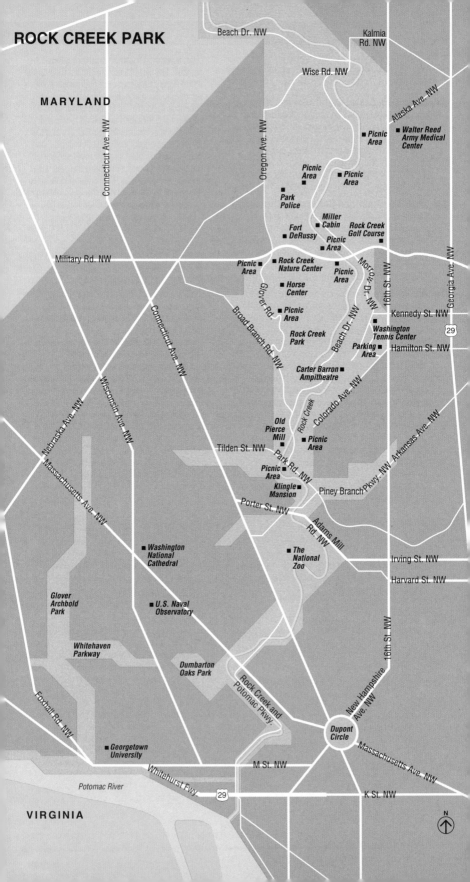

37 Rock Creek Park In 1890 President Benjamin Harrison signed Congress's million-dollar endowment mandating the preservation of this rugged 1,800-acre stretch, once the home of Algonquin Indians. Over the centuries it has nurtured bear, elk, and even bison; early settlers tapped the creek's swift waters to power their grist- and sawmills. Later, the woodlands served as a retreat for harried leaders such as John Quincy Adams and Teddy Roosevelt.

The park still stubbornly maintains its sense of ruggedness as it winds for miles along Rock Creek. Wildlife and wildflowers are abundant here, and you can still see the occasional deer and perhaps even a fox. Nature lovers haunt the place, searching for thrushes, chickadees, and ducks. **Fort DeRussy,** a link in the capital's chain of defenses against the Confederate Army, is still in evidence. (If all this seems too idyllic to be true, you're right; it is. Unfortunately, Rock Creek's waters are sour with pollution, and many of the fish have died. Fishing, swimming, and wading are prohibited.)

The park's bike/foot path begins along the **Potomac,** just below the **Kennedy Center,** and winds along the creek and beside park roads. Sites near the route include the **Watergate** complex and the **National Zoo,** where the hilly terrain is a pleasant challenge for running enthusiasts. The path ends behind **Hillwood,** a six-mile trek from **The Mall.** ♦ Information 282.1063. Metros: Foggy Bottom/GWU, Dupont Circle, Woodley Park/Zoo, Cleveland Park, Van Ness/UDC, Takoma, Silver Spring

Within Rock Creek Park:

Rock Creek Nature Center This National Park Service facility is the place to stop first to orient yourself within the park. It's especially great for kids, who can view wild-animal exhibitions or watch the workings of a beehive behind glass. The center also offers nature films, planetarium shows, and guided hikes. ♦ Free. W-Su. 5200 Glover Rd NW (just south of Military Rd). 426.6829 ♿

37 Bicycle Path It runs from the **Lincoln Memorial** into Maryland, and connects via the Memorial Bridge to the Mount Vernon bike trail in Virginia. Beach Drive, between Broad Branch and Military Roads, is closed to cars from 7AM Saturday until 7PM Sunday.

37 Rock Creek Golf Course This 18-hole public course has a clubhouse where clubs and carts are available for rental; it also has lockers and a snack bar. ♦ Daily dawn-dusk. Joyce Rd NW (between 16th St and Beach Dr). 882.7332

37 Carter Barron Amphitheatre Operated by the National Park Service, this open-air performance venue (seating 4,250) holds a yearly summer festival that showcases live pop, rock, and jazz bands. Free Shakespeare productions, courtesy of the **Shakespeare Theater,** downtown, are also held here. ♦ Colorado Ave NW and 17th St. 426.6837 ♿

37 Picnic Areas Thirty of them are scattered throughout the park, and some can accommodate groups of up to 100. Advance reservations are required year-round and must be made in person or in writing. ♦ 673.7646

37 Playgrounds The large playing field at 16th Street Northwest and Morrow Drive includes soccer, football, volleyball, and field hockey areas. Some can be reserved through the **DC Department of Recreation.** ♦ 673.7646

37 Rock Creek Park Horse Center Located near the **Nature Center** (see above), it offers guided trail rides. Riding lessons include special classes for the disabled. Children under 12 may not go on trail rides. ♦ Admission. Trail rides: Tu-W 3PM; Su noon, 1:30PM, 3:15PM. Prepaid reservations accepted for all but the noon ride. Glover Rd NW (south of Military Rd). 362.0118 ♿

37 Washington Tennis Center The center features 15 soft-surface and 10 hard-surface courts, which are open April through November; 10 courts are covered and remain open throughout the winter. Reservations must be made through **Guest Services, Inc.** (722.5949), and you must pay in person on the day of reservation. Six soft-surface courts off Park Road, just east of **Old Pierce Mill,** are open May through September. Go to the courts to make reservations in person through the **Washington Tennis Foundation.** ♦ 16th St NW (between Colorado Ave and Morrow Dr). 291.9888

38 Sedgwick Gardens This is the highlight of several blocks of subdued Art Deco apartments along this stretch of Connecticut Avenue. Architect **Mihran Mesrobian** animated the building's expanse of brick with rich detailing, giving the private residence a splendid porte cochere. ♦ 3726 Connecticut Ave NW (between Rodman and Sedgwick Sts). Metros: Cleveland Park, Van Ness/UDC

39 Ivy's Place ★★$ Indonesian and Thai specialties such as stuffed squid and shrimp with broccoli are served here. It's a good place for a bite after a movie at the nearby **Uptown Theater** (see page 152). ♦ Indonesian/Thai ♦ M-Sa lunch and dinner; Su dinner. 3520 Connecticut Ave NW (between Ordway and Porter Sts). 363.7802. Metro: Cleveland Park

Restaurants/Clubs: Red		**Hotels:** Blue
Shops/ 🌳 Outdoors: Green		**Sights/Culture:** Black

The sandwiches are enormous and the pastries, tasty, but the real specialty here is fresh bread, baked daily (except Monday), including Cuban, pumpkin, and sourdough. ♦ American ♦ M-Th, Su 7:30AM-8PM; F-Sa 7:30AM-10PM. 3411 Connecticut Ave NW (between Macomb and Ordway Sts). 362.2253; www.firehook.com ₺ Metro: Cleveland Park. Also at: Numerous other locations in the city

40 Whatsa Bagel Where New York bagel aficionados go when they want the real thing. Quite simply, they feature the best bagels in town. ♦ M-Sa; Su 7AM-3PM. 3513 Connecticut Avenue NW (between Ordway and Porter Sts). 966.8990. Metro: Cleveland Park

40 Kohr Brothers Frozen Custard In the early 1900s, when the three Kohr brothers brought their fledgling ice-cream business to Coney Island, they began adding eggs to the product to make it stand up to salt-air breezes. Hence, a star was born: frozen custard. Especially popular flavors include traditional vanilla and chocolate (or the two swirled together), but banana strawberry and a dozen other flavors are also offered. ♦ Daily. 3501 Connecticut Ave NW (at Ordway St). 686.2910 ₺ Metro: Cleveland Park

41 Uptown Theater This much-beloved, 1,500-seat Art Deco theater was built in 1936, and renovated in 1996. With its wide screen and capacious balcony, it's considered DC's best movie theater. Spotlights crisscrossing the night sky signal the occasional Hollywood openings held here, complete with celebrities and stretch limos. In 1998, *My Giant* with Billy Crystal and *Enemy of the State* with Will Smith opened here. ♦ 3426 Connecticut Ave NW (between Newark and Ordway Sts). 966.5400. Metro: Cleveland Park

41 Ireland's Four Provinces ★$ Gaelic music, from local Irish musicians, is the big draw, but don't overlook the Harp on tap, shepherd's pie, and other authentic touches in this cavernous club. There's a sidewalk cafe for warm-weather dining. ♦ Irish ♦ M-F dinner; Sa-Su brunch and dinner. 3412 Connecticut Ave NW (between Newark and Ordway Sts). 244.0860. Metro: Cleveland Park

42 Yes! The Natural Gourmet Organic fruits and vegetables, bulk grains and spices, fresh milk and yogurt, and organic toiletries are on hand here. ♦ M-Sa 9AM-9PM; Su 10AM-8PM. 3425 Connecticut Ave NW (between Macomb and Ordway Sts). 363.1559. Metro: Cleveland Park

42 Firehook Bakery and Coffee House Formerly home to an Italian restaurant, this bakery/cafe inherited a lovely outdoor garden, complete with grape arbor and fountains—the perfect setting for lunch after a trip to the zoo.

43 Spices ★★$ A strong performer in the crowded Cleveland Park restaurant scene is this lovely all-Asian spot, serving Chinese, Malaysian, Korean, and Vietnamese cuisine. Start with the Korean spring onion cake appetizer. Follow up with Penang curry (a Malaysian-style noodle soup), Thai shrimp, or ginger salad. ♦ Asian ♦ M-Sa lunch and dinner; Su dinner. 3333 Connecticut Ave NW (between Macomb and Ordway Sts). 686.3833. Metro: Cleveland Park

43 Lavandou ★★★$$ Cleveland Park's best bistro has ultracozy surroundings, dotted with paintings of the Provençal landscape and dried-flower arrangements. Don't be discouraged by the inevitable wait for a table—your patience will be rewarded with excellent Provençal cooking and attentive service. The soups—*pistou*, especially—and stews (either beef or lamb) are wonderful. ♦ French ♦ Daily lunch and dinner. Reservations recommended. 3321 Connecticut Ave NW (between Macomb and Ordway Sts). 966.3002. Metro: Cleveland Park

43 Nanny O'Brien's ★$ Drop by this friendly neighborhood pub for the burgers, Irish stew, a pint of Guinness, and live music. Some of the region's best Irish musicians gather informally for Monday night *sesiuns;* and folk, bluegrass, or Irish bands perform Wednesday through Saturday. Sunday is open-mike night. ♦ Irish/American ♦ Daily lunch and dinner. 3319 Connecticut Ave NW (between Macomb and Ordway Sts). 686.9189. Metro: Cleveland Park

43 Vace A real Italian deli, this place offers fantastic homemade pasta and sauces, pizzas, cheeses, and salamis—everything for a great meal. ♦ M-F 9AM-9PM; Sa 9AM-8PM; Su. 3315 Connecticut Ave NW (between Macomb and Ordway Sts). 363.1999. Metro: Cleveland Park. Also at: 7010 Wisconsin Ave (between Bradley Blvd and Leland St), Bethesda, Maryland. 301/654.6367. Metro: Bethesda

43 Uptown Bakers ★★$ Mouth-watering specialty sandwiches on freshly baked breads are served at this very popular cafe/bakery. The chocolate babka and apple tarts are wonderful, as are the big fat oatmeal cookies. ♦ Cafe/bakery ♦ Daily 7AM-8PM. 3313 Connecticut Ave NW (between Macomb and Ordway Sts). 362.6262. Metro: Cleveland Park

43 Palais du Chocolat Don't miss the seductive chocolates and marzipan offered here. Tasty quiche, sandwiches, and salads are also available. ♦ M-Tu 9AM-10PM; W-Th, Su 8AM-10PM; F-Sa 8AM-midnight. 3309 Connecticut Ave NW (between Macomb and Ordway Sts). 363.2462. Metro: Cleveland Park

44 The National Zoo Established in 1889 under the direction of the **Smithsonian Institution,** the zoo moved from **The Mall** to Rock Creek Valley when Samuel Pierpont

Langley, the **Smithsonian**'s third secretary, persuaded Congress to provide funds to establish a site to protect the American bison from extinction. When you enter the 163-acre zoo (see map below) follow **Olmsted Walk,** the main pedestrian pathway. Along the walk you'll find the *Gibbon Exhibit,* the **Great Ape House,** and invertebrate exhibitions. A circular walkway overlooks the great cats—full-maned Atlas lions and rare blue-eyed white tigers, plus leopards and cheetahs. All of the zoo's tigers are descendants of Mohini, a white tiger brought from India in 1960.

At least a dozen species call the **Monkey House** home, including the Celebes crested macaques, and the endangered lion-tailed macaques from India. In the **Reptile House** is a collection of 91 species of amphibians and reptiles, from the smallest snakes to the venomous king cobras, giant pythons, and anacondas. Designed in 1931 by **Albert Harris,** the building is an Italian Romanesque–style structure. Its stone corbels are carved with intricate reptilian heads and its columns rest on carved stone turtles.

Outside the Reptile House, 550-pound Aldabra tortoises wander in the summer months. Crocodiles bathe in shallow pools—indoors in winter, outdoors in summer. Also watch for the giant Komodo dragon lizards and alligators. The *Invertebrate Exhibit,* behind the reptile building, includes octopuses, giant crabs, cuttlefish, spiders, and microscopic organisms. The **Great Ape House** gives you and the apes a perfect look at

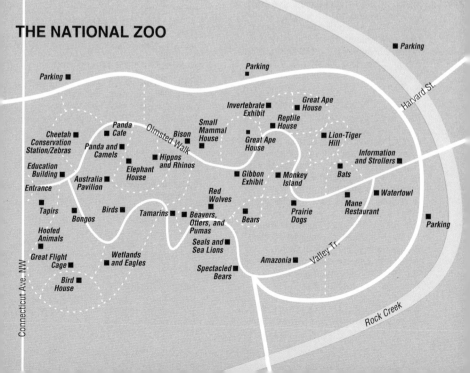

THE NATIONAL ZOO

one another. Lowland gorillas weighing in at 400 pounds watch visitors from indoors and out. The building, specially designed for apes, features sculptured steel-frame trees. All of the **Great Ape House** orangutans were born in zoos. Their housing is carefully constructed, as orangutans like to unbolt and take things apart.

The **Small Mammal House**'s exotic creatures include golden lion tamarins—small, blond, monkeylike creatures; meerkats; the foxlike fennecs; and tiny elephant shrews. Going from the extra small to the extra large, the **Elephant House** guides you to elephants, hippos, rhinoceroses, and giraffes. Favorites include the versatile-trunked Asiatic elephant and the African elephant with its large ears.

By far the most popular animals for decades have been the giant pandas, a gift from the People's Republic of China in 1972. Sadly Ling-Ling died in 1992 and Hsing-Hsing has fallen ill (at 27 years old, he's quite old for a panda). Repeated attempts to breed the pair proved disappointing: Five tiny cubs were either stillborn or died within a few days of birth. Pandas are among the rarest of animals—with about 1,000 left in the wild in China—making it very difficult for the zoo to replace the long-adored pair.

At the upper west end of the zoo roam kangaroos, antelopes, zebras, and deer. The **Bird House** has more than one thousand birds comprising 155 species, from the seldom-seen kiwi to the endangered Bali mynah. Special features include the **Indoor Flight Room** and the outdoor *Great Flight Exhibit*. Along the **Valley Trail** are otters, gray seals, sea lions, beavers, and red wolves. Visitors are treated to zoology lessons at **Zoolab** in the **Education Building, Herplab** in the **Reptile House,** and **Birdlab** in the **Bird House.** The zoo offers free films, lectures, slide shows, and wildlife films in the **Education Building** auditorium.

The zoo also runs a 3,100-acre preserve near Front Royal, Virginia, for the study of endangered species. Parking is accessible from Connecticut Avenue Northwest and Rock Creek and Potomac Parkway in Rock Creek Park. Lots fill by 10AM on busy days, and parking on nearby side streets is limited. The zoo also can be reached from the bike path in **Rock Creek Park** (see page 151). No bicycle riding is allowed within the zoo, however. Gifts are available at the **Panda Gift Shop,** the **Mane Gift Shop,** the **Bookstore/Gallery, Gibbon Gallery,** and the **Seal Shop.** ♦ Grounds: daily Jan–mid-Apr, mid-Oct–mid-Dec; daily 8AM-8PM mid-Apr–mid-Oct. Buildings and gift shops: daily. 3001 Connecticut Ave NW (between Hawthorne and Macomb Sts). 673.4717, recording 673.4800. Metros: Woodley Park/Zoo, Cleveland Park

45 Mrs. Simpson's ★★$$ This jewel box of a dining room is wittily decorated in honor of the Duchess of Windsor. A frequently changing menu of American dishes, including grilled chicken and a lemon mousse to die for, is featured. ♦ American ♦ M-Sa lunch and dinner; Su brunch and dinner. Reservations recommended. 2915 Connecticut Ave NW (between Cathedral Ave and Hawthorne St). 332.8300 & Metro: Woodley Park/Zoo

46 Marriott Wardman Park $$$ Almost a city in itself, this vast 1,505-room hotel (formerly the **Sheraton Washington**) is usually filled with visiting executives taking advantage of the exhibition-, meeting-, banquet-, and ballrooms. Escapes from the workaday world include two huge outdoor swimming pools (one open April through October, the other May through September), barber shops, and lounges. Culinary pleasures range from the pies, cookies, and European-style pastries at **Espresso** to fine American cuisine at **Americus.** Amenities include multilingual concierge service, nonsmoking rooms, exercise facilities, a post office, a flower shop, and a gift shop/newsstand. Children under 18 stay free. ♦ 2660 Woodley Rd NW (between Connecticut Ave and 29th St). 328.2000, 800/228.9290; fax 234.0015 & Metro: Woodley Park/Zoo

47 Petitto's ★★$$ This charmingly intimate Italian restaurant, tucked away in a turn-of-the-century Victorian brownstone, specializes in pasta but is also known for its fresh veal and seafood dishes. Choose among four separate dining areas, all with working fireplaces. After dinner, head downstairs for dessert to **Dolce Finale** (see below). ♦ Italian ♦ Daily dinner. 2653 Connecticut Ave NW (between Calvert St and Woodley Rd). 667.5350. Metro: Woodley Park/Zoo

Downstairs at Petitto's:

Dolce Finale ★★$ Located in the wine cellar, this place is entirely devoted to desserts—more than 25 of them, all homemade. Try the excellent tiramisù, made with mascarpone cheese, espresso, and cocoa. This is also a perfect place for a late-night sweet. Food is available for carryout, too. ♦ Desserts ♦ Daily evenings. 667.5350 &

Lebanese Taverna ★★$$ Feast on traditional three-course meals or graze on *mazas*—the Lebanese version of tapas. Rotisserie chicken or any of the pilafs are good choices. ♦ Lebanese ♦ M-Sa lunch and dinner; Su dinner. 2641 Connecticut Ave NW (between Calvert St and Woodley Rd). 265.8681 & Metro: Woodley Park/Zoo

Saigon Gourmet ★★$$ Some say that this is the best Vietnamese restaurant in Washington—although with so many very good ones around now, that's no longer the great distinction it used to be. Nevertheless, the caramel chicken or roasted quail are two of the stars on the moderately priced menu. ♦ Vietnamese ♦ Daily lunch and dinner. 2635 Connecticut Ave NW (between Calvert St and Woodley Rd). 265.1360 ₺ Metro: Woodley Park/Zoo

48 Jandara ★★$$ Despite new owners, the former **Thai Taste** has retained its chef and menu. This revamped Art Deco diner offers an intricate menu complemented by an attentive, extremely helpful staff. The chicken satay, *yum nua* (salad with beef and spicy sauce), rockfish grilled in banana leaves, and deep-fried flounder with basil, garlic, and hot pepper are particularly worth trying. ♦ Thai ♦ Daily lunch and dinner. 2606 Connecticut Ave NW (between Calvert and 24th Sts). 387.8876 ₺ Metro: Woodley Park/Zoo

48 New Heights ★★★$$$$ New chef John Wabeck, formerly of **Restaurant Nora,** specializes in New American cuisine from the food-as-art school. His dishes are as exciting to the palate as they are beautiful to the eye: crunchy buttermilk-fried oysters with corn, scallops with eggplant curry, foie gras with mango salsa, and filet mignon with fennel and blue cheese. Overlooking Rock Creek, the dining room is a knockout, decorated with

American Crafts furniture. ♦ New American ♦ M-Sa dinner; Su brunch and dinner. Reservations recommended. 2317 Calvert St NW (between Connecticut Ave and 24th St). 234.4110. Metro: Woodley Park/Zoo

OMNI ❀ SHOREHAM HOTEL

49 Omni Shoreham Hotel $$$$ This historic hotel—designed in 1929 by **Harry Bralove**— has been the site of many presidential inaugurations from Franklin Roosevelt's to Bill Clinton's. President Harry Truman held his private poker games in Room D-406, and the 770-room hotel's luxurious ambience has attracted such luminaries as Clark Gable, Rudy Vallee, Marilyn Monroe, and Gary Cooper. Amenities include a floor of nonsmoking rooms, limousine and baby-sitting services, three clay tennis courts, an olympic-sized pool, and a fitness center. The hotel's dining room, **Monique Cafe et Brasserie,** serves French and American cuisines; the **Marquee Lounge** offers cabaret entertainment in an Art Deco setting; and the faux-tropical **Garden Court** is an elegant lobby lounge and bar. ♦ 2500 Calvert St NW (between Connecticut Ave and 28th St). 234.0700, 800/THE OMNI; fax 265.7972 ₺ Metro: Woodley Park/Zoo

Bests

Sherri Dalphonse
Senior Editor, *The Washingtonian*

Marveling at the view from the rooftop cafe of the **Hotel Washington.**

Taking an early-morning ride on one of the many bike paths in Virginia, especially the **Mount Vernon Trail** along the **Potomac River** and the **W&OD Trail** through the countryside.

Seeing a movie in the restored splendor of the **Uptown Theater.**

Getting a half-price ticket 90 minutes before any play (that's not sold out) at **Arena Stage.**

Wandering about the **National Zoo** on a warm spring day, stopping to see the exotic Komodo dragons and to watch the orangutans on their high-wire act.

Catching dinner and a show in **Adams-Morgan:** Start with wonderful Ethiopian food at **Meskerem,** then head to **Café Lautrec** for live jazz.

Going to the little-visited **National Building Museum,** which is in a grand space and has a terrific gift shop.

Seeing the azaleas in bloom at the **US National Arboretum.**

Taking visitors to the **Einstein** statue on **Constitution Avenue.**

Idling away some time at **Kramerbooks & afterwords, A café,** a bookstore-and-cafe that has a

wonderful selection of books and a good brunch—and it's open 24 hours on weekends.

Arnold Berke
Senior Editor, *Preservation* magazine

The District of Columbia memorial to World War I veterans, a domed tempietto in the woods south of the **Reflecting Pool,** would be delightful for a clandestine dinner al fresco.

Franklin School, the most winning work of prolific architect **Adolf Cluss,** survives as a sumptuously modeled Victorian among the modern office blocks lining **Franklin Square.**

The noble Italianate fountain that cascades down **Meridian Hill Park** on **16th Street** brings both visual and aural relief from urban overload.

Few would dispute that the house designed by **John Russell Pope** on **Crescent Place,** now used by **Meridian House International,** is his finest gift to the capital.

The grouping of three church steeples at **16th Street** and **Columbia Road** pops up unexpectedly from prospects all across the city.

> "Washington talks about herself and about herself and about nothing else."
>
> Henry James

Suburban Maryland

Although it has grown by leaps and bounds over the last two decades, suburban Maryland is for the most part resisting the kind of large-scale development that has obliterated much of the green from Northern Virginia's landscape. However, you may find this difficult to believe when traveling northwest from DC along **Interstate 270.** The extra lanes for express traffic cut through a long corridor of business parks and shopping centers, giving the impression that the entire state of Maryland has been completely paved over.

The diverse ways in which each suburb handles the area's growing population make for an interesting study in contrasts. **Bethesda** is now dominated by gargantuan office buildings but has the biggest concentration of good restaurants outside DC, while **Potomac** and **Chevy Chase** remain largely residential. **Silver Spring,** in need of a face-lift, struggles with redevelopment—many of its residents are opposed to its becoming another Bethesda. **Glen Echo** and **Old Town Rockville** are still "undiscovered" and hope to remain so, although **Rockville** proper is already a nightmare of congestion. **Takoma Park,** more like a village than a suburb, maintains its strong sense of community, thanks to its residents, who fiercely resist

unbridled development, while **Columbia**—a planned city begun in the 1960s for commuters to the equidistant cities of Washington and Baltimore—owes its very existence to the region's growth.

Area code is 301 unless otherwise noted.

1 Glen Echo Nestled off **MacArthur Boulevard,** this tiny incorporated town is an enclave of narrow, tree-lined streets and an eclectic mix of houses. It has a loyal community of residents proud to be in on a well-kept secret.

Within Glen Echo:

 Glen Echo Park Built in 1891, this park originally provided a base for the then-emerging Chautauqua movement, which offered education and entertainment for adults in a summer-camp environment. The park's next life, as a 70-year incarnation as an amusement park, is better remembered. Declared a National Park Service site in 1971, the park includes artist studios, classroom space, children's theater performances, and a wonderful Spanish ballroom, which hosts folk, big-band, and ballroom dances. Call ahead for schedule information. Young and old alike still take turns on the recently renovated **Dentzel Carousel** (installed in 1926), which boasts its original 256-pipe Wurlitzer organ; rides cost 50**c**. ♦ Daily 6AM-midnight; carousel W-Su May-Oct. 7300 MacArthur Blvd (at Oxford Rd). 492.6282

Within Glen Echo Park:

Discovery Creek Children's Museum This Washington-based museum recently began offering programs in a historic stable at Glen Echo. Through innovative art projects, nature and history are brought to life for children (best suited for ages 6-11). ♦ Admission. Daily. Reservations required for activities. 202/364.3111; www.discoverycreek.org

Clara Barton National Historic Site In 1897, 86-year-old Clara Barton, founder of the American Red Cross, moved to the **Glen Echo House,** originally built as a warehouse for the organization's supplies. After removing some of the 72 concealed closets, deep enough to store wheelchairs, the indefatigable Barton expanded the house to 36 rooms. Her personal effects and furniture remain as they were during her last years. Tours are given upon request. ♦ Free. Daily. 5801 Oxford Rd (south of MacArthur Blvd). 492.6245 ♿

Potomac

Probably the toniest of DC's Maryland suburbs, Potomac is home to diplomats, politicians, and celebrities. Ted Koppel and Lynda Carter have homes here. Drive northwest from the city on **River Road** and you'll soon be in horse country, where mansions set on vast grounds are visible from the

road. Millions of dollars change hands when these estates are bought and sold.

2 Old Angler's Inn ★★★$$$ Under the guidance of chef Tom Power, the food at this romantic country inn measures up to its fine Edwardian-style decor. Rack of lamb and lobster tail are just two of his standout creations; other favorites include seared salmon with crispy potato cake and saffron fettuccine with mussels. The true magic is not in the food, but in the atmosphere (many a marriage proposal has taken place here). Nothing beats a cup of hot chocolate next to the lounge's roaring fire or, in warm weather, dining on the terrace. ♦ American ♦ Tu-Su lunch and dinner. Reservations required. 10801 MacArthur Blvd (between Brickyard and Falls Rds). 365.2425 ♿

3 C&O Canal National Historic Park This park offers scenic overviews of the Great Falls of the Potomac, as well as access to the 184-mile C&O Canal, which is operated by the National Park Service; its paths are great for walks and bicycling. The cliffside **Billy Goat Trail,** overlooking scenic Mather Gorge, is not for the timid, however. Rides on the mule-drawn *Canal Clipper* (fee) are offered April through October. ♦ Admission. Daily. 11710 MacArthur Blvd (west of Falls Rd). 299.3613

Within C&O Canal National Historic Park:

Great Falls Tavern Despite the name, this isn't a restaurant but a tiny museum with photographs and artifacts reflecting 19th-century life in this area of Maryland. ♦ Free, with park admission. Daily

4 Normandie Farm ★★$$ Traditional French country cooking is served here in an almost rural setting, which also happens to be *très romantique.* Best known for its popovers, the restaurant offers other specialties as well, including beef Wellington and poached salmon. ♦ French ♦ Tu-Sa lunch and dinner; Su brunch and dinner. Reservations recommended. 10710 Falls Rd (between Glen Rd S and Eldwick Way). 983.8838 ♿

The longest escalator in the world (outside of the Soviet Union) is at the Bethesda Metro stop. It is 218 feet long.

Chevy Chase

Centered around **Chevy Chase Circle** (the intersection of Connecticut and Western Avenues), this suburb straddles both Montgomery County and DC, but the town of Chevy Chase proper sits squarely on the Maryland side. The site of two of Washington's most exclusive country clubs, **Chevy Chase Club** and **Columbia Country Club**, it offers real estate as pricey as Potomac's—the per capita income in the 20815 ZIP code is one of the highest in the country—but with more history behind it. Chevy Chase predates Potomac by several decades.

Chevy Chase has its own mini–"Fifth Avenue" enclosed within a two-block stretch of **Wisconsin Avenue** (between Willard and Dorset Avenues). Among the high-toned names to be found there are **Tiffany's, Gianni Versace, Cartier, Brooks Brothers, Gucci,** and **Saint Laurent Rive Gauche.**

5 Clyde's of Chevy Chase ★★$$ This popular restaurant celebrates the 1920s and 1930s age of elegant travel with a re-creation of the Orient Express dining car and displays of antique cars. Adding to the fun, an electric train chugs along the ceiling. The innovative menu changes often, with burgers and rotisserie chicken consistent favorites. Desserts, especially chocolate bread pudding and cappuccino custard, are sinfully good. ♦ American ♦ Daily lunch and dinner. Reservations recommended. 70 Wisconsin Cir (between Western and Wisconsin Aves). 951.9600 & Metro: Friendship Heights

5 Tweeds 'n Things This is where the country club crowd browses for sportswear. All kinds of casual clothes—in muted khakis, plaids, and bright colors—are available, along with wool skirts and tweed jackets. Everything's tasteful, albeit preppy. Accessories (hats, belts, jewelry, and umbrellas) are also stocked. ♦ M-W, F-S; Th 9:30AM-8PM. 29 Wisconsin Cir (between Western and Wisconsin Aves). 656.2230 & Metro: Friendship Heights

5 Saks Fifth Avenue Across the street from the boutiques lining Wisconsin Avenue is this grande dame of department stores. Women's, men's, and children's clothing and accessories with a generous sprinkling of designer names, as well as beauty and fur salons, are found here. ♦ Daily. 5555 Wisconsin Ave (between S Park Ave and Oliver St). 657.9000 & Metro: Friendship

Heights. Also at: 2051 International Dr (between Chain Bridge Rd and Westpark Dr), Tysons Corner, Virginia. 703/761.0700 &

6 Lemon Drop This quaint little shop has a unique variety of high-quality children's clothes and accessories. For women's clothes, visit the **Lemon Twist** next door. ♦ M-Sa. 8530 Connecticut Ave (at Manor Rd). 656.1357

7 Audubon Naturalist Society The society makes its home in a Georgian mansion designed in 1928 by **John Russell Pope,** the architect of the **Jefferson Memorial.** Located on 40 acres of wildlife sanctuary, the estate, known as **Woodend,** is traversed by a three-quarter-mile nature trail. Self-guided tours can be taken daily. ♦ Free. Daily. 8940 Jones Mill Rd (between Jones Bridge Rd and Woodhollow Dr). 652.9188

Bethesda

Virtually unrecognizable today to anyone who knew it as a quiet outpost, Bethesda has experienced some of the most phenomenal commercial growth of any local suburb. The transformation has been largely a successful one, with new office buildings balanced by an influx of restaurants and creative architecture. This growth has come at the expense of a good number of the mom-and-pop operations that had once given the area its character, however, and many longtime residents are unhappy. Compensating somewhat for this loss are the diversions available at the **Bethesda Metro Center Plaza** (information 652.4988, ice rink 656.0588). Here, in the **Metro** station in front of the **Hyatt Regency,** dance concerts are offered in the summer every Friday evening from 6-9PM, and in the winter, ice skating (daily from Thanksgiving through early March).

8 Writer's Center A haven for both amateur and professional writers, this modest building in downtown Bethesda is the location for writing workshops in fiction, nonfiction, and poetry. Also offered are workshops in editing, desktop publishing, and basic graphic design. The center sponsors frequent poetry and fiction readings, as well. For a schedule of area literary events, call 656.1638. The center also holds workshops at the **Gunston Arts Center** (703/228.6960) in Arlington. ♦ 4508 Walsh St (between West and Wisconsin Aves). 654.8664 & Metro: Bethesda

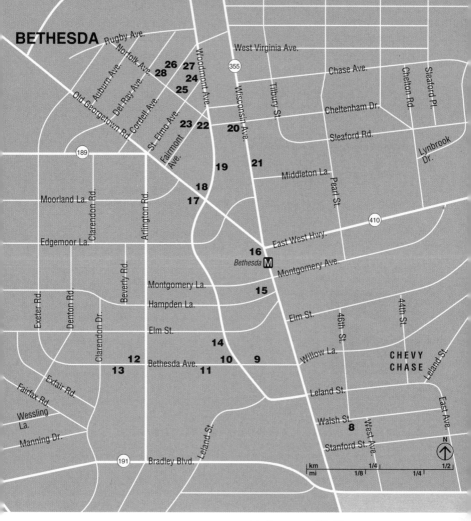

BETHESDA

9 Thyme Square ★★★$$ This eatery pays homage to its star dishes with colorful murals of vegetables on ochre walls. A delightful choice of mainly vegetarian dishes (many made with local organic ingredients) includes wild mushroom and spinach lasagna, curry roasted vegetables on Israeli couscous, and several wood-oven pizzas. Pasta with lemon prawns and chicken Havana style are among the better non-veggie choices. Have a fresh juice concoction made to order. ◆ Vegetarian ◆ Daily lunch and dinner. 4735 Bethesda Ave (between Wisconsin and Woodmont Aves). 547.9077 ♿ Metro: Bethesda

10 Barnes and Noble This bright, airy megastore offers a huge selection of books, plenty of comfortable seats in which to enjoy them, and a **Starbucks** to keep you from dozing off. ◆ Daily 9AM–11PM. 4801 Bethesda Ave (at Woodmont Ave). 986.1761 ♿ Metro: Bethesda

11 China Village Restaurant ★★$ Hunan and Szechuan dishes are the specialty of this casual eatery, where all of the classics are done well. Takeout available. ◆ Chinese ◆ Daily lunch and dinner. 4820 Bethesda Ave (between Woodmont Ave and Arlington Rd). 654.7787/8 ♿ Metro: Bethesda

12 Louisiana Express Company ★$ Cajun food is no longer the rage, but that hasn't dimmed the popularity of the jambalaya, gumbo, or terrific rotisserie chicken available

here. It's convenient to the **Metro** stop, so you can pop in for carryout, but dining on-site allows you to soak up the grungy but friendly atmosphere. ♦ Cajun ♦ Daily lunch and dinner. 4921 Bethesda Ave (between Arlington Rd and Clarendon Dr). 652.6945. Metro: Bethesda

13 Bethesda Crab House ★★★$$ Fresh, perfectly cooked crabs are served in a setting that focuses on the business at hand: The tables are covered with newspapers, and utensils consist of a wooden mallet and a small knife. An outdoor patio adds to the fun. Be sure to call ahead and arrive on time—the crab supply may be limited. ♦ Seafood ♦ Daily lunch and dinner. Reservations recommended. 4958 Bethesda Ave (between Arlington Rd and Clarendon Dr). 652.3382 ⅃ Metro: Bethesda

14 Levante's Rome ★★$$ This high-style, chrome-and-tile restaurant has been a hit since it opened in 1998. The Eastern Mediterranean menu fuses Greek, Italian, and Middle Eastern fare in its salads, pita-wrapped sandwiches, and brick-oven pizzas. ♦ Eastern Mediterranean ♦ Daily lunch and dinner. 7262 Woodmont Ave (between Bethesda Ave and Elm St). 547.2441 ⅃ Metro: Bethesda

15 Pines of Rome ★$ Popular with families, this casual restaurant is known for its white pizza (a fontina pie flavored with garlic), which makes a good appetizer. Entrées include mussels in marinara sauce and stewed octopus. ♦ Italian ♦ Daily lunch and dinner. 4709 Hampden La (between Wisconsin and Woodmont Aves). 657.8775 ⅃ Metro: Bethesda

16 Hyatt Regency Bethesda $$$ An elegant 381-room hotel, it has an indoor pool, an exercise area, and the **Plaza Cafe,** a casual restaurant with an American menu. Membership in the hotel's **Regency Club** offers special amenities, such as a complimentary breakfast and morning paper. Nonsmoking rooms are available, and children under 18 stay free. ♦ Bethesda Metro Center, Wisconsin Ave and Old Georgetown Rd. 657.1234, 800/233.1234; fax 657.6453 ⅃ Metro: Bethesda

17 Mystery Book Shop Bethesda Everything for the armchair detective, with a solid selection of British whodunits and that Washington favorite, the spy thriller, is sold here. ♦ Daily. 7700 Old Georgetown Rd (at Woodmont Ave). 657.2665 ⅃ Metro: Bethesda

18 Bean Bag Before gourmet coffee became all the rage in Washington, as elsewhere, this store was here, dispensing fresh-brewed cups of regular java, espresso, and cappuccino and selling bags of imported beans, as well as sandwiches, soup, and pastries. Take your purchase home or sample it right at a table indoors or out. A second location nearby also sells 20 varieties of loose tea. ♦ Daily. Woodmont Corner Shopping Center, 7704 Woodmont Ave (at Old Georgetown Rd). 652.6812 ⅃ Metro: Bethesda. Also at: 10400 Old Georgetown Rd (at Democracy Blvd). 530.8090 ⅃

19 Tastee Diner ★$ This popular spot is the genuine article, replete with wood paneling and chrome throughout. The food is exactly what you'd expect: meat loaf and mashed potatoes, thick shakes, homemade pies and cakes—in other words, all of your classic diner favorites. However, you may have to wait for seating. ♦ American ♦ Daily 24 hours. 7731 Woodmont Ave (between Old Georgetown Rd and Cheltenham Dr). 652.3970 ⅃ Metro: Bethesda. Also at: 8516 Georgia Ave (between Wayne Ave and Colesville Rd), Silver Spring, Maryland. 589.8171 ⅃ Metro: Silver Spring; 118 Washington Blvd (between Little Montgomery and Main Sts), Laurel, Maryland. 953.7567 ⅃

20 Tako Grill ★★$$ For most people Japanese food means sushi, teriyaki, and tempura, all of which are served here, but the specialty at Tako's is *robatayaki*—grilled meats and fish. You can make a meal of a host of small dishes priced as low as $2 apiece. Though this popular restaurant is spacious, you still may have to wait. ♦ Japanese ♦ M-F lunch and dinner; Sa-Su dinner. 7756 Wisconsin Ave (at Cheltenham Dr). 652.7030. Metro: Bethesda

21 Bethesda Theatre Cafe ★$ Second-run movies are accompanied by beer and wine, pizzas, wings, nachos, and sandwiches at this cinematic "dinner theater." Swivel chairs allow the audience to attend to both the food on the table and the action on the screen. You must be 21 or accompanied by a parent to enter. Sunday is "no smoking" day. The box office opens a half hour before showtime; call for schedule information. ♦ Deli ♦ Daily dinner. 7719 Wisconsin Ave (between Middleton La and Cheltenham Dr). 656.3337 ⅃ Metro: Bethesda

22 Georgetown Book Shop One of Bethesda's best secondhand bookstores, this shop specializes in history—particularly military and Soviet. But a good variety of other items, including pre-1945 magazines and used jazz and classical compact discs, are also available. ♦ Daily. 7770 Woodmont Ave (at Norfolk Ave). 907.6923 ⅃ Metro: Bethesda

22 Foong Lin ★★$$ The menu, which includes Cantonese, Szechuan, Hunan, and Peking dishes, changes daily. Peking chicken, crispy rockfish, steamed oysters, and General Tso's chicken are just a few of the offerings. ◆ Chinese ◆ Daily lunch and dinner. 7710 Norfolk Ave (between Woodmont and Fairmont Aves). 656.3427 ᕫ Metro: Bethesda

23 Rio Grande Cafe ★$$ This bustling Tex-Mex joint looks like a roadhouse—its wooden walls are hung with spurs and license plates and its concrete floor is stacked with cases of beer. The menu offers standard southwest favorites—from tortillas and sizzling fajitas to chili rellenos and potent, icy margaritas. ◆ Tex-Mex ◆ Daily lunch and dinner. 4919 Fairmont Ave (between Old Georgetown Rd and Norfolk Ave). 656.2981 ᕫ Metro: Bethesda. Also at: 4301 Fairfax Dr (at N Taylor St), Arlington. 703/528.3131 ᕫ Metro: Ballston

24 Tung Bor ★$ Good Chinese food is surprisingly hard to find in restaurant-rich Bethesda, which is why its fans welcomed the arrival of this restaurant. Stick to the house specialty—dim sum—and be prepared to contend with the noisy crowd; it'll be worth it. ◆ Chinese ◆ Daily lunch and dinner. 4819 St. Elmo Ave (between Norfolk and Woodmont Aves). 656.3883 ᕫ Metro: Bethesda

25 La Miche ★★$$$ French country cuisine is served here in a gracious farmhouse setting replete with lace curtains and fresh flowers. The menu offers generous portions of such favorites as rack of New Zealand lamb and baked trout stuffed with crabmeat. ◆ French ◆ M, Sa-Su dinner; Tu-F lunch and dinner. 7905 Norfolk Ave (between St. Elmo and Cordell Aves). 986.0707 ᕫ Metro: Bethesda

26 Ricky's Rice Bowl ★★$ Healthful, inexpensive food is served in this clean and efficiently run restaurant. Steamed rice dishes topped with vegetables and grilled meat are the house specialty. The Seoul Bowl (a stew of beef or chicken, broccoli, carrots, cabbage, and rice, flavored with Korean-style barbecue sauce) is a favorite. ◆ Japanese ◆ Daily lunch

and dinner. 4865 Cordell Ave (between Norfolk and Woodmont Aves). 652.7423 ᕫ Metro: Bethesda

27 Cottonwood Cafe ★★$$ The chef prefers to describe the fresh, imaginative cooking served here as "Southwest cuisine" instead of Tex-Mex. But, by any name, the seafood paella and beef or pork tenderloin are standouts. If you go in the evening, be prepared to brave a considerable crowd. ◆ Southwest ◆ M-Sa lunch and dinner; Su dinner. Reservations recommended. 4844 Cordell Ave (between Norfolk and Woodmont Aves). 656.4844 ᕫ Metro: Bethesda

28 Bacchus ★★$$ A larger outpost of the DC restaurant, this branch serves the same excellent hummus, lamb- or chicken-topped pilafs, stuffed eggplant, and *lahm mechwi* (lamb shish kebab). The appetizers are so good you may want to order a *mezza,* which is a feast of three or four of them. ◆ Lebanese ◆ M-F lunch and dinner; Sa-Su dinner. 7945 Norfolk Ave (between Cordell and Del Ray Aves). 657.1722 ᕫ Metro: Bethesda. Also at: 1827 Jefferson Pl NW (between Connecticut Ave and 19th St), DC. 202/785.0734. Metros: Dupont Circle, Farragut North

29 National Institutes of Health (NIH) Professionals affiliated with the medical sciences as well as interested laypeople are welcome to come to Building 10, the **Visitors' Center** (496.4000), for a slide show and tour of the clinical center, which is given Monday, Wednesday, and Friday from 11AM to noon and by appointment. In Building 38, the **National Library of Medicine (NLM)** (594.5983) is the world's largest research library in a single professional field. Library tours are given Monday through Friday at 1PM; meet in the lobby of **Lister Hill Center** (Bldg 38A). ◆ Visitors' Center: M-F. NLM: M-Sa. 9000 Rockville Pike (between Woodmont Ave and Cedar La). 496.4000. Metro: Medical Center

30 Marriott Bethesda $$$ A step up from the usual suburban accommodations, this 407-room hotel features a large outdoor swimming pool, an indoor pool, an exercise room, and lighted tennis courts. Two restaurants—Northern Italian and family-style American—provide a choice of prices and cuisines. For an extra treat, ask about the **Executive Kings** room, an upgraded minisuite. Nonsmoking rooms are available, and children under 17 stay free. ◆ 5151 Pooks Hill Rd (west of Rockville Pike). 897.9400, 800/228.9290; fax 897.0192 ᕫ

31 White Flint Mall Even the mannequins are perfectly coiffed and manicured at this three-tiered fashion mall, with an interior inset with rosewood and copper terrazzo floors. **Bloomingdale's** and **Lord & Taylor** are the big-leaguers anchoring more than 120 smaller shops and fashion boutiques, as well as **The Cheesecake Factory, Bertolini's Restaurant, Dave & Busters,** and **Borders Books and Music.** ♦ M-Sa 10AM-9:30PM; Su noon-6PM. 11301 Rockville Pike (between Strathmore Ave and Nicholson La), North Bethesda. 468.5777 ᕗ Metro: White Flint

JEAN · MICHEL
RESTAURANT

32 Jean-Michel ★★$$ Although located inside a suburban shopping center, this French restaurant can hold its own with many of the better ones in Downtown DC. And no wonder: It's run by Jean-Michel Farret (formerly of K Street's **Jean-Pierre**), whose highlights include osso buco with noodles in a light sauce, panfried salmon, and grilled Dover sole. ♦ French ♦ M-F lunch and dinner; Sa-Su dinner. Wildwood Shopping Center, 10223 Old Georgetown Rd (between Cheshire Dr and I-270). 564.4910 ᕗ

Rockville

This town is the **Montgomery County** seat and, as such, the center of its municipal activity. **Rockville Pike,** the main commercial strip, is chockablock with shopping centers and is notorious for its traffic congestion. Little known even to most DC residents, **Old Town Rockville** with its lovely Victorian architecture still has the quaint feel of a small town.

33 Cabin John Regional Park This 500-acre park is run by Montgomery County. Ice-skating, outdoor tennis courts (on a first-come, first-served basis), miniature train rides, and summer concerts attract lots of locals. ♦ Fee for ice-skating, tennis, and train rides. Ice-skating rink: Jan-June, late Oct–Dec; call for hours. Train rides: daily Apr-Sept. Tennis: daily. 7400 Tuckerman La (between Westlake Dr and Seven Locks Rd). Park 299.4160, ice rink 365.2246, train 469.7835, tennis 469.7300

34 G Street Fabrics Despite the name, this shop is no longer located on G Street in downtown Washington. Nevertheless, if you're in the market for fabrics, it's worth making a special trip here for designer textiles, a full bridal facility, and sewing classes. ♦ Daily. 11854 Rockville Pike (at Montrose Rd). 231.8998 ᕗ Metro: White Flint

34 Seven Seas ★★$ Here diners are sure their meal is fresh— they can see the live lobsters, crabs, and assorted fish swimming in the tanks at the restaurant's entrance. The tasty shrimp are served with the heads on; the deep-fried oysters and whole fish steamed with ginger and scallions are also excellent. Ask for the Chinese menu, which has English translations—it offers selections that the standard English menu doesn't. ♦ Chinese ♦ Daily lunch and dinner. 1776 E Jefferson St (between Montrose Rd and Rollins Ave). 770.5020 ᕗ

35 Yesterday and Today Records This record shop gives equal play to the current and the obscure. Vinyl lovers should check out the collection of LPs and 45s. ♦ Daily. Sunshine Square Shopping Center, 1327 Rockville Pike (between Halpine Rd and Edmonston Dr). 279.7007 ᕗ Metro: Twinbrook

36 St. Mary's Church Novelist F. Scott Fitzgerald and his wife, Zelda, are buried in the cemetery of this Roman Catholic church, built in 1817. The resting place may seem an unusual choice for the fast-living expatriate couple, but it makes some sense, considering Zelda was born here in Rockville. ♦ 520 Veirs Mill Rd (between Stonestreet Ave and Hungerford Dr). 424.5550 ᕗ Metro: Rockville

37 Beall-Dawson House Upton Beall (of the prominent colonial family of merchants and landowners) entertained General Marquis de Lafayette here. Now owned by the Montgomery County Historical Society, the house features furnishings dating from 1815 through the Victorian era. Also on the grounds are a small medical museum and the office of Dr. Stonestreet, with medical implements from 1852-1903, and a gift shop. Dr. Stonestreet was the Beall family doctor and first practicing MD in Rockville. Tours are given on a walk-in basis; group tours can be arranged by appointment. ♦ Admission. Tu-Sa noon-4PM; first Su of the month 2-5PM. 103 W Montgomery Ave (at N Adams St). 762.1492. Metro: Rockville

37 Taste of Saigon ★★★$$ This family-run Vietnamese place is one of the best values in the entire area. A very pleasing ambience, with murals of the homeland and lacquered chairs, complements such superb dishes as rockfish with black-bean sauce, caramel chicken, and Cornish hen stuffed with pork. ♦ Vietnamese ♦ Daily lunch and dinner. Reservations recommended. 410 Hungerford Dr (at Beall Ave). 424.7222 ᕗ Metro: Rockville

Restaurants/Clubs: Red   **Hotels:** Blue
Shops/ ♀ Outdoors: Green   **Sights/Culture:** Black

38 Il Pizzico ★★$ Simple but very good Italian fare, including homemade ravioli, is offered here. The pizzas are an outstanding value, as are the veal dishes. Lines form early, since the restaurant doesn't take reservations. ♦ Italian ♦ M-F lunch and dinner; Sa dinner. 15209 Frederick Rd (between Westmore Rd and E Gude Dr). 309.0610 &

39 That's Amore ★★$ The quantities of food served at this busy and fun restaurant are abundant. But refreshingly, the quality of the Southern Italian fare doesn't suffer. It's best to go with a big group and eat family-style. ♦ Italian ♦ M-F lunch and dinner; Sa-Su dinner. 15201 Shady Grove Rd (between W Gude Dr and I-270). 670.9666 &

Kensington

Pleasant and mostly residential, this community has some attractive, family-oriented neighborhoods. Because it's one of the few suburbs not directly accessible by **Metrorail** (although it's within easy bus or driving distance), it maintains a lower profile than some of its neighbors—and residents seem perfectly happy to keep it that way.

40 Antique Row One of the best places in the area for antiques and collectibles, these blocks boast more than 40 shops, offering a variety of styles, periods, and prices. Items range from Art Deco and railroad memorabilia to stained glass, folk art, and vintage clothing. ♦ Howard Ave (between Montgomery and Connecticut Aves)

40 Noyes Children's Library Focusing on preschoolers, this Montgomery County library offers more than 10,000 volumes and story-reading programs. ♦ Tu, Th, Sa. Montgomery Ave and Carroll Pl. 929.5533

41 Temple of the Church of Jesus Christ of Latter-day Saints This massive traffic-stopper stands on a 57-acre hill overlooking the Beltway. The $15-million building, designed by **Wilcox, Markham, Beecher & Fetzer** in 1974, is 248 feet long and 136 feet wide and stands 16 stories high. Built on a solid rock foundation, it is sheathed in 173,000 square feet of Alabama white marble, enough to cover three-and-a-half football fields. Even the windows are made of marble (five-eighths of an inch thick and translucent), casting an otherworldly light on the interior. The fortress is topped with six gold-plated steel spires, the highest of which supports a gold-leaf statue of the angel Moroni. While passersby are welcome to admire the architecture and Irwin Nelson's landscape design, the temple is open to members only. Its many rooms, on nine levels, are reserved for important occasions, such as weddings and baptisms. A 30-minute tour guided by volunteers is offered to the public, however, and includes a stop at the **Visitors' Center,**

where photographs, sculptures, and lifelike mannequins tell the story of Mormonism. ♦ Tours: daily 10AM-9PM. 9900 Stoneybrook Dr (west of Capitol View Ave). 587.0144 &

42 Round House Theater Provocative productions of contemporary plays are offered here. The five-play season runs from September to June. During June, the theater hosts a series devoted to new voices from the local scene. ♦ Shows: W-Su. Box office: Tu-Sa 11AM-5PM and one hour before performances. 12210 Bushey Dr (between Veirs Mill and Randolph Rds). 933.1644, 933.9530 &

Wheaton

The **Metro**'s **Red** line finally reached this suburb in late 1990. But despite the accessibility, this place has managed to remain fairly low-key, with plenty of mom-and-pop shops. A plethora of ethnic restaurants adds spice to the area, and the **Wheaton Plaza** shopping mall (Georgia Ave and Veirs Mill Rd; 946.3200) offers almost everything else.

43 Good Fortune ★★$ Excellent dim sum is why you should visit this nondescript but pleasant Chinese restaurant near the **Metro** stop. The large number of Chinese customers is a good endorsement. ♦ Chinese ♦ Daily lunch and dinner. 2646 University Blvd W (between Georgia Ave and Veirs Mill Rd). 929.8818 & Metro: Wheaton

44 Brookside Gardens Possibly the most beautiful outdoor spot in the area, this section of **Wheaton Regional Park** includes a conservatory, fountains, a Japanese teahouse, ponds, and 35 acres of green grass, trees, and meticulously landscaped gardens. This is the place to get the answers to all of your questions about horticulture; you can also call 949.8227 between 9:30AM and noon, on Tuesdays and Thursdays. ♦ 1500 Glenallan Ave (between Kemp Mill and Randolph Rds). 949.8230

45 National Capital Trolley Museum Built as a replica of an old terminal, this trolley museum in **Northwest Branch Regional Park** offers memorabilia from Austria, Germany, and DC. While you're there, take the 1.5-mile trolley ride though park grounds, and visit the gift shop. ♦ Admission. Sa-Su noon-5PM Jan-Dec; W 11AM-3PM, Sa-Su noon-5PM July-Aug. 1313 Bonifant Rd (between Carona Dr and Layhill Rd). 384.6088, 384.6352

In 1883 developer Benjamin Franklin Gilbert bought a 90-acre parcel of land that straddled both the District of Columbia and Maryland. He named his new suburb Takoma Park: Takoma is an Indian word meaning "high up, near heaven," and at the time the area had an abundance of trees and two healthful natural springs.

Silver Spring

Originally this suburb's revitalization was patterned after Bethesda's, but heated controversy over the scope of the development has undercut the project's momentum. When the Mall of America developers proposed a shopping-entertainment facility, residents rejected the plan as incompatible with the scale of their neighborhood. But encouraging signs are emerging: The **American Film Institute**'s move into the Art Deco **Silver Theater** could be the anchor that Silver Spring needs. A number of restaurants and small businesses have also persevered in the area and some are worth seeking out.

46 Old St. John the Evangelist Church and Cemetery Jesuit churchman John Carroll founded his private Evangelist Mission chapel on this site in 1774 and served here until his appointment as official head of the newly legislated US Roman Catholic Church 10 years later. The small frame building is an exact reproduction of the original 1790 structure, with all the original fixtures and sacred vessels intact. A testament to Maryland's influential Carroll family, the church now serves the area's Polish residents, to whom it is known as "Our Lady, Queen of Poland." ♦ Services: Su 10AM (in English), 11:30AM (in Polish). 9700 Rosensteel Ave (at Forest Glen Rd). 681.7663 ♿ Metro: Forest Glen

In 1792, a competition was announced for the design of the Capitol and the President's House. It read, in part, "A premium lot in the city of Washington . . . and $500 shall be given by the Commissioners of the Federal Buildings to the person who before the 15th of July 1792 shall produce to them the most approved plan for a Capitol to be executed in this city."

The Architecture of Washington,
American Institute of Architects

47 Parkway Deli and Restaurant ★★$ Regularly voted the best deli in the Washington area (admittedly, there isn't much competition in this category), this place offers big bowls of matzoh ball soup, kosher sandwiches, and delicacies that include chopped chicken liver, herring, whitefish, and, of course, lox and bagels. ♦ Deli ♦ Daily breakfast, lunch, and dinner. 8317 Grubb Rd (between Washington Ave and Colston Dr). 587.1427

48 American Film Institute (AFI) At press time, the **AFI** was expected to reopen in 2001 at the former **Silver Theater.** A $7.8-million restoration of the old, 400-seat theater will add an adjacent 200-seat theater, a small screening room, offices, and retail space. Offerings will include some of the earliest films ever made (shown with live musical accompaniment), classics like *Casablanca,* film festivals, and educational programs. Call for schedule. ♦ 8619 Colesville Rd (between Georgia Ave and Fenton St). 202/785.4600. Metro: Silver Spring

49 Thai Orchid ★$$ This unpretentious restaurant serves satay, greaseless deep-fried chicken wings, excellent hot and spicy salads, and such entrées as squid with hot pepper and scallions. ♦ Thai ♦ M-F lunch and dinner; Sa-Su dinner. 8519 Fenton St (between Ellsworth Dr and Colesville Rd). 587.2192 ♿ Metro: Silver Spring

50 Town Center Hotel $ In addition to 236 well-appointed rooms, this former **Quality** property offers an American restaurant, as well as **Sergio's Italian Restaurant,** a Northern Italian dining room. The health club—indoor pool, sauna, and exercise room—is open to patrons and their guests. Children under 18 stay free. ♦ 8727 Colesville Rd (between Fenton and Spring Sts). 589.5200; fax 588.1841. Metro: Silver Spring

51 China ★★★$$ Although this comfortable, family-run restaurant specializes in elaborate banquets (a minimum of four guests; call at least one day in advance), feel free to wander in for an excellent meal of authentic lemon chicken, panfried dumplings, Hong Kong pork, and Szechuan beef. ♦ Chinese ♦ Daily lunch and dinner. No credit cards accepted. 8411 Georgia Ave (between Bonifant St and Wayne Ave). 585.2275 ♿ Metro: Silver Spring

52 Crisfield ★★★$$ A no-nonsense, 1930s black-and-white tile interior allows outstanding regional specialties to shine here. Chincoteague oysters, Maryland crabs (every which way but steamed), and fresh clams are offered on a menu that hasn't changed in 50 years. ♦ Seafood ♦ Tu-Su lunch and dinner. No credit cards accepted. 8012 Georgia Ave (between East West Hwy and Blair Mill Rd). 589.1306 ♿ Metro: Silver Spring. Also at: 8606 Colesville Rd (at Georgia Ave). 588.1572 ♿ Metro: Silver Spring

Takoma Park

Founded more than a hundred years ago, this unique spot has retained a strong sense of its past (see the meticulously renovated Victorians) while distinguishing itself through civic and political activism (the city has designated itself a nuclear-free zone and a sanctuary for non-American refugees). The ethnic diversity and rejuvenated **Old Town** business district make this pretty town, nicknamed "Azalea City," well worth a visit.

53 Everyday Gourmet ★★$ Homemade breads, pastries, and luscious desserts, plus sandwiches, salads, and entrées can be consumed on the spot or carried out. Gift baskets and catering are available, too. ♦ American ♦ M-Sa breakfast, lunch, and dinner; Su lunch and dinner. 6923 Laurel St (just south of Carroll Ave). 270.2270 ♿ Metro: Takoma

53 Now & Then The vintage clothing, T-shirts, cards, gifts, and inexpensive toys for sale here are all distinguished by their sense of fun. ♦ Tu-Su. 6939 Laurel St (just south of Carroll Ave). 270.2210 ♿ Metro: Takoma

Chuck&Dave's

53 Chuck & Dave's Books Et Cetera The only independent general bookstore for miles, this shop offers a good selection of fiction and African-American studies as well as an array of New Age, self-help, and recovery titles. Alternative periodicals, jewelry, crafts, and toys also line the shelves. The store will fill special orders. ♦ Daily. 7001 Carroll Ave (at Laurel St). 891.2665. Metro: Takoma

53 House of Musical Traditions Area musicians and music lovers flock to this shop that sells, rents, and repairs all kinds of musical instruments—from kazoos and tambourines to concertinas, fiddles, drums, guitars, and banjos. An extensive line of records, tapes, and CDs in a wide variety of musical styles, including a special section of local artists, are also in stock. Lessons are available. ♦ Tu-Th noon-7PM; F noon-9PM; Sa-Su. 7040 Carroll Ave (between Tulip and Willow Aves). 270.9090. Metro: Takoma

53 Royal Bengal ★★$ This family-run Indian restaurant features beef, chicken, lamb, fish, and vegetable dishes in a quiet atmosphere. The chili chicken and tandoori chicken are particularly good, but don't shy away from the best vindaloo in the area. ♦ Indian ♦ M-F lunch and dinner; Sa-Su dinner. 6846 New Hampshire Ave (between Ray Rd and Ethan Allen Ave). 270.6054

Prince George's County

Covering a large area east of DC, from **Laurel** to the **Potomac River,** Maryland's second-largest county is the most populous jurisdiction in the Washington area. Already more than 775,000 residents call it home, and the community of rolling hills is still growing. Prince George's also claims some historic firsts: Captain John Smith landed here in 1608, and the first American airport was built in **College Park** in 1908—Wilbur and Orville Wright were teachers here. NASA's **Goddard Space Flight Center** is here in **Greenbelt** (one of the country's first planned communities, dating from the 1930s), and so the pioneering tradition continues.

54 Ledo ★$ Among the many pizza variations served here, a bacon-cheese pie with a thin, flaky crust is the ticket at this long-standing hangout. ♦ Italian ♦ Daily breakfast, lunch, and dinner. 2420 University Blvd E (between West Park Dr and 24th Ave), Hyattsville. 422.8622 ♿ Also at: Numerous other locations throughout the area

55 University of Maryland The main campus of this coeducational state-supported facility has more than 30,000 students and 1,638 faculty members. Its physics, mathematics, and computer science departments are highly regarded among the country's public universities. Free walking tours are given by the admissions office Monday through Friday. ♦ Baltimore Ave and Regents Dr, College Park. Main campus 405.1000, admissions office 314.8385 ♿ Metro: College Park/U of Md

56 Recreational Equipment Inc. (REI) This indispensable cooperative for backpackers, climbers, and other outdoors types gives members a substantial year-end rebate on purchases. Fortunately, you don't have to be a member to take advantage of the reasonable prices offered here. Watch for end-of-season sales. ♦ M-F 10AM-9PM, Sa-Su. 9801 Rhode Island Ave (at Muskogee St), College Park. 982.9681 ♿ Metro: Greenbelt. Also at: 3509 Carlin Springs Rd (at Leesburg Pike), Baileys Crossroads, Virginia. 703/379.9400 ♿

57 Prince George's Publick Playhouse Housed in a renovated Art Deco movie theater, this performing arts center hosts dance, music, and theatrical events, with special attention to ethnic artists. ♦ Shows: F-Su. Box office: M-F and one hour before performances. 5445 Landover Rd (at 55th Ave), Cheverly. 277.1710

The Roving Capital

The Continental Congress first convened in 1774, and from then until 1800, when the country's legislative body moved into official headquarters in the District of Columbia, it resembled nothing so much as a band of nomads in knee breeches. During these years the members met in eight cities, each having the right to call itself the capital—at least for a while. Congress was so transient that when a statue in honor of George Washington was proposed in 1783, Francis Hopkinson, a representative from Pennsylvania, suggested that it be mounted on wheels—the better to follow Congress in its wanderings.

Philadelphia was the capital more frequently than any other city, but in 1777, with the British closing in, Congress hightailed it to the town of Lancaster, Pennsylvania. From Lancaster, Congress moved across the Susquehanna River to York, where it remained until June 1778. The Articles of Confederation (the first constitution of the 13 American states) was passed there, and Benjamin Franklin had his press moved up so he could print a million dollars worth of much-needed Continental money. Congress moved back to Philadelphia but was again threatened by the British and moved to Baltimore, Maryland, in 1779.

In 1783 the Revolutionary War ended, leaving the nation broke and the union tenuous. Congress once again was meeting in Philadelphia and might have remained there had a group of soldiers not invaded the city and rioted for back pay. Congress fled to Princeton, New Jersey, where it met in Nassau Hall (still part of Princeton University's campus and then the largest building in the country). However, there wasn't enough room in town for the growing bureaucracy, so the federal government moved on to **Annapolis,** Maryland, where there was presumably more hotel space. In Annapolis, Congress decided that the new government needed its own city, but no one could agree on which one.

Every town in the country began lobbying to be named capital, including Trenton, New Jersey (Congress met there briefly in 1784 before rejecting the proposal). New

York City became the capital in 1784, and five years later George Washington was inaugurated there. Later in 1789, Congress moved back to Philadelphia and stayed put until 1800.

Debate on where to put the capital grew fierce. Northerners wanted it near a financial center, while agrarian Southerners feared the power of northern financiers and special interests. A political compromise between Alexander Hamilton and Thomas Jefferson settled the issue in 1790. During the Revolutionary War, the South had managed to pay its soldiers, but the North had not. Led by Hamilton, the northern states wanted Congress to absorb their debt. The South, led by Jefferson, opposed this. Finally the two men worked out a deal whereby the North was relieved of its debt and the South gained the prestige of a national capital.

Congress specified the size of the site, but the choice was left to George Washington, a former surveyor. Although hounded by land speculators, he made an independent choice: a diamond-shaped area where the **Potomac** and **Anacostia Rivers** merged. He hoped the Anacostia would provide a deep-water naval port, while the Potomac would be a link to western provinces by way of the proposed **Potowmack Canal.** Perhaps it was no accident either that the capital would be an easy day's ride from Washington's home at **Mount Vernon.**

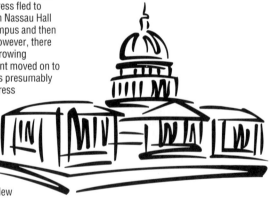

appointment. ♦ Free. M-F. Powder Mill Rd (between Baltimore Washington Pkwy and Edmonston Rd), Beltsville. 504.5755

61 Goddard Space Flight Center This research facility and museum offers a solar telescope for sunspot viewing, several dismantled rockets and other space objects, and exhibitions ranging from outer-space satellite transmissions to everyday TV weather maps. Film clips of NASA's adventures in space are screened continuously. You can even watch outtakes from the drama at ground control before a rocket takeoff or landing. Model rocket launches are held on the first and third Sundays of each month at 1PM. ♦ Free. Daily. Tours: M-Sa 11:30AM, 2:30PM; group tours by appointment. Soil Conservation Rd (just north of Greenbelt Rd), Greenbelt. 286.8981

62 Jack Kent Cooke Stadium Named for the **Washington Redskins'** late owner of 25 years, the new home of the beloved football team opened with great fanfare in 1998. (Ironically, John Kent Cooke, who was widely assumed to replace his father—who died in 1997—was forced to sell the **Redskins** in 1999, as he was not left controlling interest in his father's will.) This 80,000-seat arena—including 208 luxury suites, a 14,000-square-foot locker room, and 3.5 miles of concourse railings—makes their former home, **RFK Stadium,** seem cozy by comparison. The natural-turf field is kept from freezing by underground pipes, giant (24-by-32-foot) video screens run replays and highlights in each end zone, and 38 concession stands sell everything from pizza and hot dogs to Mexican food and desserts.

The difficulty is in actually getting tickets for a game. The **Redskins** have been sold out for years and have thousands on their season-ticket waiting list—despite their glorious new stadium. For those who do score a ticket, allow plenty of time to compensate for often-heavy traffic. Shuttle buses (fee) run constantly from the **Cheverly** and **Landover** Metro stations (a 10- to 15-minute ride). ♦ Box office and information office: M-F. Arena Dr (off Lottsford Rd), Landover. Information 276.5000, ticket office 276.6050 ♿ Metros: Cheverly, Landover

63 US Airways Arena Once one of America's foremost showcase auditoriums, the former **Capital Centre** is still the area's largest arena. It was the scene of President Reagan's second Inaugural (forced indoors by cold weather). The facility's design hasn't aged well since its opening in 1972; today it feels dark and gloomy in comparison to more recently designed spaces, which make better use of natural light.

Often used as a concert hall, over the years it has hosted such luminaries as Bruce

Springsteen, Michael Jackson, the Rolling Stones, the Grateful Dead, and Bob Dylan. Sports events also held here have included the World Professional Ice Skating Championship, professional hockey games **(Capitals),** professional **(Bullets,** now **Wizards)** and collegiate basketball games **(Georgetown Hoyas),** professional wrestling, and closed-circuit boxing. The **Capitals** and **Wizards** have since moved to the new **MCI Center** (see page 92) in downtown Washington, but the **Washington Warthogs** (soccer) and the **Hoyas** (college basketball) still play here.

In addition to 12 concession stands, there are two full-service restaurants on the premises: the elegant French-American **Captain's Club,** open to members only but available for private parties, and the **Showcase Pub & Eatery,** a deli/restaurant and bar, which seats patrons on a first-come, first-served basis. The arena's most unique feature is the **Parents' Quiet Room,** a soundproof area where adults can wait in peace while their children scream their heads off at the rock concert upstairs. ♦ Box office: daily. 1 Harry S. Truman Dr (west of Lottsford Rd), Landover. 24-hour information 350.3400 ♿

64 Six Flags America Formerly known as **Adventure World,** this amusement park is now filled with even more rides, shows, concessions, and attractions guaranteed to drive youngsters wild and parents crazy. Assorted water slides, an innovative children's pool, and **Wild Wave,** one of the world's largest wave pools, provide big splashes of fun. There are three shows and special events each weekend and sometimes during the week. Though this one suffers in comparison to **Kings Dominion** two hours south, it's still the biggest theme park in the DC area. ♦ Admission. F-Sa 4-10PM early June; M-Sa 10:30AM-9PM, Su 10:30AM-8PM mid-June–Aug; F-Sa 10:30AM-9PM first and last weekends in Sept. 13710 Central Ave (between Church and Enterprise Rds), Largo. 249.1500

65 Watkins Regional Park The authentic hand-carved, hand-painted, 80-plus-year-old carousel here is worth seeing. The park also has train rides, miniature golf, and a snack bar. ♦ Admission. Tu-Su June-Sept; Sa-Su Oct-May. 301 Watkins Park Dr (between Largo Rd and Central Ave), Largo. 390.9224

The Gridiron Club is a venerable Washington institution, limited to 50 Washington press correspondents. Their annual Gridiron Dinner presents skits lampooning current affairs and politicians. The President is always invited and usually attends.

66 Paul E. Garber Facility The **National Air and Space Museum**'s preservation, restoration, and storage facility exhibits some 90 wondrous aircraft, along with models, kites, and astronautical artifacts. Many of the antique foreign planes are war prizes collected by the US Air Force at the end of World War II. The *Bell Model 30,* the first two-bladed helicopter, and the nose cone from the *Jupiter* craft, which carried two monkeys into space in the 1960s, are also here. This is where the *Enola Gay,* the aircraft that dropped the atomic bomb on Hiroshima, was restored in preparation for the controversial 1995 exhibit at the **Air and Space Museum.** Plan ahead: Tours require reservations two weeks in advance. ♦ Free. Tours daily; reservations required. 3904 Old Silver Hill Rd (between Silver Hill Rd and Bonita St), Suitland. 202/357.1400 ♿

67 Oxon Hill Farm City folks can get a taste of country life at this working farm, where rural charms abound. Farm animals provide plenty of diversions for wide-eyed urban kids, who can watch as the cows are milked and the fields plowed. Family activities include hayrides and special events, such as a cornhusk doll-making workshop and "Jimmy Crack Corn," at which you can help shuck, shell, and grind corn for poultry feed. A forest, an orchard, and a vegetable garden complete the rustic picture. Activities are administered by the National Park Service. ♦ Free. Daily. 6411 Oxon Hill Rd (just west of Indian Head Hwy), Forest Heights. 839.1177

68 Rosecroft Raceway Enjoy the excitement of nighttime harness racing, and the view, from the raceway's restaurant. ♦ Post time: Tu-Sa 7:30PM. 6336 Rosecroft Dr (south of Brinkley Rd), Oxon Hill. Restaurant reservations 567.4045, raceway information 567.4000

"Note that the city of Washington is always referred to as the capital spelled with an *al,* as in accumulated wealth or excess of assets over liabilities. The building occupied by the Congress of the United States and the surrounding Hill are always referred to as the Capitol with *ol* and an upper case initial. That is, the Capitol building is always spelled with a capital C but the capital city is spelled without." Is that clear?

E.J. Applewhite, *Washington Itself*

The Secret Service has code names for each president. President Nixon was known as Searchlight, President Carter as Dixon, and President Ford as Passkey.

69 Fort Washington Built on this site to replace the original **Fort Warburton** (destroyed by British-set fires in 1814), the present structure was manned as a river defense post, at times by as many as 350 soldiers. High brick and stone walls enclose the three-acre fort; the entrance has a drawbridge suspended over a dry moat to prevent enemy attacks. Lethal bombardments could be delivered from three levels: the ramparts, the casement positions, and the water battery (designed by **Pierre-Charles L'Enfant**), which is placed 60 feet below the main fort. Volunteer guides in period costume give musket demonstrations during the summer. Several trails lead to picnic areas in the 300-acre historical park surrounding the fort. ♦ Admission. Daily. Tours: M-F. 13551 Fort Washington Rd, Fort Washington. 763.4601

70 National Colonial Farm This working re-creation of an 18th-century tobacco plantation offers a fascinating glimpse into colonial life in southern Maryland. Farm work and crafts are demonstrated. The grounds are managed by the National Park Service. Tours are available through the **Visitors' Center.** ♦ Admission. Park: daily. Visitors' Center: Tu-Su. 3400 Bryan Point Rd (at Cactus Hill Rd), Accokeek. 283.2115

71 Irish Pizza ★$ This pizza joint won't get written up in *Gourmet* magazine but it offers decent pizza, plenty of imported beers, and patrons who are either celebrating a big day at the nearby racetrack or nursing their wounds after picking the wrong ponies. ♦ Pizza ♦ M-Th, Su 11AM-2AM; F, Sa 11AM-3AM. 12629 Laurel Bowie Rd (between Baltimore Washington Pkwy and Brock Bridge Rd), Laurel. 490.7777 ♿

Howard County

Roughly midway between Washington and Baltimore, this suburb is home to people who commute to work in both cities. It includes **Savage, Jessup,** and **Ellicott City,** but its main claim to fame is **Columbia,** a planned community conceived in the 1960s.

72 Savage Mill Built in 1842 to manufacture cotton duck for sail canvas, this factory complex, which ceased operations after World War II, has been transformed into a 12-building crafts center. Today it houses artist studios, specialty and antiques shops, and cafes. ♦ Daily. 8600 Foundry St (between Gorman Rd and Washington St), Savage. 410/792.2820

73 Blob's Bavarian Biergarten ★$ Beer, sauerbraten, and live polka music draw families to this cavernous biergarten. ♦ German ♦ F-Su dinner. 8024 Blob's Park Rd (south of Jessup Rd), Jessup. 410/799.0155 ♿

74 Holiday Inn Columbia $ In addition to the 175 rooms here are meeting facilities, an outdoor pool, and an exercise room, as well as a restaurant and bar. Nonsmoking rooms are available, and children under 12 stay free. ◆ 7900 Washington Blvd (at Waterloo Rd), Jessup. 410/799.7500, 800/HOLIDAY; fax 410/799.1824 ♿

75 Columbia Hilton $$ This comfortable hotel has 152 rooms, an indoor pool, sauna, and Jacuzzi, meeting facilities, restaurant, and bar. ◆ 5485 Twin Knolls Rd (north of Thunder Hill Rd), Columbia. 410/997.1060, 800/HILTONS; fax 410/997.0169 ♿

76 Merriweather Post Pavilion Set in a 50-acre park, this outdoor amphitheater hosts major rock and pop concerts in the summer with lawn or pavilion seating; tickets are sold through major DC outlets. ◆ 10475 S Entrance Rd (between Columbia Rd and Little Patuxent Pkwy), Columbia. 410/730.2424 ♿

76 Columbia Inn Hotel & Conference Center $$$ The gracious 289-room hotel is a member of the nearby **Columbia Association,** a state-of-the-art athletic facility with full health-club services and tennis courts. Free transportation to the club is provided for guests. Also available are concierge service, meeting rooms, and a restaurant and bar. Children under 12 stay free. ◆ 10207 Wincopin Cir (just east of Little Patuxent Pkwy), Columbia. 410/730.3900, 800/638.2817; fax 410/964.3338 ♿

77 King's Contrivance ★$$ The historical country-estate setting here complements a menu of American dishes, such as rack of lamb and rockfish with crabmeat. Sample a dram or two from one of the most extensive selections of single-malt scotches in the Baltimore-Washington area. ◆ American ◆ M-F lunch and dinner; Sa-Su dinner. Reservations recommended. 10150 Shaker Dr (between Rte 32 and Wesleigh Dr), Columbia. 301/596.3455

78 Crab Shanty ★$$ Classic Maryland seafood, from steamed crabs to more formal grilled dishes, is served in this casual place. ◆ Seafood ◆ M-F lunch and dinner; Sa-Su dinner. 3410 Plumtree Dr (between Frederick Rd and Baltimore National Pike), Ellicott City. 410/465.9660 ♿

Bests

Michael Kahn
Artistic Director, The Shakespeare Theatre

Take a walk through the **Capitol Hill** district, lovely small houses and gardens. Visit **Eastern Market,** a covered food market which has open stalls on Saturdays and a huge flea market on Sundays. Be sure to have a breakfast of pancakes or a lunch of crab cakes or soft-shell crab sandwiches from the food stand in the corner.

Hire a bicycle and ride through **Rock Creek Park.** Pack a picnic and eat by a stream or under the trees. If it's summer, see a free performance at the **Shakespeare Theatre** *Free For All* at the **Carter Barron Amphitheater** or a concert by the **National Symphony Orchestra.**

Visit the **National Portrait Gallery** and if you are particularly interested in the performing arts, see the collection of paintings of great names in the American theater. You can then walk two blocks and have a meal in **Chinatown.**

Get off the **Metro** at the **National Archives** and stroll through the many art galleries of the **Penn Quarter district** in Downtown DC. Stand on the map of the world at the **Naval Memorial** and move around on it to measure how far you have traveled in your life. Have a meal of tapas at **Jaleo** in the **Lansburg** building and then see a great classic play at the **Shakespeare Theatre** next door.

Terence Winch
Poet/Musician with Celtic Thunder; Head of Publications, Smithsonian's National Museum of the American Indian

Washington Irish Music Festival at **Wolf Trap** (Sunday of Memorial Day weekend) International gathering of the best in traditional Irish music in a fabulous setting.

Kulturas Books and Records in **Dupont Circle** Best secondhand bookstore in the area.

Ireland's Four Provinces Very roomy and friendly Irish pub, with live music most nights.

The Dubliner Classic Irish pub across the street from **Union Station.**

The Irish Times Next door to **The Dubliner,** refuge for the thirsty and those in search of atmosphere.

Statue of Irish patriot Robert Emmett on **Massachusetts Avenue** right above Dupont Circle; a tiny, enchanting spot.

Dumbarton Oaks (just above **Georgetown**) The most beautiful gardens in DC, plus a great collection of pre-Columbian art.

Hillwood Seclusion in the heart of the city; a Japanese garden; a log house with beautiful Native American objects; a cafe; plus Marjorie Merriweather Post's mansion.

Baltimore

This historical city pulled off one of the great urban comebacks, managing to renew itself extensively without losing sight of its original charms. Baltimore is naturally proud of its history. At **Fort McHenry**, during the War of 1812, poet Francis Scott Key wrote "The Star Spangled Banner," while a 25-hour battle raged. Not long after that, the city became the site of the country's first public railroad, the **Baltimore & Ohio.** Between the railroad and the expansive harbor the town grew steadily well into the 20th century. A terrible fire in 1904 destroyed much of Baltimore's business district, but the city—with a unique penchant for reinventing itself—bounced back. Steel plants moved in, and Baltimore soon rivaled even Pittsburgh as a center of industrial output. But the years were unkind and, like other industrial cities, this one began to rust: Its blue-collar workforce showed signs of fraying, its inner city and harbor area was left to decay.

During the 1970s, however, a positive change began to take place, thanks to the energetic efforts of Mayor (and later Maryland Governor) William Donald Schaeffer. **Charles Center,** a 33-acre office and apartment complex, was already beginning to attract businesses and residents back to the city. With the addition of **Harborplace,** a smaller but equally impressive complex of shops and restaurants, the **Inner Harbor** area became the pride of the city, graced by the 30-story **World Trade Center,** the **Maryland Science Center & Planetarium,** the **National Aquarium,** and frequent appearances by the Tall Ships. The final jewel in the **Inner Harbor's** crown is **Oriole Park at Camden Yards,** a baseball-only stadium built near Babe Ruth's birthplace (itself a lovely museum).

Thanks to the foresight of local business and government leaders, who wisely decided to restore many of the town's magnificent older buildings rather than send in the wrecking ball, Inner Harbor is not the city's only attraction. Venture inland and check out Baltimore's other charms: **Lexington Market,** the **Walters Art Gallery, Little Italy,** the **Fell's Point** neighborhood with its heady mix of Old and New Baltimore, taverns and funky shops, coffee bars and dance clubs. The revitalization of Baltimore's harbor, the city's inherent charm and rich history, plus the genuine friendliness of its natives, make Baltimore more than the sum of its parts—a delightful blend of old and new, it's Americana at its best.

Area code 410 unless otherwise noted.

Downtown and Central Baltimore

1 American Visionary Art Museum
Homeless people, mechanics, housewives—all with zero art training—have their works on display in this three-story, turn-of-the-century building overlooking the harbor. Dedicated to the self-taught artist, the museum's offerings are often bizarre, yet powerful: a miniature tin church with a foil cross; tiny scenes embroidered with unraveled sock threads; a crazy whirligig powered by fans. Every year brings a new theme and new art; "Love: Error and Eros" and "Lifestyles of the Down and Out" are examples. Filled with crafts, the gift shop is equally appealing. ♦ Admission. Tu-Su Memorial Day–Labor Day; W-Su the rest of year. 800 Key Hwy (east of Battery Ave). 244.1900; www.avam.org ও

Within the American Visionary Art Museum:

Joy America Cafe ★★★$$$ This restaurant is rated one of the city's best by *Baltimore* magazine. The menus here, bound with sticks and twisted metal, are themselves works of art. The chef—self-taught, like the artists represented here—creates imaginative dishes such as grilled chicken with mango, mesquite-barbecued duck breast, and grilled tenderloin of beef, and for dessert, pumpkin crème brûlée. The dining room's crescent-shaped window overlooks the harbor; there's outdoor seating as well. ♦ Multicultural ♦ Tu-Su lunch and dinner. Reservations recommended. 244.6500 ♿

2 Federal Hill Park This hill, once occupied by Federal troops during the Civil War, is a nice spot for picnicking; it also affords the most photogenic view of the Inner Harbor. The Otterbein Homesteading Project is responsible for saving the 18th-century homes nearby, which were beautifully restored by modern homesteaders who bought them for one dollar each. ♦ Key Hwy and Battery Ave

MARYLAND SCIENCE CENTER

3 Maryland Science Center & Planetarium Architect **Edward Durell Stone** designed this octagonal structure to house the **Maryland Academy of Sciences**, founded in 1797. The center contains three floors of hands-on activities associated with such topics as structural engineering, energy and light, and the Chesapeake Bay. Other exhibitions focus on the latest in technology. The **Davis Planetarium** re-creates a stellar voyage with 350 simultaneous projectors and lasers; the **Boyd Theatre** houses a demonstration stage for live presentations, while the popular **IMAX Theater** features a sound system that is 8,000 watts strong, and its 70mm projectors send a giant image to a screen five stories tall and 75 feet wide. Call for up-to-date schedule information. ♦ Admission. Daily. 601 Light St (between Key Hwy and S Calvert St). Science Center 685.5225, Planetarium 539.STAR ♿

HARBORPLACE & THE GALLERY

4 Harborplace Built more than twenty years ago, when the waterfront was crumbling, these two pavilions are the keystone of Baltimore's highly successful urban renewal. The glass-sided structures, housing more than 100 shops and restaurants, rest on a promenade linked to the **National Aquarium**

in Baltimore and several museums. The more lively **Light Street Pavilion** overflows with little shops (devoted to magic, baseball, and comics, among others) and food stalls hawking seafood specialties and ethnic foods. The **Pratt Street Pavilion** offers upscale shops and restaurants, including **The Cheesecake Factory** (234.3990), **Tex Mex Grill** (783.2970), and **Planet Hollywood** (685.STAR). Both pavilions have balconies open to the public with splendid views of the harbor. ♦ Pavilions: M-Sa 10AM-9PM; Su. Restaurants: open late; call for exact times. E Pratt and S Calvert Sts. 332.4191 ♿

Within Harborplace:

Phillips HARBORPLACE

Phillips Harborplace ★★$$ The specialty here is seafood, and though the emphasis on serving as many people as possible makes for a hurried meal, this is still a good place to get acquainted with the region's bounties—oysters on the half shell, crab cakes, and fried fish fillets. There's also ocean-view patio seating, a piano bar, and live Dixieland jazz on Sunday. ♦ Seafood ♦ Daily lunch and dinner. Light Street Pavilion. 685.6600 ♿

5 Gallery at Harborplace A skywalk links this attractive four-level mall to **Harborplace.** There are more than 75 upscale shops, such as **Banana Republic** (539.1383), **Brooks Brothers** (625.0971), and **The Coach Store** (385.1772). Eateries include **Au Bon Pain** (539.9616), for baked goods and sandwiches, and **Ocean City Fries and Burgers** (547.8937), for a cup of the crinkle-cut fries beloved by locals. ♦ 200 E Pratt St (at S Calvert St). 332.4191

5 Renaissance Harborplace Hotel $$$$ Adjoining the **Gallery at Harborplace,** this luxurious, modern hotel contains 622 guest rooms, 18 meeting rooms, and two ballrooms, as well as sauna, pool, health club facilities, and 24-hour room service. It is situated just minutes from the **Convention Center** and **Oriole Park.** The hotel's restaurant, **Windows,** offers seafood specialties fresh from the Chesapeake Bay plus a grand view of the harbor; the **Lobby Lounge and Coffee Bar** offers beverages. Children under 18 stay free. ♦ 202 E Pratt St (between South and S Calvert Sts). 547.1200, 800/535.1201; fax 539.5780 ♿

6 World Trade Center The world's tallest pentagonal building and the most distinctive feature of Baltimore's downtown skyline, it reflects architect **I.M. Pei**'s propensity for geometry. From the 27th-floor observation deck you'll have great views of the entire city (and, on a clear day, all the way to the Chesapeake Bay Bridge). There's also a museum, **Top of the World**, with creative displays on Baltimore's history, port, and people, as well as a fun gift shop. A stop here will especially delight kids and first-time visitors. ♦ Admission. Daily. 401 E Pratt St (between President and S Calvert Sts). 837.4515 &

7 Baltimore Maritime Museum Here visitors climb aboard three historic ships, all National Historic Landmarks. The **Taney** cutter fought Japanese planes at Pearl Harbor; the **USS Torsk** submarine was the last warship to sink an enemy vessel in World War II; and the **Lightship Chesapeake** is a floating, 1930s lighthouse. ♦ Admission. Daily. Pier 3, E Pratt St (between President and S Calvert Sts). 396.3453

7 National Aquarium in Baltimore Located on Pier 3 of the Inner Harbor, this $21.3-million structure gives you an eye-level view of more than 5,000 fish, birds, reptiles, amphibians, and sea mammals. The skeleton of a 63-foot-long finback whale spans six stories, from the ceiling to the main lobby. In the central pool, visible from nearly every point in the building, is the country's largest collection of stingrays. The sounds of the sea and cries of seabirds and sea lions surround visitors. The **Marine Mammal Pavilion** houses Atlantic bottlenose dolphins. Under a towering glass pyramid on the aquarium's top level, the steamy **South American Rain Forest** is home to two-toed sloths, five-foot iguanas, and poison dart frogs, as well as such tropical birds as blue crowned mot-mots, tanagers, and scarlet ibis. The multilevel **Atlantic Coral Reef** offers a diver's view of the more than 20 species of stony coral and such colorful tropical creatures as spotfin butterfly fish, spotted drum, and striped sergeant. The **Open Ocean** shark tank features nurse and lemon sharks as well as sand tiger sharks weighing up to 350 pounds. Also of interest are the **Seal Pool**, a 70,000-gallon rock pool, and **Children's Cove**, a hands-on learning experience for kids. To avoid waiting in line, especially in summer, purchase timed entry tickets at the booth on Pier 3. No baby

strollers are allowed inside. School and group tours can be arranged with advance notice. ♦ Admission. Daily. 501 E Pratt St (between President and S Calvert Sts). Information 576.3800, TTY (for the hearing-impaired) 625.0720 &

8 The Power Plant Recently refurbished, this is the destination of choice for those who get their kicks through high-tech toys. The original, working power plant was impressive, but its current tenants have guaranteed it a vivid, new life. ♦ Pier 4, 601 E Pratt St (between President and S Calvert Sts)

Within The Power Plant:

Hard Rock Cafe ★$$$ This chain's neon electric guitar dominates the **Power Plant**'s rooftop and the trademark 1958 Cadillac hovers over the restaurant door, welcoming visitors to Baltimore's link. The fare is predictable and the music, very, very loud. ♦ American ♦ Daily lunch and dinner. 347.7625

Barnes and Noble With 35,000 square feet on two floors and a **Starbuck's**, this may be an oasis for some. A wondrous highlight at this site is the 3,000-gallon fish tank—home to 100 different Amazonian species, and maintained by the **National Aquarium**. ♦ Daily 9AM–11PM. 385.1709

8 The ESPN Zone This huge bilevel establishment is Disney's prototype for 22 "Zones" due to open across the country. A sports lover's paradise, it features one whole floor of interactive sports games (activated by debit cards) as well as hundreds of monitors carrying more than 35 channels, so participants can simultaneously catch their favorite live games. Downstairs is a bar and restaurant, where sports fanatics can drop a little more money. ♦ M-Th, Su 11AM–11PM; F-Sa 11AM–12:30AM. 685.3776

9 Hyatt Regency Baltimore $$$ Walkways connect this glass-paneled 487-room hotel to both the **Baltimore Convention Center** (see below) and **Harborplace**. Within the hotel, guests have access to two restaurants: **Bistro 300** offers breakfast, lunch, and dinner; the rooftop **Berry & Eliot's** affords one of the best views of the Inner Harbor, as well as a small bar, dining, and nightly music. Other facilities include three tennis courts, a health club, and a large rooftop swimming pool. Participants in the upgraded Regency Club can expect unlimited concierge assistance and complimentary continental breakfast, hors d'oeuvres, and cocktails, as well. Children under 18 stay free. ♦ 300 Light St (between E Conway and E Pratt Sts). 528.1234, 800/233.1234; fax 685.3362 &

Restaurants/Clubs: Red	**Hotels:** Blue
Shops/ 🌳Outdoors: Green	**Sights/Culture:** Black

Baltimore's Inner Harbor

To its residents, Baltimore isn't Baltimore—it's "Bawlmer." Fiercely loyal, Baltimore natives hold three things sacred: crabs, the **Orioles** baseball team, and the Harbor. A generation ago the Inner Harbor was a gritty place, made strangely exotic by vapors emanating from the McCormick spice plant.

Flash forward into a new Baltimore. Barry Levinson has made the city recognizable through his movies *Tin Men, Diner, Avalon,* and now the TV show "Homicide." The **Orioles** are in a new stadium, **Camden Yards,** that packs fans in even if the team isn't doing well. And the Harbor is revitalized, renovated, and chic.

Harborplace is the linchpin of the new Inner Harbor. Designed when festival marketplaces were new, Harborplace was the area's first glitzy presence. Inside, it's crammed with shops and restaurants; outside, the plaza's buskers draw huge weekend crowds. Encouraged by Harborplace's success the city, under the stewardship of Mayor William Donald Schaefer, added the **National Aquarium** on Pier 3 (see page 173) in the early 1980s.

Soon national and international chains wanted in on the area's profitability. The **Hard Rock Cafe** (see page 173) has a huge presence at the **Power Plant** complex on Pier 4 (see page 173), its neon guitar dominating the building's rooftop. **Barnes and Noble** (see page 173) set up shop in the summer of 1998. Both have been eclipsed by **The ESPN Zone** (see page 173), a huge restaurant and bar filled with interactive video games.

Unfortunately for some, the Harbor was beginning to look less like "Bawlmer" and more like Hollywood. The breaking point came when the Bubba Gump Shrimp Company proposed a new restaurant near the **National Aquarium.** Part of a chain, Bubba Gump is based on the 1994 movie *Forrest Gump,* which is shown continuously in all its franchises. Objections to the restaurant have ranged from its architectural incompatibility with the adjacent **National Aquarium** to its essential "un-Baltimore-ness."

The future of Baltimore's Harbor? Critics are divided. Traditionalists say that the Harbor has to return to its original mission, claiming restaurants with obtrusive signs and incompatible themes have no place in one of the country's most historic harbors. Others maintain the Harbor will only survive as one of the East Coast's mega-attractions if it changes and expands with the times. Stay tuned.

10 Baltimore Convention Center Completed in 1996, the 185,000-square-foot addition to the existing convention center cost $151 million. The revamped structure sports a futuristic pale green and gray exterior.
♦ Tours by appointment. 1 W Pratt St (at S Charles St). 649.7000 &

11 Old Otterbein United Methodist Church Built by German immigrants more than two centuries ago, this Georgian building is the oldest church in Baltimore. In the 1960s it served as one of the anchors for the city's urban renewal plan. The interior is rather unremarkable for its age, except for the original stained-glass windows. ♦ Sa Apr-Oct. Tours: by appointment. W Conway and Sharp Sts. 685.4703

12 Oriole Park at Camden Yards The exclusive home of the **Baltimore Orioles,** this popular stadium replaced **Memorial Stadium,** which the **Baltimore Colts** and **Orioles** shared for many years. Just a few blocks west of the Inner Harbor, the ball park has a vintage feel. Built on the site of a former railroad yard, it's bordered by an immense old warehouse, where the **Orioles'** administrative offices are now ensconced; on the ground floor, open to

the public, are numerous eating and drinking spots. The stadium seats up to 47,000 fans and is located on bus, light-rail, and railroad lines at the north end of the Baltimore-Washington Parkway. The site also has a connection to Baltimore's baseball past; a bar owned and tended by Babe Ruth's father once stood in what is now centerfield. Other features include a family picnic area beyond the outfield (usually reserved for private parties), John "Boog" Powell's barbecue stand, and on-site parking for 5,000 cars.
♦ Tours: daily (except on afternoon game days); call for schedule. ♦ 333 Camden St (between S Howard and S Paca Sts). 547.6234 &

13 Babe Ruth Museum and Baseball Center Turn-of-the-century furnishings and more than a thousand pieces of baseball memorabilia decorate the birthplace of the "Babe," born George Herman Ruth. Highlights at this shrine to the great American pastime include the oldest baseball in Maryland (circa

1870), the bat used by the "Sultan of Swat" to hit his 60th home run in 1927, and the **Orioles' 1983 World Championship** trophy. ♦ Admission. Daily. 216 Emory St (between Portland and Dover Sts). 727.1539

14 Baltimore Area Visitors' Center Maps, hotel information, and tour reservations are available here. Call ahead for details of the City Fair, held each September, as well as the city's many ethnic festivals. ♦ Daily. 300 W Pratt St (at S Howard St). 837.4636 ♿

15 Baltimore Arena Although the arena isn't historic—it was built during the late 1950s and early 1960s—the location is. On this site in 1774 the Continental Congress voted to give George Washington full military control. Later this spot was occupied by the Hurst Company building, where the Great Baltimore Fire of 1904, also called the "Sunday Morning Fire," began. This huge hall, with its jagged roofline, used to be Baltimore's most often used auditorium before the convention center was built on the harbor during the 1980s. However, Baltimore's **Skipjacks** soccer team plays indoor games here, and the arena hosts everything from tennis matches to children's programs. Check local listings or call for sport and concert event information. ♦ Box office: M-Sa Jan-May and Sept-Dec; M-F June-Aug. 201 W Baltimore St (at Hopkins Pl). Tickets 347.2010, recorded information 347.2000 ♿

16 Davidge Hall Home to a medical teaching facility ever since it was built in 1812—for a once-grand total of $35,000—this is the oldest medical school building in the Western hemisphere. Tours may be scheduled by appointment. ♦ M-F. 522 W Lombard St (between S Paca and S Greene Sts). 706.7454 ♿

17 Edgar Allan Poe's Grave The master of the macabre is buried at the old **Western Burying Grounds,** where some of Maryland's most prominent early citizens have been laid to rest. The former **Westminster Church,** which appears to hover over the graveyard, is built on columns above the catacombs. ♦ Catacomb tours by appointment. W Fayette and N Greene Sts. 706.7228

18 Lexington Market Exuding a hurly-burly carnival mood, this city-owned, indoor market is jam-packed with more than 100 food stalls, from **Polack Johnny's** (for "famous" Polish

sausage) to **Angie's BBQ & Soul Food.** Stacks of orange crabs, slabs of ham, pastry counters, bright lights—the sights are worthy of a Fellini film. Have a crab cake sandwich at **Faidley's** (727.4898); it's consistently voted the best in Baltimore. ♦ M-Sa. 400 W Lexington St (at N Eutaw St). 685.6169 ♿

19 Charles Center Apartments, shops, and commercial buildings are in this 33-acre development begun in 1956 and finished in the 1970s. **Hopkins Plaza,** an open-air space with fountains and benches, is the venue for weekend festivals and concerts. ♦ Charles St (between W Lombard and W Saratoga Sts)

At Charles Center:

Morris A. Mechanic Theatre The stage here often serves as a testing ground for Broadway productions and the venue for touring productions; recent shows have included *Rent* and *Evita.* **John M. Johansen**'s multifaceted concrete building is Brutalist in style (so called because it makes no concessions to visual amenities) and has been dubbed "Fort Mechanic." ♦ Box office: M-Sa; Su 1-3:30PM on performance days only. Hopkins Plaza (just south of W Baltimore St). Information 625.1400, telecharge 800/638.2444 ♿

Omni Inner Harbor Hotel $$$ With a whopping 707 rooms, this is Baltimore's largest hotel. Most of the rooms offer city views of downtown Baltimore. Two restaurants, **Jackie's Cafe** and the more formal **Baltimore Grill,** serve American fare, and the **Corner Bar** offers a Happy Hour and light lunch. Amenities include concierge service, an exercise room and outdoor pool, and access to a health club across the street. Children under 17 stay free. ♦ 101 W Fayette St (at N Hanover St). 752.1100, 800/THE.OMNI; fax 752.0832 ♿

20 Old St. Paul's Episcopal Church This stately edifice, constructed in the 1850s near the site of the original 1730 church which was destroyed by fire, is adorned with stained-glass works and mosaics created by Louis Comfort Tiffany and the Tiffany Studios; additional glasswork was designed by Maitland Armstrong and John LaFarge. ♦ Public access is limited; call ahead for an appointment. N Charles and E Saratoga Sts. 685.3404

When Washington socialite Evalyn Walsh McLean owned the Hope Diamond, she often fastened the gem to her dog's collar and let him roam around the house during her lavish parties. The Hope Diamond is now the star attraction at the Smithsonian's Museum of Natural History.

Baltimore City Hall

COURTESY OF THE BALTIMORE CITY HALL
COURTYARD GALLERIES

21 Baltimore City Hall A wonder of Victorian architecture, this building (illustrated above) features local white marble, mansard roofs, and a cast- and wrought-iron dome designed by Wendell Bollman. **George A. Frederick** created the building's fine ironwork in 1875, and about 20 years ago it was renovated and restored. Note the rotunda and galleries of artwork depicting Baltimore's history. The Women's Civic League offers tours; call 837.5424 for exact times. ♦ Free. M-F. 100 Holliday St (at E Fayette St) &

22 The Strand Cybercafe ★$$ This light-filled cafe, where Internet access can be had for a fee, gives new meaning to "surf and turf." Non-cybersurfers can simply relax on the comfortable sofas or armchairs and sip coffee, drink beer, or enjoy a light meal. ♦ American ♦ Daily breakfast, lunch, and dinner. 105 E Lombard St (between S Calvert and Light Sts). 625.8944 &

23 Custom House Walk up the front steps to the **Call Room,** where you can gaze at the 30-by-68-foot canvas on the ceiling that depicts sailing vessels ranging from ancient Egyptian boats to Baltimore clippers. ♦ Free. M-F. 40 S Gay St (at Water St). No phone

24 Eubie Blake National Museum and Cultural Center This community arts center is dedicated to the life and works of Baltimore-born ragtime and jazz pianist/composer James Hubert "Eubie" Blake. Exhibits of art by local and national artists are held here also. Tours can be arranged. ♦ M-F by appointment only; Sa noon-5PM. 34 Market Pl (between Water and E Baltimore Sts). 625.3113

25 Port Discovery Walt Disney Imagineering's new, 80,000-square-foot children's museum is high concept: Interactive exhibits help children explore their own minds. Aimed at 6- to 12-year-olds, activities—like a simulated archaeological dig, complex mazes, crossing the Nile, and using an X-ray machine—encourage curiosity, creativity, enthusiasm, and caution. Food concessions and a gift shop take care of their other needs. ♦ Admission; free for children under 3. Daily. Fishmarket Bldg, 35 Market Pl (at Water St). 468.0687 &

26 Marconi's ★★★$$$ At Baltimore's bastion of classic Italian cooking, the lobster cardinale and soft-shell crabs are justifiably famous, as is the chocolate sundae made with French vanilla ice cream and a homemade chocolate sauce. Enjoy it all in a romantic dining room, located in an 1880 row house, featuring many wonderful details—dark woodwork, chandeliers, and high ceilings—from a bygone age. ♦ Italian ♦ Tu-Sa lunch and dinner. Jacket required. 106 W Saratoga

St (between Cathedral St and Park Ave). 727.9522

27 Enoch Pratt Free Library Erected in 1933, the city's principal library has an ornate lobby atrium topped with a skylight. Among its holdings are two special collections that document the lives and works of native sons H.L. Mencken and Edgar Allan Poe. ♦ M-Th, Sa-Su. 400 Cathedral St (at W Mulberry St). 396.5430 &

28 Basilica of the Assumption Completed in 1821, the first Roman Catholic cathedral in the US was designed by **Benjamin Latrobe,** architect of the **US Capitol.** Two pointed towers separate the Greek-style portico from the main dome. ♦ Open daily; call for mass schedule. Cathedral and W Mulberry Sts. 727.3564 &

29 Brown's Arcade This Neo-Classical arcade was bought for the city and reconstructed by Governor William Brown after Baltimore's Great Fire in 1904. Since the 1970s, the ornate building has been the site of many charity benefits. ♦ 324 N Charles St (between W Saratoga and W Mulberry Sts) &

30 The Women's Industrial Exchange ★★$ In operation since 1882, this quaint ladies' tearoom was created to "help needy women help themselves." A small shop near the restaurant entrance still sells baby clothes and hand-knitted items. The restaurant has an old-fashioned feel and, it's been written, the oldest waitresses in Baltimore—yes, they have beehive hairdos and call you "hon." The menu is a 1950s holdout, with jello, deviled eggs, and ice cream sundaes. ♦ American ♦ M-F breakfast and lunch. 333 N Charles St (at Pleasant St). 685.4388

31 Tio Pepe ★★★$$ Cavelike, this Spanish bistro, one of Baltimore's best restaurants, serves incomparable pheasant Alcantara in grape sauce, mushrooms from the caves of Segovia, and exquisite seafood paella. Tables are placed close together, creating a convivial atmosphere—don't be surprised if you're caught up in cross-table consultations on what to order or friendly discussions about the **Orioles**'s prospects. Say "Ole!" if you get a Saturday evening reservation as early as two weeks in advance; during the week a two-day wait is typical. ♦ Spanish ♦ M-F lunch and dinner; Sa-Su dinner. Reservations and jacket required. 10 E Franklin St (between St. Paul and N Charles Sts). 539.4675

32 Louie's Bookstore Cafe ★$ It won't win any awards for its cuisine, but it's a great place to have a snack while diving into that book you just purchased a few feet away. The bookshop has a somewhat opulent aura, with huge chandeliers and a lovely mantelpiece. ♦ American ♦ Daily lunch and dinner. 518 N Charles St (between W Hamilton and W Centre Sts). 962.1224 &

33 Mother Seton House At the request of Bishop John Carroll of Baltimore, Elizabeth Seton founded a girls' school here in her home in 1808 and later became the first American-born Roman Catholic saint. Her family pictures hang on the walls, and her black habit and bonnet are on display. ♦ Sa-Su 1-3PM; and by appointment. 600 N Paca St (between W Franklin St and Druid Hill Ave). 523.3443 &

34 Walters Art Gallery Henry Walters bequeathed his collection of 19th-century paintings, Chinese porcelains, and other treasures to the city of Baltimore in 1931. With it came the fine Palladian-style building, designed in 1909 by the architectural firm **Delano and Aldrich** after a Renaissance palazzo in Genoa. Among the gallery's treasures are artifacts from the ancient Near East, Egyptian tomb paintings, papyrus scrolls, and Roman sculptures. The **Hackerman House,** to the north of the main building, offers a magnificent gallery of Asian art. The museum store sells reproductions of museum works. **Troia at the Walters** (752.2887), open for lunch and dinner, serves regional Italian cuisine in a beautiful setting incorporating a grand staircase from a former carriage house and a fountain. ♦ Admission; free on Wednesday. Tu-Su. Tours: W noon; Sun 1:30PM. 600 N Charles St (at W Centre St). 547.9000 &

In the February 1929 edition of *National Geographic* magazine, Gilbert Grosvenor described Maryland as "a geographic miniature of America." The sobriquet stuck; and Maryland—a state with a little of everything, from the metropolis of Baltimore to the Eastern Shore to the Allegheny Mountains—is often referred to as "America in Miniature."

35 Clarion Hotel $$ This comfortable 103-room hotel at Mount Vernon Square is one block from the **Walters Art Gallery.** Rooms are adorned with tasteful fabrics and elegant furnishings. The staff is very pleasant, and there's a cozy sitting room off the lobby. ♦ 612 Cathedral St (between W Centre and W Monument Sts). 727.7101, 800/292.5500; fax 789.3312 ᕿ

36 Maryland Historical Society Founded in 1844 by citizens concerned with preserving the city's past, the society hosts temporary and permanent exhibits, including the largest collection anywhere of 19th-century American silver, a well-known collection of Federal-style furniture, and the original manuscript of Francis Scott Key's "Star-Spangled Banner." ♦ Admission. Tu-Su. 201 W Monument St (at Park Ave). 685.3750

37 Mount Vernon Square Once known as **Howard's Woods,** it was designated a park upon the installation of the *Washington Monument,* the first formal monument to honor George Washington. The statue of Washington on top of the 178-foot marble Doric column depicts him resigning his commission from the Continental Army. (Wednesday through Sunday, between 10AM and 4PM, visitors, for a fee of $1, are welcome to climb the monument's 228 steps for a rewarding view of Baltimore.) Northeast of the monument is the Gothic **Mount Vernon Methodist Church,** built of serpentine stone in 1872 by architects **Thomas Dixon** and **Charles Carson.** It stands on the site where Francis Scott Key, author of the "Star-Spangled Banner," died. **Leakin Hall** on East Mount Vernon Place opened in 1927 as the Preparatory Department of the **Peabody Institute** (see below).

At Mount Vernon Square:

Peabody Institute Founded by George Peabody in 1856, this institute was conceived as a library, music academy, and art gallery. Part of **Johns Hopkins University,** the institute has become internationally renowned over the years, with about 450 students rigorously campaigning for election to the academy. In **North Hall,** student recitals are given throughout the year. Note the gates, which are bronze copies of the Ghiberti Gates at the Baptistry in Florence. Orchestral concerts are held in **Friedberg Hall** and **Leakin Hall.** The **Peabody Library** boasts approximately 250,000 volumes divided among six levels of stacks, which are all connected by a central wall that rises 61 feet to the ceiling. The library has been featured in several movies, such as *Men Don't Leave* and *Sleepless in Seattle.* The Institute's art collection, including painting and sculpture, is scattered throughout the buildings and maintained in archives. ♦ Box office: W-F 1-4PM and prior to concerts. Library: M-F 9AM-3PM. Information 659.8144, library 659.8197, box office 659.8124

38 Center Stage Maryland's state theater mounts distinguished productions ranging from *Hamlet* to *I Could Stop on a Dime and Get Ten Cents Change.* ♦ Box office M-F; Sa-Su on performance days. 700 N Calvert St (at E Monument St). 332.0033 ᕿ

39 Bombay Grill ★★$$ Among a number of good ethnic restaurants in the Mount Vernon area, this is one of the best. Try the Grand Platter of mixed meats grilled in the tandoor oven or *murgh mazhedhar* (chicken marinated in masala sauce). The dining room has a fireplace, mirrored walls, many Buddhas, and murals depicting scenes from the holy text "Mahabharata." ♦ Indian ♦ Daily lunch and dinner. 2 E Madison St (at N Charles St). 837.2973

40 The Ruby Lounge ★★$$ Atmospheric, arty, and dimly lit, this hip bistro offers a clever take on American cuisine, with all kinds of international options, including brick-oven-fired pizzas, pecan-fried chicken with okra, and grilled tuna with Asian vegetables. ♦ New American ♦ Tu-Su dinner. 802 N Charles St (at W Madison St). 539.8051

40 The Helmand ★★★$ Soothing Afghani music and candlelit tables create a serene backdrop for the wonderful food here. Make a meal of the appetizers, such as *kaddo borawni,* luscious chunks of fried and baked pumpkin with sugar and yogurt-garlic sauce, or *aushak,* ravioli stuffed with leeks and topped with mint-yogurt and ground beef sauce. The unusual flavors will please curious palates. ♦ Afghani ♦ Daily dinner. Reservations recommended F-Sa. 806 N Charles St (between W Madison and W Read Sts). 752.0311 ᕿ

41 Brass Elephant ★★$$ This Northern Italian restaurant is set in an exquisitely restored 1860s Victorian town house, replete with hand-carved marble and wood and hand-wrought brass appointments. Try the veal *valdostano* (sautéed with white wine and cream sauce and baked with fontina cheese) or any of the many fish dishes. ♦ Italian ♦ M-F lunch and dinner; Sa-Su dinner. 924 N Charles St (between W Read and W Eager Sts). 547.8480

42 Antique Row Collectors from all over the East Coast prowl the 60-odd antiques shops clustered along a two-block stretch of Howard Street. One antiques complex, **Antique Treasury,** alone houses 20 dealers. ♦ M-Sa. N Howard St (between W Madison and W Read Sts). 728.6363 ఱ

43 Prime Rib ★★★$$$ If you're seeking a fine beef meal, this is the place. Prime ribs, steaks, and other classics are served in a low-lit room with black-lacquered walls to a predominantly business crowd. ♦ American ♦ Daily dinner. Reservations recommended; jacket required. 1101 N Calvert St (at E Chase St). 539.1804 ఱ

44 Joseph Meyerhoff Symphony Hall The dream of the **Baltimore Symphony Orchestra**'s former maestro, Sergiu Comissiona, and its late president, Joseph Meyerhoff, this hall showcases the symphony (conducted by Yuri Temirkanov) in all its splendor. It was designed in 1982 by **Pietro Belluschi** and graced with near-perfect acoustics by **Bolt, Beranek & Newman;** the building's round shape gives an unobstructed view of the stage from all 2,400 seats. The interior surfaces are curved, and 420 tons of plaster coat the double-thick walls to protect the chamber from external noise. The grand staircases and glass-and-brick flourishes give the eye a treat as well. ♦ Box office M-Sa. 1212 Cathedral St (between W Chase and W Preston Sts). 783.8000 ఱ

45 Baltimore Streetcar Museum Founded in 1966, this museum features rides in Baltimore streetcars (elsewhere known as trolleys) that date from the 1890s through the 1950s. The mile-plus round-trip runs from the North Avenue loop to the 28th Street loop beside Falls Road. Back at the **Visitors' Center,** streetcar history is recalled through photographs, displays, and a slide show. If asked, a museum volunteer will conduct tours through the **Car House,** which contains nearly a dozen restored streetcars. ♦ Admission. Sa-Su noon-5PM June-Oct; by appointment M-F Jan-May, Nov-Dec. 1901 Falls Rd (at W North Ave). 547.0264 ఱ

46 Lovely Lane United Methodist Church Designed by **Stanford White,** this is the Mother Church of American Methodism as well as the nation's finest museum of Methodist history. The 1884 structure, Romanesque in style with Etruscan detailing, is on the National Register of Historic Places. Tours are given Monday through Friday and on Sunday immediately following services; call for an appointment. ♦ 2200 St. Paul St (at E 22nd St). 889.1512

47 Baltimore Museum of Art (BMA) One of our country's foremost museums, **BMA** was founded in 1914 and designed by **John Russell Pope;** two modern wings have since been added. The world-class holdings date from antiquity to the present. The **Cone Collection,** donated fifty years ago by two local sisters, is a huge stash of works, by Matisse primarily, as well as by Renoir, Cezanne, Picasso, Van Gogh, and Gauguin. Modernism and Pop art are well represented, too; some of Andy Warhol's finest pieces (including the Brillo boxes) are on display along with works by Lichtenstein and Rauschenberg.

Other sections are devoted to American decorative arts (including furniture), Asian art, and African and pre-Columbian objects. The elegant new **Gertrude's** restaurant celebrates the seafood bounty of Chesapeake Bay; it adjoins the **Wurtzburger** and **Levi Sculpture Gardens,** which contain works by Calder, Moore, and Rodin. For group tours, call 396.6320. There is a library (396.6317), open by appointment only, and also a museum shop. ♦ Admission; free Thursday and for those 16 and under. W-Su. For group tours, call 396.6320. 10 Art Museum Dr (between Wyman Park Dr and N Charles St). 396.7100 ఱ

48 Johns Hopkins University Founded in 1876 by Johns Hopkins, a prominent Baltimore merchant, this prestigious university was originally dedicated to graduate study and research. Today there are about 3,000 undergraduate students, in addition to its 1,200 graduate students. The 126-acre **Homewood** campus houses the schools of arts and sciences, engineering, and continuing studies. The lush grounds and elegant buildings are an exercise in aesthetics. The medical school and hospital are in East Baltimore, and the **School of Advanced International Studies** is located in DC. **Homewood Field** is home base for the lacrosse team, consistently one of the top teams in the nation. ♦ Tour information: 516.8171. N Charles St (between Art Museum Dr and W University Pkwy).

Within Johns Hopkins University:

Homewood Charles Carroll of Carrollton, a signer of the Declaration of Independence, built this Federal mansion in 1801 as a wedding present for his son, Charles Jr. The house, a National Historic Landmark, has been restored with period furnishings. ♦ Admission. Tu-Sa 11AM-3PM; Su noon-4PM. 3400 N Charles St. 516.5589

49 Great Blacks in Wax Museum The likenesses of more than a hundred prominent African-Americans, including Olympic star Jesse Owens and civil rights activist Rosa Parks, have been fashioned in wax and are on display here.

America's First Black History Wax Museum
Taking you through the pages of time

The scene dramatizing the removal of Ms. Parks from a Montgomery, Alabama bus is also here. ♦ Admission. Tu-Su. 1601 E North Ave (at N Bond St). 563.3404

50 Shot Tower More than a million handmade bricks were used to build this 234-foot-high landmark, where buckshot was manufactured between 1828 and 1892. Press a button and a slide show inside the tower explains the shot-making process: Molten lead was poured through sieves at the top of the tower and formed perfectly round spheres as it fell through space. ♦ Free. Sa-Su noon-5PM. 801 E Fayette St (at N Front St). 396.5894

51 Baltimore Brewing Company ★★$$ In 1516 the Reinheitsgebot Bavarian Purity Law stated that beer must be brewed with only four ingredients: water, malt, hops, and yeast. That law is upheld here by Dutch brewmaster Theo DeGroen, who claims that Baltimore's water is comparable in mineral content to the water used in some of Germany's greatest brewing centers. Food offerings at this microbrewery include salads, soups, and sandwiches, or heartier German entrées, such as bratwurst, knockwurst, and dumplings. In fair weather, take advantage of the outdoor terrace. ♦ German ♦ Daily lunch and dinner. 104 Albemarle St (between E Pratt and E Lombard Sts). 837.5000 &

52 Obrycki's Crab House ★★★$$ Casual atmosphere, beer, and succulent crab characterize this family-run crab house—Baltimore's most famous. Go with a group and order steamed crabs; just remember that it's a communal eating experience. ♦ Seafood ♦ Daily lunch and dinner Apr-Nov; closed Dec-Mar. Season closing date varies, so call ahead. 1727 E Pratt St (between S Ann and S Regester Sts). 732.6399 &

Fell's Point

Settled in the early 1700s by the Fell brothers from Lancaster, England, Fell's Point was once a booming port, home to brigs and schooners ferrying flour and tobacco around the globe. The area of narrow cobblestone streets is on the National Registry of Historic Places. Site of 47 pubs in 1796, it remains a bar magnet today. **Broadway Market,** the city's oldest, is not much—some butchers and tiny lunch counters—but it has an authentic, blue-collar quality. The area has gained more recent notoriety as the setting for the television show "Homicide." Actors can often be seen around the Thames Street police station set. (By the way, the "h" in Thames is not silent; lore has it that early Baltimoreans purposely mispronounced the English river to annoy the British.) To reach Fell's Point, take a water taxi from the Inner Harbor. Walking and motor coach tours are offered by **Zippy Larson's Shoe Leather Safaris** (817.4141). Larson also conducts well-researched historical theme tours of other parts of Baltimore and Maryland.

53 Market Square This public square, which has changed little since the time of the Fell brothers, hosts local ethnic festivals and promotional events during the summer. ♦ S Broadway (between Thames and Lancaster Sts)

53 Vagabond Players Opened in 1916, this establishment claims to be the oldest continuously operating little theater in the country. It seats about a hundred people. Call for current schedule information. ♦ Showtimes: F-Sa 8PM; Su 2PM, 7PM. Box office opens one hour before show begins. 806 S Broadway (between Shakespeare and Lancaster Sts). 563.9135 &

53 Admiral Fell Inn $$$ At various times a sailors' lodging house and a vinegar factory, the 80-room inn is furnished with antiques. Go up to the roof and contrast historic Fell's Point with the surrounding modern cityscape. Dining options include **Savannah,** a formal dining room serving American cuisine with a Southern accent, and a small English pub. Breakfast is included. ♦ 888 S Broadway (at Shakespeare St). 522.7377, 800/292.4667; fax 522.0707 &

54 Robert Long House The oldest house in the city was built by Robert Long in 1765 in the Quaker style with a pent roof and a shed dormer. Visitors are treated to period-style decor and garden. ♦ Admission. Call for hours. 812 S Ann St (between Thames and Lancaster Sts). 675.6750 &

55 Bertha's Dining Room ★★$$ Heed the ubiquitous bumper stickers telling you to "Eat Bertha's Mussels." It's good advice. The famous mollusks are served with a variety of mouthwatering dipping sauces, such as fresh basil with garlic, sour cream and scallion, and creamy mustard. A full seafood menu, as well as chicken, steak, and hamburgers, is also available in the warm, homey surroundings. A plus: Because the owners are of Scottish descent, high tea consisting of hors d'oeuvres, scones, dessert, and tea is served. ♦ Seafood ♦ M-Sa lunch, high tea, and dinner; Su lunch and dinner. One day advance reservations required for high tea. 734 S Broadway (between Lancaster and Aliceanna Sts). 327.5795

56 Pierpoint ★★$$ Intimate and friendly, this bistro offers both Italian fare and local American favorites. As with most Baltimore restaurants, seafood dishes reign supreme; however, don't skip the vegetables—they're wonderfully fresh and inventively prepared here. ♦ Italian/American ♦ Tu-Su lunch and dinner. 1822 Aliceanna St (between S Wolfe and S Ann Sts). 675.2080 ♿

Little Italy

Home to several excellent Italian restaurants, this stark section of humble dwellings is wedged at the eastern edge of the Inner Harbor. It's especially popular with conventioneers and tourists, though locals visit too.

57 Chiapparelli's ★★$$ This casual restaurant serves classic Southern Italian dishes at their most copious and robust. ♦ Italian ♦ Daily lunch and dinner. 237 S High St (at Fawn St). 837.0309 ♿

58 Vaccaro's Traditional Italian pastry is food for any *paesan*'s soul, and the ricotta cheese–filled confections here are more subtle than their sweet American cousins. Huge cookies are sold by the pound, and ice-cream scoops are the size of a man's fist. ♦ Daily. 222 Albermarle St (at Stiles St). 685.4905

59 Dalesio's of Little Italy ★★★$$ One of the best restaurants in Little Italy, it has a sophisticated menu that goes well beyond the usual spaghetti and clam sauce, offering such dishes as grilled salmon and *pasta puttinara* (fresh tomato sauce studded with black and green olives, capers, anchovies, and fresh basil). The traditional decor is accented with antiques. ♦ Italian ♦ M-Sa lunch and dinner; Su dinner. 829 Eastern Ave (between Albemarle and President Sts). 539.1965 ♿

Elsewhere in Baltimore

60 Baltimore Museum of Industry Once an oyster cannery, this museum details the city's industrial history. Permanent exhibitions include a 1910 garment loft, a 19th-century print shop, and a 1906 steam tugboat. ♦ Admission. Tu-Su Memorial Day–Labor Day; W-Su the rest of year. 1415 Key Hwy (between Boyle and Webster Sts). 727.4808 ♿

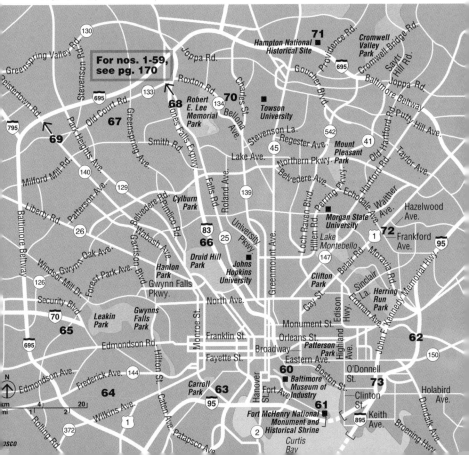

For nos. 1-59, see pg. 170

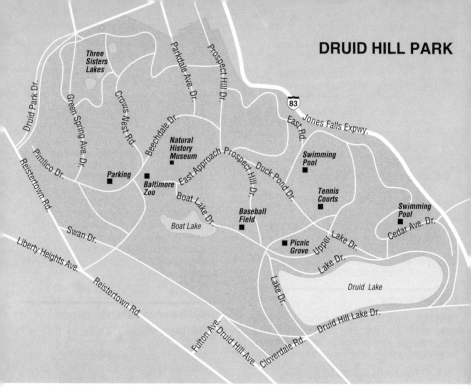

DRUID HILL PARK

Three Sisters Lakes

Druid Park Dr.

Green Spring Ave. Dr.

Crows Nest Rd.

Parkdale Ave. Dr.

Prospect Hill Dr.

Beechdale Dr.

Natural History Museum

East Approach

Prospect Hill Dr.

East Rd.

Jones Falls Expwy.

Swimming Pool

Pimlico Dr.

Parking

Baltimore Zoo

Duck Pond Dr.

Tennis Courts

Reisterstown Rd.

Boat Lake Dr.

Baseball Field

Swimming Pool

Cedar Ave. Dr.

Swan Dr.

Boat Lake

Picnic Grove

Upper Lake Dr.

Liberty Heights Ave.

Reisterstown Rd.

Lake Dr.

Lake Dr.

Druid Lake

Fulton Ave. Druid Hill Ave.

Cloverdale Rd.

Druid Hill Lake Dr.

61 Fort McHenry The 20-foot-thick brick walls of this star-shaped 18th-century fort overlooking the harbor protected the compound from British attack on 13 September 1814; the next morning, when he saw the US flag still flying, Francis Scott Key wrote "The Star-Spangled Banner," a poem about the defense of **Fort McHenry.** Set to the tune of an old English drinking song, it became the national anthem in 1931. The **Visitors' Center** offers films and exhibitions on the history of the fort and the writing of the national anthem. ♦ Admission. Daily. E Fort Ave (east of Key Hwy). 962.4290 ⅋

62 Baltimore Ravens Stadium In August 1998 this new football stadium opened with a brand-new team, the Baltimore **Ravens** (the old Cleveland **Browns,** wooed to Baltimore and renamed to reflect the city's Edgar Allen Poe connection). The $220-million, 69,000-seat arena complements nearby **Camden Yards,** but lacks the latter's vintage feel. However, the two stadiums share parking facilities and are served by the same MTA lines. ♦ Tours: Daily 10AM-2PM (except on afternoon game days); call for schedule. ♦ 1101 Russell St (between I-95 and S Martin Luther King Jr. Blvd). 230.8000 ⅋

63 Mount Clare Mansion Baltimore's only pre-Revolutionary mansion was built in 1760 by Charles Carroll. Late 18th-century furniture and mementos of the Carroll family are on display. ♦ Admission. Tu-F 11AM-3PM; Sa-Su 1-3PM. Carroll Park, 1500 Washington Blvd (between S Monroe and Bayard Sts). 837.3262 ⅋

64 B&O Railroad Museum Early locomotives stand as silent reminders of a bygone day here on the site of the nation's first passenger and freight railway station. Train fanciers will find such treasures as a steam-powered replica of Peter Cooper's early *Tom Thumb* train, an 1836 *Grasshopper* locomotive built here at the Mount Clare shops, a caboose from 1907, and a *Forty & Eight* boxcar. The museum features memorabilia, such as hand-blown whiskey flasks, station clocks and railroad watches, and, on the second floor, an elaborate model train display. Train rides are a big hit with kids. ♦ Admission. Daily. Train rides: Sa-Su 11:30AM, 12:30, 2, 3PM. 901 W Pratt St (at S Poppleton St). 752.2490; www.borail.org ⅋

65 Edgar Allan Poe House The 23-year-old Poe moved to this house in 1832 and in it wrote "MS Found in a Bottle," the first story to earn him recognition. The recently renovated house, which belonged to his aunt Maria Clemm, was almost razed in a slum-clearance project in 1935 but is now a museum. A wide range of Poe artifacts, including his old lap desk from his days at the **University of Virginia,** the telescope he used as a teenager, and a full-color reproduction of his young wife Virginia's death portrait are here. ♦ Admission. Th-Sa noon-3:45PM. 203 N Amity St (between W Lexington and W Saratoga Sts). 396.7932

66 Druid Hill Park/Baltimore Zoo What used to be a private estate in the 1800s is now Baltimore's largest public recreational area (see map on page 182). Tennis courts and play-grounds are scattered throughout the 650-odd acres; Victorian picnic shelters built in 1859 are still in use; and an Olympic-size pool is open during warm weather.

The **Conservatory**, a late 19th-century domed greenhouse, features three massive seasonal floral displays. In a smaller hothouse next door, there's a tropical collection of African violets, succulent cacti, and more than 500 varieties of orchids.

More than 1,200 species of crawling, walking, and swimming animals live within **Baltimore Zoo**'s 160 acres. The lions and giraffes are housed in an open-air exhibition; there is a hippo house and an area for rare breeds of antelope, as well as a three-acre house and exercise area for four African elephants, including the affable Dolly. The **Children's Zoo** features rabbits, sheep, and baby animals, pony rides, a minitrain, and a carousel. Watch the black-footed penguins eat their fill daily at 3PM; the Kodiak bears dine at 2PM. Group tours may be arranged in advance by calling 396.6164. ♦ Admission. Daily 10AM-4PM with extended hours in summer. 2600 Madison Ave (at Cloverdale Rd). 396.7102

67 Cylburn Arboretum Built between 1863 and 1883 by wealthy Baltimore businessman Jesse Tyson, this estate sprawls over 176 acres. The **Arboretum** contains Japanese maples, native Maryland oaks, and rare trees. The many nature trails show off Maryland's flowering plant life. Also of interest: the **Horticultural Library**, a hands-on **Children's Nature Museum, Fessenden Herbarium**, and the **Bird Museum**. ♦ Free. Grounds: open daily. Sights: M-F. 4915 Greenspring Ave (between W Cold Spring La and W Northern Pkwy). 396.0180

68 Pimlico Race Course This track is home to the mid-May Preakness race, the second leg of horse racing's Triple Crown. Watch this and other thoroughbred races from the aprons, or reserve window seating in the restaurant. There's live racing from late March to late October; at other times simulcasts are usually broadcast. ♦ Nominal admission. Live racing: Tu, Th-Su. Post time: 1PM. 5201 Park Heights Ave (at W Belvedere Ave). 542.9400

69 Linwood's Cafe and Grille ★★★$$$ Having quickly become one of Baltimore's favorites, this restaurant, a 1990s take on Art Deco—dark teak wood with black trim and blue upholstery—offers healthy regional cuisine with impressive presentations. The seasonal menu changes quite frequently, and the open-kitchen design (with counter-style seating) allows patrons to watch the chef at work. ♦ American ♦ M-Sa lunch and dinner; Su dinner. Reservations recommended for dinner. 25 Crossroads Dr (just north of McDonogh Rd), Owings Mills. 356.3030

70 Polo Grill ★★★$$$ A good place for spotting local celebrities, this attractive hunter-green dining room looks much like a hall in an English hunting lodge and is known for such specialties as roast rack of veal, Oriental barbecued salmon, and local crisp soft-shell crabs. ♦ American ♦ Daily breakfast, lunch, and dinner. Reservations recommended. 4 W University Pkwy (between N Charles St and Canterbury Rd). 235.8200

71 Hampton National Historic Site One of the largest constructed in the post-Revolutionary period, this late-Georgian mansion was built by the prominent Ridgely family. Its extensive formal gardens are particularly impressive. The estate, along with a gift shop and a tearoom, is administered by the National Park Service. ♦ Admission. Daily. Tours: hourly until 4PM. 535 Hampton La (between Providence and Dulaney Valley Rds), Towson. 962.0688

72 Bo Brooks ★★★$$ Locals stand in line here to feast on the best crabs in the city. The little critters come in all varieties and preparations (backfin, hard shell, soft shell, baked, stuffed, fried, steamed) and arrive in combination with the freshest oysters, mussels, and clams available. No steamed crabs, however, are served during lunch at this casual crab house, since they're flown in fresh daily (but later in the day) from the restaurant's own crab farm in Texas. ♦ Seafood ♦ M-F lunch and dinner; Sa-Su dinner. 5415 Belair Rd (at Frankford Ave). 488.8144

73 Haussner's ★★★$$ If you have but one meal in Baltimore, it should be eaten at this 70-plus-year-old establishment. Each day the menu offers a choice of more than 90 fresh entrées and 40 accompanying vegetables. Enjoy a feast of sauerbraten, rabbit with spaetzle, or a seafood special. But be sure to save room for one of the spectacular desserts, especially the world-famous strawberry pie. Heads of state are literally fixtures here—there's a grand collection of Greco-Roman busts and hundreds of paintings, including prints of such masters as Gainsborough and Rembrandt. The effect is pretty kitschy—and also irresistible. ♦ German-American ♦ Tu-Sa lunch and dinner. 3244 Eastern Ave (at S Clinton St). 327.8365

Alexandria

An elegant enclave tucked amid suburban Virginia's sprawl of freeways and new developments, Alexandria is a handsome, historic city. At its **Old Town** core are streets lined with redbrick homes dating back to the 19th century, a few even to colonial times. But this is no museum display like Williamsburg—people live in these homes and conduct business here, too.

Alexandria was established in 1749, serving for many years as a principal colonial port, and during the late 18th century as a vital social and political center. George Washington was a native son, as were Revolutionary War heroes General Henry "Light Horse Harry" Lee and his son, General Robert E. Lee, the commander in chief of the Confederate army. Fortunately, several generations of residents and city leaders have preserved the rich past in dozens of historic buildings.

Old Town served as the merchant district for the old seaport and is still a lively shopping and entertainment center. **King Street**, the main east-west drag, is a browser's paradise, lined with shops selling clothing, crafts, housewares, and gifts. And this is *the* place for antique hunting; no section of DC has the wealth of antiques shops that fill the western stretch of King Street. **Prince** and **Queen Streets**, east of **Washington Street**, are lined with unusually handsome early 19th-century row houses, and a riverfront park offers a retreat from the bustle of commerce. Old Town has for some years

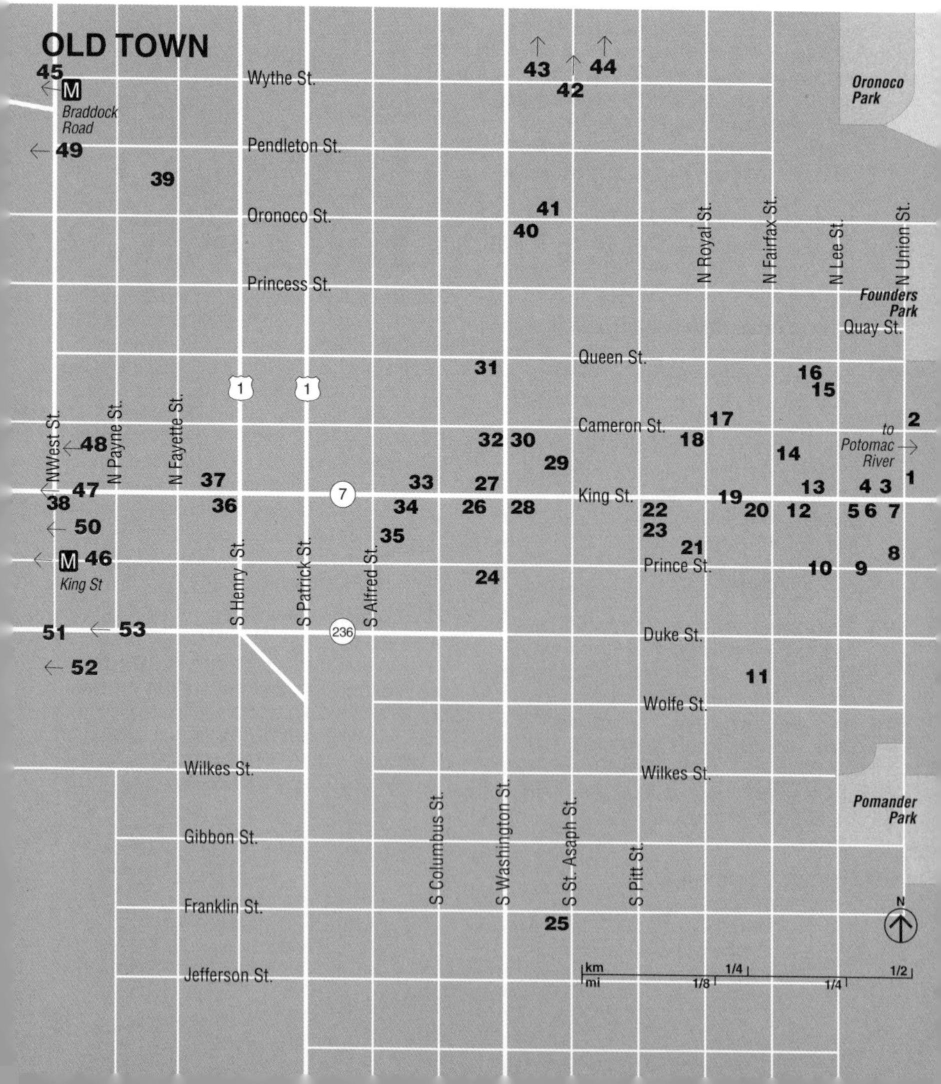

OLD TOWN

45
M Braddock Road
← 49
39
43 44
42
Oronoco Park

Wythe St.
Pendleton St.
Oronoco St.   41 40
Princess St.

N Royal St.
N Fairfax St.
N Lee St.
N Union St.
Founders Park
Quay St.

31
Queen St.
16 15
2
to Potomac River →

NWest St.
48 N Payne St.
N Fayette St.
47
38
← 50
M 46
King St

Cameron St.   17 18
32 30   29
7   33 27 26 28
34 35
24

King St.   22 23   19 20 13 4 3 1
21   12 5 6 7
Prince St.   10 9 8
14
1

S Henry St.
S Patrick St.
S Alfred St.
236

51 ← 53
← 52
Duke St.
Wolfe St.   11

Wilkes St.   Wilkes St.
Gibbon St.
Pomander Park

S Columbus St.
S Washington St.
S St. Asaph St.
S Pitt St.

Franklin St.
25
N

Jefferson St.
km   1/4   1/2
mi   1/8   1/4

presented parking challenges similar to those found in Georgetown and Adams-Morgan. Our advice: Find a garage and spend a little money for peace of mind, or take the **Metro** to King Street.

Though Alexandria proper extends far west and south of Old Town, the outer areas contain more modern (and, many say, less interesting) homes and businesses. For many years this city has served as both a bedroom community for Washington and a place with its own distinctive identity as the unofficial capital of Northern Virginia.

Area code 703 unless otherwise noted.

1 Torpedo Factory Art Center Works by some 160 artists—including photographers, jewelers, sculptors, painters, and textile designers—are displayed in five galleries within this converted munitions factory, which during World War II was the nation's major producer of naval torpedoes and parts. Although everything is for sale, the artists (many of whom work in studios on the premises) are more interested in explaining than hawking their works. ♦ Free. Daily. 105 N Union St (between King and Cameron Sts). 838.4565 & Metro: King Street

Within the Torpedo Factory Art Center:

Alexandria Archaeology Since 1961 the city of Alexandria has conducted its own excavations, unearthing everything from 10,000-year-old artifacts to 20th-century objects. ♦ Free. Tu-F 10AM-3PM; Sa; Su 1-5PM. Third floor. 838.4399

2 The Food Pavilion Located next to the **Torpedo Factory Art Center** and boasting an appropriately industrial decor, this pavilion houses food concessions selling inexpensive Chinese, Italian, deli, and Mexican fare. Kids will like the giant gumball machine, and there's outdoor seating facing the river. ♦ Daily 10:30AM-10PM. 5 Cameron St (east of N Union St). Metro: King Street

3 The Fish Market ★$$ This bustling chowder and seafood house has several cozy dining rooms rigged with nautical decor. ♦ Seafood ♦ Daily lunch and dinner. 105 King St (between N Union and N Lee Sts). 836.5676 & Metro: King Street

4 Bugsy's ★$ The former **Armand's Pizzeria** still serves pizza and sandwiches to hungry sports fans. ♦ Pizza ♦ Daily lunch and dinner. 111 King St (between N Union and N Lee Sts). 683.0313 & Metro: King Street

4 Landini Brothers ★★$ At times, this restaurant seems to be a little bit of everything—power lunch spot for local politicians and business bigwigs, watering hole, rest stop for shoppers and tourists (it's smack dab on Old Town's main drag). But the food is fine—especially the calamari and homemade pasta dishes—and the quiet, softly lit atmosphere conducive to conversation and relaxation. ♦ American/Italian ♦ M-Sa lunch and dinner; Su dinner. 115 King St (between N Union and N Lee Sts). 836.8404 & Metro: King Street

5 America! Everything here is made in the good old USA, including flag-inspired pillows, ties, jewelry, dolls, and ceramic sculptures. ♦ M-Th 10AM-10PM; F-Sa 10AM-11PM; Su 11AM-9PM. 118 King St (between S Union and S Lee Sts). 836.1491 & Also at: Pentagon City Fashion Mall, 1100 Hayes St (between S 15th St and Army Navy Dr), Arlington. 415.5252. Metro: Pentagon City; Union Station, 50 Massachusetts Ave NE (at First St), DC. 202/842.0540. Metro: Union Station

6 Hats in the Belfry Try on everything from derbies and straw bonnets to gladiator helmets and Indian headdresses. ♦ M-Th 10AM-10PM; F-Sa 10AM-midnight; Su 10AM-9PM. 112 King St (between S Union and S Lee Sts). 549.2546. Metro: King Street. Also at: 1237 Wisconsin Ave NW (between M and N Sts), DC. 202/342.2006

6 Bird in the Cage Antiques This shop sells a hodgepodge of antique wedding gowns, vintage jackets, books, glassware, political buttons, quilts, dolls, and more. ♦ Daily 10AM-9PM Mar-Dec; M-Th, Sa-Su, F 10AM-9PM Jan-Feb. 110 King St (between S Union and S Lee Sts). 549.5114. Metro: King Street

7 Ben & Jerry's If you scream for ice cream, here's the scoop: This outpost is said to be the highest-volume link in the long chain. So if plain vanilla just won't do, stop in for some Cherry Garcia or Wavy Gravy. ♦ M-Th, Su 11AM-11PM; F-Sa 11AM-1AM. 103 S Union St (between Prince and King Sts). 684.8866 ♿ Metro: King Street. Also at: 3135 M St NW (between 31st St and Wisconsin Ave), DC. 202/965.2222

8 Union Street Public House ★★$$ This popular pub features its own microbrewery beer (Union Street Draft). It's also known for its excellent steak sandwiches, pasta jambalaya, and cream of crab soup. ♦ American ♦ Daily lunch and dinner. 121 S Union St (between Prince and King Sts). 548.1785 ♿ Metro: King Street

9 Captains' Row The early 19th-century cobblestone walk from the waterfront up Prince Street is known for its charming homes, all private, built by sea captains. The rooflines, proportions, materials, and trim of these houses vary wildly, reflecting the independent spirits of their original owners.♦ Prince St (between S Union and S Lee Sts)

10 Gentry Row The houses on this mid–18th-century block form a collage of characteristic Georgian themes. All residences are private, except for the Greek Revival–style Athenaeum. ♦ Prince St (between S Lee and S Fairfax Sts). Metro: King Street

On Gentry Row:

Athenaeum This impressive example of Greek Revival architecture, originally the **Bank of Old Dominion** (in 1851), was purchased a century later by the Northern Virginia Fine Arts Association for use as an art museum and cultural activities center. Guest curators stage original exhibitions of contemporary art, and the museum hosts lectures, readings, performances, and workshops. ♦ Voluntary donation. W-Sa; Su 1-4PM. 201 Prince St. 548.0035

11 Old Presbyterian Meeting House The Scottish Presbyterians of Alexandria established this brick church in 1774. George Washington's funeral services, canceled at **Christ Church** because of muddy streets, were held here in December 1799, and the bell tolled nonstop for four days thereafter. The church was struck by lightning and burned in 1835; the following year it was rebuilt as a Greek Revival–style sanctuary. A weathered tombstone in the cemetery honors the Unknown Soldier of the American Revolution. ♦ M-F 9AM-3PM. Services: Su 8:30AM, 11AM Sept-May; Su 10AM June-Aug. 321 S Fairfax St (between Wolfe and Duke Sts). 549.6670. Metro: King Street

12 Warehouse Bar & Grill ★$$ Winners at this spiffy, popular place are the crab cakes and the 20-ounce T-bone. ♦ American ♦ M-F lunch and dinner; Sa breakfast, lunch, and dinner; Su brunch and dinner. Reservations recommended. 214 King St (between S Lee and S Fairfax Sts). 683.6868 ♿ Metro: King Street

13 Ramsay House/Alexandria Convention and Visitors Bureau Alexandria's founder, William Ramsay, shipped his house down the Potomac River and hauled it in one piece to its proper lot here. Ramsay, a merchant trader, later added a small office and otherwise expanded the house. None of his personal belongings remain, however, save for a couple of letters from his children. Several rooms have been rebuilt to accommodate the **Alexandria Convention and Visitors Bureau**, which provides free maps, hotel and group tour reservations, and lists of shops and restaurants in the area. ♦ Free. Daily. 221 King St (at N Fairfax St). 838.4200

14 Carlyle House Built in 1753 by John Carlyle to resemble a Scottish manor house, this great Georgian-Palladian home was Alexandria's first stone building. Archaeologists uncovered five privy shafts and trash chutes during the building's restoration, along with some glassware from Carlyle's time. The mansion is now decorated with authentic 18th-century furnishings. This is where General Edward Braddock and five colonial governors planned the initial campaigns of the French and Indian War. Guided tours are offered every half hour. ♦ Free. Tu-Sa; Su noon-4:30PM. 121 N Fairfax St (between King and Cameron Sts). 549.2997. Metro: King Street

15 La Bergerie ★★★$$$ Located on the second floor of the old Crilley Warehouse, this neighborhood mainstay serves such Basque specialties as *garbure* (white bean–vegetable soup), coq au vin, and an almond-filled tart. The real charm is in the handsome setting: leather banquette, exposed brick, and chandeliers. ♦ French ♦ M-Sa lunch and dinner. Reservations required on Saturday. 218 N Lee St (between Cameron and Queen Sts). 683.1007 ♿ Metros: Braddock Road, King Street

15 Ecco Cafe ★$$ Even regulars sometimes grumble about the pizza, but the homemade pasta and desserts attract an upscale crowd. ♦ Italian ♦ Daily lunch and dinner. 220 N Lee

St (between Cameron and Queen Sts). 684.0321 & Metros: Braddock Road, King Street

16 Bilbo Baggins ★$$ The quality of both food—mainly seafood dishes and steaks—and service can be spotty, but this cute restaurant has Alexandria's best wine bar. Many Alexandrians come here for Sunday brunch and the unbeatable raisin bread. ♦ Continental ♦ M-Sa lunch and dinner; Su brunch and dinner. Reservations recommended. 208 Queen St (between N Lee and N Fairfax Sts). 683.0300 & Metro: Braddock Road

17 Gossypia Mexican wedding dresses, tea-length dresses, and other unusual women's clothing, jewelry, and accessories from South America and Asia can be found here. ♦ M-Sa; Su noon-5PM. 325 Cameron St (at N Royal St). 836.6969. Metros: Braddock Road, King Street

18 Gadsby's Tavern Museum In February of 1799 John Gadsby, the proprietor, offered tribute to his friend George Washington by hosting a gala ball in his honor. It was the last time Washington would visit the tavern. He died shortly thereafter, just before his 68th birthday. For many years, the tavern has celebrated his birthday with a traditional Birthnight Ball. The inn has been completely restored, to the point of acquiring period china and silverware, although the original ballroom interior is now at the Metropolitan Museum of Art. What you see here is a reproduction. ♦ Admission. Daily. Tours: every half hour. 134 N Royal St (between King and Cameron Sts). 838.4242. Metros: Braddock Road, King Street

18 Gadsby's Tavern ★$$ This 200-year-old restaurant serves game pie, prime rib, seafood, trifle, and a rich pecan pie. There's entertainment nightly, including 200-year-old "news of the day" Wednesday through Saturday. ♦ American ♦ Daily lunch and dinner. 138 N Royal St (at Cameron St). 548.1288 & Metros: Braddock Road, King Street

19 Market Square/City Hall Established in 1749, this is the nation's oldest operating farmers' market. The U-shaped Victorian building with a central courtyard was erected in the 1870s, and in 1962 the courtyard was filled in by an addition to the building. But the farmers' market goes on, set up in arcades on the south plaza of **City Hall** each Saturday. Among the many offerings are salt-cured meats, produce, homemade baked goods, flowers, and handmade crafts. ♦ Sa 5:30AM-9AM. King St (between Fairfax and Royal Sts) & Metro: King Street

20 Stabler-Leadbeater Apothecary Patrons such as Martha Washington and Robert E. Lee once frequented this pharmacy, which first opened its doors in 1792. On sale here now are old medical books and remedy bottles, T-shirts imprinted with the Stabler-Leadbeater Apothecary label, games, and some collectibles. Adjoining the shop is a tiny museum, with the original apothecary furnishings. On display are antique medical objects, pill rollers, mortars and pestles, old potions, and vintage bottles. ♦ Admission to museum. M-Sa; Su 1-5PM. 105-07 S Fairfax St (between Prince and King Sts). 836.3713. Metro: King Street

21 British Connection & Tea Cosy A taste of England comes to Old Town in this tearoom, where you'll find all the right stuff: teas, biscuits, sweets, kippers, and Scottish meat pies. The scones with Devon cream and jam are as authentic as they get this side of the Atlantic. In the back, a shop sells jolly good provisions and wares. ♦ Daily. 119 S Royal St (between Prince and King Sts). 836.8181 & Metro: King Street

22 Holiday Inn of Old Town $$ You wouldn't guess that there is a modern 227-room hotel behind these colonial brick walls. Among the amenities are a restaurant that offers a great Champagne brunch on Sunday, a large indoor swimming pool, trail bikes, and shuttle service to **National Airport** and the **Metro** upon request. Children under 18 and small pets stay free. ♦ 480 King St (at S Pitt St). 549.6080, 800/HOLIDAY; fax 684.6508 & Metro: King Street

23 Santa Fe East ★★$$ The cooks here have a distinctive approach to New Mexican cooking (duck tostadas, for instance). If you like your nachos topped with chicken, their version is very good. The Southwestern decor has a rustic feel, with brick and stucco walls decorated with Native American artifacts. Best of all is the enclosed patio with a fountain that was made by a Native American artist to symbolize the "Trail of Tears"—a forced march to relocate the Cherokee people from North Carolina to Oklahoma that many did not survive. ♦ Southwestern ♦ Daily lunch and dinner. Reservations recommended. 110 S Pitt St (between Prince and King Sts). 548.6900 & Metro: King Street

---

Virginia just ain't what it used to be. Under its first charter in 1606, the colony extended west all the way to the Pacific Ocean.

Restaurants/Clubs: Red   **Hotels:** Blue

Shops/ ♥ Outdoors: Green   **Sights/Culture:** Black

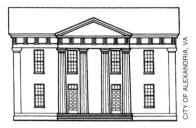

CITY OF ALEXANDRIA, VA

24 The Lyceum This two-story, Greek Revival–style brick and stucco building (illustrated above), documents Alexandria's history with memorabilia, photographs, video presentations, antiques displays, and changing exhibits. The 1839 building served as a hospital during the Civil War; it was restored in 1974 by Carrol Curtice. The Fashion Promenade features costumed historians portraying colonial celebrities in amusing vignettes. ♦ Free. M-Sa; Su 1PM-5PM. 201 S Washington St (at Prince St). 838.4994. Metro: King Street

25 Blue Point Grill ★$$$ A generally dependable kitchen makes use of the gourmet foodstuffs sold in the adjoining **Sutton Place Gourmet** shop. Though seafood (grilled or sautéed) is their specialty, chicken with rosemary and filet mignon are also good bets. ♦ American ♦ Daily lunch and dinner. Reservations recommended. 600 Franklin St (at S St. Asaph St). 739.0404 ᕫ Metro: King Street

26 Scotland Yard ★$$ Venison, quail, finnan haddie, and, of course, a grand selection of single-malt Scotch whiskies are served in the wood-paneled, clubby dining room. ♦ Scottish ♦ Tu-Su dinner. Reservations recommended. 728 King St (between S Washington and S Columbus Sts). 683.1742. Metro: King Street

26 Geranio ★★$$ This comfortable, rustic trattoria serves classic homemade pastas, like *agnolotti* stuffed with portobello mushrooms, and such seafood specialties as grilled shrimp over creamy polenta. It can be especially romantic on a cold night with a warm fire. ♦ Northern Italian ♦ M-F lunch and dinner; Sa-Su dinner. Reservations recommended. 722 King St (between S Washington and S Columbus Sts). 548.0088 ᕫ Metro: King Street

Marylanders believe that Virginia is, at best, confusing and badly laid out; at worst, redneck, backward, unforgivably homogeneous . . . Meanwhile, Virginians see Maryland as smug, yet also rootless, sprawling, untethered.

Liza Mundy *The Washington Post Magazine*, 15 September 1996

27 Murphy's Irish Restaurant & Pub ★$ On Sundays, this lively gathering spot offers an inexpensive Irish country breakfast, and it's always a good choice for dependable pub fare. Live entertainment starts nightly at 9PM. ♦ Irish/American ♦ M-Sa lunch and dinner; Su brunch and dinner. 713 King St (between N Washington and N Columbus Sts). 548.1717 ᕫ Metro: King Street. Also at: 2609 24th St NW (between Calvert St and Connecticut Ave), DC. 202/462.7171 ᕫ Metro: Woodley Park/Zoo

28 Gap Outlet Two floors stock top-quality men's, women's, and children's clothing at unbeatable discount prices. The real bargains are upstairs. ♦ M-Sa 10AM-9PM; Su. 622-28 King St (between S St. Asaph and S Washington Sts). 683.0181 ᕫ Metro: King Street

29 Silverman Galleries, Inc. This shop offers one of the area's largest collections of 18th- through 20th-century jewelry—diamonds are a specialty. Also, 18th- and 19th-century American and European furniture, silver, porcelain, and various decorative arts and furnishings are available. ♦ W-Su. 110 N St. Asaph St (between King and Cameron Sts). 836.5363 ᕫ Metro: King Street

29 King Street Blues ★$ The food may not be inspired (meat loaf and mashed potatoes, homemade desserts), but this is a fun bar, decorated with neon lights and artsy murals. The owners aren't singing the blues, however; the joint is packed on weekends. There's live music Thursday nights. ♦ American ♦ Daily lunch and dinner. 112 N St. Asaph St (between King and Cameron Sts). 836.4264. Metro: King Street

30 Le Refuge ★★$$$ A cozy, candlelit spot, it offers French-country dishes, including cassoulet, bouillabaisse, cold salmon, and other seasonal favorites. ♦ French ♦ M-Sa lunch and dinner. 127 N Washington St (between King and Cameron Sts). 548.4661 ᕫ Metros: Braddock Road, King Street

31 Lloyd House This distinguished example of late-Georgian architecture was designed in 1798 by **John Wise.** After a succession of owners, the house was saved from demolition by Alexandria's preservation-minded citizens. The interior has been restored for use by the **Alexandria Library,** which holds a large collection of books and documents on Virginia history. The friendly staff is happy to lend a hand with local history and genealogical research. ♦ M-Sa. 220 N Washington St (at Queen St). 838.4577. Metro: Braddock Road

32 Christ Church George Washington paid 36 pounds and 20 shillings for his pew as a vestryman in this 18th-century colonial Georgian-style church. Built in 1773 and originally called the "Church in the Woods," it's the oldest continually active Episcopal church in the nation. The church was occupied by Union troops throughout the Civil War, and much of the building, inside and out, is original. Incumbent presidents are invited to attend services on the Sunday closest to Washington's birthday. Shortly after Pearl Harbor, Franklin D. Roosevelt and Winston Churchill attended services here together. Robert E. Lee, a parishioner, worshiped here from the age of four until the beginning of the Civil War. Plaques mark the pews where the Washington and Lee families sat. ♦ Services: Su 8AM, 9AM, 11:15AM, 5PM. Tours: M-Sa 9AM-4PM; Su 2-4:30PM. 118 N Washington St (between King and Cameron Sts). 549.1450 ♿ Metros: Braddock Road, King Street

33 South Austin Grill ★★★$ A spin-off of the popular **Austin Grill** in DC, this restaurant offers the same mouthwatering Tex-Mex favorites—and the same long lines during peak hours. But the fajitas and margaritas, among other specialties, make it well worth the wait. The colorful dining room includes huge copper sculptures of animals and an eclectic array of tiles laid into the floor. ♦ Tex-Mex ♦ Daily lunch and dinner. 801 King St (at N Columbus St). 684.8969 ♿ Metro: King Street

33 East Wind ★★$$ Vietnamese cuisine becomes an art form here. *Cha gio* (egg rolls) makes a good starter. Delicately seasoned main courses include *bo dun* (strips of beef marinated in wine, honey, onions, and spices, and then broiled on skewers), grilled lemon chicken, and roast quail. Stylish service complements the elegant surroundings. ♦ Vietnamese ♦ M-F lunch and dinner; Sa-Su dinner. Reservations recommended. 809 King St (between N Columbus and N Alfred Sts). 836.1515 ♿ Metro: King Street

33 Barcelona ★★$$ Tapas are the specialty of this restaurant/bar—order a few and you'll have a meal. Try the delicious *pimientos de piquillo rellenos* (sweet peppers stuffed with scallops, shrimp, and spinach) or any of the several versions of scrumptious paella. Tile

floor, turquoise walls, and splashes of straw create a Spanish mood. ♦ Spanish ♦ Daily lunch and dinner. 815 King St (between N Columbus and N Alfred Sts). 548.1670. Metro: King Street

34 Taverna Cretekou ★★$$ This picturesque little restaurant has a vine-covered courtyard in back. The grilled lamb, perfectly trimmed and seasoned with a lemon-herb mixture, is recommended, as are the appetizers and homemade desserts. It's authentically rowdy on Saturday nights, when the waiters may spontaneously dance or burst into song. ♦ Greek ♦ Tu-Su lunch and dinner. Reservations recommended. 818 King St (between S Columbus and S Alfred Sts). 548.8688 ♿ Metro: King Street

35 Morrison House $$$ Most of the 45 rooms and suites in this colonial-style mansion have four-poster beds, brass chandeliers, and sconces. Tea is served every afternoon in the parlor. Amenities include a multilingual staff, concierge and valet service, indoor valet parking, and baby-sitting. ♦ 116 S Alfred St (between Prince and King Sts). 838.8000, 800/367.0800; fax 684.6283 ♿ Metro: King Street

Within the Morrison House:

Elysium ★★$$ Two dining rooms, one formal, the other clubby and more informal, feature regional specialties. Afternoon tea is a high point. ♦ American ♦ M-Sa breakfast, lunch, and dinner; Su brunch and dinner. Reservations recommended. 838.8000 ♿

36 Le Gaulois ★★★ $$ When the block on which it sat—on Pennsylvania Avenue downtown—was razed in the name of progress, this popular bistro relocated to Alexandria, but it still serves first-rate  French food at bargain prices. Its signature wintertime dish, the *pot au feu gaulois*—a dinner of boiled beef, chicken, oxtail, and vegetables—is a perennial winner, but it's hard to go wrong with anything here, including the quenelles (pike dumplings in lobster sauce). ♦ French ♦ M-Sa lunch and dinner. Reservations recommended. 1106 King St (between S Henry and S Fayette Sts). 739.9494 ♿ Metro: King Street

Virginia was the tenth of the original 13 states to ratify the Constitution.

Restaurants/Clubs: Red   **Hotels:** Blue
Shops/ ♥ **Outdoors:** Green   **Sights/Culture:** Black

Random Harvest

37 Random Harvest The owners of this shop have gleaned objects from many a tasteful household: Three floors contain handsome antique furniture, rugs, lamps, frames, and mirrors, as well as elegant new fabrics. ♦ M-Sa; Su 1-6PM. 1117 King St (between N Henry and N Fayette Sts). 548.8820. Metro: King Street. Also at: 1313 Wisconsin Ave NW (between N and Dumbarton Sts), DC. 333.5569

37 Quimper Faience The colorful plates, bowls, pitchers, and teapots here look like colonial folk art. Made in France, the pottery is molded by hand and exquisitely painted in accordance with a 300-year-old French technique. ♦ M-Sa; Su noon-6PM. 1121 King St (between N Henry and N Fayette Sts). 519.8339. Metro: King Street

38 Hard Times Cafe ★★$ This is chili heaven, with Cincinnati-style, vegetarian, and Texas-style among the options. You'll find cheap but good eats, with large portions, lots of side dishes, and, most likely, a line outside. There is a great jukebox for fans of classic country music. ♦ American ♦ Daily lunch and dinner. 1404 King St (between S West and S Peyton Sts). 683.5340. Metro: King Street. Also at: 3028 Wilson Blvd (between N Garfield and N Highland Sts), Arlington. 528.2233 ও Metro: Clarendon; 428 Elden St (between Herndon Pkwy and Grant St), Herndon, Virginia. 318.8941 ও

39 Daniel Donnelly The specialty here is 20th-century modern designer furniture and lighting by, among others, Charles Eames, George Nelson, and Gilbert Rohde. Browse through the shop's collection of modern furniture reference books. ♦ M, Th-F; Sa noon-6PM; Su noon-5PM. 520 N Fayette St (between Oronoco and Pendleton Sts). 549.4672 ও Metro: Braddock Road

40 Lee-Fendall House Philip Richard Fendall, grandson of Philip Lee (also Robert E. Lee's relation), built this Greek Revival mansion in 1785. The Lee family lived in the house from 1785 until 1903, and it was the home of labor leader John L. Lewis from 1937 to 1969. (According to legend, it was here that Henry "Light Horse Harry" Lee authored a farewell address to George Washington.) The children's room contains a dollhouse gallery and antique toys from many Lee generations. Tours are available on a walk-in basis. ♦ Admission. Tu-Sa; Su noon-4PM. 614 Oronoco St (between N St. Asaph and N Washington Sts). 548.1789. Metro: Braddock Road

41 Boyhood Home of Robert E. Lee The Lee family moved into this house in 1812 (shown below), and Robert E. Lee lived here until he enrolled at West Point in 1825. Beautifully furnished with period antiques, portraits, and family artifacts, the 1795 brick house is a showcase of the early Federal period. ♦ Admission. M-Sa; Su 1-4PM. 607 Oronoco St (between N St. Asaph and N Washington Sts). 548.8454

42 Best Western Old Colony Inn $$ Here's a moderately priced 322-room inn on the edge of Old Town that shuttles guests to the subway, **National Airport,** or Old Town's shopping district. Amenities include indoor

Boyhood Home of Robert E. Lee

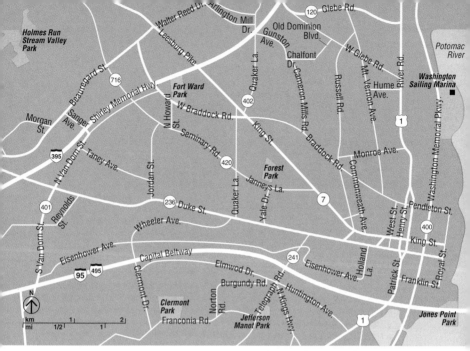

and outdoor swimming pools, a health club, lounge, and a restaurant with Sunday brunch. Nonsmoking rooms are available. Children under 18 stay free. ♦ 615 First St (between N Pitt and N Washington Sts). 548.6300, 800/528.1234; fax 548.8032 ᴋ Metro: Braddock Road

43 Executive Club $$ Suites only (78 of them) are offered in this pretty Georgian-style building. There's a health club (with Universal weights, treadmills, and bicycles), an outdoor swimming pool, and complimentary continental breakfasts. A free shuttle service takes you to **National Airport** and, in the evening, to Old Town. ♦ 610 Bashford La (at E Abingdon Dr). 739.2582, 800/535.2582; fax 548.0266. Metro: Braddock Road. Also at: 108 S Courthouse Rd (between S Second St and Walter Reed Dr), Arlington

44 Washington Sailing Marina Rentals and lessons are available in sailing and windsurfing; bicycles can be rented to ride along the Mount Vernon path on the banks of the Potomac, one of the prettiest riding routes in the area. **Spinnaker & Spoke** sells boating and biking equipment, plus there's a snack bar. ♦ Daily; hours for boat rentals vary. 1 Marina Dr (east of George Washington Memorial Pkwy). 548.9027 ᴋ

At the Washington Sailing Marina:

Potowmack Landing $$$ You'll get a splendid view of the river and DC—especially if you enjoy watching planes taking off and landing at **National Airport**—from this nautical-theme restaurant and bar, but the food is often less than splendid. ♦ American ♦ Daily lunch and dinner. 548.0001 ᴋ

45 Calvert Grille ★★$ This neighborhood restaurant has won a loyal following for its barbecued baby back ribs and chicken, hamburgers and fries, crab cakes, and meat loaf and mashed potatoes. ♦ American ♦ Daily lunch and dinner. 3106 Mt. Vernon Ave (between Kennedy St and W Glebe Rd). 836.8425 ᴋ

45 R.T.'s ★★$$ Even before the Clintons and Gores stopped here on their way to see Jerry Jeff Walker at the neighboring **Birchmere** (see below), this bar/restaurant had a loyal following. An appetizer of Jack Daniels shrimp is the best way to dive into a meal of New Orleans–style seafood. The portions are generous, the prices reasonable, and everyone seems to be having a great time. The original artwork on the walls is by Brian McCall. ♦ Cajun/Seafood ♦ M-Sa lunch and dinner; Su dinner. 3804 Mt. Vernon Ave (at Russell Rd). 684.6010

45 Birchmere This is a small venue for some big musical talent, from folk and bluegrass to light rock. The food isn't much, so eat elsewhere, especially if you have to arrive early for a big-name act. The Seldom Scene, one of the nation's top bluegrass bands, plays here a couple of Thursday nights every month. Other recent acts have included Kate and Anna McGarrigle, Junior Brown, and the Saw Doctors. ♦ Hours for performances vary. 3901 Mt. Vernon Ave (at Bruce St). 549.7500 ᴋ

46 Embassy Suites Hotel $$$ Directly across from the **King Street Metro**, this 268-suite hotel has an indoor pool, an exercise room, and free cocktails and cooked-to-order breakfasts. A free shuttle takes guests to the heart of Old Town. ♦ 1900 Diagonal Rd (between Reinekers La and Duke St). 684.5900, 800/EMBASSY; fax 684.1403 ⅃ Metro: King Street

47 George Washington Masonic National Memorial The distinctive 333-foot tower atop this memorial to George Washington is visible from many parts of Alexandria. Inside are a museum with some of Washington's personal effects, a replica of the room he presided over when he was Master of the Alexandria Masonic Lodge, and an observation deck with a superb view of Alexandria. The 45-minute tours begin approximately every hour, depending on the crowd. ♦ Free. Daily. King St and Callahan Dr. 683.2007 ⅃ Metro: King Street

48 Radisson Plaza Hotel $$$ You can't miss this 30-story, 500-room hotel as you exit the highway. Guests have the use of indoor and outdoor swimming pools, tennis and racquetball courts, a health club, 24-hour room service, four restaurants, and a lounge. Nonsmoking rooms, shuttles to the subway and **National Airport,** and limo service are also available. Children under 18 stay free. ♦ 5000 Seminary Rd (at I-395). 845.1010, 800/333.3333; fax 845.7662 ⅃

49 Fort Ward Museum and Historic Site The fifth-largest Civil War fortification protecting Washington was reconstructed with the help of photographs by Mathew Brady and dedicated in 1964. The museum, which features a collection of 2,000 Civil War items, is located in a 40-acre city park with picnic facilities and an outdoor amphitheater. ♦ Free. Tu-Sa; Su noon-5PM. 4301 W Braddock Rd (between Marlboro Dr and N Van Dorn St). 838.4848

50 Five Guys For generations raised on fast-food hamburgers, the freshly ground beef versions at these hole-in-the-wall carryouts will come as a shock. For the rest of us, it's instant (and delicious) nostalgia. The fresh-cut spicy fries are wonderful, too. ♦ Daily 10AM-11PM. 4626 King St (between Beauregard St and Dawes Ave). 671.1606 ⅃ Also at: 107 S Fayette St (between Prince and King Sts). 549.7991 ⅃ Metro: King Street

51 Generous George's Positive Pizza and Pasta Place ★★$ If your favorite part of a pizza is the crust, you'll like the doughy pies served here. Toppings range from basic to the elaborate "Positive Pizza Pie" topped with a mound of spaghetti. All pasta dishes are served in generous portions on a pizza crust with mozzarella cheese. The restaurant can get crowded and noisy, but it's a good place to take young children. ♦ Italian ♦ Daily lunch and dinner. 3006 Duke St (between Roth and Sweeley Sts). 370.4303 ⅃ Metro: King Street. Also at: 7031 Little River Tpke (at John Marr Dr), Annandale, Virginia. 941.9600 ⅃; Concord Shopping Center, 6131 Backlick Rd (between Commerce St and Essex Ave), Springfield, Virginia. 451.7111 ⅃

52 Cameron Run Regional Park If you're in DC in July or August, you'll need to escape the brutal heat and humidity by ducking inside air-conditioned museums or staying in a hotel with a swimming pool. Or you can venture to this nifty park, which has a wave pool, three water slides, a water playground for kids (inhabited by an oversize foam alligator, snake, and turtle), a batting cage, and 18 challenging and imaginatively landscaped holes of miniature golf. ♦ Admission. Daily 10AM-8PM Memorial Day–Labor Day. 4001 Eisenhower Ave (between Bluestone Rd and Clermont Ave). 960.0767

53 Doubletree Guest Quarters $$$$ This is a home away from home. Each of the 225 suites has a living room, dining room, bedroom, and a fully equipped kitchen. There is a restaurant, an outdoor pool, and a fitness center. A complimentary continental breakfast is served, and children under 18 stay free. Discount weekend rates are available. ♦ 100 Reynolds St (at Duke St). 370.9600, 800/424.2900; fax 370.0467

"The Russians did it with marble; we did it with shadows."

Harry Weese, Metro system architect

Visitors come to Washington "not to see some Claghorn on Capitol Hill or to tut-tut at the hard streets where the city's poor live, not to count the ways the Government falls short of the Founding Father's ideals, but to pay homage to the ideas themselves, to keep the ideals alive and try to imbue the kids with them."

R. W. Apple, *The New York Times,* 11 December 1998

At a White House dinner honoring Nobel Prize winners, John F. Kennedy remarked "I think this is the most extraordinary collection of talent, of human knowledge, that has ever been collected together at the White House--with the possible exception of when Thomas Jefferson dined alone."

Restaurants/Clubs: Red   **Hotels:** Blue

Shops/ ♥ Outdoors: Green   **Sights/Culture:** Black

Bests

Ann Cashion
Chef/Proprietor, Cashion's Eat Place

Of course, if you visit Washington, you can spend all your time on, or in the vicinity of **The Mall.** Between the various museums of the **Smithsonian,** the national monuments, the **White House,** the **Capitol,** and the federal bureaus and agencies, there's enough to keep a tourist going for weeks. You really can't do it all, but personal favorites of mine in and around **The Mall** are:

- **The National Air and Space Museum** . . . which, contrary to popular wisdom is not just for kids. It speaks eloquently, I think, to those of us who lived through the infancy of NASA and the Space Program. Stand beside the Mercury and Gemini capsules and weep at the courage and patriotism of men who were propelled into the great unknown in these tiny, fragile cones of rivets and corrugated metal. Be sure to catch a movie in the **IMAX Theater;** I like *To Fly* best of all.

- Visit the **Reading Room** at the **Library of Congress.**

- Don't miss the **Vietnam Veterans Memorial,** somber and understated, the only war memorial with which I am familiar that quantifies and makes concrete the magnitude of the sacrifice which war extracts from a nation.

If you have the time and inclination to go beyond **The Mall** and experience the city that a resident like myself enjoys on a daily basis, here are some suggestions.

- Stroll through residential **Georgetown** where you'll discover block after block of beautifully maintained mansions, town houses, and tiny row houses from the 19th century. Tour the grounds of the **Dumbarton Oaks Library.**

- Experience the **Potomac.** Rent a canoe at **Jack's Boat House.** Paddle downstream to get a unique view of the monuments. Stop for refreshment at the grand terraced bar at **Sequoia.** Or paddle upstream for more of a "wilderness" experience. You are likely to see herons gliding gracefully just above the river's surface. When you return, reward yourself for your exertion with dinner at **Hibiscus Cafe,** first-class Caribbean cuisine in a lively, attractive setting.

- Drive out to **Great Falls** where the national kayaking team practices.

- Tour the **Washington National Cathedral;** learn the story behind its gargoyles. Admire the herb garden.

- Visit the **Phillips Collection,** which houses a remarkable array of Impressionist and Post-Impressionist works including Renoir's *Luncheon of the Boating Party.* Lunch around the corner at **Teaism** with its astonishing variety of teas and delicious light meals and snacks.

- While in **Dupont Circle** browse the galleries that feature the work of contemporary area artists. Enjoy the remarkable number of thriving independent bookstores which the neighborhood supports. Visit **Melody Record Shop.**

- Go to **Glen Echo Park,** formerly the city's largest amusement park. Ride the old carousel. On weekends join hundreds of area residents who swing dance to live bands in the historic, Mission-style **Spanish Ballroom.**

- Ride the **Washington Metro,** a truly elegant and comfortable public transit system.

- Absolutely reserve an evening for live music. Besides **Blues Alley,** the most deluxe and well-appointed area jazz club, you could check out **One Step Down** on the edge of Georgetown or **Café Lautrec** in **Adams-Morgan,** particularly on Thursday night. (If you find yourself in Adams-Morgan, do visit me at **Cashion's Eat Place** for a memorable meal!) Excellent non-jazz venues include **The Birchmere** in **Alexandria** for bluegrass and country/folk artists of national prominence, and the **930 Club** for new music and contemporary rock.

- Attend a performance at the **Lansburg Shakespeare Theatre** where there's not a bad seat in the house from which to experience director Michael Kahn's brilliant and provocative productions. Tapas next door at **Jaleo** before or after the show.

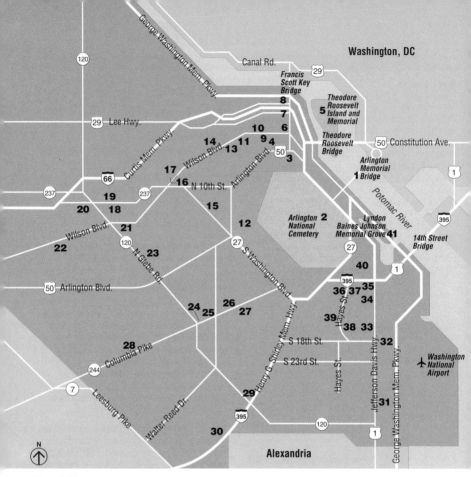

Arlington

Situated directly across the **Potomac River** from the capital, Arlington was originally part of the District of Columbia. In 1847, on what some call one of Washington's saddest days, the 25.7-square-mile parcel was ceded back to Virginia; the federal government couldn't imagine having a need for all that extra space. Today, Arlington is a booming suburban community containing many federal offices and monuments, including **Arlington National Cemetery**, the **Pentagon**, the **Iwo Jima Memorial**, and the **Netherlands Carillon. Ronald Reagan National Airport** (formerly **Washington National Airport**) stands on a landfill just south of the **Pentagon**, providing convenient access to the city for tourists and, perhaps more important, congressmen who keep voting down bills to relocate it.

This small county also contains the concrete high-rise office and hotel complexes of **Rosslyn, Pentagon City**, and **Crystal City**, which, because they have much taller buildings, seem to look more like cities than Downtown DC. However, while DC is still pulsing after dark with restaurant- and theatergoers, the streets in these "mini-cities" seem to roll up after rush hour. Other neighborhoods in Arlington are home to a lively immigrant community, where Vietnamese stores and restaurants bustle with activity. Ongoing development around the **Metro** stations at **Clarendon**, **Virginia Square**, and **Ballston** is transforming the faces of these once-sleepy communities with new shops, restaurants, hotels, and high-rise apartment buildings.

1 Arlington Memorial Bridge Although a bridge had been planned at this location for years, it took a massive traffic jam on Armistice Day 1921 to get one built. A long, low series of arches spans the Potomac with architectural firm **McKim, Mead, and White**'s usual Beaux Arts flair. ♦ Metro: Arlington Cemetery

2 Arlington National Cemetery Just over the **Arlington Memorial Bridge**, 612 acres of rolling hills dotted with simple headstones give silent testimony to US military sacrifice. The quarter of a million soldiers buried here have served in every major military action from the Revolutionary, Civil, and Spanish-American Wars and the two World Wars, to the Korean, Vietnam, and Persian Gulf conflicts. In 1868 General John Logan set aside 30 May to decorate Civil War graves in a service held at the portico of **Arlington House**.

Thus began an annual day of tribute—Memorial Day.

Space at the cemetery, reserved for officers and enlistees of the US military and government employees and their spouses, is expected to run out around 2030, so certain requirements for interment have been set: The deceased must have been on active duty, a 20-year veteran, or the recipient of a high honor such as the Purple Heart.

After parking your car in the parking lot (no cars are allowed on the cemetery grounds), start your visit at the nearby **Visitors' Center**, an imposing modern building with a giant skydome designed in 1989 by **Frances Lethbridge** and **Patricia Schiffelbein**. It houses the main information offices (where you can obtain a map of the grounds), a bookstore, and the **Tourmobile** station (202/554.7950). Guided tours aboard the **Tourmobile** stop at various monuments and

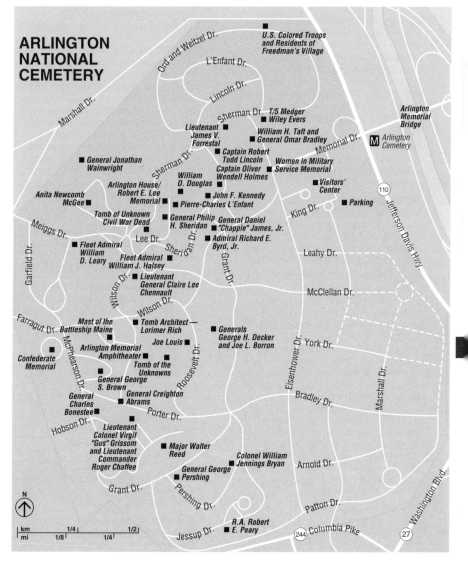

ARLINGTON NATIONAL CEMETERY

U.S. Colored Troops and Residents of Freedman's Village

Ord and Weitzel Dr.

L'Enfant Dr.

Lincoln Dr.

Marshall Dr.

Sherman Dr.   T/5 Medger
■ Wiley Evers

Arlington Memorial Bridge

M Arlington Cemetery

Lieutenant James V. Forrestal

William H. Taft and General Omar Bradley

Memorial Dr.

General Jonathan Wainwright

Sherman Dr.

Captain Robert Todd Lincoln
Captain Oliver Wendell Holmes

Women in Military Service Memorial

Anita Newcomb McGee ■

William O. Douglas

Arlington House/ Robert E. Lee Memorial ■

John F. Kennedy ■

Pierre-Charles L'Enfant

Visitors' Center ■

Tomb of Unknown Civil War Dead ■

General Philip H. Sheridan ■

General Daniel "Chappie" James, Jr. ■

Parking ■

King Dr.

Jefferson Davis Hwy.

110

Meiggs Dr.

Lee Dr.

Sheridan Dr.

Admiral Richard E. Byrd, Jr. ■

■ Fleet Admiral William D. Leary

Fleet Admiral William J. Halsey

Garfield Dr.

Wilson Dr.

Grant Dr.

Leahy Dr.

■ Lieutenant General Claire Lee Chennault

Wilson Dr.

McClellan Dr.

Farragut Dr.

Mast of the Battleship Maine

Tomb Architect— Lorimer Rich ■

Joe Louis ■

■ Generals George H. Decker and Joe L. Borron

York Dr.

Eisenhower Dr.

McPherson Dr.

Confederate Memorial

Arlington Memorial Amphitheater ■

Tomb of the Unknowns ■

General George S. Brown ■

Roosevelt Dr.

Bradley Dr.

Marshall Dr.

General Charles Bonestee ■

General Creighton Abrams ■

Porter Dr.

Hobson Dr.

Lieutenant Colonel Virgil "Gus" Grissom and Lieutenant Commander Roger Chaffee ■

Major Walter Reed ■

Colonel William Jennings Bryan ■

Arnold Dr.

General George Pershing ■

Grant Dr.

Pershing Dr.

Patton Dr.

Washington Blvd.

N

R.A. Robert E. Peary ■

244 Columbia Pike

27

km 1/4 1/2
mi 1/8 1/4

Jessup Dr.

points of interest. ♦ Nominal parking fee. Memorial Dr and Jefferson Davis Hwy. 607.8052. Metro: Arlington Cemetery

Within Arlington National Cemetery:

Women in Military Service Memorial
Dedicated 18 October 1997, this is the first national memorial to honor US servicewomen. Located at the ceremonial entrance of the main gateway to **Arlington National Cemetery,** the museum and educational center includes a hall of honor, four exhibit alcoves, and a 196-seat theater. A computerized database allows visitors to access photos and the military histories of registered servicewomen.

John F. Kennedy's Grave
This memorial, designed by John Carl Warnecke, is marked by an eternal flame and a slate headstone from Cape Cod. The simple marble terrace yields a panoramic view of the city; one low wall reminds visitors of Kennedy's power with words, showing an inscription from his inaugural address. Jacqueline Kennedy Onassis is buried beside him. Nearby in a grassy plot is Robert F. Kennedy's grave, marked by a white cross. An adjacent granite wall and fountain memorialize the words of the late attorney general and senator.

Tomb of Pierre-Charles L'Enfant
The grave of the designer of DC's city grid lies on a hillside overlooking Washington, just in front of **Arlington House.** His original plan is carved on the tomb.

Arlington House/Robert E. Lee Memorial
The story of this house is really the story of two great Virginia families—the Washingtons and the Lees—and their struggle to hold onto this 1,100-acre estate, which overlooks the Potomac River and is now **Arlington National Cemetery.**

John Custis, Martha Washington's son, purchased the land in 1778. In 1802 his son, artist George Washington Parke Custis (adopted by George and Martha), started building the Greek Revival mansion and, in turn, passed it along to his daughter Mary Anna Randolph Custis, who married Lieutenant Robert E. Lee in 1831. The mansion took its more common name, the **Custis-Lee House,** from this famous marriage. The house is preserved as a memorial to Robert E. Lee, a man highly regarded by both sides in the Civil War. It was here, in 1861, that Lee learned of Virginia's secession from the Union and decided to resign his commission in the US Army to serve his native state. "My affections and attachments are more strongly placed here," he once wrote of the house, "than at any other place in the world."

Mrs. Lee left the estate when the Union Army crossed the Potomac during the Civil War. In 1864 the federal government claimed legal title to the land for unpaid taxes that had been questionably imposed during the war. Then, in 1883, the Supreme Court ordered that the house be returned to Lee's son, George Washington Custis Lee. Because of its condition, however, he was unable to live in the house, and he sold it back to the government for $150,000. Congress approved the restoration of the ransacked house in 1925, and the estate was taken over by the National Park Service in 1933.

Thanks to extensive research and curatorial zeal, the house has largely been restored to its 1861 appearance. Each room has a few pieces of the Lee family's furniture, artwork, and housewares; others are period pieces. A portion of the double parlor set has survived and now furnishes the **White Parlor;** the violin given to Robert E. Lee's father-in-law by George Washington is also on display here. The bedchamber in which Lee resigned his commission in the US Army contains his original bedstead and writing chair. The dining room is furnished with original china, silver, and glassware. Copies of many of the paintings that once hung here—among them an 1830 Italian Madonna by William George Williams—decorate the house. Original artworks include George Washington Parke Custis's *Battle of Monmouth,* which was intended for the **Capitol** but is now on display in the **Morning Room,** and the 1831 portrait of Mary Anna Randolph Custis by August Herview, painted shortly before her wedding to Lee, which is in the family parlor. Both floors of the house are open, as are the flower garden and a museum that traces Robert E. Lee's life and includes many objects he used. This glimpse into the lifestyle of pre–Civil War Southern gentility is a must for DC visitors. Tours are self-guided. ♦ Free Daily. 557.0613

Tomb of the Unknowns
Formerly the **Tomb of the Unknown Soldier,** this memorial remains the focus of sentiment and ceremony at the cemetery. Cut from a single block of white marble, it is decorated by sculpted wreaths and a three-figure symbol representing valor, victory, and peace. The inscription on the back panel reads, "Here Rests in Honored Glory an American Soldier Known But to God." Entombed in the monument are four crypts, three of which hold the remains of unknown US servicemen, one each from World War I, World War II, and the Korean Wars. After much controversy, the Vietnam War crypt was disturbed in 1998 when the remains of First Lieutenant Michael Blassie were identified through DNA testing, subsequently disinterred, and moved to his family's cemetery in St. Louis.

At all times, a soldier from the "Old Guard" of the Third US Infantry protects the tomb and periodically performs the impressive

Changing of the Guard. This routine of heel-clicking, rifle maneuvers, and salutes takes place every half hour during summer and every hour in winter. (The **Iran Memorial,** marking the aborted rescue mission of American hostages in 1980, and the **Astronaut Memorial,** created in memory of the *Challenger,* are located near the tomb.)

Arlington Memorial Amphitheater

The 1920 memorial by **Carrère and Hastings** is dedicated to the Army, Navy, and Marine Corps. Finished in white Vermont marble, the 2,500-seat amphitheater is reminiscent of Greek and Roman theaters. Memorial Day and Veteran's Day services are held there.

Mast of the Battleship Maine

The mast—its tower still in place—was raised in 1912 from the ship, which sank in 1898 in Havana Harbor. It is set in a granite base inscribed with the names of the 229 men who died in the mysterious explosion that preceded the Spanish-American War.

Confederate Memorial

Erected in 1912 by the United Daughters of the Confederacy, Moses Ezekiel's Baroque bronze monument honors the soldiers of the short-lived Confederate States of America. A female figure in the center stands for the "South in Peace," while a frieze on the base portrays the South's women sending their men to fight. President Woodrow Wilson dedicated the statue.

3 United States Marine Corps War Memorial

More popularly known as the **Iwo Jima Memorial,** this is Felix W. Weldon's re-creation of Joe Rosenthal's Pulitzer Prize–winning photograph. Five marines and a sailor raise the American flag on Mount Suribachi, Iwo Jima. The 78-foot-high, hundred-ton sculpture represents the World War II battle site where more than 5,000 marines died. ♦ N Meade St (south of Arlington Blvd). 289.2530. Metros: Rosslyn, Arlington Cemetery

On the Marine Corps War Memorial grounds:

Sunset Parade

This takes place on Tuesdays at 7PM, from late May through late August, and features the **Marine Silent Drill Team** and **Drum and Bugle Corps.** ♦ Free. No reservations necessary. Information 202/433.6060

3 Netherlands Carillon

This gift from the Netherlands to the United States was officially presented on 5 May 1960, the 15th anniversary of the liberation of the Netherlands from the Nazis. It has 49 stationary bells with a four-octave range of notes. ♦ Concerts: Sa 2PM Apr-May, Sept; Sa 6:30PM June-Aug

4 Quality Inn Iwo Jima

$ Just four blocks from the **Metro,** this 141-room brick hotel has an outdoor pool, restaurant, and lounge. Close by the **Iwo Jima Memorial,** the gift shop features World War II memorabilia and the front desk sports more of the same. Occasional specials drop this into the one-dollar-sign range. Children under 18 stay free. ♦ 1501 Arlington Blvd (between Fort Myer Dr and N Pierce St). 524.5000, 800/221.2222; fax 522.5484 ᴗ Metro: Rosslyn

5 Theodore Roosevelt Island and Memorial

In the Potomac River, between the Roosevelt and Key Bridges, lie these gentle marshlands honoring the 26th president. The island's 88 acres allow red-tailed hawks, red and gray foxes, and marsh wrens to roam freely, along with groundhogs, great owls, and wood ducks. Old sycamore, oak, hickory, and dogwood trees shade the two-and-a-half miles of nature trails. Paul Manship's 17-foot-tall bronze memorial statue of Roosevelt stands in front of four granite tablets, each inscribed with his thoughts on nature and The State.

The parking lot and pedestrian bridge to the island are accessible from the northbound lanes of the George Washington Parkway. The island can also be reached by canoe from **Thompson's Boat House** (202/333.4861) in DC. Nature walks are available. ♦ Free. George Washington Memorial Pkwy (between Custis Memorial Pkwy and Francis Scott Key Bridge). 289.2530

FUNDED BY THE FREEDOM FORUM

6 Newseum

This high-tech, interactive museum is dedicated to free press and free speech. A blocklong **News Wall** holds 36 monitors running live news feeds from around the world. Visitors can watch programs being produced in the **News Forum/Broadcast Studio;** participate in creating broadcast news in the **Interactive Newsroom;** and view news and journalism films in the 220-seat domed theater, as well as in two smaller theaters in the **News History Gallery.** ♦ Free. W-Su. The Freedom Forum World Center, 1101 Wilson Blvd (at N Kent St). 284.3700. Metro: Rosslyn

In case of nuclear attack, federal officials would head to underground bomb shelters in the Virginia countryside. According to *The Washingtonian* magazine, the bunker at Mount Weather has streets, sidewalks, and a small underground lake. The shelter designated for the Federal Reserve Board chairperson is equipped with electronic banking equipment and, reportedly, about a trillion dollars in cash.

6 Tom Sarris' Orleans House ★★$$
Bringing New Orleans style—signature black
wrought-iron balconies and all—to Virginia,
this restaurant is best known for its huge
portions of prime rib and fully stocked salad
bar. Seafood and other grilled meat entrées
also come in hearty portions. ◆ American ◆
M-F lunch and dinner; Sa-Su dinner. 1213
Wilson Blvd (between N Lynn St and Fort
Myer Dr). 524.2929. Metro: Rosslyn

6 Hyatt Arlington $$$ This 302-room
European-style hotel is convenient to both the
Iwo Jima Memorial and **Arlington National
Cemetery.** It's also a quick walk across Key
Bridge to Georgetown. Catering to individuals
rather than conventioneers, the hotel provides
a fitness facility, in-house movies, two
restaurants, and two lounges. Discount rates
and free parking on weekends. Children under
18 stay free. ◆ 1325 Wilson Blvd (between
Fort Myer Dr and N Nash St). 525.1234,
800/233.1234; fax 875.3393 ᴧ Metro:
Rosslyn

7 Appetizer Plus ★$$ How much sushi can
you eat? Find out for a fixed all-you-can-eat
price. There's also tempura and teriyaki.
◆ Japanese ◆ M-Sa lunch and dinner; Su
dinner. 1117 N 19th St (at N Lynn St).
525.3171. Metro: Rosslyn

7 Holiday Inn Rosslyn Westpark Hotel $$
Located at Key Bridge, this 308-room hotel is
a short walk to Georgetown and close to
major highways. Decorated in a modern
contemporary style, the hotel offers a rooftop
restaurant, a fitness facility and indoor
swimming pool, and same-day valet service
except on Sunday. A room on one of the top
floors will assure you a breathtaking view.
Children under 18 stay free. ◆ 1900 Fort Myer
Dr (between Key Blvd and Lee Hwy).
527.4814, 800/368.3408; fax 522.8864 ᴧ
Metro: Rosslyn

8 Key Bridge Marriott $$$ Amenities in this
588-room hotel include indoor and outdoor
swimming pools, exercise facilities, two
restaurants, and two lounges (one offers a
spectacular panoramic view of DC). Children
under 12 stay free; up to five people in a room
can stay for the price of two. ◆ 1401 Lee Hwy
(between Francis Scott Key Bridge and N Oak
St). 524.6400, 800/228.9290; fax 524.8964 ᴧ
Metro: Rosslyn

9 Red Hot & Blue ★★★$$ It's well worth
the wait—which can be considerable during
peak hours—for this upscale BBQ joint, where
political gossip mixes with rhythm and blues
selections from the jukebox. Try one of
several microbrews on tap with hickory-
smoked pork ribs and chicken or a "pulled pig
sandwich," all served with baked beans and
coleslaw. Photos of blues artists and celebrity
customers adorn the bright red walls.
◆ Southern ◆ Daily lunch and dinner. 1600
Wilson Blvd (at N Pierce St). 276.7427 ᴧ
Metro: Rosslyn

10 Pho 75 ★★$ This kitchen serves nothing
but *pho* (beef broth with rice noodles, thinly
sliced beef, and Asian spices). Diners are
given an array of garnishes—green chilies,
limes, bean sauce, and red chili sauce—which
they can use to create just the right flavor. The
very simple dining room features pictorial
scenes of the homeland. ◆ Vietnamese ◆ Daily
lunch and dinner. No credit cards accepted.
1711 Wilson Blvd (between N Quinn and
Rhodes Sts). 525.7355. Metro: Court House

10 Village Bistro ★★$ This charming little
spot manages to feel French while offering
something for everyone. The casual, high-
ceilinged room is simple and bright. If you
pick one of the day's seafood specials or a
veal or chicken dish, you probably can't go
wrong. The numerous vegetables and side
dishes, neglected in so many other
restaurants, can be real show-stoppers here.
◆ American/Continental ◆ M-F lunch and
dinner; Sa-Su dinner. 1723 Wilson Blvd
(between N Quinn and Rhodes Sts). 522.0284
ᴧ Metro: Court House

11 Bardo Rodeo ★★$$ With a handful of its
own beers and nearly three dozen others on
tap, this eclectic establishment boasts that it's
the "largest brewpub in the Western
Hemisphere" (600 seats inside, more
outside). The menu shows plenty of
imagination, and the kitchen takes new twists
on some old standbys. Along with a satisfying
bite to eat and a tasty brew, this place offers
24 pool tables upstairs. ◆ American ◆ M-W,
Sa-Su dinner; Th-F lunch and dinner. 2000
Wilson Blvd (between Rhodes St and N
Courthouse Rd). 527.9399 ᴧ Metro: Court
House

12 Fort Myer Neat brick barracks house troops,
chiefs of staff, a clinic, and a firehouse. Its
Parade Ground nearby has held
demonstrations of aviation history's bests,

including the Wright brothers' first public display of their plane in 1909. ♦ Arlington Blvd (between Washington Blvd and N 10th St). 545.6700 ᴦ Metro: Court House

13 Pizza de Résistance ★$ Modern and casual, this restaurant serves pizza, California-style: Toppings include lamb and feta cheese, scallops and shrimp, smoked salmon, and mesquite chicken. ♦ Pizza ♦ M-F lunch and dinner; Sa-Su dinner. 2300 Clarendon Blvd (between N Veitch and N Adams Sts). 351.5680 ᴦ Metro: Court House

14 Good Taste Gourmet ★★$ Formerly called **Mandarin Cafe,** this small, plain restaurant is the spot for hot Szechuan cuisine. Wonton dumplings smothered in hot sauce are the perfect opener. Delectable entrées such as bean curd Szechuan style and shrimp sautéed with ginger and red chilies will warm your palate mighty fast. The flavors are truly special. ♦ Chinese ♦ Daily lunch and dinner. 2607 Wilson Blvd (between N Barton and Danville Sts). 527.2828. Metro: Court House

15 Whitey's ★$ You can get (just about) anything you want at this local institution, which features "roasted" chicken and burgers, and live music from folk to jazz. In keeping with its pine-paneled, old-neon character, there's also a game room with billiard tables, pinball machines, darts, and a jukebox that's stocked with CDs—the one concession to contemporary technology. ♦ American ♦ Daily breakfast, lunch, and dinner. 2761 N Washington Blvd (between N Daniel and N Ninth Sts). 525.9825 ᴦ Metro: Clarendon

16 El Pollo Rico ★★$ The only choice here is Peruvian-style chicken, fresh off the spit. A whole charcoal-grilled bird—perfect for a picnic—is about $10, including coleslaw and fries. If that's too much food, get the quarter or half chicken. ♦ Peruvian ♦ Daily lunch and dinner. No credit cards accepted. 2917 N Washington Blvd (between N 10th and N Garfield Sts). 866.1286 ᴦ Metro: Clarendon. Also at: 7031 Brookfield Plaza Rd (just west of Backlick Rd), Springfield, Virginia. 522.3220

16 Hard Times Cafe ★★$ Like its sister restaurants in Alexandria and Herndon, this honky-tonk saloon specializes in hearty chili (vegetarian, too) and ice-cold longnecks. But

before you settle into one of the wooden booths with a beer and some grub, make sure you play your favorites from the country-western jukebox. ♦ American ♦ Daily lunch and dinner. 3028 Wilson Blvd (between N Garfield and N Highland Sts). 528.2233. Metro: Clarendon. Also at: 1404 King St (between S West and S Peyton Sts), Alexandria. 683.5340 ᴦ Metro: King Street; 394 Elden St (between Herndon Pkwy and Grant St), Herndon, Virginia. 318.8941 ᴦ

16 Café Saigon ★★$ Not much more than a storefront, this place has wonderful grilled meat and seafood dishes (try the shrimp and scallops on skewers); the crispy rolls and garden rolls are great, too. ♦ Vietnamese ♦ Daily lunch and dinner. 1135 N Highland St (at Wilson Blvd). 243.6522 ᴦ Metro: Clarendon

17 Hunan Number One ★★$$ The best dishes are Cantonese offerings such as sizzling black-pepper steak, steamed shrimp in a lotus leaf with black-bean–and-garlic sauce, and fillets of flounder with asparagus. But perhaps the best reason to stop here is the dim sum—served daily from 11AM to 3PM. ♦ Chinese ♦ Daily lunch and dinner. 3033 Wilson Blvd (between N Garfield and N Highland Sts). 528.1177. Metro: Clarendon

17 Cafe Dalat ★★$ The decor may not be much, but the friendly service and low prices of this Vietnamese restaurant make it a popular spot, even in this neighborhood saturated with Asian culinary options. Soups and noodle dishes are standouts. ♦ Vietnamese ♦ Daily lunch and dinner. 3143 Wilson Blvd (between Herndon and N Hudson Sts). 276.0935 ᴦ Metro: Clarendon

17 Atami ★★$ With tiny quarters and a friendly staff, this restaurant serves both Japanese and Vietnamese specialties. The all-you-can-eat sushi special is a great way to g et your fill; the sukiyaki is also good. ♦ Japanese/Vietnamese ♦ M-Sa lunch and dinner; Su dinner. 3155 Wilson Blvd (between Herndon and N Hudson Sts). 522.4787 ᴦ Metro: Clarendon

17 Nam Viet ★★$ Stop in for crispy rolls, orange beef, and other spicy Vietnamese dishes. ♦ Vietnamese ♦ Daily lunch and dinner. 1127 N Hudson St (between Wilson Blvd and N 13th St). 522.7110 ᴦ Metro: Clarendon

17 Queen Bee ★★★$ It's well worth the wait for a table at Arlington's most popular Vietnamese restaurant. The spring rolls, noodle soups, chicken in ginger sauce, grilled jumbo shrimp, skewered beef, and deep-fried whole fish are highly recommended. The decor—a country mural, a mirrored wall—is standard Oriental. ♦ Vietnamese ♦ Daily lunch and dinner. 3181 Wilson Blvd (between N Hudson and N Irving Sts). 527.3444 ᧒ Metro: Clarendon

18 Arlington Renaissance Hotel $$$
Directly over the **Metro** stop, this 209-room hotel has two restaurants, a lounge, and privileges at the downstairs health club, which features a lap pool and a whirlpool. Rooms on the top floor—the concierge floor—are larger and include hors d'oeuvres and continental breakfast. ♦ 950 N Stafford St (at Fairfax Dr). 528.6000, 800/2-RAMADA; fax 528.4386 ᧒ Metro: Ballston

19 Food Factory ★$ Bare-bones but cheap—everything in this Middle Eastern cafeteria is less than seven dollars. The kabobs are the best choices. No alcohol is served. ♦ Middle Eastern ♦ Daily lunch and dinner. No credit cards accepted. 4221 Fairfax Dr (between N Stafford and N Stuart Sts). 527.2279 ᧒ Metro: Ballston

19 Rio Grande Cafe ★★★$$ Excellent Tex-Mex staples (enchiladas, tacos, and most popular, fajitas), as well as such surprises as frogs' legs, are served in a fun, lively setting. The hour-plus wait for a table is easily soothed by the swirled margaritas. ♦ Tex-Mex ♦ Daily lunch and dinner. 4301 Fairfax Dr (at N Taylor St). 528.3131 ᧒ Metro: Ballston

20 Holiday Inn Arlington at Ballston $$
The main features of this 221-room hotel are the large meeting rooms, complete with state-of-the-art video equipment, and an outdoor swimming pool. The lobby and restaurant are decked out in the style of an old railroad depot, upon which the restaurant was built. Extras include a fitness facility, a nearby jogging trail, and a free shuttle to local restaurants, shopping, and the **Metro.** Children under 18 stay free with parents. ♦ 4610 Fairfax Dr (between N Glebe Rd and N Buchanan St). 243.9800, 800/HOLIDAY; fax 527.2677 ᧒ Metro: Ballston

21 Ballston Commons Though the **Commons** has seen better days, this enclosed mall still features 100 shopping spots. Included are **Hecht's** and **JC Penney** department stores; **B. Dalton Booksellers, Victoria's Secret,** and a raft of other chain stores; specialty shops such as **The Artists Proof** (415.3939) which sells signed photographs of sports heroes and Hollywood celebrities; and a food court with 10 choices. ♦ M-Sa 10AM-9:30PM; Su noon-6PM. 4238 Wilson Blvd (between N Randolph St and N Glebe Rd). 243.8088 ᧒ Metro: Ballston

22 Layalina ★★$$ This friendly, homey Middle Eastern eatery serves such Syrian specialties as stuffed grape leaves with lemon, *soujok* (hot sausage), and *fattoush* salad. The *mezze* combination, which serves two to three, and vegetarian sampler are good introductions to the menu. ♦ Syrian ♦ Tu–Su lunch and dinner. 5216 Wilson Blvd (between N Frederick and N Greenbrier Sts). 525.1170. Metro: Ballston

A Taste of Italy
PINES OF ITALY
Ristorante Italiano
Southern Italian Cuisine

23 Pines of Italy ★★$ Neighborhood Italian at its simple, casual best: good fried zucchini, fried artichoke hearts, homemade pasta, and white pizza. If you're on a budget, ask for the prices of the specials before ordering—they can be relatively high. ♦ Italian ♦ Daily lunch and dinner. 237 N Glebe Rd (between Piedmont St and N Pershing Dr). 524.4969 ᧒

24 Thai Square ★★★$ Thought by many to be the only authentic Thai restaurant in the metropolitan area, this small, tidy establishment is a find. Try to order from the Thai rather than the English menu, but beware dishes of searing intensity. Especially fine are long stewed pig (like Chinese pork) served with rock sugar, and spicy grilled catfish with wide rice noodles. ♦ Thai ♦ Daily lunch and dinner. Reservations required for parties of 5 or more. Free parking in back. 3217 Columbia Pike (between S Highland St and S Glebe Rd). 684.7040

25 Matuba ★★$$ Excellent sushi, tempura, and teriyaki are the specialties of this friendly spot. For a great bargain stop in on Monday, when the sushi is sold for $1 a piece. ♦ Japanese ♦ M-F lunch and dinner; Sa-Su dinner. Reservations recommended. 2915 Columbia Pike (between Walter Reed Dr and S Garfield St). 521.2811 ᧒

25 Arlington Cinema 'n' Drafthouse This big old movie theater serves beer, wine, pizzas, and snacks while showing second-run movies. Relax in the comfy sofas and chairs.

It's very popular with residents of the nearby military installations. You must be 21 to enter. ◆ M-Th, Su doors open 7PM, movies 7:15PM, 9:45PM; F-Sa doors open 6:45PM, movies 7:30PM, 9:45PM, midnight. No credit cards accepted. 2903 Columbia Pike (at Walter Reed Dr). 486.2345 &

26 Atilla's ★★$ You can tell that this small pastel-colored restaurant and carryout place is something of a local institution because it's almost always packed. Choose from two menus: Indian and Middle Eastern. The housemade pita and hummus are as good as any in the area, and, best of all, the first round is set upon your table without charge for your munching pleasure. ◆ Indian/Middle Eastern ◆ Daily lunch and dinner. Reservations recommended. 2705 Columbia Pike (between S Adams St and Walter Reed Dr). 920.4900 &

27 Bob & Edith's Diner ★$ A bona fide old-fashioned diner—counter, booths, formica aplenty—it's a local favorite and your best bet for eggs and hash browns at 3AM. ◆ American ◆ Daily 24 hours. No credit cards accepted. 2310 Columbia Pike (between S Wayne and S Barton Sts). 920.6103 &

28 Atlacatl II ★★$ Recommended Mexican and Salvadoran specialties at this place include fried yucca, *pupusas* (corn tortillas filled with pork and cheese), and tamales. ◆ Mexican/Salvadoran ◆ Daily lunch and dinner. 4701 Columbia Pike (at S Buchanan St). 920.3680 &

29 Econo Lodge $ This 164-room hotel features an outdoor swimming pool, meeting rooms, a restaurant, and free morning and late afternoon shuttle service to **National Airport** and the **Pentagon Metro.** Children under 18 stay free. ◆ 2485 S Glebe Rd (at Henry G. Shirley Memorial Hwy). 979.4100, 800/446.6900; fax 979.6120 &

BISTRO
BISTRO

30 Bistro Bistro ★★★$$ Here's one of the area's most pleasant and imaginative restaurants and watering spots. The bi-level dining room is casually elegant with marble-top tables, a large dark wood bar, floor-to-ceiling windows, and murals on the walls. Oyster stew, fried calamari with three dipping sauces, pizza, and roast chicken with mashed potatoes are among the hits. And don't pass up the crème brûlée. The fare, invariably good,

often verges on great. An added bonus: a terrific (and reasonably priced) selection of single-malt scotches. ◆ American ◆ M-Sa lunch and dinner; Su brunch and dinner. Reservations recommended. 4021 S 28th St (between S Quincy and S Randolph Sts). 379.0300 &

30 Carlyle Grand Cafe ★★★$$ A restaurant that really lives up to its middle name. This 350-seat set of dining rooms has a lot going for it, from the striking Art Deco posters on the walls to the no-smoking-anywhere policy, but head upstairs if you want to relax (the bar downstairs is boisterous and noisy). The two menus aren't identical, but they overlap in all the right places. The kitchen particularly shines when it comes to grilling and smoking, so fish (particularly salmon) and chicken are nearly always perfect. ◆ American ◆ Daily lunch and dinner. 4000 S 28th St (at S Quincy St). 931.0777 &

31 Hyatt Regency Crystal City $$$ The big, shiny 685-room hostelry offers all you'd expect from a Hyatt, plus the convenience of this location near **National Airport.** Amenities include a restaurant (with a lovely view across the Potomac), lounge, health club (with a whirlpool), outdoor swimming pool, and shuttle service to **National Airport** and **Crystal City.** The hotel also offers special weekend packages and meeting facilities. ◆ 2799 Jefferson Davis Hwy (at Crystal Dr). 418.1234, 800/223.1234; fax 418.1289 &

32 Crystal City Underground and Crystal Plaza Shops Beneath an area of glass-and-concrete high-rises that shoot out of the flatlands near **National Airport,** this gem of a small mall contains 120 shops, services, and dining establishments. Winding cobblestone walkways and twisting alleys connect to the **Metro** and the two **Marriott** hotels. Stores include **The Crystal Boutique** (415.1400), for designer women's fashions, and **The American Phone Center** (413.7175), with fun phones in every conceivable shape and design. ◆ M-Sa; Su some shops open. Crystal Dr (between S 23rd and S 18th Sts). 413.4380. Metro: Crystal City

32 Crystal City Marriott Hotel $$$ The lodge is connected to the **Crystal City Underground** shops and the **Metro** station, and it's just five minutes from **National Airport** (a shuttle service runs every 15 minutes from 6:05AM to 11PM). The 345-room hotel has a restaurant and lounge, a health club (with an indoor swimming pool, whirlpool, and sauna), and meeting facilities. The lobby is decorated in traditional Northern Virginia style with hunter green and deep reds, but the color scheme in the rooms is much lighter. ◆ 1999 Jefferson Davis Hwy (at S 20th St). 413.5500, 800/321.9879; fax 413.0192 & Metro: Crystal City

Pillars of Strength

Egyptians created the first obelisks, using pairs of the graceful geometric figures to adorn the doorways of temples. The tall, slender, four-sided pillars were most often carved of red granite and honored Ra, the Egyptian sun god. Traditionally, an obelisk was designed so that its height equaled 10 times the width of its flat bottom. The stone column usually sat upon a circular base and tapered to a point or pyramid.

Several Egyptian obelisks have survived the ages, including those at the Great Temple at Karnak in Thebes. During the period of European colonialism, several of these Egyptian treasures were moved to Europe and the US. The obelisk at Paris's Place de la Concorde once stood at Luxor. Twin obelisks, each known as Cleopatra's Needle, have been separated: One now stands at London's Embankment, the other in New York City's Central Park.

Of course, the **Washington Monument** is obelisk-shaped and follows the Egyptian formula for such a pillar's height. But the fact that it isn't a single, solid stone—a monolith—keeps it from being a true obelisk.

COURTESY BUREAU OF ENGRAVING & PRINTING

CRYSTAL GATEWAY
Marriott.

33 Crystal Gateway Marriott $$$ This second—and larger (697 rooms)—Marriott fixture is also connected to the **Underground** shops and subway line, and is an easy five-minute drive to **National Airport.** Amenities include a six-story sunlit atrium, indoor and outdoor swimming pools, a health club, concierge service, four restaurants, and facilities for disabled guests. The lobby and rooms are done up in pastels; the concierge-level rooms are the nicest. ♦ 1700 Jefferson Davis Hwy (between S 18th and S 15th Sts). 920.3230, 800/228.9290; fax 271.5212 ⑁ Metro: Crystal City

During the Civil War, Theodore Roosevelt Island was taken over by the Union Army to house the First US Colored Troops, a black unit.

34 Embassy Suites Hotel $$$ The upscale all-suite property has 267 suites, all outfitted with the comforts of home: hair dryers, microwaves, irons and ironing boards, on-command VCRs, and voice mail. The hotel also has a tropical atrium, meeting facilities, a fitness center (with indoor swimming pool), and complimentary parking and shuttle service. **Scrimmages** offers American fare and guests receive a complimentary breakfast. Children under 12 stay free. ♦ 1300 Jefferson Davis Hwy (between S 15th and S 12th Sts). 979.9799, 800/EMBASSY; fax 920.5947 ⑁ Metros: Pentagon City, Crystal City

35 Doubletree Hotel—National Airport $$$ Conveniently located near the **Pentagon City** shopping complex and its **Metro** stop, this 632-room high-rise includes 152 suites, some with spas and balconies. Rooms on the upper floors offer spectacular views of the Potomac River and the Washington skyline. Two restaurants, **Skydome** (a rooftop, revolving lounge), a health club, an enclosed rooftop swimming pool, and shuttle service to the **Pentagon, National Airport,** and the **Crystal City** office complex are among the amenities offered. ♦ 300 Army Navy Dr (at Jefferson Davis Hwy). 416.4100, 800.222.8733; fax 416.4166 ⑁ Metro: Pentagon City

THE
FASHION CENTRE
AT
PENTAGON CITY

36 The Fashion Centre at Pentagon City One of Washington's most elegant malls is also one of the few with its own **Metro** stop. Some of the 160 shops and restaurants under the stunning glass atrium include **Nordstrom, Macy's, The Museum Company, Crate & Barrel, Eddie Bauer,** and **The Disney Store;** there's also a six-screen movie theater and large food court on the lower level. ♦ M-Sa 10AM-9:30PM; Su. 1100 Hayes St (between S 15th St and Army Navy Dr). 415.2400. Metro: Pentagon City

36 Ritz-Carlton Pentagon City $$$$ This plush 345-room hotel features a complete fitness center with indoor lap pool, Jacuzzi, and massage; afternoon tea to the strains of classical music; valet parking, concierge, baby-sitting, and 'round-the-clock room service; shuttle service to **National Airport;** plus **The Grill** restaurant (notorious as the site where Monica Lewinsky blabbed to Linda Tripp) and nighttime entertainment. A gracious environment, the decor includes Oriental rugs, gilt mirrors, fine oil paintings,

Pentagon

antiques, and freshly cut flowers in porcelain vases. Guests on the top two floors have access to a cozy little club that features five food presentations daily (from a continental breakfast to dessert and after-dinner drinks), a friendly concierge who aims to please, and a terrific view. As an added bonus, the hotel is connected to **The Fashion Centre at Pentagon City.** Discounted weekend rates are available. ♦ 1250 Hayes St (between S 15th St and Army Navy Dr). 415.5000, 800/241.3333; fax 415.5061 ♿ Metro: Pentagon City

37 Pentagon Centre For an alternative to the higher prices and smaller stores of **The Fashion Centre at Pentagon City,** try this collection of superstores and reasonably priced restaurants across the street. (One of the escalators from the **Pentagon City Metro** exit leaves you right at its door.) **The Price Club** is a warehouse discounter open to members only, but you can stroll through **Marshall's** for discounted fashions; **Best Buy** (414.7090) for amazing values on home electronics and recordings; **Linens 'n' Things** (413.0993) for housewares; and **Borders Books and Music** (418.0168) for a terrific selection of reading and listening matter. Of the restaurants, the best is **Chevy's** (413.8700), whose friendly staff serve better-than-average Mexican food in a friendly barn of a room. ♦ Daily 10AM-9PM; restaurants open until midnight. 1201 S Hayes St (at S 12th St). 413.8700. Metro: Pentagon City

38 Arlington County Visitors' Center Stop here for information on hotels, restaurants, and sights. ♦ Daily. 735 S 18th St (between Hayes and Ives Sts). 228.5720 ♿ Metro: Pentagon City

39 Woo Lae Oak ★★$$ Decorated with ancient ceramics, the restaurant specializes in Korean barbecue (which you cook on the grill built into your table). You can't go wrong with the dumpling and noodle dishes or hot pots of vegetables in spicy sauce. ♦ Korean ♦ Daily lunch and dinner. Reservations recommended. 1500 Joyce St (between S 16th St and Army Navy Dr). 521.3706 ♿ Metro: Pentagon City

40 Pentagon The world's largest office building, this five-sided structure has three times the floor space of the Empire State Building. The headquarters of the Department of Defense covers 29 acres, with a five-acre courtyard at its center. There are 17.5 miles of corridors, yet no office is more than seven minutes from any other. Built during World War II, the structure took only 16 months to complete. During the hourlong guided tours (first-come, first-served; bring a photo ID), which leave from the concourse, the guide walks backward the entire time. Call ahead to arrange tours for the physically disabled. ♦ Tours: M-F 9:30AM-3:30PM every half hour. Jefferson Davis and Henry G. Shirley Memorial Hwys. 695.1776 ♿ Metro: Pentagon

41 Navy and Marine Memorial This is a simple, graceful representation of seven seagulls in flight, sculpted in 1930 by Ernesto Begni dei Piatti. ♦ George Washington Memorial Pkwy (just north of I-395)

42 Lyndon Baines Johnson Memorial Grove At the south end of **Lady Bird Johnson Park** stretch 15 acres of pines, flowering dogwoods, and daffodils planted to commemorate the 36th president and his first lady. The memorial site, marked by a large Texas pink-granite monolith, is surrounded by stones inscribed with quotations by Johnson. A picnic in the park brings you frighteningly close to the planes landing at nearby **National Airport.** ♦ George Washington Memorial Pkwy (between Henry G. Shirley Memorial Hwy and Washington Blvd)

The Potomac River was known as Co-hon-go-roo-ta to the indigenous people, Espiritu Santo to the Spanish, and the Elizabeth to the English.

Restaurants/Clubs: Red **Hotels:** Blue
Shops/ Outdoors: Green **Sights/Culture:** Black

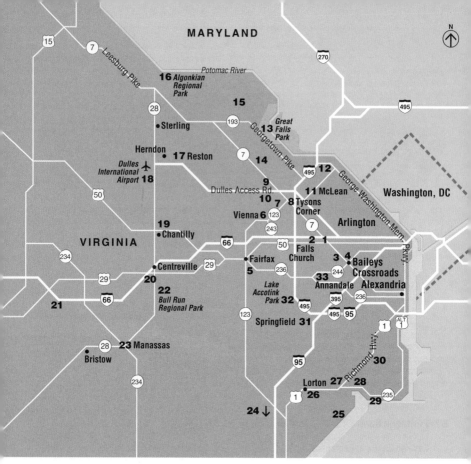

Northern Virginia

Much of the DC area's wealth is concentrated across the **Potomac River**, within the rapidly growing Northern Virginia suburbs. The region's prosperity is readily evident in the enormous **Tysons Corner** complex of malls and office buildings and **Dale City**'s **Potomac Mills Mall**, as well as in the paralyzing rush-hour traffic. Other shops and some of the area's best ethnic kitchens can be found on **Route 7**, the main thoroughfare between **Falls Church** and **Baileys Crossroads**. Beneath all the hustle and newness, however, lies the subtle dignity of the Old Dominion in the shape of such gracious colonial mansions as **Mount Vernon**, such Civil War battlefields as **Manassas**, and the rolling green **Hunt Country** to the west. Even some of the newness has its own charm, particularly in the planned community of **Reston**, with its million-dollar residences. Rural Virginia, just an hour's drive from downtown Washington, remains remarkably similar to the pastoral ideal so admired by Thomas Jefferson.

Area code 703 unless otherwise noted.

1 Falls Church The original wooden church was erected in 1733 near a road leading to the Potomac waterfalls. In 1769, a new structure was completed on the same site. The church served as a recruiting station during the Revolutionary War, a federal hospital during the Civil War, and later as a stable. It was completely renovated in 1959. ◆ M-F. Services (Episcopal): W noon; Su 8AM and noon. 115 E Fairfax St (between E Broad St and S Washington St), Falls Church. 532.7600 &

1 Haandi ★★★$$ If you like pink, this is the place: walls, tablecloths, nearly everything is pink. And if you don't—well, the spring chicken marinated in yogurt and spices and *murgakhani* (chicken in tomato, cream, and curry sauce) more than compensate. The menu also offers kabobs, lamb chops, tandoor-cooked dishes, delicious mango chutney, and other Indian favorites. ♦ Indian ♦ Daily lunch and dinner. 1222 W Broad St (at Haycock Rd), Falls Church. 533.3501 ♿

1 Bangkok-Vientiane ★★$ Laotian and Thai dishes such as pork-filled spring rolls and seafood soup with bean thread are served. Look for the excellent daily specials such as Thai eggplant, shrimp with zucchini and basil, and beef with green curry. Laotian rice tends to be more glutinous than Thai, and the spices less fiery. ♦ Laotian/Thai ♦ M-Sa lunch and dinner; Su dinner. Reservations recommended. 926A W Broad St (between N Spring and N West Sts), Falls Church. 534.0095

1 Panjshir ★★$$ This cozy place serves up top-notch *aushak* (a ravioli-like creation stuffed with scallions and topped with meat sauce, yogurt, and mint), kabobs (beef, chicken, and lamb), and a nice selection of Afghan vegetarian dishes. Afghan rugs and ornate mirrors add to the charm. ♦ Afghan ♦ M-Sa lunch and dinner; Su dinner. Reservations recommended for groups. 924 W Broad St (between N Spring and N West Sts), Falls Church. 536.4566. Also at: 224 Maple Ave W (between Courthouse Rd SW and Pleasant St SW), Vienna. 281.4183 ♿

1 Secret Garden ★★$$ Hardly a secret in Falls Church, this Korean restaurant delights patrons with *galbi* (barbecued short ribs), *bulgogi* (thinly sliced beef marinated and grilled), and a sushi bar. If you prefer your fish cooked, choose your own flounder from the huge aquarium and the chef will cook it to order. ♦ Korean ♦ Daily lunch and dinner. 6678 Arlington Blvd (at Annandale Rd), Falls Church. 533.1004 ♿

1 Taco Baja ★$ When you want a good meal fast, this Mexican cafe obliges. Bulletin boards list the offerings, which you carry to your table. Try the vegetarian special; it includes a guacamole-filled taco. ♦ Mexican ♦ Daily lunch and dinner. No credit cards accepted. 6136F Arlington Blvd (at Patrick Henry Dr), Falls Church. 534.5434 ♿

2 National Memorial Park This vast cemetery is noted for its gardens and sculptured fountains. The *Fountain of Faith,* the centerpiece of the grounds, was created by Swedish sculptor Carl Milles. Thirty-seven graceful bronze figures—each with a face depicting one of the sculptor's friends—seem to hover in a spray of water. ♦ 7400 Lee Hwy (between S West St and Hollywood Rd), Falls Church. 560.4400

3 Peking Gourmet Inn ★★★$$ George Bush's favorite Chinese restaurant (when he was president) was equipped with a bulletproof window. Many political photos, of the Republican bent, still grace one wall. Three generations of the Tsui family provide dedicated service and a consistently high

standard of classic dishes in a handsome, Oriental setting. The Peking duck is unusually crisp and fat-free; other specials include pork with garlic sprouts, Szechuan beef proper, duck with spring onions wrapped in flour pancakes, and Jou-Yen shrimp. Surprisingly inexpensive, this place is even worth a wait on the weekends. ♦ Chinese ♦ Daily lunch and dinner. Reservations recommended. 6029 Leesburg Pike (at Glen Carlyn Dr), Baileys Crossroads. 671.8088 ♿

4 Fortune Chinese Seafood Restaurant ★★$$ Despite the European decor, this spacious, comfortable restaurant sticks with Chinese tradition where it matters—the menu. Dim sum is served from rolling tea carts every day of the week. The regular menu offers beautifully prepared seafood specialties (try the steamed flounder or crabs with ginger and onions), along with meat and noodle dishes. On Saturday and Sunday afternoons, the restaurant is packed with Chinese families. ♦ Chinese ♦ Daily lunch and dinner. 5900 Leesburg Pike (at Glen Forest Dr), Baileys Crossroads. 998.8888 ♿

DUANGRAT'S
THAI RESTAURANT

4 Duangrat's ★★★$$ Recently voted "Top Thai Restaurant" by *Zagat Survey*, this spot offers superb Thai specialties. The crispy flounder with chili sauce is terrific, as is the trout wrapped in banana leaves, and the *bhram* (chicken with cabbage, shallots, and peanut sauce). On Friday and Saturday nights, Thai dancers perform in the upstairs dining room. If you want to re-create your favorite dish, try the Thai grocery store a few doors down, which is owned by the same folks. ♦ Thai ♦ Daily lunch and dinner. 5878 Leesburg Pike (at Glen Forest Dr), Baileys Crossroads. 820.5775 ♿

5 George Mason University A branch of the University of Virginia until 1972, the university enrolls nearly 20,000 students. Its major emphases are the humanities, public policy, and high technology. The Sports Recreation Complex, commonly known as the "Field House," boasts 69,000 square feet of basketball, tennis, and volleyball courts, a 200-meter indoor track, and archery and fencing facilities. Concerts, dance, theater, and seminars fill the university's **Center for the Arts**. The **Patriot Center** hosts concerts as well as sporting events. Tickets are sold through **Ticket Center** outlets. ♦ Patriot Center box office: M-Sa. 4400 University Dr (off Rte 123), Fairfax. University information 993.1000, Patriot Center box office 993.3000, Center for the Arts 993.8888, Ticket Center 202/432.SEAT, 800/448.9009

6 Nizam's ★★★$$$ From suburbia to Istanbul: Middle Eastern delicacies, including *doner kebab* (grilled lamb, pita bread, and yogurt sauce) and *manti* (ground lamb with a tomato sauce and yogurt), are served in romantic settings on two floors in this elegant restaurant. ♦ Turkish ♦ M-F lunch and dinner; Sa-Su dinner. Reservations recommended. 523 Maple Ave W (at Nutley St NW), Vienna. 938.8948 &

7 Wu's Garden Restaurant ★★$$ Among the ordinary restaurants in the Vienna area, this comfortable Chinese dining place stands out. Enjoy exceptionally good Mandarin cuisine amid rosewood partitions and Oriental decor. Try the shrimp imperial or the sesame beef. ♦ Chinese ♦ Daily lunch and dinner. 418 Maple Ave E (between East St NE and Beulah Rd), Vienna. 281.4410 &

8 Tysons Corner The largest of the suburban cities that have developed around DC, this one is known primarily for two things: high-rise office towers and shopping malls. In fact, the city has so much office space that only about a dozen other downtowns in the US have more. That, plus two megamalls and assorted strip malls on Routes 7 and 123, can bring traffic to a standstill. But the area does have hidden charms, including a quiet park and the **Wolf Trap Performing Arts Center.**

In Tysons Corner:

Tysons Corner Marriott Hotel $$$ Adjacent to the shopping center, this 390-room hotel matches the surrounding area—pleasant suburbia with a touch of class. The traditional rooms are done in forest green and blond wood. In addition to such regular amenities as free parking, cable TV, and a restaurant, the hostelry sports a health club, complete with an indoor swimming pool,

whirlpool, sauna, and exercise room with locker facilities. ♦ 8028 Leesburg Pike (between I-495 and Gallows Rd). 734.3200, 800/228.9290; fax 734.5763 &

Tysons Corner Center The original Tysons Corner mall offers more than 230 stores aimed at a middle-income clientele. Major department stores are **Bloomingdale's, Hecht's,** and **Nordstrom;** kids will gravitate to the **Sesame Street General Store.** Dining options include the **Rainforest Café,** a marvel with waterfalls, live birds and tropical fish, rainfall, and simulated thunder and lightning. ♦ M-Sa 10AM-9:30PM; Su noon-5PM. 1961 Chain Bridge Rd (between I-495 and International Dr). 893.9400 &

Within Tysons Corner Center:

America ★$$ Like its sister location in **Union Station** on **Capitol Hill,** this vast room with marbled floor and wall murals is hard-surfaced and rather noisy when it's full. But it does serve the most eclectic menu of American food imaginable, virtually one dish for every state in the union. Fortunately, most of them are nicely executed; try the Wyoming barbecued chicken or the Iowa loose-meat sandwich. ♦ American ♦ Daily lunch and dinner. 847.6607

8 Galleria at Tysons II More upscale than the megamall across the street, this specialty mall has 110 stores of its own, including **Macy's, Saks Fifth Avenue, Neiman-Marcus,** and more one-of-a-kind boutiques. ♦ M-Sa 10AM-9:30PM; Su noon-6PM. 2001 International Dr (between Chain Bridge Rd and Westpark Dr). 827.7700 &

8 Fairfax Square Across from **Tysons Corner Center,** this complex gives spendthrifts five more reasons to shop. The chic, but by no means cheap, retailers include **Tiffany & Co., Fendi, Gucci, Hermès,** and **Louis Vuitton.** ♦ M-Sa. 8045 Leesburg Pike (at Old Gallows Rd). 391.8644 &

Within Fairfax Square:

Morton's of Chicago ★★$$$ This well-known establishment serves steaks no less legendary than those of its Georgetown namesake. Set on the basement level with a clubby mahogany interior, the restaurant features prints by LeRoy Neiman. Everything on the menu is huge, including the house specialty: "The Porterhouse" is a 24-ounce half fillet and half New York strip, served with a 16-ounce baked potato. ♦ American ♦ M-F lunch and dinner; Sa-Su dinner. Reservations recommended. 883.0800. Also at: 3251 Prospect St NW (between Wisconsin Ave and Potomac St), Georgetown. 202/342.6258 &

8 Clyde's of Tysons Corner ★★$$ Classier than the Georgetown original, this popular outpost serves equally reliable burgers and omelettes, as well as seafood. Choose from four dining rooms, each with a different theme: The **Palm Terrace** boasts a 75-foot mural of nymphs and satyrs; **The Cafe** style is Art Nouveau; a seashore motif appropriately dominates the **Oyster Bar**; and **The Grill** is done in Art Deco. ♦ American ♦ M-Sa lunch and dinner; Su brunch and dinner. 8332 Leesburg Pike (between Gallows and Chain Bridge Rds). 734.1901 ⅃ Also at: 3236 M St NW (between Wisconsin Ave and Warehouse Pl), DC. 202/333.9180; 11905 Market St (at Bluemont Way), Reston, Virginia. 787.6601

8 Embassy Suites Hotel at Tysons Corner
$$$ A stone's throw from **Tysons Corner Center,** this large and glitzy hotel has 232 two-room suites and an indoor swimming pool, sauna, and Jacuzzi. Amenities include complimentary breakfast and shuttle service within a five-mile radius. Children under 16 stay free. ♦ 8517 Leesburg Pike (between Chain Bridge and Dulles Access Rds). 883.0707, 800/EMBASSY; fax 883.0694 ⅃

WOLF TRAP FOUNDATION
FOR THE PERFORMING ARTS

9 Wolf Trap Farm Park Situated on 117 acres of woodland, this concert/arts facility has brought the best of the performing arts to Virginia. The Wolf Trap Foundation presents events ranging from **Metropolitan Opera** stars to folk singers, the **Alvin Ailey Dance Theatre,** and a variety of comedians. In recent years *Riverdance* has been drawing crowds here. The concert hall, called the **Filene Center,** comprises a stage, a lofty tower, and a soaring, open-sided wood canopy that shelters 3,500 seats built into a natural slope. Higher up there's unprotected lawn seating for 3,000 more. The romantic setting is matched by fine acoustics. Tours of the center and the park are available from the **Visitor Services Office** (225.1800). ♦ Tickets required for performances. Filene Center box office: daily noon-6PM; performance days: noon-9PM May-Sept. 1624 Wolf Trap Rd (between Dulles Access Rd and Leesburg Pike). Recording 255.1860, information 255.1900

Within Wolf Trap Farm Park:

The Barns at Wolf Trap During "off-season," when the weather's too chilly, this intimate concert stage, just down the road from **Filene Center,** offers an intriguing blend of folk, international, bluegrass, and pop music. There's not a bad seat in the house, and beer and wine are available. ♦ 1635 Wolf Trap Rd. Information 938.2404, tickets 218.6500 ⅃

Potomac Vegetable Farms This is one of the few remaining undeveloped plots in an area that is being overtaken by shopping malls, offices, and housing developments. Established in 1963 by the Newcomb family, the 28-acre farm grows vegetables (including beans, Chinese cabbage, Japanese eggplant, mustard greens, sweet corn, and Swiss chard), fruit (blackberries, blueberries, raspberries, and strawberries), and a variety of flowers and herbs—all without chemical pesticides. Organic methods, including natural fertilizers, cover cropping; and such predator insects as ladybugs, praying mantises, and lacewings enrich the soil and help keep pests at bay. Pick up some produce at their farm stand. ♦ Daily July-Oct. 9627 Leesburg Pike (at Beulah Rd). Recording 759.3844, information 759.2119

10 Meadowlark Gardens Regional Park Just five miles from Tysons' high-tech towers is this 95-acre oasis of woods and gardens, including three lakes and an herb garden. Swimming and boating are not allowed. ♦ 9750 Meadowlark Gardens Ct (off Beulah Rd). 255.3631

11 McLean This wealthy suburb, best known as the home of the Central Intelligence Agency, offers a few tourist stops and several fine restaurants. Its town center is relatively small and can be navigated on foot. Most of its businesses and homes seem to have sprung up in the last 25 years, so it offers more Southern hospitality than historic charm.

In McLean:

Giant Gourmet—Someplace Special Finally, here's a supermarket that excels in selection and quality, carrying food from all over the world, freshly baked (in-house) breads and pastries, more than 300 wines, 60 imported beers, and such exotic meats as bear and pheasant. Full-service catering is also available. ♦ M-Sa 9AM-8PM; Su. 1445 Chain Bridge Rd (at Old Dominion Dr). 448.0800 ⅃

Kazan ★★$$$ The exotic tented ceiling and tuxedoed captains are in tune with the tab, which is slightly higher than at your usual ethnic hangout. The cuisine is a superior representation of what the Middle East has to offer, from Turkish moussaka to *borek* (pastry filled with cheese, spinach, or meat). ♦ Turkish ♦ M-F lunch and dinner; Sa dinner. Reservations recommended. 6813 Redmond Dr (between Chain Bridge and Beverly Rds). 734.1960 ⅃

As President Ford led Queen Elizabeth to the White House dance floor the US Marine Band struck up *The Lady Is a Tramp.*

12 Claude Moore Colonial Farm at Turkey Run You can take an amazing look at an authentic pre-Revolutionary War farm, including a costumed "family" (acting courtesy of staff members) that uses reproductions of period tools to perform household chores and farm work that vary with the seasons (spinning, churning, breaking flax, cultivating, and harvesting). The third weekend of every month features either a fair or a harvest. ♦ Admission. W-Su Apr–mid-Dec; closed on rainy days. 6310 Georgetown Pike (between Dolley Madison Blvd and Balls Hill Rd), McLean. 442.7557 &

13 Great Falls Park The best view of the imposing 76-foot-high waterfall is from the Virginia side; during full spring floods the volume of water surpasses that of Niagara Falls: 480,000 cubic feet per second. To watch kayakers at the base of the falls, head for the **Observation Deck.**

Swamps and a forest along the Potomac's banks offer spectacular displays of wildflowers in their seasonal blooms. Bird watchers claim that this park—a migration stop for many birds—provides one of the East Coast's best vantage points; even bald eagles have been spotted here. Natural pools along the river attract deer, foxes, muskrats, beavers, opossums, and rabbits. An excellent system of hiking trails leads you through the woods and along the river, and picnic areas are located throughout the park (no open fires, please). At the **Visitors' Center,** rotating exhibitions about nature, conservation, and safety are offered; the helpful staff answers questions and will direct you to the season's special vistas.

In the late 1700s George Washington came here to oversee the building of the Potowmac Canal, a bypass of the falls and other unnavigable parts of the river. Locks 1 through 5 and part of the canal are still visible, and the National Park Service works constantly to prevent further deterioration. Ruins of the canal are located southeast of the **Visitors' Center.** Also visible are a chimney, a spring house, and other remnants of Matildaville, the city founded by Henry "Light Horse Harry" Lee in honor of his first wife.

Note: This waterfall is a beautiful yet extremely dangerous section of the river; currents are swift and the rock faces sheer. Everyone is urged to stay off the rocks near the river and out of the water near the falls. Drownings occur several times yearly when the swift current pulls careless climbers and waders into the torrent. Parents: Watch your children! Experienced rock climbers with proper equipment can register at the **Visitors' Center.**

Take Route 193, Exit 13 from the Beltway; the park entrance is six miles west; the **Visitors' Center** is a quarter mile past the entrance on the right. ♦ Admission. 9200 Old Dominion Dr (at Georgetown Pike), Great Falls. 285.2965

14 Colvin Run Mill Historic Site This 19th-century gristmill still grinds grain. Throughout the year, special weekend events include an Easter egg hunt, Civil War reenactments, puppet shows, and concerts. Call for schedule. ♦ Admission for mill tour. Sa-Su Jan-Feb; M, W-Su Mar-Dec. 10017 Colvin Run Rd (between Leesburg Pike and Walker Rd), Great Falls. 759.2771 &

15 L'Auberge Chez Francois ★★★★$$$$ Fresh country cooking is served in a magical sylvan setting at this country inn (pictured above). Large bay windows overlook the garden and, inside, three fireplaces and white stucco walls with exposed beams lend warmth and coziness. Chef and owner Francois Haeringer turns out such delicacies as *choucroute garnie,* a collection of sausages and duck served atop Alsatian-style sauerkraut, as well as bouillabaisse, cassoulet, and roasted rabbit with wild mushrooms. Reservations are required four weeks in advance, especially for weekends. The terrace is perfect for alfresco dining on a warm evening. ♦ French ♦ Tu-Su dinner. 332 Springvale Rd (between Georgetown Pike and Beach Mill Rd), Great Falls. 759.3800 &

16 Algonkian Regional Park This 511-acre park overlooks the Potomac and features an 18-hole golf course, 12 vacation cottages, miniature golf, a swimming pool, boat launching ramp, walking trail, and picnic areas. ♦ Fee for boat launch. 47001 Fairway Dr (at Cascades Pkwy), Sterling. 450.4655 &

17 Reston Envisioned by Robert E. Simon in the mid–1950s and begun in 1962, this is one of the nation's few remarkable "new towns." (Simon's initials form the basis of the city's name.) It is conveniently located between Downtown DC and **Washington Dulles Airport,** and is a completely planned city, covering 11.5 square miles. When it is completed in 2001, more than 65,000 people are expected to live around the four lakes that dominate the community's design.

Forty percent of all the land is open and/or public space. Homes are arranged in small neighborhood clusters, which are distributed evenly throughout the city. Recreational amenities include golf courses, pools, ballparks, tennis courts, bridle paths, and a **Nature Center.** This picture of suburban serenity also has been very successful in attracting many high-tech industries, and the presence of the US Geological Survey and such companies as GTE, AT&T, and Unisys has guaranteed at least one job per city household.

Development is supervised by Mobil Land Development Corporation, which coordinates the design and construction of homes (ranging from small apartments to town houses and minimansions, of varied quality and styles), schools, business complexes, and shopping centers. Away from the central core, the landscaping far outshines the architecture.

In Reston:

Reston Town Center This outdoor shopping mall—framed by sleek office buildings, a **Hyatt** hotel, and parking lots—has brick-and-marble walkways open only to pedestrian traffic. Among the upscale stores are **Appalachian Spring** (wooden crafts), **Ann Taylor, Talbots, Hold Everything, The Gap,** and **Gap Kids.** Most of the restaurants in the complex offer alfresco dining, and the green serves as a venue for summer concerts. ♦ New Dominion Pkwy (off Reston Pkwy). 689.4699

18 Washington Dulles Airport Marriott $$ This is the closest hotel to the airport, with indoor/outdoor pools, a Jacuzzi, weight rooms, outdoor tennis courts, and a picnic pavilion. The 360 rooms are typical Marriott, done in neutral beige and forest green with dark wood furniture. The hotel's dining room, **The Grill,** serves American-style fare for breakfast, lunch, and dinner; the lobby bar offers the same menu for lunch and dinner. Children under 12 stay free. ♦ 45020 Aviation Dr (at Dulles Access Rd). 471.9500, 800/462.9671; fax 661.8714

18 Holiday Inn Dulles Airport $$ The convenient airport location, as well as an indoor pool, sauna, whirlpool, and lounge, make these accommodations pleasant. Children under 18 stay free. ♦ 1000 Sully Rd (at Dulles Access Rd). 471.7411, 800/HOLIDAY; fax 834.7558 ext 575

19 Sully Historic Site In 1794 Richard Bland Lee—uncle of General Robert E. Lee and Northern Virginia's first representative to Congress—built this plantation, which is furnished with Federal-period antiques. Tours, given every half hour, include the smokehouse and stone dairy. ♦ Admission.

M, W-Su. 3601 Sully Rd (between Hwy 50 and Wall Rd), Chantilly. 437.1794

20 Sweetwater Tavern ★★$$ Part of the Great American Restaurant chain, this brewpub gives Oktoberfest a Western theme. The cowboy menu—baby back ribs, chicken tenders—receives a little kick from crab cakes and jambalaya pasta (sausage, shrimp, and chicken in a spicy sauce) . . . and, of course, the requisite home brew. ♦ American ♦ M dinner; Tu-Su lunch and dinner. Reservations required for parties of 8 or more. 14250 Sweetwater La (off Multiplex Dr), Centreville. 449.1100 ♿

at STONE RIDGE

21 Nissan Pavilion at Stone Ridge The area's newest and most elaborate outdoor concert facility opened in May 1995 to rave reviews for its state-of-the-art presentation. Seating over 21,000, between its covered pavilion and gently sloping lawn, the concert venue offers an advantage over its two competitors (**Wolf Trap Farm Park** and **Merriweather Post Pavilion**): Giant video screens give even back-row patrons a good view of the stage. While the schedule emphasizes popular rock and country music acts, a few classical performances by the **National Symphony** are given. A new bypass around Manassas and the addition of exit 43B from Interstate 66 (which was widened to eight lanes) has made the trip to an evening concert shorter, maybe even sweeter. ♦ Wellington Rd (off Hwy 29), Bristow. Recorded information 754.6400, tickets 432.SEAT ♿

22 Bull Run Regional Park These several thousand acres include 150 campsites, a swimming pool, miniature golf, a skeet and trap range, a clay-target range, indoor archery, picnic areas, nature trails, and an amphitheater for concerts. There are dog shows in the spring and fall, a yearly country jamboree in June, and a craft show in September. From late November through early January, the *Miracle of Lights*—two miles of colored-light displays—dazzles visitors, and the holiday fair in early December features carolers, craftspeople, and Santa himself. ♦ Mid-Mar through early Jan. 7700 Bull Run Dr (off Rte 28), Centreville. 631.0550, Miracle of Lights 709.KIDS

Restaurants/Clubs: Red   Hotels: Blue

Shops/ 🌳 Outdoors: Green   **Sights/Culture:** Black

23 Manassas Although the town didn't exist when the famous battle took place, it boasts a pretty Victorian-era downtown with a courthouse built in 1892 and a bank built four years later. It's a pleasant surprise in the midst of booming suburbia. A few years ago, locals interested in preserving the tranquillity of this area took on and defeated the folks from Walt Disney who wanted to erect a theme park devoted to American history.

In Manassas:

THE MANASSAS MUSEUM

Manassas Museum Here you can see displays of the history of Manassas as well as of the entire Piedmont region, including Civil War and railroad memorabilia. There are quilts and other textiles, agricultural implements, and a section devoted to African-American history. The museum provides maps for walking, driving, and architectural tours of downtown and the surrounding area. There's also a gift shop. ♦ Admission; free Tuesday. Tu-Su 10AM-5PM. 9101 Prince William St (at Main St). 368.1873 &

Carmello's Ristorante Italiano ★$$ This Northern Italian restaurant spices up the traditionals: chicken, seafood, and veal dishes. The Mediterranean decor creates an elegant yet casual atmosphere. ♦ Italian ♦ M-F lunch and dinner; Sa-Su dinner. Reservations recommended. 9108 Center St (at Battle St). 368.5522

Laws Antiques Complex The H.L. Sonny Laws auction house has offered one-stop antiques shopping for more than 30 years, with two malls on either side of Route 28 lined with 40 antiques shops. The auctions include three-day catalog affairs, first-weekend-of-the-month estate sales, and Friday night disposals of household goods. ♦ Auction house: daily. Antiques shops: M, W-Su. 7209 Centreville Rd (north of Rugby Rd). 631.0590

24 Potomac Mills Mall One of the world's largest discount and outlet centers, **Potomac Mills** contains more than 220 stores, including **Ikea**, a Swedish furniture store, and outlets for such major designers and retailers as **Laura Ashley, Nike, Nordstrom, Macy's,**

Eddie Bauer, Calvin Klein, Donna Karan, and **The Gap.** Weekend shoppers are advised to arrive early; the crowds can be overwhelming. There are many food vendors (the **Ikea** restaurant is terrific), as well as a 15-theater cinema. Drive south on Interstate 95 and take the exit marked **Potomac Mills.** ♦ M-Sa 10AM-9:30PM; Su. 2700 Potomac Mills Cir (south of Prince William Pkwy), Dale City. Information 643.1770

25 Gunston Hall This was the home of George Mason, a Virginia farmer who authored the Virginia Declaration of Rights in 1776 and helped to frame the Bill of Rights. The Georgian-style home, replete with 18th-century English and American furnishings, overlooks the Potomac River. **William Buckland,** a joiner-turned-architect, designed the sumptuous Palladian drawing room and Chinese Chippendale dining room, as well as the two distinctive porches (one Gothic, the other 18th-century-style). Equally glorious are the boxhedge gardens behind the house. Occasionally there are special events—costumed guides cooking in the restored kitchen, for example. Guided tours of the house are given every half hour; self-guided tours of outbuildings, gardens, and other areas of the plantation can be taken daily. ♦ Admission. Daily. 10709 Gunston Rd (southeast of Hwy 1), Mason Neck. 550.9220

25 Pohick Bay Regional Park This water-oriented park has 150 campsites, an 18-hole golf course, miniature golf, Frisbee golf, sailboat and paddleboat rentals, a swimming pool, and nature trails. ♦ Admission. 10651 Gunston Rd (off Hwy 1), Mason Neck. 339.6104

26 Pohick Church George Washington and George Mason were on the select building committee that influenced the design of this 18th-century country church. The simple block of brick is set off with handsome quoins and pediments of Aquila Creek stone cut from Washington's own quarries. ♦ Services (Episcopal) Su 8AM, 9:15AM, 11:15AM Jan–Memorial Day, Labor Day–Dec; Su 8AM, 10AM Memorial Day–Labor Day. 9301 Richmond Hwy (between Gunston Rd and Mount Vernon Memorial Hwy), Lorton. 339.6572

27 Woodlawn Plantation This estate was bequeathed by George Washington to his

Woodlawn Plantation

COURTESY OF WOODLAWN PLANTATION

adopted daughter, Nellie Parke Custis, and his nephew, Lawrence Lewis. The late-Georgian Federal-style mansion (illustrated above) is architecturally more coherent and impressive than **Mount Vernon** (three miles to the east), and its rooms and restored formal gardens (managed by the National Trust for Historic Preservation) are well worth the trip. There is also a gift shop. Guided tours are given every half hour. ◆ Admission. Sa-Su Jan-Feb; daily Mar-Dec. 9000 Richmond Hwy (at Mount Vernon Memorial Hwy), Mount Vernon. 780.4000

At Woodlawn Plantation:

HISTORIC AMERICAN BUILDING SURVEY

Pope-Leighey House Originally located in Falls Church, this early 1940s house by **Frank Lloyd Wright** (pictured above), was rescued from destruction in 1964, when it was moved to **Woodlawn Plantation** and donated to the National Trust for Historic Preservation. Built of cypress, brick, and glass, the house contains features that were uncommon in their time: heated concrete floors, a flat roof, and windows vital to the structural integrity of the wall. This is a rare example of what Wright called Usonian architecture—well-designed housing for moderate-income families. Guided tours are given every half hour. ◆ Admission. Sa-Su Jan-Feb; daily Mar-Dec

28 George Washington Gristmill Historical State Park The original foundations (circa 1770) remain at this restored mill. George Washington owned the mill for almost 30 years, but after his death it fell into disrepair and by 1850 was in shambles. During the Depression, the Civilian Conservation Corps and local artisans and historians worked to restore it, rebuilding the walls and foundation in time for the bicentennial (1932) of Washington's birth. Although it hasn't turned since 1987, the mill's machinery is visible; taken from Front Royal, it dates to 1770 and was forged by millwright Oliver Evans of Philadelphia. Fishing and picnic areas, as well as tours, are available. ◆ Admission. M, Th-Su Memorial Day–Labor Day. 5514 Mount Vernon Memorial Hwy (just east of Richmond Hwy), Mount Vernon. 780.3383, 550.0960

29 Mount Vernon While today's presidential home is characterized by privacy and security—sliding iron gates, video cameras, and guard posts—no such security was needed in the early days of the Republic. What presidential homes then had in common were wheat and tobacco fields, mills, smokehouses, and stables. In a time of broad personal mastery, a gifted leader was often able to administer a nation, lead troops in battle, design a building, and run a profitable farm. George Washington exemplified this spirit, and his estate (illustrated on page 212) is its testimony. He lived here from 1754 until his death in 1799.

In its prime, the plantation comprised 8,000 acres divided into five working farms, and it was self-sufficient in almost every way. There were orchards, a gristmill, and facilities for making textiles and leather goods. "No estate in United America is more pleasantly situated than this," Washington wrote, but the proprietor was allowed little time here. First there was the French and Indian War and then the Revolutionary War, which kept Washington away for eight years. When he returned, he was determined to become a successful planter, experimenting with crop rotation and comparing notes with like-minded growers. His harvests were good, and he even won a "premium for raising the largest jackass" from the Agricultural Society of South Carolina. But only four years later, he went to Philadelphia as a delegate to the Constitutional Convention and then served two terms as president. Finally, in 1797, he returned home, where he lived contentedly until his death two years later.

The current estate, a more manageable 400-plus acres, is probably the best-preserved 18th-century plantation in the country, and in the summer as many as 6,000 people visit it daily. The best strategy is to arrive early and tour the mansion before seeing the outbuildings and grounds. The inside of the white Georgian mansion has been lovingly restored: All wallpaper, drapery, and upholstery are exact replicas, and the walls were repainted with the original colors. Note the Palladian window in the large dining room and the harpsichord Washington imported for his adopted daughter, Nellie, in the **Little Parlor.** Upstairs, the master bedroom holds a trunk Washington carried with him during the Revolutionary War, as well as the bed in which he died. (Washington—who stood 6 feet 2 inches—had the extra-long bed made to order.)

Visitors have access to 10 of the outbuildings, including the spinning room and open-hearth kitchen house. (In days when fires were common and virtually unstoppable, the kitchen was often set apart from the main house.) Be sure to visit the stable, where a rare 18th-century coach is on display, and the small museum with exhibitions of Washingtoniana, colonial silver, and china. In

the reconstructed greenhouse/slave quarters is a fascinating exhibition about archaeology at the estate. (Ongoing digs take place on the premises.) And up on a hill, where the hundreds of slaves who lived and worked here are buried in unmarked graves, stands a stone memorial in their honor.

On either side of the gracious bowling green are period gardens with flowers, vegetables, and boxwood hedges. Note the partially submerged walls called ha-has that separate tended lawns and gardens from pasture. It's a pleasant walk down to the family vaults where George and his wife, Martha, are buried. Check out the newest addition to the grounds: a reconstruction of a 16-sided barn that once stood about three miles from the house. The working unit demonstrates Washington's method of separating grain from chaff.

Plan to spend about two hours touring the grounds; tours of the mansion are self-guided, but there are also several special tours—offered at no extra charge, and with no reservations required—that take in the gardens and an overview of the slaves' living quarters and working conditions. Call ahead for tour schedule. There's a gift shop, and outside the gates is a restaurant. Parking is free. **Tourmobiles** (202/554.7950) stop here, too. ♦ Admission. Daily. George Washington Memorial Pkwy and Mount Vernon Memorial Hwy. 780.2000, TDD 799.8121

30 Thieves Market Browse through more than a dozen antiques shops under one roof. Collectibles include furniture and Oriental rugs, paintings, china, and silver. ♦ M-Sa; Su noon-5PM. 8101 Richmond Hwy (at Rte 235), Alexandria. 360.4200 ♿

31 Talbots Surplus Store You'll save money but still look soigné at this outlet store, a popular purveyor of the town-and-country look. ♦ M-F 9:30AM-8PM; Sa; Su noon-5PM.

Mount Vernon

CHRIS MIDDOUR

6815 Old Springfield Plaza (between Amherst Ave and Commerce St), Springfield. 644.5115

32 Lake Accotink Park Meandering through

479 acres of a landscaped park area, Accotink Creek flows into a pretty lake. A historical four-mile hiking trail follows along the **Old Alexandria Railroad,** whose tracks once ran through the park. Canoes, paddleboats, and rowboats can be rented at the marina facility, which also operates a miniature golf course and a seasonal concession stand. There are

playgrounds, baseball fields, and a carousel, and fishing is permitted (with a license). ♦ Apr-Oct; call for marina hours. 7500 Accotink Park Rd (between Old Keene Mill and Braddock Rds), Springfield. 569.3464

33 Duck Chang's ★★$ Peking duck is the specialty of this modest neighborhood establishment, and nobody does it better. ♦ Chinese ♦ Daily lunch and dinner. 4427 John Marr Dr (between Little River Tpke and Columbia Pike), Annandale. 941.9400

Vantage Points

For a glorious view of Washington, especially at dusk, visit the **Iwo Jima Memorial,** just across the **Potomac River** in **Arlington.** After you've inspected this huge bronze statue, which commemorates the raising of the American flag over Mount Suribachi during World War II, enjoy the twinkling displays of the **Lincoln** and **Jefferson Memorials,** the **Washington Monument,** and the **Capitol** in the distance.

In warm weather, relax with a cool drink at the **Sky Terrace,** the canopied rooftop of the **Hotel Washington** in **Downtown DC.** From there you can take in the **Treasury Building** and the **White House** or contemplate the view south toward **The Mall** and the banks of the Potomac.

If you're visiting the nation's capital on the holiday weekends of Memorial Day, the Fourth of July, or Labor Day, pack a picnic supper and head for the west lawn of the **US Capitol** grounds (between the **Capitol** building and its reflecting pool), where the **National Symphony Orchestra** offers a free, first-class performance. The wonderful music enhances the twilight scene as you gaze down **The Mall** toward the **Washington Monument** and the **Lincoln Memorial.** (Check local newspapers for programs.)

Thrusting 555 feet into the sky, the **Washington Monument** is the city's highest and most spectacular viewing station (you can see to distant horizons from the top). But if vertigo is your middle name, the view from the obelisk's base is perfectly fine. Call ahead to check on the wait, which can be as long as three hours. During the tourist season, the memorial stays open late enough for you to enjoy the sparkling lights of DC at night.

Heading south on **16th Street NW** toward Downtown DC, pause at the top of **Meridian Hill Park.** The sight of the **White House** directly ahead and the **Washington Monument** and **Jefferson Memorial** beyond is a dramatic reminder of the city's historical and political importance.

From the **Clocktower Pavilion** at the **Old Post Office** (315 feet), you can see Downtown DC and the monuments. Victorian brass fittings, red oak woodwork, and frosted glass decorate the atrium of the **Old Post Office,** and the **Capitol** looks especially magnificent from this lovely spot.

Take the elevator up to the roof terrace of the **Kennedy Center for the Performing Arts** for a panorama of the city and the Potomac. You can also enjoy the view while dining at the **Roof Terrace Restaurant.**

The Potomac looks glorious up close, too. In the light of day, sit on its banks in **East and West Potomac Park;** the prime stretch is from just south of the **Lincoln Memorial** to Hains Point.

Due west of DC, across **Arlington Memorial Bridge,** is **Arlington House** (also called the **Custis-Lee House**). From its portico on the bluff, you can look across the Potomac directly to the **Lincoln Memorial.** Below lie the graves of President John Kennedy and wife Jacqueline (marked by an eternal flame) and his brother Robert. **Arlington National Cemetery,** carved from the plantation that Robert E. Lee's family abandoned during the Civil War, stretches through the hills around the mansion.

From the **Pilgrim's Observation Gallery** of **Washington National Cathedral** in **Upper Northwest,** you can survey **Wisconsin Avenue** down into **Georgetown** and beyond to Northern Virginia. Turn in the other direction, and you'll see suburban Maryland. Crowning the highest hill in the District, the cathedral's tower, accessible by elevator, provides a vista like no other in the city.

To gain a perspective on **Old Town Alexandria,** venture to the top of that city's **George Washington Masonic National Memorial.** Its observation deck, more than 300 feet high, furnishes a breathtaking, and sometimes windy, view of Alexandria. On a clear day, you can see into Washington.

For a trip through time, pause on the grounds of **Mount Vernon** in Northern Virginia. From here, it's easy to imagine the way the Potomac River and the surrounding countryside looked in George Washington's time. (Every effort is being made to keep the scenery free of suburban sprawl.) With nothing but trees, water, and sky in all directions, it's among the area's best vistas.

History

1607 The first permanent English settlement is founded at Jamestown, Virginia.

1608 Captain John Smith sails up the **Potomac** to where Algonquin-speaking Indians live. Henry Fleete, a British fur trader, is the first European known to visit the area. He's captured by Indians and held prisoner for several years.

1662 The Maryland Colony is divided into large plantations. The first land patent on the future site of the District is granted.

1749 The city of **Alexandria** is laid out along the northern edge of the Virginia Colony.

1751 The Maryland Assembly establishes **Georgetown** along the southern border of the colony.

1765 The **Old Stone House** is built on what is now **M Street** in Georgetown.

1783 The US and Britain sign a peace treaty ending the American Revolution. Congress meets in Philadelphia to discuss the future of the newly independent colonies. There is no president, no money, and no strong unifying interest now that the war is over. Unpaid soldiers march on Congress to demand back pay. The legislatures discuss the possibility of establishing a federal capital where they could conduct the business of government without fear of intimidation. Several ideas are discussed but no agreement is reached because of conflicting interests between northern and southern delegates.

1787 The Constitutional Convention meets in Philadelphia and frames the federal constitution. It provides for the selection of a tract of land on which to build the federal capital.

1788 Virginia and Maryland offer parcels of territory for the establishment of a federal district.

1789 The US Constitution is ratified. George Washington is elected the first US president.

1790 The nation's capital is moved to Philadelphia. A political compromise is reached to build the federal capital on the Potomac River. Congress authorizes George Washington to choose the exact site on a federal territory, but stipulates that it be not more than 10 square miles in total size. Washington selects an area that includes Georgetown on the north and Alexandria on the south. He envisions the growth of a great commercial port city on the Potomac, much like New York on the Hudson or Philadelphia on the Delaware.

1791 Washington appoints Andrew Ellicott to survey the area and **Pierre-Charles L'Enfant,** a French military engineer who served in the Continental Army, to draw up plans for the city, to be known as the Territory of Columbia. Work is slow and difficult. The terrain is swampy, there is little infrastructure, and no place for workers or government officials to live. As a result, there is constant agitation in the press and in Congress to relocate to more civilized surroundings.

1792 Influenced by the Baroque landscape architecture of Paris and Versailles and envisioning a vast country with an enormous population, **L'Enfant**'s plans for the capital reflect a sense of grandeur and scale. His design calls for a broad milelong road (now **Pennsylvania Avenue**) to connect the **Capitol** with the **President's House** (the Executive Mansion). Public buildings are to be set widely apart on broad open roads. **L'Enfant** is soon dismissed from the job because he is late completing the plans and is unable to work with the commissioners overseeing the building of the city. His plan, though not followed in its entirety, nonetheless serves as the blueprint for Washington, DC. The cornerstone is laid for the **White House.**

1793 Washington lays the cornerstone of the **Capitol** building designed by **Dr. William Thornton.**

1800 Inadequate finances lead to delays in finishing the government buildings. When John Adams and other officials of the federal government move into the District, the **White House,** designed by **James Hoban,** is still under construction and only one wing of the **Capitol** is complete. Despite its incomplete state, the District becomes the nation's capital.

1801 Congress formally designates as federal territory the District of Columbia, which includes the town of Alexandria on the Virginia side of the Potomac.

1802 The City of Washington is incorporated with an elected council and a mayor appointed by the president. City population: 3,000.

1808 Construction begins on the **Washington Canal** along current-day **Constitution Avenue.**

1810 Population: 24,000.

1812-14 Barely 25 years after the American Revolution, the former colonies are again pitted against England in the War of 1812. British armies under Admiral George Cockburn invade the District and burn the **Capitol,** the **White House,** and other public buildings. The image of Washington as the nation's capital is actually strengthened by its destruction. Although the city is devastated it rebuilds within five years. The **Library of Congress** is burned and its collection of 3,000 books destroyed. Thomas Jefferson sells his personal collection of 6,500 volumes to Congress to start a new library. Today, the **Library of Congress** holds over 90 million items and is the largest in the world.

1815 President Madison signs the Treaty of Ghent, ending the War of 1812. **Washington Canal** is finished, running along what is now **Constitution Avenue.**

1820 Congress votes to give Washington residents the right to vote for a mayor and city council. However, the power of self-government is extremely limited. Population reaches 33,039 persons.

1829 James Smithson, a British professor of chemistry at Oxford, dies. Although he had never visited the US, he greatly admired the new nation and leaves his considerable fortune to the US government to establish an institute for research and public education in Washington. His only stipulation is that his name be on the institute. It takes more than a decade for Congress to act on Smithson's wish. Today, the **Smithsonian** is the largest museum complex in the world.

1842 Although Washington has recovered from the destruction of the British invasion in 1814, the city remains a bit rough around the edges. English author Charles Dickens describes it as a "monument raised to a deceased project," consisting of "spacious avenues that begin in nothing and lead nowhere."

1846 Although Virginia donated land for the District in 1788, its citizens change their minds and ask for it back. The District territory south of the Potomac is returned to Virginia, reducing the capital by one-third of its original size. Alexandria, Virginia, becomes an independent city again.

1848 The cornerstone is laid for the **Washington Monument.**

1850 Congress abolishes slave trade in the District, though owning slaves remains legal.

1855 The **Smithsonian**'s first building, the **Castle,** designed by **James Renwick,** is completed.

1860 City population: 75,000.

1861 Abraham Lincoln is sworn in as the 16th president. When the Civil War breaks out, the population of the city explodes with an influx of Union soldiers, workers, and escaped slaves. An all-out effort is made to protect Washington from Confederate troops, many of which are billeted dangerously close to the Capital. Government buildings are converted to hospitals and barracks for Union soldiers. A network of forts is erected around the city's southern perimeter.

1862 Congress frees all slaves in the District.

1863 President Lincoln issues the Emancipation Proclamation. **Ford's Theater** opens.

1864 The war gets dangerously close to the District. Confederate General Jubal Early threatens to overrun the city but is defeated at nearby Fort Stevens. The Confederacy never again comes close to capturing the Union capital.

1865 End of the Civil War. Confederate General Robert E. Lee surrenders to Union General Grant at Appomattox. Five days later, President Lincoln is assassinated at **Ford's Theater.**

1867 Congress gives Washington residents the right to vote. **Howard University,** the capital's first black university, is chartered by Congress.

1870 Spurred by the influx during the Civil War, Washington's population nearly doubles to about 132,000.

1871 Congress creates a territorial government for the District. All local officials are appointed by the president.

1874 The territorial form of government is abandoned. Congress resumes direct control of the District. A panel of three commissioners appointed

by the president administers the city. Voting rights for Washington residents are stripped. The city's first art museum, the **Corcoran Gallery,** opens on Pennsylvania Avenue.

1880 The construction of streetcar lines hastens the growth of outlying areas. The population reaches about 178,000.

1885 Nearly one hundred years after Congress passed a resolution to build a monument to the hero of the American Revolution, the **Washington Monument** is completed.

1890 **Rock Creek Park** and **Potomac Park** are established. The cornerstone of the **Library of Congress** is laid. Population reaches about 230,000.

1895 Washington annexes Georgetown.

1897 The first permanent **Library of Congress** building opens. (Previously, the **Library** had been housed within the congressional complex.)

1900 Washington celebrates its centennial. Population reaches about 279,000.

1902 The McMillan Commission is established to ensure that construction in Washington remains true to **L'Enfant**'s original plans: There is to be an emphasis on wide avenues and open spaces punctuated by great monuments.

1907 **Union Station** is completed. President Roosevelt lays the cornerstone for the **National Cathedral.**

1912 First Lady Helen Taft and Japan's Viscountess Chinda (wife of the Japanese ambassador) plant the first of two cherry trees as Japan's gift to Washington; the total gift is 2,000 trees.

1914 Construction begins on a memorial to Lincoln.

1917 As the nation enters World War I, Washington experiences a construction boom. Rows of buildings, intended to be temporary, are erected around **The Mall.** (So much for **L'Enfant**'s plan for wide-open spaces.)

1918 By the end of World War I, Washington's population has reached nearly 400,000.

1922 The **Lincoln Memorial,** designed by Henry Bacon, is dedicated. Black officials are segregated at opening ceremonies.

1926 The National Capital Parks and Planning Commission is established. The Public Buildings Act leads to the construction of many federal buildings.

1931 The nation is in the midst of the Great Depression. Marchers demonstrate in Washington seeking relief from economic hardship.

1932 The election of Franklin D. Roosevelt and the launching of the New Deal results in an explosion in the size of the federal government; new buildings change the Washington landscape. Over 17,000 Army veterans march on Washington demanding back pay.

1937 Congress grants a charter to establish a **National Gallery of Art.** Andrew Mellon, the financier, donates a building to house the museum.

History

1940 The District's population soars to about 663,000, spurred by New Deal programs and black migration from the South.

1941 **National Gallery of Art** opens.

1943 The **Jefferson Memorial** is dedicated, and the **Pentagon** is completed.

1950 During the Korean War, the population of Washington peaks at approximately 802,000.

1960 The District's population drops for the first time, to about 764,000.

1961 John F. Kennedy is inaugurated the 34th president. Congress ratifies the 23rd Amendment to the Constitution, giving Washington residents the right to vote in presidential, not local, elections.

1963 Civil rights leader Martin Luther King Jr. leads 200,000 demonstrators in a "March on Washington for Jobs and Freedom." King delivers his "I Have a Dream" speech on the steps of the **Lincoln Memorial.** John F. Kennedy is assassinated in Dallas and buried in **Arlington National Cemetery.**

1964 The **Capital Beltway** is completed.

1967 Congress reorganizes the District's government. The three-commissioner system is replaced with a mayor, an assistant commissioner, and a city council, all appointed by the president. Although pressure grows for self-rule, it remains elusive.

1968 Race riots rock the city following the assassination of Martin Luther King, Jr. Twelve people are killed, and $24 million of property is damaged.

1970 Anti–Vietnam War demonstrations in **The Mall** reach enormous proportions. District residents are given the right to elect one non-voting delegate to the House of Representatives. Population: about 757,000.

1971 The **John F. Kennedy Center for the Performing Arts** opens.

1973 Limited local self-rule is achieved. Residents of the District are given the right to vote for their

local leaders. Congress reserves the right to veto any action that threatens the federal interest. Moreover, the city budget must be reviewed and enacted by Congress.

1975 Walter Washington is the first popularly elected mayor of Washington, DC.

1976 The US celebrates its bicentennial. The modernistic Washington subway system, called the **Metro,** begins operation.

1978 The **East Building** of the **National Gallery,** designed by **I.M. Pei,** opens.

1979 Continuing in a long tradition of civil protest, farmers demonstrate for farm relief in Washington.

1980 Washington's population falls to approximately 638,000.

1982 Amidst controversy, the **Vietnam War Memorial,** designed by Maya Ying Lin, is built. Known as "The Wall," it contains the names of all US casualties in Vietnam. Contrary to expectations, the popular reaction is clear, powerful, and favorable. It becomes one of the most visited Washington attractions.

1984 The **Washington Convention Center** opens.

1987 Opening of the **Smithsonian Quadrangle.**

1990 The **National Cathedral,** begun in 1907, is finally completed.

1992 Near the **Vietnam War Memorial,** the *Women's Memorial,* Glenna Goodacre's bronze sculpture of two uniformed women tending a wounded male soldier, is dedicated; it honors the estimated 10,000 women who served in the war. William Jefferson Clinton, Democratic governor of Arkansas, is elected the 41st president of the US.

1995 Pennsylvania Avenue closes to motorists between 15th and 17th Streets to protect the **White House** from terrorist attacks.

1997 Washington's first memorial to Franklin D. Roosevelt is dedicated. The **Women in Military Service Memorial** opens, honoring women who serve in the US armed forces.

1998 Anthony Williams is elected mayor, ending nearly two decades of local rule by former mayor Marion Barry.

1999 Bill Clinton becomes the second US president ever to be impeached by the House of Representatives; like Andrew Johnson before him, Clinton is found not guilty (of high crimes and misdemeanors) by the Senate.

Index

Index

Index

F

G

Index

Restaurants

Only restaurants with star ratings are listed below. All restaurants are listed alphabetically in the main (preceding) index. Always call in advance to ensure a restaurant has not closed, changed its hours, or booked its tables for a private party. The restaurant price ratings are based on the average cost of an entrée for one person, excluding tax and tip.

★★★★ An Extraordinary Experience
　★★★ Excellent
　　★★ Very Good
　　　★ Good
　$$$$ Big Bucks ($25 and up)
　$$$ Expensive ($15-$25)
　$$ Reasonable ($10-$15)
　　$ The Price Is Right (less than $10)

★★★★

★★★

Hotels

The hotels listed below are grouped according to their price ratings; they are also listed in the main index. The hotel price ratings reflect the base price of a standard room for two people for one night during the peak season.

$$$$ Big Bucks ($180 and up)
$$$ Expensive ($120-$180)
$$ Reasonable ($80-$120)
$ The Price Is Right (less than $80)

$$$$

Features

Page	Entry #	Notes